GRAMMAR
OF THE
FILM
LANGUAGE

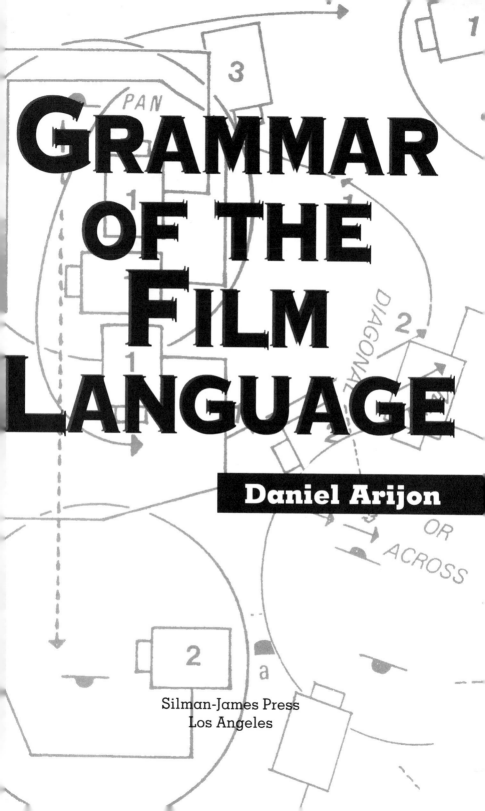

GRAMMAR OF THE FILM LANGUAGE

Daniel Arijon

Silman-James Press
Los Angeles

First Silman-James Press Edition

10 9

Library of Congress Cataloging-in-Publication Data

Arijon, Daniel
Grammar of the film language / by Daniel Arijon
p. cm.
Includes index
1. Cinematography.
2. Motion pictures--Production and direction.
I. Title
TR850.A8   1991   778.5'3—dc20   91-28390

ISBN: 1-879505-07-X

Cover design by Heidi Frieder

Printed in the United States of America

Silman-James Press
1181 Angelo Drive
Beverly Hills, CA 90210

CONTENTS

The heading "4 THE TRIANGLE PRINCIPLE" has page number 26.

FOREWORD TO THE PRESENT EDITION

The hardcover edition of this book has enjoyed a successful life during the past fifteen years under the imprint of Focal Press. It saw several reprints in English and translations were published in Japanese, French, Serbo-Croate, and Spanish. I've had the pleasure of seeing it used as a textbook in several film and television schools around the world. That kind of reception to my work has made my modest contribution to the understanding of the visual grammar of the moving image a worthwhile effort.

Now, Silman-James Press grants my work an extended life in this paperback edition. I hope that their effort will benefit all those interested in pursuing a career in the communication wonder of this age: the moving image in all its diffuse variants—film, tape, disk, and whatever may come in the future.

The true and tested rules of visual language outlined in this book will remain constant for a long time to come. You can be sure of that. As I said in the hardcover edition, the greatest movies of our age are still unmade. Let us try to be the ones who will make them. There is an expanding audience all over the world waiting for these stories.

Daniel Arijon
Montevideo, Uruguay
April, 1991

INTRODUCTION

There are so many books on film making, that one is tempted to ask why there should be yet another. And why this one? The author feels, and this conviction stems from his own case histories, that for the last twenty years there has not been a book on the market that chronicles the developments in the narrative techniques of the cinema in a practical way.

A young person not lucky enough to be associated with good film makers, usually seeks the information he needs in books. He will find many books that discuss various theories about film, or contain criticism and interviews or essays. A highly complicated endeavour such as film making, requires the effort of many specialists, some of whom have written good technical books. But one sector of the subject has been neglected in recent years—which may be termed the organizing of images for their projection on a screen. Existing books on the subject are outdated or incomplete. And few of them have any tangible practical information that the budding film maker can assimilate and apply in his own work. The aim of this book is to fill the gap that has opened since those works were originally written.

The cinema has evolved at a wondrous pace, especially in its narrative forms. With new lightweight cameras, portable recorders and other technical developments on the one hand, and economic hire charges for good equipment, cheap raw stock and processing on the other, the possibility of making a professional full length low-budget film is almost within the reach of everyone. If the dream of the former generation was to write the great novel of their time, the aim of the younger generation seems to be the making of very good films. To them, and the many other persons who are increasingly turning to film as a medium of expression, this book is mainly dedicated. It is designed to shorten the years of apprenticeship and avoid the uncertain task of collecting scraps of information here and there and to assemble the basic rules of film narration. You will not find theories here, but facts, tested and proven over a long period by diverse film makers all over the world, which can be readily applied to any film project you might be considering.

Work on this book has taken up nearly twelve years alongside with my own career in film making. I hope that my humble effort will also help anyone who, like the author, began their career or is about to begin it in countries or areas where an industry that absorbs new blood does not exist.

Age, nationality or background does not matter. What is important is that you have something to say that can, and must, be expressed through the film medium in your own way and in your own terms. The greatest movies of our age are still unmade. Let us try to be the ones who will make them.

Daniel Arijon
Montevideo, Uruguay, 1975

ACKNOWLEDGEMENTS

This book would not have been possible without the help of *Carrillon Films del Uruguay*, where I found unlimited support for my project, and where moviolas and projectors were freely put at my disposal over a number of years.

Luis Elbert and *Nelson Pita* located and obtained many of the film prints used by the author in his research. *Manuel Martinez Carril* of *Cinemateca Uruguaya* also helped provide film prints for viewing and analysis expressly for this manuscript. The late *Jorge Calasso, Miss Elena Iuracevich, Raul Fernandez Montans,* and last but not least, *Milton Cea,* made invaluable contributions and suggestions. To all of them, my heartiest thanks.

Daniel Arijon

This book is dedicated
to Delmer Lawrence Daves
who ignited the spark
and to Hector Mario Raimondo Souto
who propelled my efforts
into reality

1

FILM LANGUAGE AS A SYSTEM OF VISUAL COMMUNICATION

Across the open door of my office, I can see the editing equipment we have been using for several weeks in putting together our last film. From my desk I can partially see the small screen of the editing machine. Now it is only a white rectangular spot—lifeless, just a piece of coated glass. On a sudden impulse I rise and walk into that room. I stop at the door and survey it in a way I have never done before. The objects are familiar—the cans of film, the bins full of strips of celluloid, the scissors, the splicing machine. On small hooks hang numerous strips of film, some of only a few frames length, other of countless feet unreeling loosely into the bins.

I select one of the strips of film at random and thread it into the moviola. I pull some switches and the strip of film starts to move. On the small screen suddenly an image appears. We are inside a church, large, modern, ascetic. A girl, young and innocent, walks towards us. We follow her until another figure appears on the screen. It is an actor dressed in a dark spacesuit and wearing a strange and brilliant helmet. We only catch a glimpse of the lone glass eye on the projecting front of his helmet and there the shot ends. The small screen becomes blank again with only a flickering light shining beneath the glass.

What I have seen is just a fragment of a photographed reality. A reality that was carefully arranged and rehearsed in front of a movie camera. A similar process was registered on the other strips of film. Here, reality is broken down into little frames and here in the cutting room I stand, thinking about this aspect of my craft.

Those pieces of film were selected by me, recorded on film by a photographer, immersed in chemicals in a laboratory until the images were clearly visible and fixed on the celluloid base. And

1

they are destined to be shadows, ungraspable, ever-changing patterns of light when projected on a screen in the moviola, the cinema theatre or a million television sets across a nation.

What had we been doing in that room for the last few weeks? We played with fragments of recorded time, arranged shadows and sounds to convey a story, pursued some moments of truth, tried to communicate some feelings and reached for the clues that would grant those images the power to grasp the attention and emotions of an audience that will always remain anonymous to us.

And how did we attempt to do it? The answers would be multiple and all interdependent. But they rest on a common base, which is both solid and yet shifting—*the knowledge of our craft*. Film editing, montage, schnitt are the words used to describe it. And in its most simple sense they also define a simple operation: the joining together of two strips of celluloid. That is the final step in a long process. Good film editing starts with the writing of the script intended for representation in front of a registering mechanism, the movie camera. Where do we learn the process? How has it evolved? What are its tangible rules?

Beginnings of film language

Film language was born when film makers became aware of the difference between the loose joining together of small images in various states of motion, and the idea that these series of images could be related to one another. They discovered that when two different symbols were combined, they were transmitted into a new meaning and provided a new way of communicating a feeling, an idea, a fact—one plus one equalled three—as in other systems of communication. Theorists began to experiment. There were no signposts to guide them towards the language they needed. Many of the concepts evolved were so cerebral, so abstract, that they bore no relation to reality. In spite of all their mistakes, delusions and false discoveries, those film makers were a painstaking lot. If any value is to be found in their rules, it is that they are the product of experimentation, an accumulation of solutions found by everyday practice of the craft. Those rules really worked for them and their epoch. The drawback was their limited use and the impossibility of being transformed into constant principles. Few film makers have the ability to rationalize their creative mental processes in the form of written, analytical theory.

2

All languages are types of accepted convention. A society agrees or is taught to interpret some symbols with uniform meanings for everyone belonging to that group. Storytellers, men of ideas, have first to learn the symbols and the rules of combination. But these are always in a state of flux. Artists or philosophers can influence the group by introducing new symbols or rules and discarding ancient ones. The cinema is not alien to this process.

The history of the progress of the cinema as a medium of visual communication, is directly related to the ability of film language to grasp reality. But reality is an ever-changing concept, an ever-changing form of perception. Film editing is the reflex of the sensitivity of its user, of his attunement to the current moods of the medium.

Types of film maker

The difference between the creator and the artisan lies in the fact that the first has the courage to innovate, experiment and invent. He is not afraid of his mistakes and is therefore always advancing, whereas the artisan uses the best pieces of knowledge gained by the creators and avoids the experimentation stage, incorporating the new advances into his repertory only when they have been accepted by the mass.

Both types of film maker are necessary to the craft. Films made between 1910 and 1940 were rich culture pods on which were tried different visual and audio experiments in an industry producing an enormous output of films for popular consumption. Perhaps this factor contributed most to the evolution of film language. The steady work of the artisans provided the means for the industry to function and then, as now, a healthy industry continued to give opportunities to the creators to go on experimenting.

A good film is not the product of total improvisation, but the result of knowledge, not only of the life and the world that it portrays, but of the techniques that render the ideas more expressive.

Forms of film expression

All forms of film language are artistically licit, except perhaps the use of the medium as an empty play of forms. The contemporary film goer registers a natural repugnance for the abstract and abstruse use of film narration. He seeks a representation of reality, whether external, internal or imagined, that is less loaded with clues, charades and unintelligible symbols.

Film as a medium has limitations, you must understand its strong points and its shortcomings. Conflict and movement are close to its soul. But peace, hope and great truths are all of a static nature and can be but poorly served by the film medium. Thoughts and ideas, especially abstract ideas, cannot be expressed on film as clearly as by the written word; they must be shown as acting upon the behaviour of the characters, animals or things recorded by the camera. Film portrays only the external result— the actions and reactions created by motivations, thoughts or desires. Robert Flaherty remarked once: 'You can't say as much as you can in writing, but you can say what you say with great conviction.' He was right.

Defining our aims

The purpose of the notes that follow is very simple, and perhaps very ambitious too. All the rules of film grammar have been on the screen for a long time. They are used by film makers as far apart geographically and in style as Kurosawa in Japan, Bergman in Sweden, Fellini in Italy and Ray in India. For them, and countless others this *common set of rules* is used to solve specific problems presented by the visual narration of a story. This book sets out to record systematically the contemporary solutions to those specific problems. We are dealing with a craft that is constantly subject to change; the practices compiled here have proved to be stable for a very long time and hopefully they will continue to be for a long time yet.

Richard S. Kahlenberg, of the American Film Institute, has pointed out that never before has the aspiring film maker had such a wide opportunity of learning his craft as today. Films used to be made to be shown for a few weeks and then they were shelved. Now, thanks to TV they are replayed at our homes, as by a nostalgic time machine, enabling film buffs to see the works of past masters. Television 'cools' the images and technique can be readily appreciated. Kahlenberg pointed out that many film makers have learned their craft studying these old films. Peter Bogdanovich is a well known example of that approach.

4

Like any written work on a practical subject this is not, of course, without limitations. You will not learn film language by example, or by analyzing other people's work only. Not until the film is running through your fingers will you complete your education. The knowledge of others and personal experience are both essential to acquire film sense. Sadly we can only offer the first half of the job. We hope it will encourage you to undertake the other half. In this context it is well to remember the following comment, that Anthony Harvey, a film editor and director, made in an interview for the British magazine *Sight and Sound*[1]:

'My greatest fear has always been that of becoming too technical. Sitting at a moviola day after day, year after year, one is in danger of becoming obsessed with the mechanics so that they take over everything else. You can lose the whole point of a scene that way. Of course, you have to know all the technical possibilities, but you need to know them so well that they become second nature, not so that you use them to distort the material you've got.'

Wise film makers stick to their visions. That should be their prime concern. The complexity of the inbetween processes involved in the translation of a vision from the brain of its author to a strip of celluloid, must not blind the creator and distract him from his own, personal, unique conception of the theme that motivated his desire to use film as his system of communication.

1 *Sight and Sound* Spring 1966 Vol. 35 No. 2. "Putting the Magic in It" by Roger Hudson.

2

THE IMPORTANCE OF PARALLEL FILM EDITING

The movie camera, in spite of its complexities as an instrument and the specialized knowledge needed to operate it, must be for the film maker only a registering mechanism, such as the pen or the typewriter are to a writer. To handle a camera, only an efficient crew is needed. Far more important to a film maker is the ability to handle ideas and concepts.

Once these ideas have materialized on strips of film they must be assembled. For that he relies heavily on an editing principle: the alternation of two or more centres of interest. This 'parallel film editing' is one of the most frequently used forms of film language. It serves to present clearly conflicting or related story lines by moving alternately from one centre of interest to the other. The technique is so common that audiences take it for granted in every film. A film which avoids use of the technique irritates the viewer even though if pressed to supply a reason for his discomfort he would not be able to give the right answer.

Two basic types

To clarify what parallel film editing is, here is an example—a rough description of the first sequence of a well known film.
1   Elio Petri's film *The Tenth Victim*, begins with Ursula Andress being pursued on a New York street by a hunter (George Wang). The hunter is momentarily detained by a policeman who checks the validity of his 'licence to kill'.
2   A man seen in close up, begins to explain what the Great Hunt is. In the not so distant future citizens exercise 'licences to kill' in government sponsored duels to the death.
3   The film returns to Ursula Andress being chased around the

scenic sites of New York by the hunter, who keeps firing his gun, and misses every time.

4   Again the unknown man is presented in close up, and gives more information about the Great Hunt.

5   Miss Andress teases the hunter to keep on firing, until he runs out of bullets.

6   Once more the unknown man appears in close up and details the advantages of succeeding, in ten consecutive chases, alternating as hunter and victim.

7   Ursula Andress, followed at a short distance by her pursuer, steps on a car's hood, jumps over a net fence and runs into the 'Masoch Club'.

8   Her pursuer arrives and, after a pause, also enters the club. He moves in the futuristic interior, walking among the seated patrons.

9   A master of ceremonies on the stage (the man we had previously seen in close up explaining the mechanism of the Great Hunt) introduces a dancer. She emerges, wearing a mask and a costume of blue and silver sequins, and starts to dance.

10   The hunter sits down and watches her.

11   She moves among the club's patrons who remove pieces of her dress, until only two small garments remain.

12   The hunter watches her.

Two types of parallel film editing are to be found in the sequence described. Firstly, two different situations are alternately presented to the audience:

the chase on the streets of New York, and
the explanation of what the Great Hunt is.

Each story line develops separately, contributing more information on each successive appearance. On the external views of the chase (the first story line) we become aware that something unusual is happening. Then we see how the victim is controlling the hunter at will. Later we see how she leads him to a site she has pre-selected (paragraphs 1, 3, 5 and 7). The close ups of the club's master of ceremonies (the second story line) explain what the Great Hunt is, then what its mechanism is, and later what are the advantages of surviving in ten consecutive chases (paragraphs 2, 4 and 6):

Second, two related situations in a common site are alternated:
the dancer, and
the hunter.

Once inside the club, the parallel film pattern changes, and concentrates on the relationship between the dancer (as shown in paragraphs 9 and 11), who is really the victim in disguise, and the confused hunter (shown in paragraphs 8, 10 and 12).

The task of relating two story lines, or two characters, or two different events, or a larger number of story lines, characters and events, is assigned to parallel film editing. These types of parallel editing could be defined as follows:

1   The lines of interaction are close together, in the same space.

2   The lines of interaction are far apart, in different places, and only a common motivation provides the link.

The first type of parallel film editing is exemplified by the confrontation of the dancer and the hunter. A dialogue between two persons, where both are separately observed by the camera, falls in the same category.

The chase on the streets of New York alternating with the explanations of the master of ceremonies, exemplifies the second type of parallel film editing. Their interrelation can be immediate (as in a race where two opponents are moving towards a common goal), or delayed to the end, such as in the example quoted, where the identity of the man who speaks (he is the master of ceremonies) is carefully hidden from the audience at the beginning of the story. This man is the link between both story lines.

Interrelating two story lines in a parallel pattern gives them a mutual dependence, since the average film viewer has been conditioned to expect such a response from this combination.

Comparative behaviours can be presented on the screen with this method. The documentary film form is very apt to obtain remarkable image associations by the conscious editing of several events in parallel patterns, i.e. various athletes in different sports prepare to compete, the competition begins and some of the participants fail. By observing the same athletes in the three stages of behaviour and seeing them alternately at each stage, a space-time relationship unique to the cinema is obtained.

Action and reaction

When we are told a story we unconsciously want to know two things:

what *action* is going on, and

how the people involved are *reacting* to that action.

If the storyteller forgets to keep track of those two things his audience will be confused or unsufficiently informed. If you were telling the story personally, your audience would ask you about the missing facts, which you would then supply.

But telling a story on the screen is an impersonal act because you seldom see your audience or hear their reactions. The film is already printed, the story inmutable and if you forget something you cannot stop the film and supply the missing information. Most film takes contain action and reaction within the length of the shot. Witness this example where two shots are used:

Shot 1: a hunter moves his rifle from side to side and fires.

Shot 2: a flying bird is suddenly hit and falls.

Shot 1 shows the hunter aiming (an action) and then he fires (a reaction). Shot 2 shows the bird flying (an action) and its flight is suddenly interrupted (a reaction).

But if we showed Shots 1 and 2 without grouping the actions and reactions, our understanding of what is going on would not be as effective as if we grouped them as follows:

(*Action*)

Shot 1: the hunter moves his rifle from side to side, aiming off screen.

Shot 2: a bird is flying in the sky.

(*Reaction*)

Shot 1: the hunter fires his rifle.

Shot 2: the bird is hit and falls.

In this way we have grouped first the informative parts of the shots, enabling us to show the outcome more comprehensibly. That alternation of shots: Shot 1—Shot 2—Shot 1—Shot 2, is known as parallel film editing, and is only one of its forms. In this example we were dealing with two lines of action, but the number of lines involved might be increased for a different situation.

This grouping of action and reaction permeates the whole structure of a film: from the union of two shots, to the juxtaposition of two or more sequences, and to a greater extent the construction of the whole story itself.

Peak moments and the understanding

The process of manipulating action just described forces a selectivity process in working out a film story. Only the *peak moments* of a story are shown on a screen, and all the events or actions that delay or do not add new, significant material, are deleted from the narrative.

Selection of peak moments implies the control of time and movement. An expert film maker is always compressing or expanding time and yet he gives the illusion of supplying us with the entire real time of the event: movement may be fragmented and controlled according to a dynamic criterion. Film editing demolishes the old dramatic unities of place and time. The audience is moved from here to there, from the present to the past, without warning. And the viewer accepts all this quite naturally.

This process originates from when man invented his first written language. Written thoughts force the reader to analyze and assimilate each graphic symbol individually to obtain meaning, and that developed capacity for instant analysis and comparison differenciates us from primitive man, who lived in a true unity with his environment, always conscious of the whole and unable to conceive an abstraction. To properly understand the visual language of film, the viewer needs to have passed through the experience of learning a written language made of conventional signs particular to his community. With this same ability he can assimilate a conventional way of linkage between the moving images on a screen.

As long as a succession of *actions* and *reactions* is maintained the interpretation of that visual language does not demand of the viewer an understanding of its physical construction. But for the film maker this action-reaction pattern dictates all the formulas for camera placement and sequence construction and the needs of editing.

How parallel editing is obtained

Parallel film editing to cover a story point, can be achieved using two approaches:

single shots of short duration and/or

long master shots.

If short single shots are used, the two or more related actions involved are covered individually by using diverse and multiple camera set ups.

These shots are edited in such a way that they shift the viewpoint alternately from one action to the other, thus piecing together the whole event or scene. Each shot used, each piece of

10

film, is a peak moment in the series of actions and reactions that all story lines contain.

With this method, the whole event can be appreciated only when all the shots have been cut together. That is the main difference between the single shot and the master shot approach. As the name implies, a master shot is a single camera position from which the event is recorded in its entirety. In practice two or three camera positions may be used simultaneously to provide several such master shots. If fragments of those master shots are selected, and edited in parallel, the total event recorded can be reconstructed using the best or most significant segments of each master take, presenting a fragmented view similar to the short single shot process. A good film maker uses either method. Both are quite dynamic and offer definite pictorial advantages over a single shot recording of a scene.

A wider perspective

Parallel editing covers greater possibilities in the interaction of two narrative lines. Where the degree of knowledge shared between the characters of the story, or between the film and its audience is variable the alternatives can be seen as those in which:

1 Both story lines support each other, and the data that both contribute (alternately) builds up the story.

2 In one line, the movement or intention is kept the same, while on the other the reactions to that steady repetition are varied.

3 The characters involved in both narrative lines are unaware of what the other group is doing, and only the audience has all the facts.

4 The information given in both narrative lines is incomplete, so that the characters have all the facts, but the audience is purposely kept in the dark, to stimulate its interest.

Which one of these approaches is to be used must be decided by the story writer and the film maker concerned. But one fact remains, parallel film editing will always provide the best way of conveying the desired information to the audience. The two basic elements, action and reaction, will help complete the presentation.

11

3

DEFINING THE BASIC TOOLS

Films made with a camera almost always tell a story. Usually in these movies, real persons and objects are recorded on film and reproduced on the screen at the same film cadence: 24 frames per second. But on some occasions that procedure is altered and man-made drawings, patterns, objects, animals, and persons projected at 24 frames per second, may have been recorded at speeds that go up to hundreds of frames per second, or down to frame by frame photography with variable time lapses between each exposure.

In the first group, we can place the following film forms:
newsreel
documentary, and
fiction.

In the second category we can include all the films that require a radical change in recording techniques. This second category would cover:

animated cartoons,
animated puppets,
time lapse photography of objects,
plants, animals or human beings.

We are particularly concerned here with film techniques applicable to the first three.

Newsreel

Newsreels attempt to cover an unrepeatable act or event. The film maker has minimal control over the incident he records. He is a spectator with a visual recording mechanism. In its crudest form this coverage produces a series of disconnected shots that register portions of the total event but when projected on the screen present

12

total chaos. Many things are missing but a narrator can give some unity to the ensemble. A middle stage is reached if these shots are bridged by others where spectators are seen reacting. This creates a sort of action-reaction relationship, which the audience accepts though still conscious that they are seeing an incomplete occurrence.

The most complete film record is obtained by using one or more motor driven cameras synchronized with a tape recorder registering all the events, interesting or dull, as in some "verité" films.

But on film, there is no such thing as the ideal camera position to cover a situation fully and impartially. Camera operators have to choose their sites, heights, lenses, lights. All this leads to a compromise—an unavoidable selection. And even then, few people would cover a situation in exactly the same way.

Documentary

The documentary film form offers further variants. To start with, most documentary films deal not with one, but with a succession of occurrences that take place under a common motivation. When presenting this material on the screen, changes are introduced in the real order in which the situations occurred. Many motives may be involved, such as the following:

a Several situations that respond to a common stimulus are grouped into a sequence. As the nature of the stimulus is changed, the subjects are grouped in new sequences. Each individual subject was perhaps filmed reacting consecutively to the chain of stimuli, but now his actions are fragmented and put together in patterns of behaviour, thus disrupting the temporal continuity to achieve an idea progression.

b The linear recording of an event is interrupted to introduce an explicative visual variant different in nature, i.e.: animated drawings to show a process that cannot be photographed using the real elements.

c The series of events are repeated in different patterns or order of presentation, to explore diverse approaches and solutions.

The list can be longer. But the fact remains that *manipulation is necessary*—facts have to be arranged to be shown at their best and an event is often repeated to be filmed several times. Repetition means staging.

13

We are manipulating the occurrence, selecting with a technique that cloaks our tampering with reality. The result borders on the realm of fiction.

Fiction film

Many of the best documentaries have profited from a dual approach that blends unadulterated reality with carefully recomposed fiction. This statement leads us to the ultimate film form—total fiction. Here the events are also real, but can be repeated at will as many times as necessary, until the exact nuance of behaviour or acting is captured on film from one, two or several angles. Each situation is carefully planned and enacted for the benefit of the cameras. The end result strived for is an imitation of reality. In fact, what we see is a richer version of reality. There is not a single viewpoint, but a plurality of them, such as no human being is able to obtain in real life. Reconstructed reality is the most popular of film forms.

Film stories may be planned or unplanned. The techniques to be discussed here mostly concern the planned approach where events are selected, arranged and staged for a series of related actions. Unplanned events must be treated in a way that permits them to blend with planned scenes.

Three types of scene

Film stories usually have a structure that progresses scene by scene from the statement of a situation, through a development of the conflict, to a *dénoument* that closes the play. All scenes fall within these three categories:
1   dialogues without action
2   dialogues with action
3   actions without dialogue
These are of course simplified categories. Actors may not move while they talk, but the vehicle on which they are placed can, and the camera also can be in motion. When actors move during their exchange of dialogue the camera can be fixed, or move with them. And in the third instance the voice of a narrator or the internal thoughts of the characters may accompany the pure movement framed on the screen. Furthermore, all three techniques can be used together within a single sequence. But this classification is essential to the study of grammatical rules.

Elements of film grammar

To translate scenes from script to picture any rules must have a twofold effect:
1 We must shoot film that can later be joined in continuity.
2 We need solutions for the editorial problems that will arise in different situations.
To achieve this we must control two things:
1. The distances from which we record the event.
2 The motions of the subjects performing that event.
By selecting the distance, we control what the audience sees and the number of performers and objects shown in the different shots. Points or moments of emphasis in a story, can be governed by approaching or moving away from our main subjects.

With the second device, without hampering the free movement of our performers we impose a measure of control on the recording process of that motion.

The shot

Now, let us define which are the grammatical tools of the film language. First of all we have the shot.

The length of the shot or take is limited only by the amount of film that can be exposed in the camera without reloading—say, four, ten or thirty three minutes. The shot can be used in its entirety in an uninterrupted flow, or broken up into smaller strips of film to be intercut with other shots. A staged event can be shot repeatedly, in whole or part from the same or different positions. Generally, when the scene does not play too well the repeat shots are taken from the same position. Changes of camera position are used more conciously, to allow the film editor to cross-cut.

Movement

During a shot the camera can remain *fixed*, or it can pan (sweep horizontally on its axis), or it can *tilt* (pivoting either up or down) or it can travel at different speeds attached to a moving vehicle.

It can record simple or complex events. It can move supporting the action that it records.

It can do all that from different distances. Those distances can be obtained either physically or optically.

15

Distances

The gradation of distances between the camera and the recorded subject can be infinite. Actual practice has taught that there are five basic definable distances. They are known as:

    close up, or big close up
    close shot,
    medium shot,
    full shot, and
    long shot.

However, these denominations do not imply a fixed measurable distance in each case. The terminology is quite elastic, and deals mainly with concepts. It is obvious that the distance between camera and subject is different between a *close shot* of a house and *close shot* of a man.

Figs. 3.1 to 3.5 illustrate the areas that each camera position covers.

FIGURE 3.1　Close up.

FIGURE 3.2　Close shot.

Through actual practice it has been discovered that the human figure has 'cutting heights' from which pleasing compositions can be obtained, whether one or more bodies are shown on the screen.

These cutting heights are:
under the arm pits,
under the chest,
under the waist,
under the crotch, and
under the knees.

16

FIGURE 3.3 Medium shot.

FIGURE 3.4 Full shot.

FIGURE 3.5 Long shot.

If a full shot of the human figure is framed, the feet of the subject must be included. Cutting above the ankles will not give a pleasant composition. Figure 3.6 illustrates the diverse cutting heights.

Types of editing

There are three main ways in which a scene can be edited:

1 A master shot registers the whole scene. To avoid monotony, there are several techniques for editing 'within the film, frame or 'in camera'.'

2 A master shot is inter-cut with other shorter takes. These other takes cover fragments of the scene from a different distance or introduce subjects in another place, and are intercut into the

17

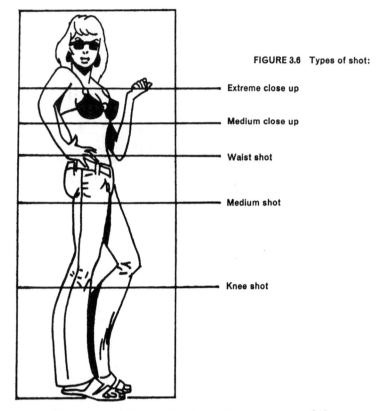

FIGURE 3.6 Types of shot:

Extreme close up

Medium close up

Waist shot

Medium shot

Knee shot

master shot to provide emphasis on key passages of the scene.

3   Two or more master shots are blended together in parallel.

Our point of view alternates from one master shot to the other. By using any or all of the three methods we can cover a *sequence*. A sequence envelopes a scene or a series of related scenes that have a time and space continuity. Usually a sequence has a beginning, a middle and a conclusion. This conclusion ends either on a high point or a low point or a low moment of intensity of the story.

Visual punctuation

Sequences are joined together by two types of *punctuation*:

1   A straight cut.
2   An optical.

In a straight cut the transition is visually abrupt. The several ways of achieving it will be discussed later on. In the case of an optical, a *fade out, fade in, dissolve* or *wipe*, can be employed to obtain a smooth visual transition.

Scene matching

In matching scenes the following three requirements must be satisfied. It is necessary to match:
1 The position.
2 The movement.
3 The look.
The movie screen is a fixed area. If a performer is shown on the left side of the screen in a full shot, he must be on that side if there is a cut to a close shot placed on the same visual axis. If this rule for matching the position is not respected, awkward visual jumps on the screen will result, so that the audience has to switch attention from one sector to another to locate the main character

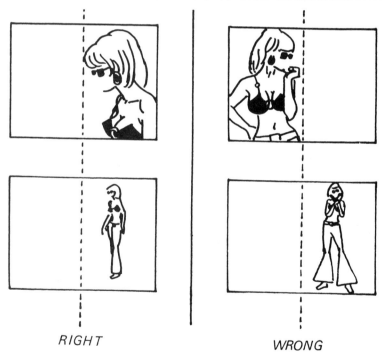

RIGHT   WRONG

FIGURE 3.7   The central subject of the scene should, in normal cases, be kept in the same frame position, as in the first example, when making a cut from one shot to another.

19

whose adventures they are following. This is both annoying and distracting. The spectator must be given a comfortable eye scan of the shots with a constant orientation that allows him to concentrate on the story (Fig. 3.7).

For this purpose the screen is usually divided in two or three vertical parts, in which the main performers are placed. All position matching is done in any or all of these areas.

Matching the movement has a similar logical base. Direction of movement should be the same in two consecutive shots that record the continuous motion of a performer otherwise the audience will be confused about the supposed direction of movement (Fig. 3.8).

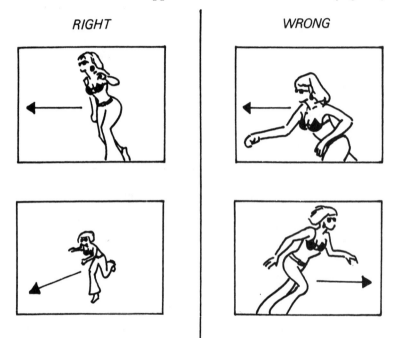

RIGHT   *WRONG*

FIGURE 3.8 Movement is of a similar kind and in the same direction in the first example illustrated. The audience follows the motion of the subject easily. But if the direction of movement is suddenly reversed in the second shot, there will be confusion as to where the subject is going.

Matching the look is the third requirement to be taken into account when assembling shots where players appear individually or in groups. Matched looks on the screen *are always opposed*. Two subjects who exchange looks, do so in conflicting directions, as shown in Fig. 3.9.

FIGURE 3.9 When two people face each other, their glances are in opposed directions.

If the actors are framed in separate shots, this opposition in directions must be maintained for a proper visual continuity.

FIGURE 3.10 If both players are featured in separate shots, their glances should still be in opposed directions.

If both players were looking in the same direction in both shots, they would logically be looking at a third person or object, and not at themselves, as demonstrated in Fig. 3.11.

FIGURE 3.11 When both players look in the same direction, they are not looking at each other, but at something or at somebody else.

Without this opposition of glances, scenes become weak and sometimes meaningless.

Opposed glances

Establishing and maintaining a constant opposition in the direction of a look exchanged between two players, can be achieved

21

very simply. The only requisite is that their heads face each other. The physical distance between them is unimportant. If a player moves to a position where he now has his back to his fellow player, the opposition of looks is maintained as he periodically glances at the other person over his shoulder, or if after a moment, he turns to face his interlocutor again. In a group of *three*, one of them is the arbiter of attention. When one of the actors speaks, the other two look at him. As the interest shifts, one of the players looks to the new centre of attention, making an effective and clear change for the audience to follow. See Fig. 3.12.

FIGURE 3.12   Player B acts as the arbiter of attention, shifting the interest from A to C. He achieves this change by moving his head from one player to the other.

In the first example in Fig. 3.12 attention is centred on player A, and in the second illustration the interest is on performer C. We must see the arbiter of attention, subject B in this case, move his head from one side to the other, to guide the audience in following the displacement of the point of interest from A to C.

This also happens if we frame each player in separate shots. Interest in a scene can be destroyed by allowing the players to look at the wrong places, in two or more directions. We must guide the audience, not confuse them (Fig. 3.13).

RIGHT   WRONG

FIGURE 3.13 In the first example two players concentrate on the person in the foreground, who thus becomes the dominant one. In the second case, B looks in another direction, drawing away the attention of the audience, who are forced to choose and are unable to. Either player C is important or something off screen is really upstaging her. The audience cannot know.

Centre of interest alternates

When large groups have to be presented, two possibilities arise:
1 All players focus their attention on a central character, changing in unison to a second centre of attention as the point of interest in the scene shifts.
2 Several groups are present in the scene. Each group has two basic centres of interest. A predominant group is chosen.

In the first case two subjects are the centre of interest in the group. The attention of the audience (and that of the remaining players on the screen) moves from one to the other, and back again. The silent performers are the arbiters of attention. They look in unison at the actor holding the interest, and shift their looks to the other performer as the centre of attention is transferred. Sometimes a third centre of interest is introduced to break the monotony of continually shifting between two points, especially in lengthy scenes from a single camera position.

23

FIGURE 3.14 Here a large group is seen throwing attention first on to A and then on G. These two players are the centre of attention in the group, and the silent performers decide with the direction of their glances, cast in unison, which of the two is dominant at any one time.

In the second situation stated above two approaches can be applied. In both the dominant group is nearly always placed near the camera.

In the first approach we have two, three or more static groups framed on the screen. The one that interests us is located near the camera.

The other groups are in the background. All of them present closed circles of interest, being independent from each other.

Logically, the group closest to us demands immediate attention, while we are just conscious of the existence of the others and would miss them only if suddenly removed.

To stress the foreground situation dramatically the other groups could at a certain moment break the closed circles of attention and turn to look at the forward group.

FIGURE 3.15 With several groups of people in the scene, the group closest to the camera is the dominant.

The second approach offers a variant: the foreground group remains static, but the subordinate groups in the background are given movement across the screen. Such can be the activity of traffic in a street, or of dancers in a ballroom.

These movements must be inconspicuous, or they interfere with the foreground action.

4

THE TRIANGLE PRINCIPLE

Basic body positions

All dialogued scenes have two central players. These two dominant players in a film scene can be deployed in a pair of linear arrangements:
a straight line composition, and
a right angle relation.
Figure 4.1 illustrates the concept.

Within those arrangements four body rapports can be assumed during a conversation between the players.
1 The actors face each other,
2 the actors are placed side by side,
3 one player has his back to the other.
4 They are placed back to back.

A human body can assume one of the following positions:
1 lying down (either face up or down or lying on his side)
2 kneeling (either the torso straight up, or sitting on the heels, or bent forward with the elbows on the ground)
3 sitting (from a squatting position to any height afforded by the instrument used to support the body)
4 reclining (either backwards on a supporting surface or forwards by using the elbows as support)
5 standing (either up or leaning sideways using a hand for support)
These body positions might be assumed simultaneously by both players or different body attitudes could be chosen for each. In the later case various combinations are afforded: different linear compositions, body rapports and body positions, provide in toto

FIGURE 4.1   Two players can be deployed in the linear arrangements depicted in these illustrations, either as straight line or a right angle.

a wide range of visual presentations, for dramatically underlining the dialogue of exchange between two static characters.

It can be said that between two talking partners a *line of interest* flows. This line has a straight path.

Line of interest

The line of interest between two central players in a scene is based on the direction of the looks exchanged between them. A line of interest can be observed from three extreme positions, without crossing to the other side of the line. These three extreme positions

27

FIGURE 4.2 The four basic body rapports that can be assumed by two players engaged in a conversation.

28

form a triangular figure with its base parallel to the line of interest (Fig. 4.3).

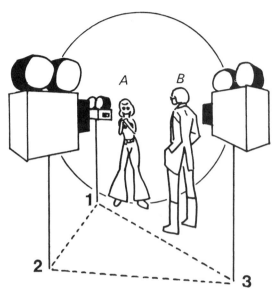

FIGURE 4.3 Basic positions into the triangular method of covering two players located on a common line of interest.

Camera viewpoints for master shots, are on the angles of this figure. The main advantage is that each performer is framed on the same side of the screen in each shot with player A on the left side and player B on the right.

Two triangular camera formations can be set, one on each side of a line of interest (Fig 4.5).

But we cannot successfully cut from a camera position in one pattern to another on the other triangular arrangement. If we do that, we will only confuse our audience, because using two camera positions located on different triangular formations will not present a steady emplacement of the players on the same areas of the screen, as mentioned in the previous chapter when discussing matched shots.

A cardinal rule for the triangular camera principle then, is to select one side of the line of interest and stick to it. This is one of the most respected rules in film language. It can be broken of course. The proper way to do that is discussed later.

29

FIGURE 4.4 Constant screen position for both players is assured by using the triangle principle for camera coverage of a dialogued scene between two static players. Notice how the girl A is always on the left side of the screen in the three shots. The young man B also remains framed on his own side, the right sector of the screen.

Importance of the heads

When two performers are standing face to face, or sitting facing each other, it is quite simple to draw the line of interest flowing between them. But when the actors are lying down with their bodies parallel or extended in opposite directions, it seems more

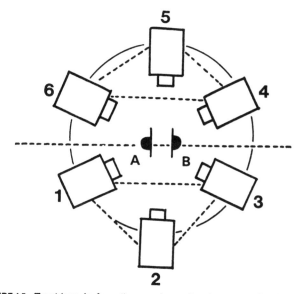

FIGURE 4.5 Two triangular formations can be employed one on each side of the line interest. One of them has to be chosen, excluding the position on the other.

FIGURE 4.6 The two incompatible right angle positions relative to the line of interest, position 2 and position 5.

31

difficult. Yet it is quite simple if we remember only that the central points of two persons talking to each other are their heads.

They attract our attention immediately, regardless of the positions of the bodies, because the head is the source of human speech and the eyes the most powerful direction pointers that a human being has to attract or direct interest. The positions of the bodies therefore do not really count, it is the heads that matter. Even in situations where one actor has his back to the other, or they are back to back, a line of interest passes between their heads. In all film scenes, the line of interest must flow between the heads of the two central performers.

Five basic variations of the triangle principle

A straight line composition can be covered visually by using three different arrangements of the triangular camera principle, with the players in a right angle relation only two triangular figures can be applied for visual coverage of the scene. Let us examine each one of these *five variants* separately.

EXTERNAL REVERSE ANGLES. The two sites on the base of the triangular camera locations (parallel to the line of interest of the scene), provide the three variations with which a linear disposition of the players can be covered. The cameras placed on those two viewpoints can be pivoted on their axis, obtaining three well differentiated positions. Each one of those positions is applied in pairs. We mean by this that both camera angles on the base of the geometric figure assume identical positioning in their relation to the players covered.

In the first case, both camera positions on the base of the

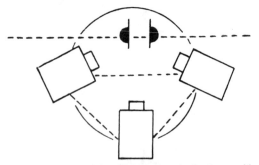

FIGURE 4.7 External reverse angles. The cameras in the two positions parallel to the line of interest are directed inward towards the players. Note that the symbol represents a human figure—the flat side indicates the front of the figure.

triangle are behind the backs of the two central players, angled in, close to the line of interest between the performers and covering them both.

INTERNAL REVERSE ANGLES. In the second variant, the cameras are between the two players, pivoted outwards from the triangular figure, and close to the line of interest though not representing the viewpoints of the performers. In either case the rapport is not that of a head-on confrontation, though quite close to it in effect.

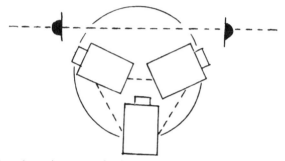

FIGURE 4.8 Internal reverse angles. In this variant the two camera positions parallel to the line of interest point outwards, covering each player individually.

With the cameras back to back anywhere on the base of the triangle the effect represents the subjective viewpoint of the player excluded from the shot.

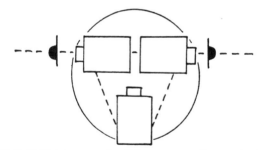

FIGURE 4.9 Subjective camera angles. If the camera positions are back to back on the line of interest itself, they each become the subjective point of view of the player excluded from the shot.

PARALLEL POSITIONS. With the third variant the camera sites are on the base of the triangular figure close to the line of interest, deployed with their visual axes in parallel, (Fig. 4.10) and cover the performers individually.

33

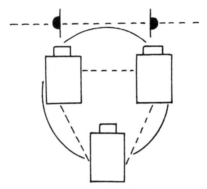

FIGURE 4.10 Parallel camera positions. When both camera positions have their visual axes in parallel, they cover each player individually giving us a profile view.

The three situations outlined above can be combined to multiply the camera placements. Fig. 4.11 shows how the combination looks. Seven camera viewpoints contained within a triangular figure. All positions can be combined in pairs to cover both players, except for the internal and parallel sites that cover each of the subjects individually.

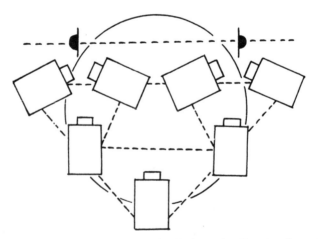

FIGURE 4.11 The three basic variants outlined in the previous figures can be combined into a major triangular deployment. Thus, varied and ample camera coverage is obtained for two static players during their exchange of dialogue.

RIGHT ANGLE POSITIONS. When the actors are placed side by side in an 'L' formation, the camera viewpoints on the base of the imaginary triangle acquire a *right angle* relationship, close to the line of interest passing between the players. In this case with the camera in front of the performers.

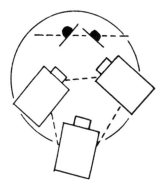

FIGURE 4.12 When the players are placed side by side in an L formation, a right angle camera relationship is assumed by the two sites located on the base of the triangular figure for camera placement.

The same arrangement can be placed behind the players, with which a new variant for dialogue coverage is achieved, shown in Fig. 4.13.

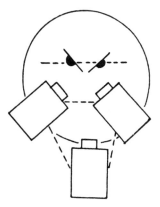

FIGURE 4.13 The right angle camera positions cannot only be in front of the actors, but behind.

COMMON VISUAL AXIS. To cover only one of the players in a master shot while framing both players on the other, the camera in one of the two viewpoints on the triangle base, must be *advanced on its visual axis*.

Advancing on either of the two viewpoints (optically or physically) we obtain a closer shot of the selected performer, thus emphasizing him over his partner. Fig. 4.14 shows the arrangement.

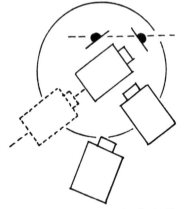

FIGURE 4.14 Advance on a camera common visual axis. To obtain coverage of a single player in the group, one of the cameras is moved forward on the visual axis line of either of the two positions on the base of the triangle.

The above mentioned five basic variations are used not only to cover static conversations of a group of players, but also the movement of those players on the screen.

Emphasis by composition

When two speaking performers face each other, the strongest camera positions to record their dialogue, are located on the base of the triangle, parallel to the line of interest. Positions 1 and 3 of the *external reverse* camera arrangement, have two immediate advantages over the camera site situated on the apex of the triangle. They give composition in depth, because from their viewpoints, the actors are placed on two different planes: one close to the camera and the other further back.

The second advantage is that one of the actors faces the camera, getting our full attention, while the other has his back to us. In theatrical terms, the second actor has an open body position (face to the audience), while the first has a closed body position

36

(his back to the audience). Therefore the performer facing the camera is the dominant one.

On the screen this is accentuated further by the distribution of screen space in the composition of the shot, as shown in Fig. 4.15.

FIGURE 4.15 Emphasis by composition on the two external reverse master shots can be achieved by giving two-thirds of the screen space to the player who faces the camera, and the remaining third to the one with his back to the camera.

On normal screen sizes (3 × 4 ratio) the actor who speaks is given two-thirds of the screen space, while his interlocutor has only one-third.

If the latter is slightly out of focus, the emphasis on the speaking performer will be strengthened.

The second position in the triangular arrangement is the weakest of the three. It views the actors from the side (a half-open body position), and pictures them on the same plane and with equal screen space. It is reserved for the opening or closing of a conversation sequence. It is also used to introduce a pause in the cutting rhythm of the sequence or to precede a change in editorial pattern.

The one-third, two-thirds, space of relationship just described works also wide screen frames, as Fig. 4.16 shows.

FIGURE 4.16 The one-third—two-thirds space distribution principle is maintained for visual compositions on the wide screen.

But a dialogue between two persons seen in close shots on such a screen becomes too jarring from a visual standpoint, due to the great volumes of screen image being shifted from take to take. A solution can be found however. The screen is divided in three equal parts for compositional purposes. The player featured in each reverse shot is always put in the central sector of the screen. This means, that player B is in the centre of the screen from Position 1, and performer A is in the middle of the picture from Position 3. In Fig. 4.17 the pictorial composition in the foreground rests heavily on the left and on the right respectively. The remaining third of the screen space may be filled only by a background object or busy detail to balance the foreground composition.

Audience attention is thus focused on the centre of the screen at all times, without breaking the triangle principle for the placement of the camera. This visual solution can be used with a normal screen size composition too, but not with such spectacular results as a large screen affords, especially in close and medium shots.

Types of visual emphasis

Now that the wide screen is in general use many film makers take advantage of the long rectangular shape to practise adventurous compositional contrasts in their use of what I have called external reverse shots.

The player in the foreground blocks half of the screen with his body. Usually, he is sparsely illuminated, his figure totally in silhouette. The actor facing the camera in the background is brilliantly lit, so that the lighter areas shift from left to right, and back again, as each alternate reverse shot is used (Fig. 4.18).

The next recourse is to increase the area of the screen given to the player in the foreground, who has his back to the audience and is minimally lit. Most of the screen space is allocated to this

FIGURE 4.17 By dividing the screen into three equal sectors, the dominant player in each master shot can be placed in the centre of the screen without breaking the triangle principle for camera deployment. Thus attention is always retained in the centre of the screen.

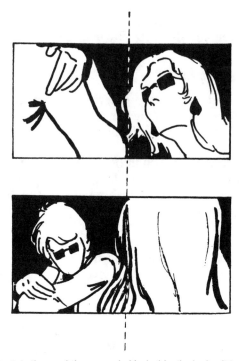

FIGURE 4.18 A half area of the screen is blocked by the body of the player in the foreground, whose back is minimally lit, to emphasize the lighter figure in the background.

foreground player and a small sector of the screen is left free for you to see the dominant actor in the background (Fig. 4.19).

The device is particularly emphatic, because our attention is centred on a small (usually upper, occasionally lower) area of the screen. Right and left top angles of the screen are contrasted from shot to shot, as the two extreme external reverse camera positions are edited in parallel.

When an internal and an external reverse camera position are combined, some film makers place the performers off-centre in both shots, close to one of the lateral sides. The empty two-thirds of the screen are filled with colour, or inert shapes that do not interfere with the players. Fig. 4.21 illustrates the concept.

On other occasions a dark area that blocks the same two-thirds of the screen in both shots is employed to obtain the same effect, as seen in Fig. 4.22.

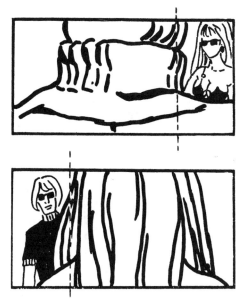

FIGURE 4.19   Here a very small upper area of the screen is used to frame the dominant player in each reverse master shot.

FIGURE 4.20   In this example a small lower area of the screen is used to compose the key figure in each of the reverse master shots.

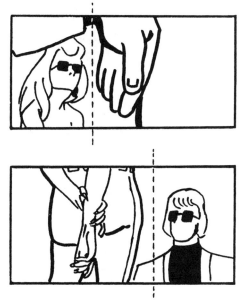

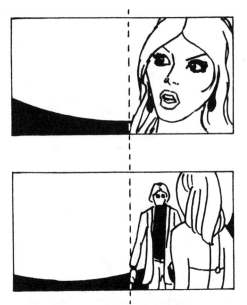

FIGURE 4.21 An internal reverse angle and an external reverse camera position use pictorial compositions that concentrate the players in the same lateral area of the screen.

FIGURE 4.22 The centre of interest in both master shots is retained on the left side of the picture. The rest of the screen is darkened to stress the key, well-lit area. Director Sidney J. Furie uses many compositions of this type in his films, especially in *The Ipcress File*, *The Apaloosa* and *The Naked Runner*.

This technique is also extended to internal reverse camera positions. These camera sites cover each of the two central figures individually. Both players occupy the same screen area in each reverse shots.

Two-thirds of the screen in both pictorial compositions are kept empty (Fig. 4.23).

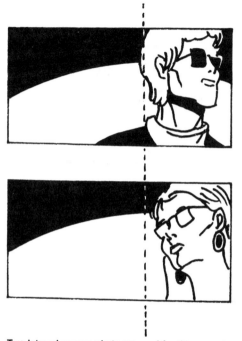

FIGURE 4.23 Two internal reverse shots are used for this example, and the same area of the screen is employed to frame the players. Note the opposed glances that relate the players to one another visually.

The usual rapport for two internal reverse shots is to fill two thirds of the screen area with the figure of the player featured in the shot, leaving the third area in front of him free, so that the composition has breathing space in front. (Fig. 4.24).

J. G. Albicocco in the film *Le Rat D'Amérique* used the wide screen to compose unusual pairs of external reverse shots. Fig. 4.25 shows how he framed the players on opposed sides of the screen from shot to shot.

He applied the same compositional concept to the juxtaposition of internal reverse shots, as depicted in Fig. 4.26.

FIGURE 4.24 Two-thirds of the screen area are used in each master shot to compose the lone player, leaving 'air' in front of him to achieve a pleasing pictorial composition.

FIGURE 4.25 Bizarre way of framing two players for a pair of reverse master shots. Its shock effect can often help to obtain an alienated mood in the scene.

FIGURE 4.26 Here, the player's face is placed close to one side of the screen frame, leaving half the screen empty behind. This unusual way of composing two related internal reverse master shots brings a special visual enhancement to the scene.

Those types of composition quickly grasp attention and tend to distract from the mood of the scene. And yet, to certain types of situations such as intimate love scenes, they bring a strange imbalance that can enhance the situation. External reverse angles

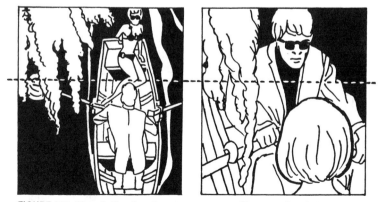

FIGURE 4.27 Here, both external reverse camera positions are directly behind the players, on the line of interest itself. Only high angles permit this alignment.

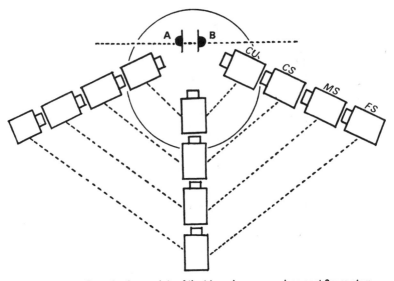

FIGURE 4.28 From the three points of the triangular camera placement figure stem axis lines on which the camera can be placed at any distance to cover the two central players in a scene.

from different heights located on the line of interest itself can be applied if you put one player low in the frame and the other in the upper half. You can interchange their locations on the screen in the reverse shot (Fig. 4.27).

These principles do not apply only to close ups. From the three points of the triangular figure, stem axis lines on which the camera can be placed to obtain close ups, close shots, medium shots and full shots (Fig. 4.28).

We will now see this principle applied to dialogue scenes involving two or more persons. Each camera position in the triangular layout will be used to produce a master shot. The scene will be covered in full from each set-up and from at least two camera viewpoints. The intention is to edit these master shots to give full visual coverage.

Before going on to these formulas let us examine how the triangle principle applies to the coverage of a single player.

Triangle principle: One person

In a film, as in life, one person can monologue or dialogue with himself. But in a film the internal thoughts can be made audible.

46

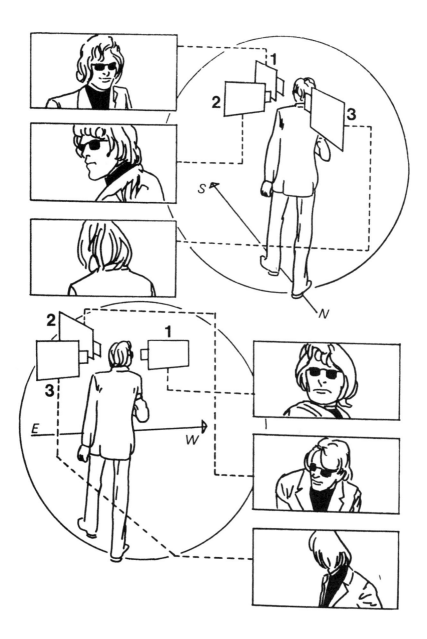

FIGURE 4.29 The direction in which the lone player is looking governs the placement of the camera within the triangular figure, as illustrated above.

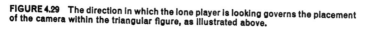

47

The device is used in literature, theatre, and radio transmitted to the present, past, or future tense. But with film the capturing of our inner self is most direct, whether the internal or external voice of the player speaks, or whether they conduct a dialogue with one another. When the internal voice is heard, the performer has his lips closed. He may react facially but there is no lip synchronization. The internal voice can be replaced by the remembered or imagined voices of the protagonist.

At all times the direction of his gaze dominates the visual presentation of the lone player. A line of interest extends between his eyes and the object gazed upon. Once this line of interest has been established, the triangular camera placement principle can be applied. Even if we are not shown the object he is looking at, or he stares into space. The subject need not remain static—he can write, paint, or be engaged in a manual activity, all without moving from a fixed place. The direction of his gaze becomes our line of interest, even when his head is turned sideways (Fig. 4.29).

If the lone player is looking straight ahead, our line of interest runs north-south to his body. With his head on one side, it extends along an east-west axis.

If the player looks straight ahead, an east-west axis cannot be used to position the camera. The sense of direction is broken if either reverse shot is used consecutively. Examine Fig. 4.30.

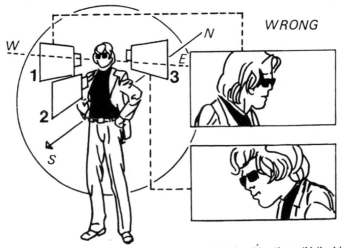

FIGURE 4.30 When the lone figure is looking straight ahead (north-south) the triangular camera placements cannot be in an east-west direction. The external reverse angles will present conflicting directions of gaze, which is incorrect.

Likewise, if the camera is on a north-south axis when our lone player is looking sideways it will not work. The direction of his gaze must be adhered to as the line of interest, with the triangular camera deployment set parallel.

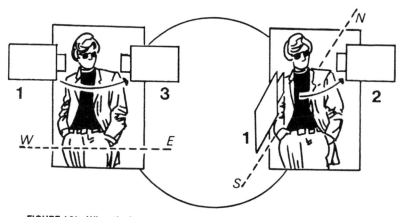

FIGURE 4.31 When the lone player turns his head in a half circle this is covered by east-west camera position. With a right angle turn a north-south camera placement will suffice.

The direction of the line of interest will shift when the lone player moves his head from one side to the other and two coverages are possible:

1   a head turn of almost 180° is covered by the camera using an east-west axis:
2   a head turn of 90° is covered by the camera using a north-south axis.

Fig. 4.31 illustrates both cases, for which the triangular camera coverage must be shifted.

5

DIALOGUE BETWEEN TWO PLAYERS

Visual formulae to cover dialogue are few in number—though variations can be achieved through dress, background, lighting, etc.

The two strong camera positions parallel to the line of interest are those from which master shots are made to cover the static dialogue. The scene is first covered partially or in full from one camera position, and then repeated from the other to be edited in parallel later.

Working from the two dominant camera positions, the following analysis uses as a basis the five triangular variations for camera deployment examined in the preceding chapter.

Face to face

The most simple approach with face to face dialogue is to use a set of external reverse angles. With the performer appearing in foreground (with his back to us) in external reverse shots the tip of the nose should not extend beyond the line of his cheek—we do not see his nose at all from such an angle. The one third/two-thirds screen space distribution is basic, although the variants already discussed in the examination of the triangle principle can be used if desired.

Fig. 5.1 shows the classic arrangement, which is the one more widely favoured by film makers all over the world.

An *internal* reverse angle can be combined with an *external* reverse camera position. The performer singled out is the more prominent. Two solutions are available (Fig. 5.2).

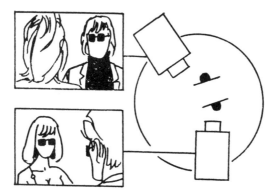

FIGURE 5.1 Dialogue between two players. This is the most common framing for external reverse master shots of two players who face one another.

FIGURE 5.2 Two combinations of an external reverse angle and an internal camera position are possible.

51

The next possibility is to cover both subjects individually by using internal reverse shots. Only one of the actors is shown in each master shot (Fig. 5.3).

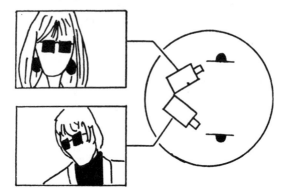

FIGURE 5.3   Two internal reverse master shots cover the players individually.

Number contrast

The combination of an external reverse and an internal reverse position creates *number contrast* on the screen. External reverse shots include both players, while internal reverse shots feature only one actor.

Thus we have the following three positions:

2 performers to 2—both master shots are external reverse camera position;
2 performers to 1—one master shot is external, and the other is internal;
1 performer to 1—both master shots are internal reverse angles.

Performers side by side

Two players placed side-by-side on a linear arrangement, have a common sense of direction—both look forward. Yet, this is not the direction of our line of interest—that runs *across* the heads of the performers—the direction of their gaze when they look at each other, and of psychological rapport between them. Even if they do not look at each other at all during the whole scene, if they are in a withdrawn mood, their heads lowered, eyes shut perhaps, with their voices occasionally breaking a long silence—even then, it is no deterrent to the subjacent link between them.

One possibility is with external reverse angles (Fig. 5.4).

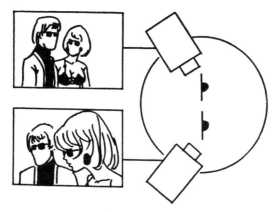

FIGURE 5.4 External shots applied to a linear arrangement for the actors, where both are looking in the same direction.

Another might employ internal reverse angles as seen in Fig. 5.5.

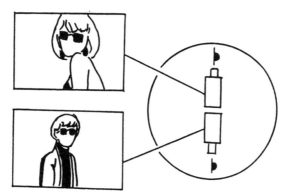

FIGURE 5.5 Internal reverse shots applied to a couple of performers sitting on the front seat of a car.

A third possibility is the use of parallel camera positions for a frontal coverage as Fig. 5.6 shows.

When two persons are shown in the front seat of a vehicle moving along a road, those three side-by-side coverage formulae find an immediate and natural application.

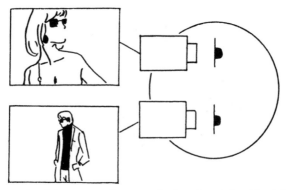

FIGURE 5.6 Parallel camera positions covering two players placed frontally to the cameras.

Several variants can be obtained with side-by-side positions where both players adopt a right angle body rapport. The first is the most simple, see Fig. 5.7.

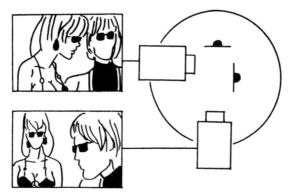

FIGURE 5.7 Right angle camera arrangement to cover two actors who assume an L formation.

The next variant is achieved by advancing along one of the camera axes, so that only one of the players is featured. Two solutions are available, seen in Fig. 5.8.

In the foregoing examples, the players' bodies face the inside of the angle formed by their figures. Positioned to face outwards, the three previous solutions would appear as in Fig. 5.9.

In all these right angle, side-by-side examples, the players are covered from the front. A rear camera coverage is also possible. Fig. 5.10 shows three approaches.

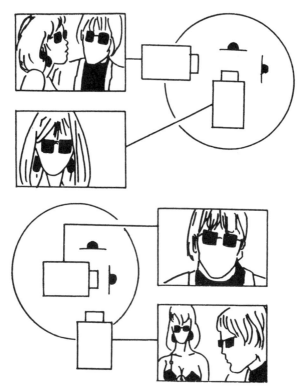

FIGURE 5.8 Two possibilities for an advancement along one of the camera axes; a close shot of one of the players is obtained.

Players behind one another

This situation occurs only in very special circumstances: two persons ride the same horse, or bicycle, a motor scooter or a canoe, and they are conversing from that forced position. The person in front usually turns his head to look at the other from the corner of his eye. The most used cinematic variations, employed to record dialogues in such scenes, are the external triangular camera deployment and the parallel camera positioning.

The situations covered involve the use of a moving vehicle. This complicates the scene because we must theoretically put the camera on another vehicle moving at the same speed. Establishing shots (the number 2 position in the apex of the triangle principle) are usually from a moving camera platform. But closer shots of the performers riding in the moving vehicle, are more difficult to

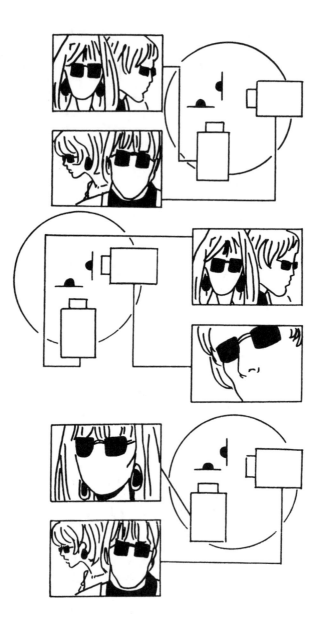

FIGURE 5.9 The players look outside their angular formation. The three approaches shown all have a right angle relationship.

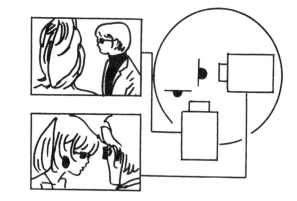

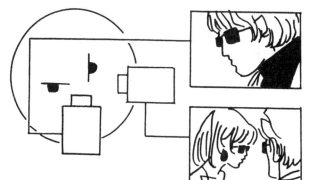

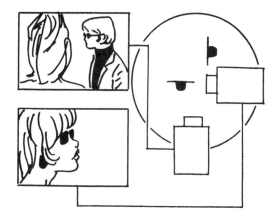

FIGURE 5.10 With a similar arrangement of players as that depicted in Fig. 5.9 the camera coverage is now from behind.

57

obtain with precision and safety for those involved. So, for close shots at speed a static vehicle is filmed in the studio, with either back projection or travelling matte, to provide a moving background. Some obstructions rotated in front of the actors complete the illusion. By resorting to this visual sleight of hand, the shots are obtained under controlled conditions. The vehicle is placed upon a base that can be rotated in front of the projection screen or blue-backing employed for travelling matte, so that by pointing the players towards or away from the camera, Positions 1 and 3 of the triangle camera coverage can be achieved. Positions 1 and 3 as seen in Fig. 5.11 cover external reverse positions.

FIGURE 5.11   External camera coverage for two players aligned one behind the other.

The second approach is a parallel camera coverage. Positions 1 and 3 individually cover each one of the players, while Position 2 frames both players on the screen (Fig. 5.12).

An advance on a common visual axis can be applied by using positions *1 and 2* or *3 and 2* of the parallel camera arrangement. By cutting from shot to shot, not only is there number contrast, but one of the players is emphasized as well.

On other occasions this type of dialogued scene is covered in a single shot from a single camera position, and this position is usually the number 2 (apex) in the triangular camera arrangement.

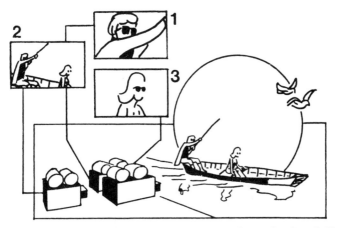

FIGURE 5.12   A parallel camera deployment to cover two players placed one behind the other.

Word of caution

When filming individual shots of two or more players, mistakes may occur. When the camera is repositioned on the set, and lens and lights changed and adjusted, frequently the direction in which the player was looking is forgotten, especially if the new shot is a head-on close shot.

An actor who was previously looking to the left, may now unconciously deliver his lines looking to the right, thus ruining the sequence.

When making individual shots of a player engaged in conversation, it is a good idea to keep the second actor in his former place, but out of camera range, for two reasons:
1   it will ensure that the camera is not placed on the other side of the line of interest;
2   the acting of the player on camera will be more natural, since he has someone to whom his lines can be delivered, instead of addressing them into empty space.
If for any reason, the second player is not available when the single shots are recorded on film, a reference point beside the camera hood (sun-shade) must be given to the performer.

Either a technician stands there substituting the missing player, or an object is selected for that purpose. Some technicians prefer to put their clenched fist against the hood as a reference point. Fig. 5.13 shows the situation.

59

FIGURE 5.13 The omitted player is kept out of camera range to ensure proper placement of the camera position. The actor or substitute B is positioned out of shot to provide the correct reference point for actress A whose attention is supposed to be fixed on a definite object or person who might have been seen in the previous shot.

Performers must avoid looking into the camera lens. It violates the direction of the line of interest and the audience feels that the player is looking at them directly and not at the other players. In a fiction film players may look into the camera lens only for a special purpose.

1 The performer monologues with the audience, as Laurence Olivier did in his film *Richard III*. It is a recourse derived from the theatre, where players break the flow of the scene and address the audience to give their own personal view of the events. It is an accepted convention but can destroy the flow of a staged event.

2 A more legitimate use is when the player addresses the audience as a radio or TV announcer.

In the first case, the player relates directly with the audience. We suddenly become participants and not spectators of a staged story. It shocks our feeling of security in the darkness of the movie theatre, while in the second instance the performer relates with another player (shown or not in the preceding or following shots).

That is why in the second case the audience accepts the actor looking straight into the camera lens as more natural.

These scenes must be used sparingly, and with strong dramatic motivating. The player need not continually look into the camera lens. He may look elsewhere, with a detached gaze not particularly fixed on a given point, and suddenly turn to the camera and look into it as he delivers the important lines of his monologue, thus stressing that passage.

Camera distance

Looking back at the examples given for the coverage of conversations between two players in a film scene, we notice three limitations:

1 All the takes were close shots;
2 The two players had the same body level;
3 The camera had the same level in both shots.

Further variations are available. The three points of the triangle principle generate axis lines on which the camera can be moved. Different camera distances can emphasize a dialogue visually, and afford a livelier presentation of the scene. In an example involving external reverse angles, Position 3 can be a medium shot, while Position 1 is a close shot. Fig. 5.14 illustrates such a case.

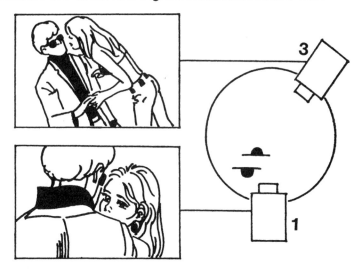

FIGURE 5.14 Different camera to subject distances on a set of external reverse camera positions.

61

Likewise, when covering two actors placed wide apart, this difference in distances is useful to concentrate attention on the most important of the two.

Let us say for example, that in a bare prison cell a lawyer questions a prisoner, and the lawyer dominates the scene. His questions and the way he waits for the answers are vital to the story, but the prisoner's attitude is passively uncooperative.

Changes of camera to subject distance would stress this situation by alloting a close shot to the lawyer, and a full shot to the prisoner (Fig. 5.15).

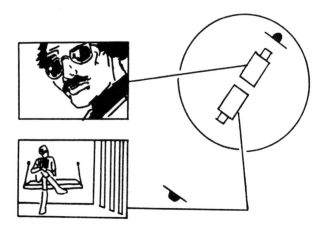

FIGURE 5.15 Different camera to subject distances on a set of internal reverse camera positions.

These distances should be exploited in pairs. No more than four different distances (two pairs) are needed to obtain good results.

For example, half the dialogue scene can be covered with a medium shot from Position 1, and a close shot from Position 3. The other half of the scene is then covered with a close shot from Position 1, and a medium shot from Position 3. By reversing the play of distances in the second pair of master shots, an effective and simple though dynamic presentation is obtained.

Camera and actor height

Camera height influences presentation. In conversation, the lens is usually at the same height as the actors, sitting or standing.

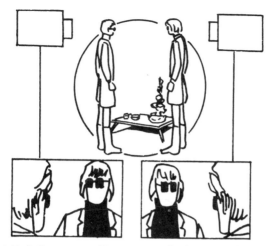

FIGURE 5.16 Both camera positions are on a level with the players they cover.

If an actor stands and the other is sitting, the camera height can vary for the reverse shot (Fig. 5.17).

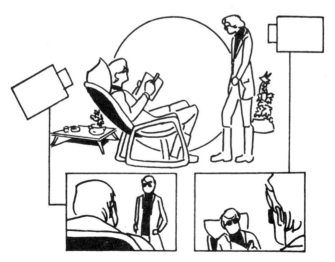

FIGURE 5.17 Suitable heights must be selected for each camera position to accommodate the differing heights of the players themselves.

The previous examples used external reverse angles. If internal reverse positions are used to cover the same situation (one actor stands, the other sits) for single shots of each player the camera is alternately high and low, as if seeing the scene from each player's viewpoint (Fig. 5.18).

FIGURE 5.18 Different camera heights are applied to a pair of internal reverse shots.

If the camera tilt is too acute the effect will be unreal, since we normally do not look at other people from such extreme low or high viewpoints. Such angles should be reserved as shockers to stress important story points or special events. On other occasions when both players are standing, we can obtain a contrast in heights by merely placing the camera low in both external reverse master shots (Fig. 5.19).

One player can be stressed with a different camera height on the external reverse shot coverage of two players who are standing up (Fig. 5.20).

A line of interest is not necessarily horizontal. When one player lies flat while the other stands or kneels, and using the triangular camera disposition, Positions 1 and 3 (those close to the line of interest) are near the heads of the performers, and therefore have different heights. A vertical line of interest is also possible (Fig. 5.21).

The head of each player is covered by vertical camera positions shown in the diagram.

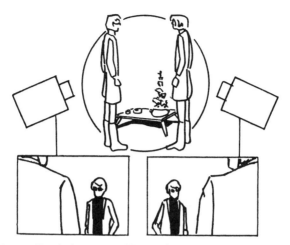

FIGURE 5.19 When both camera positions are low they create an interplay of heights between the players.

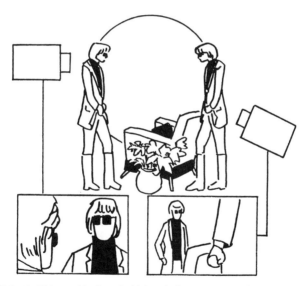

FIGURE 5.20 This combination of a high and a low camera position serves to throw emphasis on to one of the players.

If the line of interest runs horizontally, obliquely or vertically, the triangle principle for camera coverage can be adapted to it.

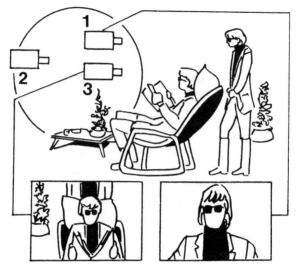

FIGURE 5.21   A vertical line of interest is covered by a triangular camera deployment.

Subjects lying side by side

Two players lying on the ground, face to face, or both on their backs, can be covered by a right angle placement to feature each actor alternately on the screen.

The camera is level with the actors on the ground, or framing the players from above, either from a slanted angle or from a vertical position (Fig. 5.22).

The players heads are kept in the same sectors of the screen. There is, perhaps, an alternation in heights within the screen. Fig. 5.22 shows (in the illustration corresponding to Position 1 of the camera) the head of the man on the left placed low on the screen, while camera Position 2 his head is high on the left. The same happens to the woman on the right, who without abandoning her area of the frame, shifts up and down from shot to shot. The higher position in each shot is occupied by the dominant player. With one camera placed lower than the performer's position, there is a reverse play of master shots. For this purpose the players must be placed in such a way that the camera has full scope for changing position above or below the level of the artists where the ground

FIGURE 5.22 A right angle camera deployment used to cover two players lying side by side.

slopes away sharply below and in front of them. In a studio set up this is quite easily arranged, but even on location if the shot is vital the performers can lie on a platform or over a hole dug in the ground so that the camera can be placed comfortably below their level for one of the reverse shots, especially if an immovable background object is to be included (Fig. 5.23).

Many film makers prefer to shoot such establishing shots on location with surroundings and closer shots under studio conditions subject, of course, to budget.

67

FIGURE 5.23 An external reverse camera set-up to cover two players lying side by side: a platform may be used to aid the shooting of one by a low level shot.

Telephone conversations

Two players talking to each other on the phone, are seen in single takes, and edited alternately to cover the length of their conversation. But to obtain the feeling of a normal conversation the actors should look in *opposite directions* especially with split screen sequences.

For the performers are filmed separately and combined in printing with mattes (Fig. 5.24).

FIGURE 5.24 Opposed glances are usually maintained between shots of two people talking on the phone.

Opposed diagonals

When people talk to each other they do not necessarily keep their bodies erect.

Sometimes the head is unconsciously tilted to a side to express a mood of ease or intimacy—an opportunity for interplay of opposed diagonals in composing close shots (Fig. 5.25).

This can be achieved with any one of the triangular camera set-ups already discussed. Wide screen compositions can also benefit from this treatment. Fig. 5.26 gives an example.

People have particular ways of standing when facing each other and in a conversation. Their bodies are seldom perfectly aligned. Standing a little to one side of the other is psychologically a more comfortable position. So, from the two external reverse camera positions the players may be aligned or there might be a small or large lateral gap between them.

If the players are perfectly aligned the reverse camera positions must be close to the axis line formed by their line of interest, not parallel to the line itself which would give a muddled view of the dominant player. A good result will register a diagonal composition of both bodies on the screen. The tip of the nearby actor's nose

69

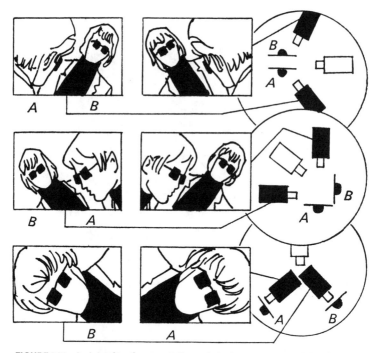

FIGURE 5.25   An interplay of opposed diagonals in the composition of the shots can be obtained with any one of the triangular camera set-ups.

FIGURE 5.26 Wide screen compositions can also benefit from diagonal pictorial arrangements.

should remain within the profile. When one small lateral gap exists between both players, the external reverse camera positions assume the relationship shown in Fig. 5.27.

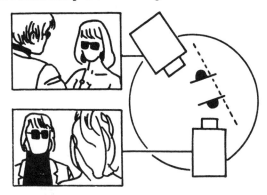

FIGURE 5.27 External reverse angles featuring a small gap in the alignment of the players.

In one of the shots the diagonal composition is maintained, but in the other the camera shoots over the shoulder of the player with his back to the camera.

If the lateral gap between them is wider (such cases occur when an object or piece of furniture is placed between the players), the external reverse camera positions assume a right angle relationship as seen in Fig. 5.28.

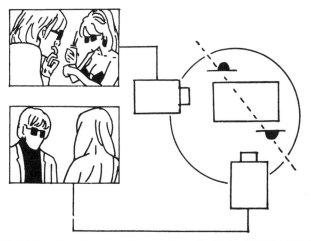

FIGURE 5.28 Right angle camera deployments applied to a wide gap between the players.

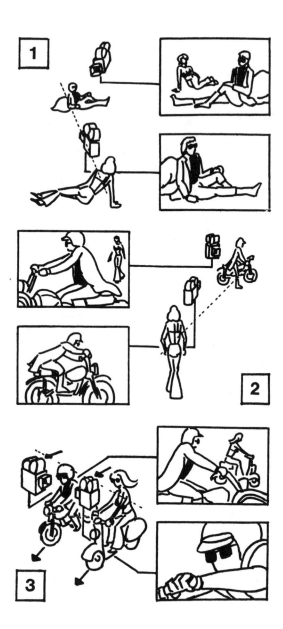

FIGURE 5.29 Three examples where the positioning of the actor's bodies or their direction of travel appears to violate the triangular camera placement principle. Yet all these examples are correct because they adhere to the line of interest.

72

Often, the opposition of an internal and external reverse shot violates the sense of direction of one of the players portrayed. Nevertheless their use is correct, since the line of interest is always dominant (Fig. 5.29).

In these cases the camera remains on the same side of the line of interest. It is the direction in which the bodies point from shot to shot that makes it appear as a blunt reverse. In the first example for instance, the legs of one player extend to the left on the external reverse shot, and to the right on the internal reverse. But bodies do not count, only the line of interest flowing between both heads matters, and all these examples adhere to this rule. If both reverse takes are tracking shots, such as in the third example, the directions of travel appear opposed on the screen.

Translucent density masks

The Japanese director Kihachi Okamoto in his film *Ankokugai no Taiketsu* (*The Last Gunfight*), starring Toshiro Mifune, successfully employed this daring technique. The process is not new. Directors of photography have repeatedly employed filters that fade gradually from dark to clear, using them to mask out clear skies as seen in exterior long shots to give them a night effect. In colour films sometimes a blue, green or red filter of that type is used for the same purpose. But the masks used by Kihachi Okamoto and photographer Kazuo Yamada on Agfacolor film and Tohoscope screen size, were translucent density masks of a consistent shade, with a definite edge to them that photographed in a blurr due to the out of focus position of the mask. These masks were placed obliquely on the screen and seldom placed vertically or horizontally, they were used singly or in pairs. The success of the technique was based on the wise criterion with which it was applied. Basically they were used to enhance sombre compositions in gun fight scenes. The director seldom used these masks on scenes shot under broad daylight or where the lighting was bright. He kept masks of different sizes, changing from place to place on the screen as shot followed shot, without diverting from the usual patterns of master shot editing. The masks were changed on an opposition principle similar to those portrayed in Figs. 5.25 and 5.26. In several instances he kept the same mask for two shots in a row, before shifting to another mask position. Unmasked shots were intercut into the sequence along with the masked shots. He

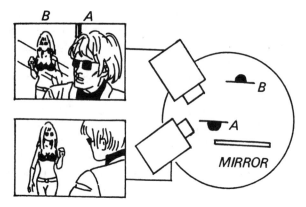

FIGURE 5.30 A simple case of a reverse shot where one of the players is reflected in a mirror.

even panned the camera keeping the mask on, and did forward tracking shots to which the mask conferred a rare method of isolation as darkness crept around the main subject as it was approached.

Players reflected on mirrors

Mirrors have always fascinated film makers. One, two or more mirrors have been employed in a surprising gallery of effects designed to be used with two master shots edited in parallel.

The most favoured effects use only one mirror, in one of three key positions in relation to the two players involved: behind, between, or sideways to the performers. For example, if the mirror is behind the players, in the first shot one of the performers is placed in the foreground, his back to the mirror, while the second player is reflected in its surface, but is out of shot (Fig. 5.30).

6

THREE-PLAYER DIALOGUE

Several different visual approaches have been evolved for covering three-player dialogue in a film. There are three basic linear dispositions:
1 a straight line,
2 a right angle or 'L' shaped formation,
3 a triangle.
Each arrangement requires different solutions to bring out its best possibilities.

Regular cases

As before, for the master shots the camera is positioned close to the line of interest. It is an easy situation if the three players are in a straight line—each player maintains his screen area from shot to shot (Fig. 6.1).

Here, two players are placed one behind the other, and face the third. But they could be placed on the extremes of the line, facing in towards the central performer (Fig. 6.2).

All the players are standing. Further variations are possible by having one or two players seated, or at different heights on a multi-level stage. These subtle variations, including different spacing between the figures, will help disguise the too formal pictorial composition that a straight line arrangement on a plane setting is apt to give. An 'L' shaped formation covered by right angle camera positions, will also maintain the same regular order of the players in both master shots as in Fig. 6.3.

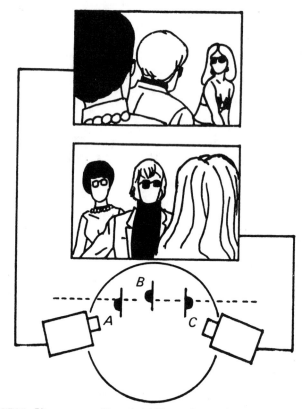

FIGURE 6.1 Players arranged in a straight line and covered by two external reverse camera positions; all the players retain their screen area in both shots.

Irregular cases

When the players are arranged in a triangle, two lines of interest converge on the dominant performer, and one line prevails. The centre of attention for the audience, and for the group on the screen, can be shifted by any subordinate player. He becomes the arbiter of attention. By turning his head from the dominant performer to the other, the second person becomes the important character in the scene. This recourse can be applied in two ways:

1 the centre of attention moves back and forth between two players. The third has only a passive role, deciding with the movement of his head which of his two companions predominates.

2 the centre of attention moves in a full circle around the triangle of players, each successively becoming the centre of attention.

FIGURE 6.2 The three players standing in a C formation are covered by two external reverse camera positions. They all maintain the same screen area in both shots.

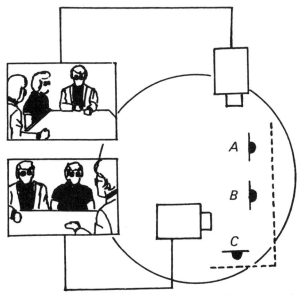

FIGURE 6.3 An L shaped arrangement of actors, covered by two external reverse camera positions, where all the players keep their screen areas in both shots.

There are three basic formulas for external reverse camera shots. They provide irregular variants because this geometric arrangement of players does not give each player a steady screen area.

The camera sites for these formulas are obtained by selecting two of the six positions depicted in Fig. 6.3A. In the illustration each player, acting as the apex of their triangular arrangement, is given two external reverse camera shots.

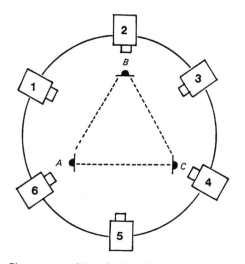

FIGURE 6.3a Players arranged in a triangle with six possible external camera sites.

Formula A

The dominant player, in the centre of the group, remains in his place in both master shots, while the players at either side exchange positions from shot to shot.

In this formula the three players (placed on a neutral line of interest) are located precisely between both reverse camera points, which give alternately a rear and a frontal view (Fig. 6.4.)

This solution is best applied to closely knit groups, where the intimacy or bluntness of the situation requires scrutiny of the action and reaction of the players, divided into two sections and featured alternately.

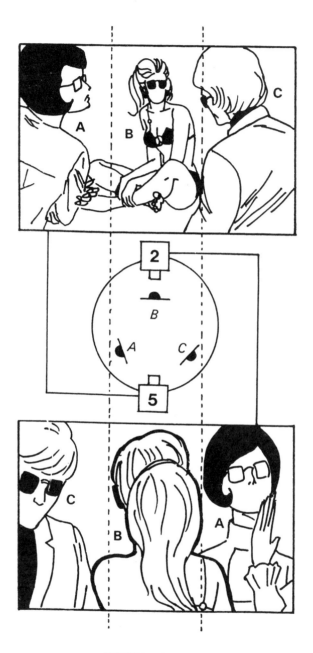

FIGURE 6.4 Formula A

Formula B

Here the performer acting as arbiter of attention (as a silent spectator) is placed at one side of the screen. In the next shot she appears on the opposite side.

The other two players, conversing (along a diagonal line of interest) maintain their relative positions and occupy the screen area shown in Fig. 6.5.

Combinations of seated and standing players and different shooting distances add variety.

Formula C

The dominant player, placed on one side of the screen, stays in that area in both shots, while the other two performers exchange their positions from take to take.

In Formula B, the dominant line of attention flowed diagonally to the background, and the arbiting actor was close to the side of the screen.

In Formula C the dominant line flows horizontally between the two players in the foreground, and the arbiting actor is placed beyond (Fig. 6.6.).

Notice that in all three figs. the order of players (shown above) remains A, B, C.

The shift in order (shown below) demonstrates the effect of the different formulas.

External/internal reverse camera positions

Opposing external/internal reverse camera positions provide what one might call 'number contrast' on the screen, because the external position covers the whole group, while the internal placement frames only a segment. This can provide variety in presentation.

Two approaches are possible. Fig. 6.7 shows a 3 to 1 number contrast.

The second variation, a 3 to 2 number relationship from shot to shot, is illustrated in Fig. 6.8.

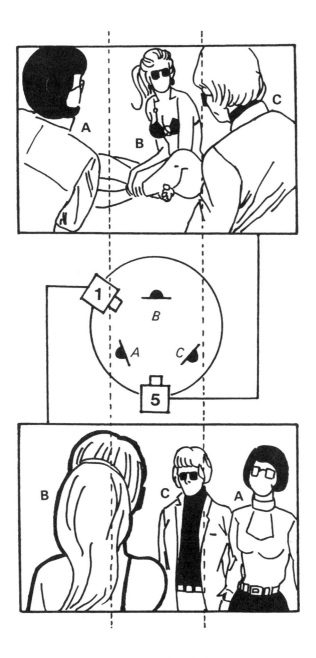

FIGURE 6.5   Formula B

81

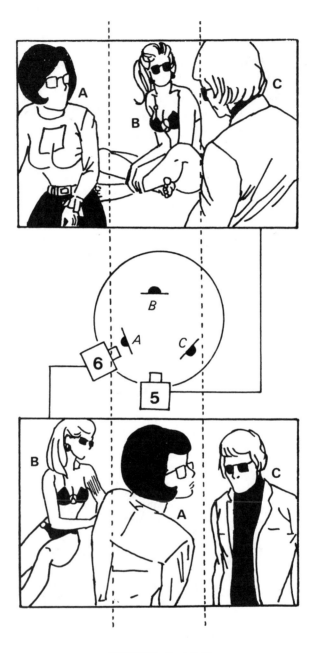

FIGURE 6.6 Formula C

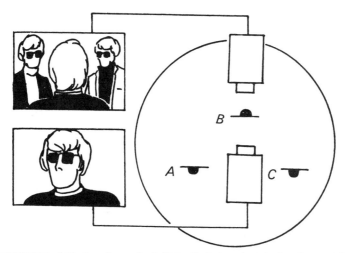

FIGURE 6.7   A 3 to 1 number contrast obtained by juxtaposing an external reverse shot with an internal one.

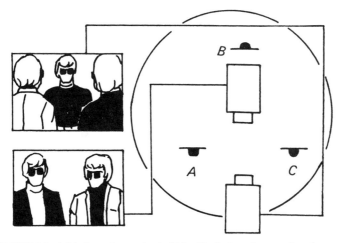

FIGURE 6.8   A 3 to 2 number contrast obtained by juxtaposing an external reverse shot with an internal one.

Once more we stress the fact that all players need not stand in the scene. One or two of them can be seated, reclining or lying down. This will add variety to the pictorial compositions chosen for the scene.

Internal reverse camera positions

With a group of three human figures divided in two, the 2 to 1 number contrast is added to the range of possibilities for covering a trio of players (Fig. 6.9).

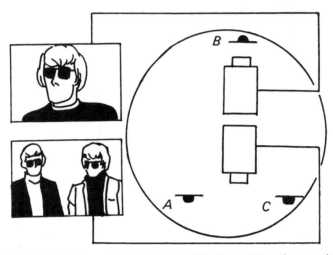

FIGURE 6.9   A 2 to 1 number contrast obtained by using two internal reverse shots.

Three internal reverse shots can be used to cover, individually three players arranged in a roughly triangular form. An external camera position frames the whole group and might serve as an establishing shot—and could be re-inserted from time to time to remind the audience of the group as a whole. Observe Fig. 6.10.

It is important to retain the correct interplay of directions of interest between the actors where one holds the attention of the other two.

Parallel camera positions

If a group of three, seen from dominant parallel camera positions, is divided into two units, the players present profiles to the camera positions.

There is no arbiter of attention, since two players face the third who dominates. Number contrast is obtained by this method (Fig. 6.11).

84

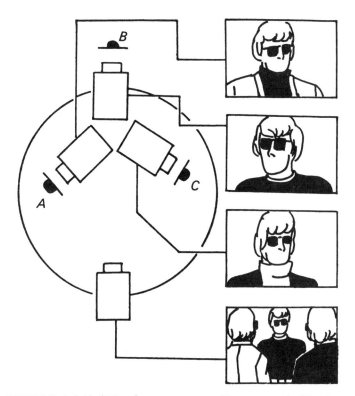

FIGURE 6.10 Individual internal reverse camera positions cover each of the players in the group separately; an establishing shot reminds the audience of the ensemble of the whole group.

An establishing shot encompasses the whole group, and is traditionally used at the beginning, middle or end of the scene.

If the central player acts as an arbiter of attention, the group can be divided into three—those at the extremes of the group are in profile and the centre player faces the camera (Fig. 6.12).

Cameras on a common visual axis show the whole group from the first position and only the dominant actor in a closer view. He may be at the centre or side of the group (Fig. 6.13).

Placing actors at different levels and distances apart, as in the other approaches, provides new screen compositions.

Pivoting point

Three players can be shown in a filmed scene by including only two in each master shot. The person appearing in both can occupy

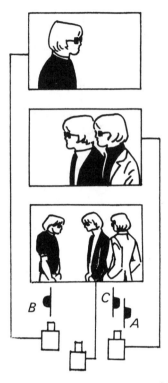

FIGURE 6.11 Parallel camera positions applied to a group of three persons, Number contrast, 2 to 1, is obtained in this way.

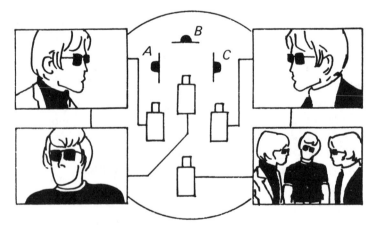

FIGURE 6.12 Individual coverage of each player in a group of three performers achieved by using parallel camera positions.

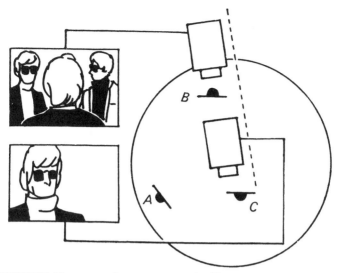

FIGURE 6.13 Two camera sites on a common visual line cover a triangular group of three performers. One of the shots emphasises the central player in the scene.

the same place on the screen for both shots or he can be shifted from one side of the screen frame to the other as the shot is changed.

The first possibility applies when covering an approximately triangular arrangement of actors, the other is useful where actors are placed more or less in a straight line. In both cases one actor provides a pivoting point for the two dominant camera positions.

Fig. 6.14 shows a triangular composition where the centre actor acts as pivot.

In the example examined, the scene is established at position 1. Positions 2 and 3 are master shots. As in this case, the establishing shot is sometimes positioned on one of the axis lines stemming from the two strong camera positions of the triangle principle.

Notice that the dominant camera sites are a right angles to each other, and both include the centre actor (B) on the same side of the screen.

In the preceding example the pivoting actor was kept in the foreground in both master shots. A shift in distance from shot to shot (in one master take the pivoting player is near the camera and in the reverse shot he is in the background) will work smoothly if the pivoting performer is kept on the same side of the screen in both takes (Fig. 6.15).

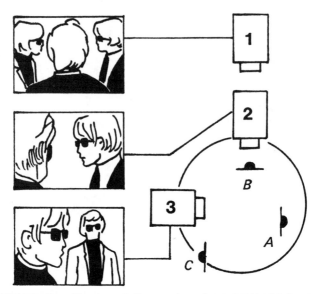

FIGURE 6.14 One of the players in the group is used as a pivot to relate two master shots placed at right angles. This pivoting actor is placed on the same side of the screen in both takes.

FIGURE 6.15 In this example the pivoting player shifts from foreground to background as each master shot is edited in parallel with the other while keeping a constant screen area.

The actor used as a pivot must move his head to vary the centre of interest that shifts from player B to player C in reverse shots.

In our next example the two camera positions are external reverse angles around the player used as pivot in the scene (Fig. 6.16).

FIGURE 6.16   A set of external reverse camera positions around a side player use him as a pivot to cover the group of three players.

If three actors are in a line and two of them face the third person, the centre pivoting player is included in both takes, but he shifts from one side of the screen to the other, as shown in Fig. 6.17.

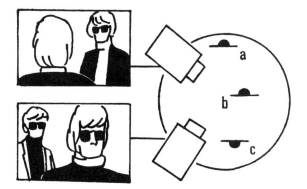

FIGURE 6.17   Irregular coverage of a straight line arrangement of players, where the pivoting performer shifts from one side of the screen to the other as each master shot is alternated in parallel editing.

In the cases examined the pivoting player was dominant, as he had an important role in the scene. But a passive stance for him is also possible. In Fig. 6.18 players A and C are dominant. Performer B in the centre may be just listening to a heated discussion between the other two. Yet player B has been used as a pivot for the camera sites, and is featured in both shots, on the left and right sides of the screen respectively. His passiveness can be stressed by the profiled position, eyes downcast, purposely to avoid throwing emphasis on either of the others. His role is also minimized by being given only a third of the screen area.

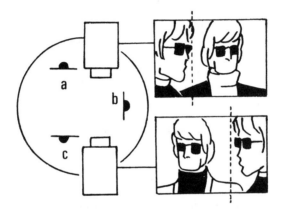

FIGURE 6.18 In this example the pivoting player has a passive role. His figure shifts from one side of the screen to the other as the master shots are alternated.

Not only can one actor be used as a pivoting point, but also a camera position can be employed as such. This pivoting camera position is an advance on the same visual axis of one of the two dominant external reverse camera sites, providing a close shot of the player chosen as the centre of interest in the scene.

A close-up of the dominant performer B (Fig. 6.19) inserted between shots from sites 1 and 3 masks the change in screen position of A and C when seen from the second position.

Emphasizing the centre of interest

When a conversation between three actors develops in such a way as to stress two and reduce the involvement of the third, this could be treated in two ways:

90

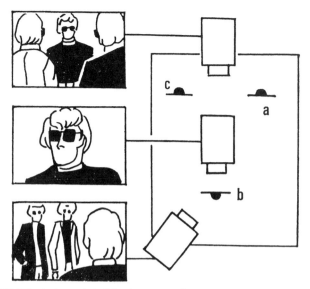

FIGURE 6.19 A closer shot of the dominant performer is used as a pivoting shot to relate two external reverse shots of the group of three players.

1   Emphasis is applied over a single line of interest;
2   The line of interests in the scene shifts to a crosswise direction. In the first approach the line of interest is unique for the three players. Emphasis can be partial or complete: partially, if in the first master shot the three players are shown but in the second only the two dominant performers, totally by moving from a 3 to 3 group relationship to a pattern of 2 to 2, showing only the two main protagonists.

Partial emphasis

Partial emphasis is possible by using any one of the three basic linear arrangements: a straight line, an 'L' shape or a triangle. Fig. 6.20 shows partial emphasis being applied to a straight line arrangement of players.

A variant is shown in Fig. 6.21, where the set of external-internal camera sites is moved to the other end of the straight line composition.

An 'L' shaped arrangement of the players can be easily treated with partial emphasis. Fig. 6.22 gives a simple case.

FIGURE 6.20 Partial emphasis applied to a line formation of the group of three players.

FIGURE 6.21 A variation of partial emphasis applied to the group of three players in a straight line arrangement.

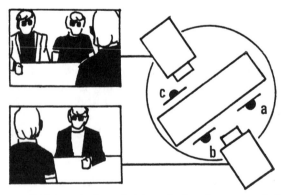

FIGURE 6.22 Partial emphasis applied to an L shaped arrangement of players.

For a triangular grouping two main solutions are available. Fig. 6.23 shows the first, where the subdued performer is placed on one side of the screen.

FIGURE 6.23 The secondary performer is placed on one side of the screen in this variant of partial emphasis applied to a triangular composition.

The second variation is obtained by placing the secondary actor in the centre of the screen in the master shot where all the players are shown (Fig. 6.24).

FIGURE 6.24 The secondary player is placed in the centre of this other variant of partial emphasis applied to a triangular formation of players.

Total emphasis

Total emphasis, as we said before, can be obtained by two pairs of master shots—featuring three, and two players respectively. All four camera positions are external reverse coverage points of the group. Fig. 6.25 shows a simple case.

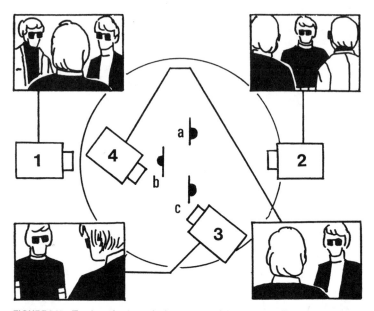

FIGURE 6.25 Total emphasis applied to a group of three players. The editing pattern progresses from a 3 to 3 relationship to a 2 to 2 opposition of the principal performers in the group.

An ordinary editing pattern for these four master shots would be like this:
Shots 1—2—1—2—1—3—4—3—4—3—1—2—1—2
       (——)   (——)

By using that combination one player is excluded from the scene in the middle of the sequence, to re-appear at the end.

When you cut from three-person to two-person coverage, the cut is more effective if the shot of the two players is a reverse of the position where the three were shown, rather than an advance on the same visual axis line. For example: Shot 1 covers three people. Shot 3 covers two. If you are editing shots 1 and 2 in parallel, your move to a shot featuring only two players will start with shot 3 after shot 1, because shot 3 is a reverse of shot 1. Your editing pattern will look like this:
Shots 1—2—1—2—1—3—4—3—4
             (——)

This is visually more effective than if you moved in on a common visual axis position as depicted in the following editing pattern:
Shots 1—2—1—2—1—4—3—4—3
(——)

The return from a two-person coverage to three person shots follows the same rule.

The three irregular formulas for external reverse coverage of a group of three persons, where the three are included in each master shot, can be treated with total emphasis, where two of their components are selected to be virtually stressed.

A 'north-south' to 'east-west' change

Examples so far have dealt with emphasis applied over to a single line of interest extending from 'north' to 'south'. If we emphasize the two players located 'north', the line of interest will shift to a dominant direction from 'east' to 'west', excluding the actor placed 'south'.

This new line of interest can be placed on either side of the two players that it covers, as we will soon see. Camera positions must be deployed that allow a smooth passage from one line to the other as interest is shifted and two of the players emphasized. A set of external-internal reverse shots can be applied to each line of interest, as depicted in Fig. 6.26.

Let us begin by simple cases and move on to those gradually more complex:

Using only four camera positions

The most elementary coverage of a crosswise change in the direction of interest, is obtained by using four master camera positions —two for each direction of the line of interest. All four positions are external reverse angles. The three players are first shown in a 'north-south' line of interest. One of the three irregular formulas for external coverage of groups of three persons is chosen to frame the players along this line of interest. The shift of interest when the two players facing the third, turn toward each other is shown from a north-south camera position. This change in direction is very simply achieved. Following that, two external

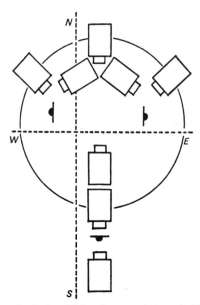

FIGURE 6.26 Two sets of external-internal reverse shots applied to a group of three players to cover a change in the line of the interest, which shifts from an east-west to a north-south coverage.

reverse camera positions can cover, and stress, both players on the new line of interest, excluding the third.

Fig. 6.27 shows the four camera positions. Positions 1 and 2 are alternated by parallel editing, until from position 1 we see the change in direction take place in the line of interest. To emphasize the two dominant players we alternate between positions 3 and 4 and frame only them.

If the third actor is to become involved again this can be reversed to the north-south position framing the whole group. A simple editing pattern for these four camera positions would look like this:

Shots 1—2—1—2—1—3—4—3—4—1—2—1—2

Note: in the example given the shift of interest was seen from site 1. If it had been seen from behind the players (site 2) the east-west camera sites should be behind the players. Why?

Referring once more to Fig. 6.27, the 'north-south' line is covered by positions 1 and 2, the two dominant reverse angles

96

FIGURE 6.27 A north-south line of interest changes to a dominant east-west line of interest. Four main camera positions are used, and all are external reverse shots. Position 1 is chosen as the camera site from which the change in the line direction is witnessed.

of the triangular principle for camera deployment whose apex is the neutral site 0, the one chosen to establish the scene.

When the line of interest shifts to an 'east-west' direction as seen from site 1, this camera position becomes the apex of a new triangular formation consisting of sites 3—1—4, and angles 3 and 4 must be on the side of the new line of interest. So, if the change is seen from site 2, positions 3 and 4 must be on the side of the line of interest that faces the apex of *that* new triangular formation. Fig. 6.28 shows this.

To return to a 'north-south' direction where the whole group is seen, position 2 must be used to effect the change in direction. A sequence using position 2 for the shift in the line of interest, would look like this:

Shots 1—2—1—2—3—4—3—4—2—1—2—1

The formula just described is admittedly a bit complicated to describe, though once grasped is simple to put into practice.

Introducing internal shots

In the cases just discussed all the positions were external reverse shots.

By introducing an internal reverse camera site, we have a new way of covering the group, still using four camera sites. Once more these master shots are employed in pairs.

In such a sequence, position 1 becomes the establishing shot, position 2 and 3 the main masters, and position 4 is a reaction shot.

The conversation begins by alternating Shots 1 and 4 along a 'north-south' line. In this way number contrast is obtained on the screen.

When the shift to a dominant 'east-west' line is desired, we show it happening from position 1, and move to an external reverse coverage of the two emphasized players. Occasionally we intercut shot 4 where performer A (as seen in Fig. 6.29) looks on, reacting silently or occasionally speaking. An editing order for a typical sequence using this set-up could be like this:

$$(-)\quad(—)$$
Shots –1–4–1–4–1–4–1–2–3–2–3–4–2–3–1–4–2–3–2–3–4–1–
$$(————————)\,(——————————————)\,(—)$$
$$\text{'a'}\qquad\qquad\qquad\text{'b'}\qquad\qquad\qquad\text{'c'}$$

In the first part of the sequence ('a') the dominant line of interest runs in a "north-south" direction, and players B and C talk directly to A. When players B and C turn to each other to exchange dialogue, A becomes a silent onlooker, and thus sub-

FIG. 6.28 This line of interest shifts from a north-south to an east-west direction in a similar way to that preceding except that in this case the change is seen from the second position.

ordinate. The 'east-west' interest established, this section of the sequence ('b') uses predominantly masters 2 and 3 edited in parallel. Master 4 is intercut twice to show the silent reaction of the subordinate player. Mid-way position 1 is introduced, (with a dominant east-west line at work) to re-establish the whole group. Near the end ('c') player A talks as seen from position 4, and we close the sequence from camera site number 1, where the players in the background (B and C) turn towards A, re-establishing the dominance of the 'north-south' line of interest. Fig. 6.29 illustrates the case under discussion.

FIGURE 6.29 Four camera positions are used for this shift in the line of interest but one of them is an internal reverse shot.

Eight camera sites are employed

The next development is to apply a full set of external-internal camera positions to each direction of the line of interest. As shown in Fig. 6.26, at least eight camera sites are brought into play to cover the sequence.

You might heighten this 3-person dialogue sequence with the sequence using a combination of external-internal reverse shots that cover or relate the three actors (along a 'north-south' line), and then move to a set of external-internal reverse shots that cover only the two actors emphasized (on an 'east-west' line), excluding the third.

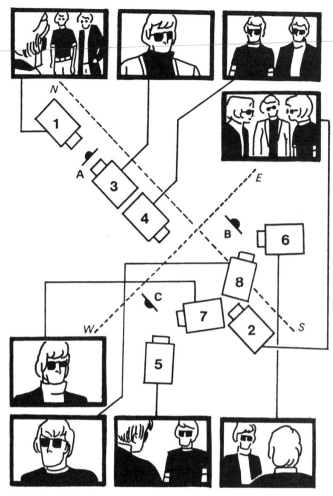

FIGURE 6.30 Eight basic camera positions as described in the text.

Figure 6.30 shows the eight basic camera positions. The order of the sequence could be something like this:

Shot 1   Players B and C in the background talk with performer A who is in foreground, his back to the camera.

Shot 3   A replies. He looks off screen, right.

Shot 4   B and C as seen from A's viewpoint, look to him off screen, left.

Shot 3   A still talking.

Shot 4 B and C answer A.

Shot 3 A ends talking.

Shot 2 C and B in foreground turn to look at each other. Player A in the centre of the screen becomes unimportant.

Shot 5 Reverse. C and B talk.

Shot 6 Reverse. C and B talk.

Shot 5

Shot 6

Shot 8 B is featured alone.

Shot 7 C is featured alone.

Shot 8

Shot 7

Shot 3 A re-enters the conversation. He is facing us, looking off screen, right.

Shot 4 B and C turn their heads to us to look at A off screen left.

Shot 3 A talks again.

Shot 1 The whole group again: A—B—C.

Fig. 6.30 shows how sites 1—2—3 and 4 cover the 'north-south' line of interest, while positions 5—6—7 and 8 frame an 'east-west' shift.

To show the shift of the line of attention from N-S to E-W position 2 is used. Notice that this differs from position 4 (previously used to show the players on whom visual emphasis is now brought to bear) in that the actors exchange positions on the screen. In position 4 the order on the screen is B—C, while from position 2 these players are seen arranged in the foreground as C—B.

Shot 3, however, (an internal reverse position) bridges this anomaly. And it works because shots 3 and 4 have a reverse angle relationship, while shots 3 and 2 are placed on a common visual axis. In fact, Player A is used as a pivot to effect the bridge between those two positions.

If the direction is reversed E-W to N-S later in the sequence, this is achieved by using the same principle. Shot 3 is once more bridged between 7 and 4 which are covering an E-W line from each side of it. The shift from E-W to N-S actually takes place at site 4, which starts covering a E-W line and ends as an extreme of the N-S line that dominates again.

A sequence featuring three persons, employing a crosswise shift of the line of interest covered by sets of external-internal

102

reverse camera sites, can be filmed using fewer than the 8 positions given. Only those positions needed are brought into play.

In the example just examined, the actor excluded by the shift of the line of interest, was placed in the centre of the group. The same principle applies if you want to exclude either of the other two, placed on the base of the triangle.

The two previous approaches may seem a bit complicated to someone not familiar with the workings of the triangular camera placement for coverage of static dialogues. Perhaps it will help to fix the simple principles just described, in which the line of interest shifts from north-south to east-west, if we keep in mind that the camera positions deployed around the players assume the form of a cross. The two emphasized players become the arms of the cross or 'T' figure, while the lone player from whom attention is momentarily released, is positioned at the bottom of the cross or T figure. Whether you use four camera positions (all external reverse shots or a combination of internal-external reverses) up to the full eight camera sites, the basic pattern assumed by the camera coverage is a cross or T figure. Two simpler methods that cover a players' L configuration are discussed next.

A simple method using three camera sites

There is a simple method by which the centre of interest in a conversation between three persons can be emphasized using only three camera positions. One acts as the main master shot and covers the three performers. The other two positions cover only two different sets of actors. These subordinate masters are edited in parallel with the main one.

In this grouping the most important actor is placed in the centre: player B (see Fig. 6.31). When she talks with C (an E-W direction) the relationship is shot 1 and shot 2. Shot 2 is a right angle position in relation to shot 1.

When performer B turns (this turn is always seen from position 1) to talk to A (a 'N-S' direction) the relationship becomes shot 1 —shot 3. Shot 3 is a reverse angle position in relation to shot 1. Number contrast is constantly opposed from shot to shot, as we cut between from three and two-persons. Shots 2 and 3 cannot be edited together in parallel.

A typical sequence using this solution would look like this:
Shots 1—2—1—2—1—3—1—3—1—2—1—3—1
(——)   (——) (——)

103

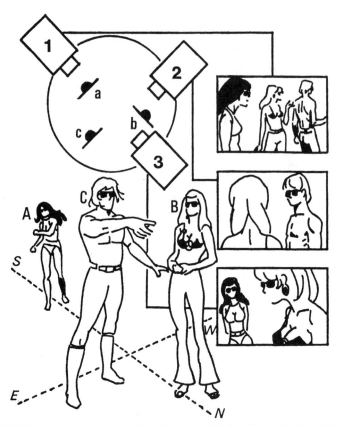

FIGURE 6.31 An east-west to north-south change of the line of interest achieved with only three camera sites.

The marks under the numbers underline the points where the shift of direction of the line of interest takes place.

Using a pivoting shot

A variation of the previous example would make use of a close shot of the central performer (player C, as seen in Fig. 6.32) to serve as a pivoting shot. This close shot replaces the establishing shot of the previous example and serves the same purpose: it documents when the central performer throws attention from one player to the other.

This close shot (1) is the key master position in the sequence,

104

and is intercut with two subordinate masters (2 and 3) to cover the dialogue.

Once again, masters 2 and 3 cannot be edited together in parallel. A simple sequence using this procedure would be edited like this:

Shots 1—2—1—2—1—3—1—3—1—2—1—3—1

      (—)   (—)   (—)

Notice how the editing order of these shots resembles the pattern in section 4.

The marks below the numbers in the editing pattern given above indicate again where player C in master 1, moves his head from side to side shifting the line of interest.

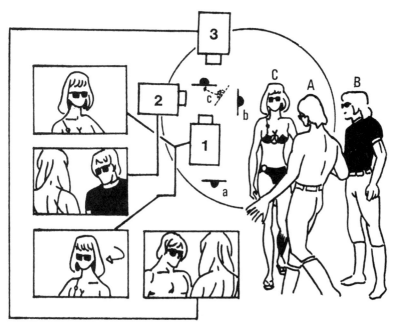

FIGURE 6.32 A player is used as a pivot to achieve a change of direction for the line of interest in the scene.

Deliberate omission

Suppose one of the players is to be deliberately omitted, as we cut from take to take using reverse shot positions giving the apparent illusion that all rules are broken.

105

Fig. 6.33 shows an example where advantage is taken of an obstruction in the set decoration to hide the player located in the centre (and also in the background) of the triangular arrangement of performers.

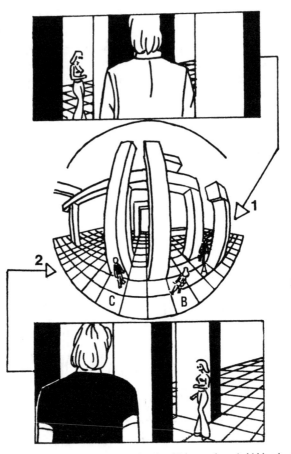

FIGURE 6.33   A case of deliberate omission, in which one player is hidden by an element of the décor.

As can be seen, actress B changes her screen position from shot to shot, while the two actors appear and disappear at opposite sides of the screen. The actor furthest away in any of the two reverse shots should appear in the centre of the screen, in the background, but the set decoration (in this case the columns) hide him.

106

While what we see on the screen is the following composition:
Shot 1: B—A
Shot 2: C—B
the true composition is really:
Shot 1: B—C—A
Shot 2: C—A—B.
In the following example both reverse camera positions were moved in close to the central character in the triangular arrangement of the performers, changing a contrast that should be:
Shot 1: A—B—C
Shot 2: B—C—A
into a two to two relationship, that looks like this:
Shot 1: A—B
Shot 2: C—A
In this way players C and B are alternatedly omitted, while performer A shifts his position from one side of the screen to the other. Different camera levels are used to add variety. (Fig. 6.34).

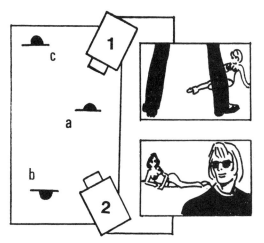

FIGURE 6.34 In the preceding example the pivoting player was located in the background in both shots. Here, he is in the foreground and shifts from one side of the screen to the other as either one of the other two players is consciously omitted from each alternate master shot.

Summing up

A brief review of the topics covered in this chapter is now given to underline the essential points examined in relation to dialogues among static groups of three persons. We have seen that:

1   Three players can be deployed along three linear arrangements: a straight line, a right angle and a triangle.

2   With three performers engaged in conversation, and where there are two dominant centres of attention and a silent arbiter, the actors can remain in the same screen sector by employing the triangular camera site principle.

3   A triangular arrangement of players can be covered by fifteen pairs of external reverse angles. These sets of takes fall within three main irregular formulas.

4   Number contrast can be obtained by combining an external and an internal reverse shot, or by using internal reverse shots exclusively. Parallel camera sites give the same effect.

5   A player featured in both reverse shots can be used as a pivot to relate the takes that cover the three players.

6   A pivoting shot can be used to ease the transition between two takes where the players exchange their screen positions.

7   Visual emphasis can be applied over a single line of interest using external reverse shots exclusively. This emphasis can be partial or total.

8   The line of interest in a scene can be shifted to a crosswise direction. Five different methods were outlined. In the first three a combination of external-internal reverse shots were applied, while in the last two a pivoting player was used.

9   One of the players can be deliberately omitted from shot to shot giving the illusion that all 'rules' are broken in the coverage of actors arranged in a triangular form.

Scope for covering a group of three static persons is wide enough to offer some visual variety.

7

DIALOGUE INVOLVING FOUR OR MORE PERSONS

Basic techniques for the coverage of two- or three-person static dialogues are also valid for larger groups. Rarely is a dialogue carried on by four people simultaneously. There is always a leader, conscious or unconscious, acting as a moderator and shifting attention from person to person so that the dialogue moves by zones. In simpler cases two central speaking players are only occasionally interrupted by the others. In such a group it is more pleasant to the eye if some stand and some sit, perhaps in geometric patterns (triangles are common, but also squares and circles). If some are much closer to the camera than others it adds to the illusion of depth.

There is a very subtle way of putting emphasis on any person within a group. In the theatre this technique is known as occult balance. A group of sitting people is balanced by a standing figure. The reverse is also true (Fig. 7.1).

The use of lighting patterns is also important when covering a group. Conventionally, light on the main characters is stronger while all the others receive a subdued illumination that keeps them visible but subordinate.

The variations applied to groups of two and three persons will now be shown in a comprehensive pictorial coverage of four persons or more.

Simple cases

If both the whole group and the centre of interest must be covered visually this presupposes at least two basic master shots—one framing the group full view, the other a close shot of the main actor/s. Some examples:

FIGURE 7.1 The principle of visual balance in action. A standing player can balance a group of seated performers, and vice versa.

1 Using a common visual axis

Two shots on the same visual axis are intercut alternately. This serves to cover a conversation in depth. When players B and D talk (see Fig. 7.2) Shot 1 is used. But when B turns to C, we move in to close Shot 2 and back again to Shot 1 as D cuts into the

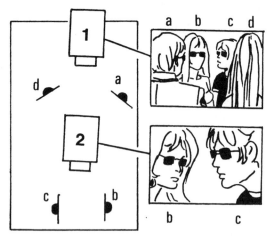

FIGURE 7.2 A group is covered using two master shots arranged on a common visual axis. In one of them the whole group is framed, in the other the centre of interest of the group is visually emphasized.

conversation and then, turning, makes a comment to A. If players A and D have their backs to us they throw audience attention on to performers B and C, but if A and D turn to face us, they themselves become the centre of attention.

A further variation is for A and D to act only as witnesses to the conversation, and then only find their facial or body reactions to it are important. Shot 1 serves merely as a re-establishing shot and is periodically intercut into master Shot 2 to give colour to the dialogue by expanding the group.

2. Using a right angle camera site

Figure 7.3 shows another variant. The purpose here is similar to the previous case. Either a dialogue between all the performers and the two central ones can be covered, or a discussion between A and B is watched by the rest of the group. The variation is in the use of a right angle for the camera position of the closer second shot.

FIGURE 7.3 The right angle camera arrangement used here covers the whole group and its centre of attention.

111

Groups arranged round a table

Groups of people around a table are common in film scenes. Ways have been found to present them clearly to the audience. The triangular camera placement principle is valuable for solving many tricky script situations in this type of scene. Once more the two extremes of the centre of interest dominate in the scene.

Case A

The visual axis and right angle sites outlined above can be used together to cover two important actors in a group by giving them individual attention (Fig. 7.4).

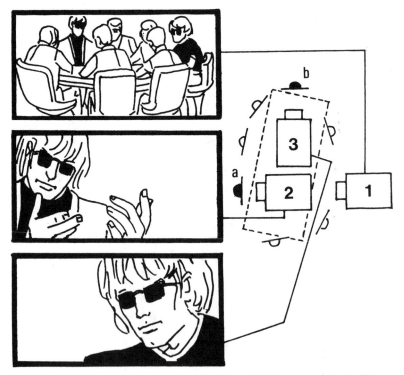

FIGURE 7.4 Coverage of a group where the two central players are emphasized by individual shots.

112

The procedure is simple. *Shot 1* shows the whole group. Actors A and B are the centre of attention. Player A addresses the whole group. When he turns his attention on B, cut to Shot 2, where A speaks his lines to B off screen. Now cut to Shot 3, to show B replying. Then cut back to shot 2 where A replies to B, and again to Shot 3 where B makes his point clear.

Now we re-establish by going back to Shot 1 to show the group reacting. If A and B speak to one another again, we may cut once more to an interplay of their individual shots and then return to the full shot number 1 to hear the comments of another in the group.

Case B

In Fig. 7.2, 7.3 and 7.4, the second camera was placed closer to the group, thus excluding some actors from the shot. In Fig. 7.5, the camera distance is the same in both positions.

This *right angle* set up creates on the screen a visual rule similar to one of the three irregular formulas employed for covering roughly triangular groups of three. With the second camera on the left, the first actor on that side in position 1 shifts to the right in position 2. Other actors remain in the same order:

Shot 1: *A* B C D E
Shot 2: B C D E *A*

With the second camera on the right, the reverse occurs: the first actor on the right in Shot 1 moves to the left in camera position 2.

Shot 1: A B C D *E*
Shot 2: *E* A B C D

Groups of four and five persons can be visually covered using these *right angle* camera sites.

Case C

A group of five persons covered by external reverse angles, although adhering to the same rule, offers a slight variant that is simple to define. Fig. 7.6 shows two possibilities for the same example. In one of them the line of interest flows between players C and E, and in the other between C and A. The two actors on the opposite side of the line of interest shift from one side of the screen to the other and interchange positions, while the others

FIGURE 7.5 Irregular camera coverage, where a player at one extreme of the frame area shifts to the other side as the shot is changed. The remaining group maintain the same visual order on the screen.

114

maintain the same order. Where players C and E dominate, the coverage is as follows:

Shot 1: *A B C* D E

Shot 2: C D E *B A*

In the instance where C and A dominate, the formula is reversed:

Shot 1: A B C *D E*

Shot 2: *E D* A B C

Study Fig. 7.6 and you will see how the formula works for *diagonal* lines of interest.

FIGURE 7.6 A group with a diagonal line of interest covered by external reverse shots obeys the visual rule shown. The two players not involved in the line of interest move to the other side of the screen in the second shot and exchange positions. The illustration features the solutions available for both diagonal lines of interest.

Case D

In our next case, external reverse angles are also applied to a group of persons seated at a table, but with different results.

The important conversation is between B and C (Fig. 7.7). Our camera positions are concentrated on one side of the line of interest generated between the two central actors.

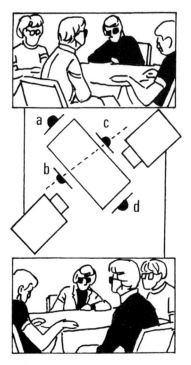

FIGURE 7.7 When the dominant players are placed in the centre of the screen for an interplay of external reverse shots, the players on the extremes of the frame change position from shot to shot.

Notice how actors A and D exchange sites on the screen in the reverse shot, while in the centre of the screen B and C always remain in their sectors.

Subdividing the group

So far, we have applied external camera positions to medium sized groups. Internal reverse camera sites, on the other hand, can divide the group, oppose its parts and achieve a visual interplay where number contrast adds variety to the screen image.

This division can assume three basic forms:
1 an actor is opposed to the rest of the group;
2 the group is split into two equal or unequal portions; and
3 the subdivision produces several groups.

In each, an establishing shot is needed (conventionally, at least) to open the sequence and may appear again in the middle and at the end. Fig. 7.8 shows the first variant. With two internal reverse camera positions within the group, one player is placed in opposition to the others.

In a short dialogue the sequence could be edited:
Shots 1—2—3—2—3—2—3—1
A longer one:
Shots 1—2—3—2—3—2—3—1—2—3—2—3—1

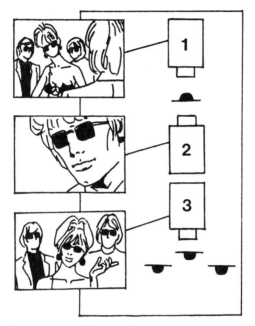

FIGURE 7.8   The group is subdivided, and the dominant player is placed in opposition to the rest of the group.

The actors may, of course, be at different heights (Fig. 7.9).

The floor plans of Figs. 7.8 and 7.9 show site 1 corresponding to the establishing shot, and sites 2 and 3 (inside the group) as internal reverse angles.

The next development involves subdividing the group into two smaller units. An even number of players may appear as two sets of equal parts on the screen, but this is not as interesting as having different numbers in each section as in Fig. 7.10.

117

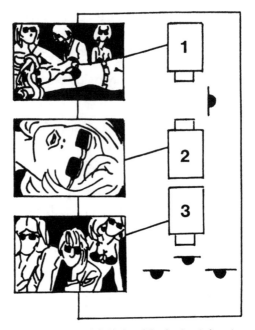

FIGURE 7.9 When a group is subdivided, and the dominant player is opposed to the rest of the group, different body levels can be assumed by the players without reducing the effectiveness of the visual formula shown.

The editing principle is similar to the preceding one: an establishing shot can start the sequence, we then move in to internal reverse camera positions at right angles to that. For a while these two closer shots are intercut and finally there is a return to the first camera position.

The next development is combining internal and external reverse angles. Five players deployed in a straight line can be covered by using opposed diagonals from shot to shot, and a sector of the line stressed by means of the internal reverse angle (Fig. 7.11).

Geometrical patterns

A group may be assembled in one of many geometrical shapes— a circle, rectangle, square, triangle, etc., or an amorphous shape with no clear pattern at all. But the screen composition is governed by the floor plan distribution and the heights of the players. Both present balanced screen compositions. The floor plan distribution

FIGURE 7.10 The ensemble is subdivided into two smaller groups, and the resultant master shots are edited in parallel.

determines the plane in which each player is viewed. The other variable refers to their position—lying, seated, reclined or standing up. The two factors combined give composition in depth, as opposed to a flat arrangement.

Sometimes dominant geometrical shapes are applied only to central characters, allowing a loose pattern to supporting figures.

In the triangular composition for dialogue (Fig. 7.12) for example, the first of only two camera sites views the whole group but emphasizes the apex of the 'triangle'. The second frames only the two players on the base of the triangle.

119

FIGURE 7.11 The group, in straight line arrangement, is covered using an external and an internal reverse shot.

FIGURE 7.12 The group of players covered in Shot 1 has a dominant triangular formation. The reverse shot conforms to one of the irregular rules applied to this form of arrangement, using internal reverse shots.

120

Several opposed sectors

In a group distributed in three or more sectors, using establishing and internal reverse shots, the dialogue coverage is similar to single shots of three persons in a triangular formation except that here, from some angles, more than one person is framed. (See Fig. 7.13 for a three-sector group covered by four camera sites.)

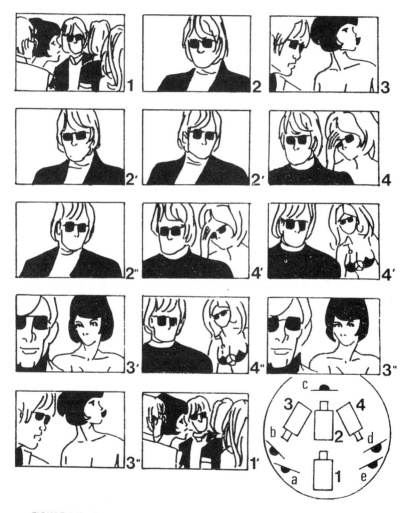

FIGURE 7.13 A progressive change of interest moving in a circle.

A sequence using this principle, could be edited as follows:

Shot 1   Whole group is established.
Shot 2   Performer C throws attention to the left.
Shot 3   Performer A and B talk to C off-screen.
Shot 2' C replies and moves his head to right.
Shot 4   Performers D and E reply to C off-screen.
Shot 2" C replies.
Shot 4' Performers D and E reply and then move their heads, and instead of looking to the left where C is off-screen, they now look off-screen right.
Shot 3' Performers A and B looking off-screen left, reply to D and E.
Shot 4" D and E reply. Still looking off-screen right.
Shot 3" A and B end talking to D and E off-screen left, and turn their heads right, towards C, who is out of the screen on that side.
Shot 1' Whole group. Performer C is again dominant. The other four players are looking at him.

In the sequence just described the line of interest moved in a full circle shifting from group to group (see Fig. 7.13).

The multiple plane arrangement has endless variations. One, for example, (illustrated in Fig. 7.14) deals with triangular arrangements of six players, composed in depth. The whole group is established in the first master shot. Of two vertical triangular formations the one on the left has its apex in the foreground on A, seated; the other has its base in the foreground and its apex on F, beyond. Camera sites 2 and 3, frame these triangular formations separately but parallel. Site 4, at right angles to 2 and 3, frames the seated foreground figures in a triangular composition.

In this group the dominant players are sitting in the foreground, while the subsidiaries stand.

A further variation is to split the group in *changing patterns*, ie: the whole group is established and then broken up in three parts, each covered by different camera set-ups. After returning to the establishing shot they are seen again in other, closer, shots. But this time the group has been divided only into two parts, presenting visual arrangements that differ from the previous three master shots. A step further is to mingle these five master shots into a free-form editing pattern, where the establishing shot picks up the whole group again from time to time.

FIGURE 7.14 A large group subdivided into triangular pictorial compositions for each of the master shots.

Handling large groups

If, instead of being so closely knit, several groups are scattered about the set, fixed camera set-ups can still cover a dialogue that moves by zones. It is advisable to have a central group or person on whom the action is hinged, showing him as speaker and listener, and shifting audience attention from player to player.

Master shots can be used, edited in pairs, occasionally re-establishing larger sections of the group. If the line of interest is constantly changing direction, keep these changes simple. Use a player as pivot in two master shots (or in a re-establishing take) to clearly indicate the change of direction when he moves his head from one centre to another.

Most film makers prefer simpler situations or, if faced with such a complex set-up, move the camera or the players during the sequence to simplify the problem. The measure of a good director is seen when he handles such a complex dialogue situation using only static camera set-ups, with a minimum of movement for the players and then only when strictly necessary for the requirements of the story. Alfred Hitchcock handles a sequence like this in his film *The Birds*. This is the scene in the cafe, after the birds have attacked the schoolchildren, and where an elderly woman specializing in ornithology puts the whole event in doubt. Notice how Melanie Daniels, the barman, the lawyer, the lady ornithologist, a mother with two children, the cook, the waitress, the travelling salesman, the local barfly and a sea captain, are all involved in a conversation that covers a whole reel of the film (around 8 minutes). Hitchcock handles them separately or in groups using static camera set-ups.

A performer faces an audience

On many occasions in films there is a need to present the central protagonist facing a crowd. Perhaps he is a flight instructor talking to a group of pilots, or a football coach addressing his team, or a politician addressing a crowd or, perhaps, a musician performing for an audience. The size of the crowd does not matter, there are two ways of dealing with it—to treat it as a single group, of an impersonal nature or, to treat it as a series of small groups related to the central performer.

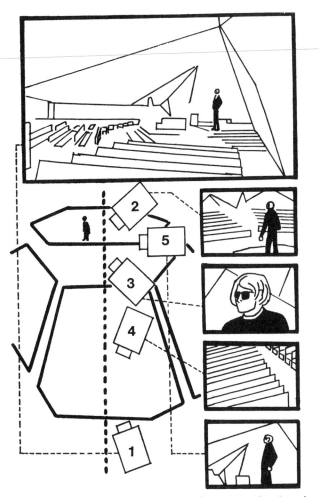

FIGURE. 7.15 Impersonal treatment of a large crowd, where the direction of gaze of the dominant player establishes the line of interest. One of its sides is chosen for the camera positions.

In the first case the audience and our central protagonist form the two poles of attention with an imaginary line of interest flowing between them. Having chosen one of its sides, the camera is sited according to the triangular camera disposition where two sets of reverse camera positions (one external and the other internal) can easily be adopted (Fig. 7.15).

The protagonist stares straight ahead—an impersonal way of dealing with his crowd. In the example here, for instance, he will be looking to the left in all shots.

Members of the crowd do not participate individually. Nobody stands up and speaks to our performer. The crowd (large or small) of passive spectators are there to be entertained or instructed.

If our main performer shifts his gaze from side to side, answering questions or replying to observations made by individual members of the audience, the camera treatment is similar to the one used for covering triangular groups.

When the crowd acquires identifiable faces, it becomes subdivided into sectors. All these sectors radiate toward our protagonist who can have two body rapports with the crowd by being on the rim of the crowd or in the centre. In the first case at least two groups or a series of small groups deployed in an arc face the performer. Between him and the individual member of the group, two sets of camera positions can be located, one external, one internal (see Fig. 7.16).

Our central protagonist acts as an arbiter of attention, shifting his gaze from group to group. If the individual players in the audience talk between themselves, momentarily excluding the central player, we have a triangular formation of centres of interest.

Those people are the ones who count, those around them are secondary and anonymous. They serve only to reinforce the importance of the main characters by looking at them directly—thus acting as a chorus that stresses any shift in interest. Fig. 7.17 shows a simple sequence with the main player as centre and arbiter of attention.

The numbers identifying parts of Fig. 7.17 correspond to the floor plan shown in Fig. 7.16.

In the example shown, external reverse shots (1–2 or 5–6) establish the locale, while individual close internal reverse shots (all the others) focus attention on the centres of interest.

If our main protagonist faces more than two groups, shifting his attention to a third or fourth subject, *opposed looks will always occur*. If both persons are looking at the same side of the screen in individual close shots, they are not relating to each other, but to somebody else off-screen.

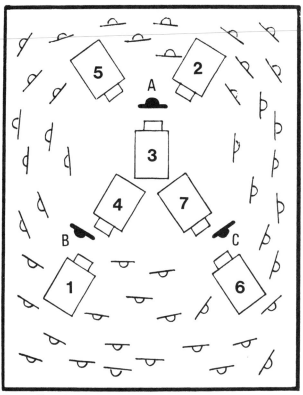

FIGURE 7.16 Floor plan showing the camera positions used when lone player facing a crowd shifts his gaze from one side to the other changing the direction of the line of interest.

A crosswise change of the line of interest

A 'north-south' to 'east-west' change in the line of interest, emphasizing either the subjects on the stage or those on the audience, can be applied to the two central points of interest located in a crowd.

In the first example in Fig. 7.18 the emphasis is put on the players on the stage, who relate with the crowd and between themselves. The 'east-west' line dominates. The players talk among themselves and occasionally look towards the audience, shifting the direction of the line of interest. The crowd is treated as an impersonal mass.

The second example, on the right of Fig. 7.18, could be a night-club set-up, where two customers at a table are emphasized rather

FIGURE 7.17 Storyboard development of the sequence following the floor plan depicted in Fig. 7.16.

than the lovely female singer on stage who stands in front of the orchestra. When the players at the table talk among themselves an 'E-W' line is dominant, but when they watch the singer a 'N-S' line of interest prevails.

FIGURE 7.18 Placements for a crosswise change of direction, either on the stage or on the floor.

You need not, of course, use all the key camera positions shown on the floor plans in Fig. 7.18. The numerous editing combinations give adequate coverage for situations in this category, with fewer camera positions.

Crowd with main player at centre

If our main player stands alone in the centre of a crowd, she relates only with half of it—those in front of her. Those behind have only an indirect rapport with her.

Camera placement principles are the same as before—two sets of external and internal reverse shots. In Fig. 7.19 positions 1 and

FIGURE 7.19 The dominant player stands in the centre of the crowd. The direction of her look determines the line of interest of the scene, and one side of this line is chosen to position the camera.

2 are external; 3 and 4 internal. As our protagonist is in the centre of the crowd, she acts as a central pivot around whom the camera can be placed to relate her to the surrounding crowd (as in Shots 5 and 6).

Actors as pivots

When dealing with examples with three players, we explained how one of those players could be used as a pivot to assemble the interplay of master shots covering the group. There we said that the player used as a pivot could be on the same side of the screen in both shots, or assume an irregular solution where he alternated between sides of the screen from shot to shot. Both rules apply to a performer in relation to a crowd. He can be placed in the centre of the crowd (large or small) or on the rim. In this example a central performer is used as a pivot within a small group.

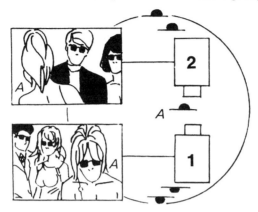

FIGURE 7.20 A central player is used as a pivot within a group to present it as sub-divided into two smaller units. The pivoting player is used in an irregular manner, shifting his position from one side of the screen to the other.

Fig. 7.20 clearly shows that the central actor is the most important. The players facing her in shot 2 are her opponents, and those behind, in Shot 1, are her friends or her audience. Actor A shifts from right to left on the screen as we cut from shot to shot.

This is a closely knit group and we are dealing with medium shots to frame the scene. But the group behind and in front of actor A can be larger and further apart. In that case she truly becomes an island between both masses, and the camera coverage is as if for a closely knit group (Fig. 7.21).

Two players, dominant or passive, can also be used as pivots in a scene. Fig. 7.22 shows a simple case where both central performers are dominant and located in the centre of the group.

Actors A and B do the talking, while the others just stand in the background watching the main actors play out the core of the scene.

If these players are on the edge of the group, the crowd is omitted from one of the reverse shots. Fig. 7.23 visualizes one of those situations. In the first shot the group beyond the central players is included, while in Shot 2 only the central performers are featured.

131

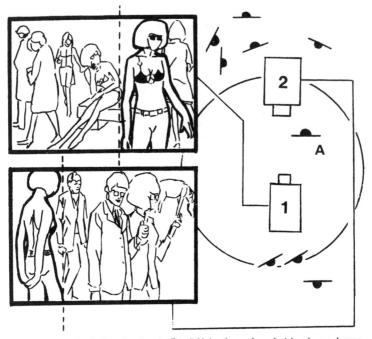

FIGURE 7.21 A similar situation to Fig. 7.20 is shown here but involves a larger group.

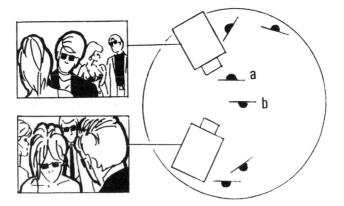

FIGURE 7.22 Two central players in the group used as visual pivots to show the whole group around them. The key performers in this instance are located in the centre of the group.

FIGURE 7.23 The two dominant players in the group are placed on the rim of it. For this reason the group is featured in only one of the shots.

When the pivoting performers have a passive role in the scene, they can be placed in foreground to help relate a group divided into sectors. These two players always remain on the sides of the screen, but the person or persons in the centre change from shot to shot. This is achieved by placing both camera positions at right angles. Fig. 7.24 shows a simple case involving only four persons seated at a table.

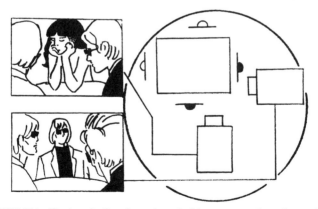

FIGURE 7.24 The two pivoting players have, in this case, a passive nature and the dominant players appear alternately in the centre of the screen as each master shot is edited in parallel.

133

The parallel editing of the master shots obtained from those two right angle camera sites, allows a little trickery in shooting the scene.

Two groups of players who, for some reason, cannot be present on the stage or on the location at the same time, can be related perfectly by arranging two pivoting players in the foreground in both shots. The only requisite is that these two performers be available for filming both shots. In the first take, a group of persons situated in the centre of the screen talk to someone off-screen whose place is taken by a substitute who provides the replies in the conversation.

Later on, a week or a month afterwards, the second shot is filmed with the missing group framed between the two pivoting players in the foreground. The second camera site is used. The central players look off-screen, too, but in the opposite direction to that in the first master shot.

When, at the editing stage, both takes are combined (in parallel) the difference will not be noticeable if the lighting has been matched carefully. This formula allows for further trickery: two different sets or locales can be used, one for each take—producing on the screen an imaginary set which is an amalgam of both.

8

EDITING PATTERNS FOR
STATIC DIALOGUE SCENES

In any dialogue situation where actors move *on* but not *from* their sites, and there is no camera movement, variety and comprehensive coverage relies purely on a cutting pattern.

A motion picture must move. Therefore, our cutting pattern cannot always be the same, so there must be more than one pair of key positions from which master shots are produced.

A master shot (the long take obtained from a single camera position) covers a complete sequence, or a complete dialogue. If the actors move within the frame in that long take, the shot can be self-sufficient, provided that certain rules are respected. In such a case a shot would need no 'toning up' by inserting cut-aways or closer shots.

In the passive kind of scene we are concerned with now, this would seldom be enough. Such scenes are too static to remain visually interesting—unless the situation and dialogue are so full of meaning and dramatic force that any visual variation would disturb the mood of the scene.

Except in those cases, a master shot covering a whole conversation would be very much enhanced by stressing certain passages with close shots or cut-aways.

Another solution is to present the scene with two master shots edited in parallel. But generally that is not enough. As a dialogue builds up in interest we tend to wish to be closer to the performers to catch every nuance of movement and fleeting reactions in their faces.

In using an editing pattern the simplest solution is to cover the first half of the dialogue with two master shots, preferably medium shots, and the final part with another pair both close shots.

Approaching and receding patterns

A lengthy dialogue should have certain peaks of interest and should not demand a high degree of concentration throughout otherwise the effect of a denoument is weakened and even lost.

This recommended peak-pattern allows the audience some emotional repose, and they can respond more fully to the really important passages. The auditive part of the scene must receive a corresponding visual counterpart that works hand in glove with the intentions of the dramatist.

The film director must resort to a visual 'approaching and receding' editing method. The performers may be presented in medium shots, proceeding to close shots or close ups as peak moments are approached, and then again medium shots as we give the audience a rest before building up to the next peak.

This approaching and receding method must not appear too obvious. So different editing patterns should be used in each section of the dialogue covered from peak to peak, in order to mask the means being used as a guide to the audience. The actors could also be moved from zone to zone on the set after each peak moment for further variations—but for the moment we are concerned only with static situations.

How a sequence begins

On the screen we do not usually begin a conversation with the actors already in their allotted places, have them say their lines, and cut straight to the next sequence. We normally record a more natural order of events. Our performers meet first, then talk, and finally, part. There are variations *to* this, but not *from* this need. On other occasions, when the sequence begins the characters in the story are already in position and needing no introduction to one another. Nevertheless, we like to meet them visually before we can listen to what they have to say. We are then led in to a closer view for the dialogue.

But such sequences seldom begin with the players already on the screen speaking their first lines from the beginning of the first shot. There is nearly always a movement at the beginning or at the end of the sequence. Here are six generic variants where such movement lapses into static body positions from which a conversation can be comfortably developed.

1 Both players enter into camera range, walk towards us, and stop to talk.

2 One performer is already on the screen, the other enters and stops beside him and they start talking.

3 In the two previous examples the camera was fixed, but it could have panned or travelled following both or one of the actors to their stopping places.

4 If the panning or travelling technique is used, a third character can start the sequence by walking up to the couple, giving them something and going away. The camera remains with the our two main performers (or larger group) who would then begin to speak.

5 A panning or tracking movement that starts on an empty part of the set and moves to one side to frame the main players can also be used to begin the scene. The voices of the players are heard before their figures are revealed.

6 The opening movement in the sequence can be covered in several shots prior to the start of the static dialogue.

The possibilities outlined can be applied to larger groups. For the exits at the end of the sequence we would only have to reverse the movements described above. It must be understood that these opening and closing motions are an essential part of the dialogue sequences where the performers stop to talk in a fixed place.

Re-establishing shots

To keep our interest adequately aroused in the situation, we must be reminded from time to time of the place in which the action that attracted our attention is happening. This presupposes the use, at least once, of a re-establishing shot halfway through the sequence. The shot can serve several purposes:

1 It re-estates the place, reminding us of the spatial relationship between the performers and their placement on the set—something we tend to forget as we concentrate on the closer shots.

2 It serves as a pause in the narration—a visual pause that breaks the saturation of the close shots accumulated during the development of the dialogue.

3 It serves to end the sequence, giving the performers space in which to part or go away together.

4 If the sequence continues, it serves to mask a change in editing patterns, or allows the actors to move from zone to zone before the new editing pattern is introduced.

5 If some actor is temporarily excluded in an interplay of close shots that concentrate on the central performers, a re-establishing shot reminds us of his presence. If he is not re-established his disappearance would be baffling to us, since we would not have been aware of his exit.

Of course, there are exceptions to this pattern of establishing shot dialogue in closer shots—re-establishing shot. We can start a scene with close shots and establish the locale after a suitable period has elapsed (the opening of the Masoch Club sequence in *The Tenth Victim*, (see Page 6) where the announcer is first introduced alone, in close up, and his location is revealed at a later stage in the story). That procedure is correct. But what we can seldom do is dispose completely of the establishing shot.

Importance of silent reactions

Often the silent reaction of a listening performer is more expressive than the face of the performer speaking to him. For example, the sequence starts with one player speaking his first lines, and in mid-speech we cut to the other listening in silence, with the voice of the first actor continuing. When he finishes, the image of the second player remains on the screen and he then replies. Now we can reverse the formula, cutting in the middle of his lines to the first master shot where his partner is reacting in silence. This is a scene tackled in the crudest form. Refinements in cutting the master shots to determine how much a voice overflows into the next shot, or providing a series of muted reactions to statements from a player, must be dictated by the context of the scene and its meaning and position in the story as a whole.

If one actor is confronted by a group, to whom he has a long speech to deliver, we cannot effectively sustain interest with a single shot of that lone performer; we must occasionally insert various silent shots of the listening group as the voice continues.

Having outlined the most general principles, let us now get down to particulars by investigating some current editing practices of static diologues covered from fixed camera positions.

Inserts and cut-aways

Many directors and editors still tend to shoot and edit a static dialogue in a continuous static single shot. This last vestige of the theatrical influence in film work is a practice still transmitted from one generation of film directors to another. It allows screen performers to approach the scene in a similar way to their experience in the theatre. The scenes covered tend to be lengthy and the players have time to sink their teeth into their roles and bring out the best in their acting.

But the camera is relegated to the role of passive spectator and its cinematic possibilities are denied to it. Many film technicians have felt secure with this type of coverage and dreaded experimentation with the montage method that breaks the natural tempo of the scene and brings one of its own to bear, whose rules must be mastered by continuous practice in editing.

Early film directors and editors who were aware of the limitations of such a shallow approach, introduced inserts and cut-aways in their first efforts to break away from it. The insert would be a shot spliced in to substitute a part of the main master shot. It shows a section of the scene framed by the master shot in greater detail. A cut-away is a shot inserted on the master shot that shows something or somebody not covered by the master camera position. If both such shots are used repeatedly within a main master shot they themselves become subordinate master shots. This approach to static dialogue editing, although basic, is still useful today.

Case A

Let us examine the use of inserts first. Let us say that we have a scene where one player is explaining something to another. There is a map on the wall behind them (Fig. 8.1). Suddenly, to make a point clearer, one of the players indicates a section of the map. If we cut to a close shot of him on the same visual axis of the master shot, the audience, too, will be able to appreciate the point.

We then return to the former master shot. That small shot spliced into the master shot served to highlight a part of the dialogue and its use was justified. In fact, it would have been a mistake not to avail ourselves of the situation to present a clearer visual story to the audience.

The next possibility is to make the insert shot from a reverse camera position. For instance, a car is on the road parked beside a policeman who is admonishing its driver. We cover this dialogue from a full shot position (see Fig. 8.2). As the policeman hands a

139

FIGURE 8.1 The insert has the same visual axis as the master shot.

ticket to the driver, we cut to a close reverse shot in which we catch that delivery being made. The reverse position in this case affords us a better view of the proceedings. Now we return to the full shot master shot to complete the scene and witness how the driver pulls away and the policeman watches him go.

The insert serves not only to pinpoint attention on an object, but also to show in detail an emotional reaction as portrayed on the face of a player. The approach is similar to the cases just described.

Case B

An insert can be used twice within a master shot. For example, Two persons talking as seen from a master shot that frames them in full shot. Two inserts of the same performer are made where he reacts silently to the words of his partner. As these moments come

140

FIGURE 8.2 The insert has a reverse angle relationship with the master shot.

in the master shot, the reaction seen in full shot is substituted by the insert where that same reaction was filmed in close shot. The editing order would be simple:

Master
Insert 1
Master
Insert 2
Master

In such a situation both inserts corresponded to the same player, but both performers can be highlighted alternately, by showing one of them in the first insert, and the other in the second.

This second insert need not always be placed within the main master shot. It can be used at the end of it, to cap the sequence with the detail that the insert affords.

Case C

An insert shot is often used as hinge to unite two master shots.

141

For example: Three officers are discussing a situation in front of a military map. The map is placed sideways to the audience and cannot be clearly seen. When one of the players points to it, we cut to a close shot of the map and the hand of the performer roaming over it. This shot could be from a right angle camera position, and is our insert.

But then, instead of returning to the previous master shot, we cut to a second master shot that continues the scene (Fig. 8.3). This second master shot can be made from any one of the points of the triangle camera disposition for coverage of a group, and this group can be framed in its entirety as before. Or the view may become selective and frame only a section of it.

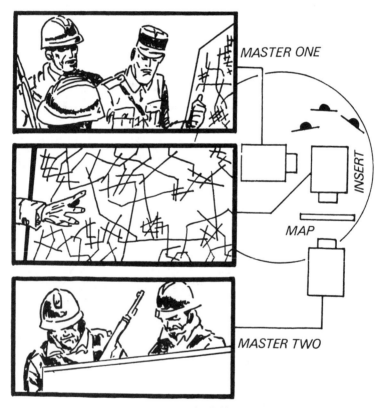

FIGURE 8.3 An insert is used to bridge two master shots.

Case D

In the old days, and in fact in quite recent times, especially in America, static dialogued scenes were shot according to a standard procedure:

1 A master shot, (usually a full shot), is made of the scene all the way through.

2 The ensemble of players is split in groups, and each group is photographed repeating the whole scene from beginning to end with the other players sitting or standing out of camera range all through the scene.

3 Close-ups of every player involved are shot covering the whole event.

This means that the film editor has a wide field of selection when editing the scenes, since he has all the lines of dialogue and silent reactions he needs. He is the one who selects the camera angles to appear on the screen. If the director later wants to delete some piece of dialogue or phrase, the editor can do that very easily, because he has numerous cover shots (inserts and cut-aways) to choose from to bridge the gap where the words were removed.

Case E

In scenes which are essentially psychological and greatly depend on dialogue, the performance and truthful staging must take precedence over the arrangement of the shots. The classical method of shooting the scene, as described above in case D, is the easiest way out, but perhaps not the most economical. It allows the director and film editor to try several different versions of the scene till they arrive at the most satisfactory.

If the scene has special bits of business worth stressing visually, the director shoots them for the editor to use at the proper time in the sequence. Such inserts can be simple facial reactions, the movement of a hand, the motion of a mechanism seen in detail, etc. In fact, the word insert is often synonymous with close shot. It is not necessary for the film editor to use them all, perhaps none may be used in the final version of the scene. But a wise director shoots them anyway to be adequately covered. On the stage floor, among all the rush and excitememt of getting the scene on film, the quality of all ideas cannot be assessed properly, and the final editing pattern may not yet, perhaps, have been decided.

143

On other occasions an insert is used to repair technical errors unwittingly committed—for example, if a piece of film has been fogged for some reason or someone out of camera range moved in front of a light during the shot. Such errors might not be seen until printed, at which stage it is perhaps too costly or impossible to reshoot the scene. An insert spliced in place of the damaged spot of film often saves the day.

Case F

Sometimes during the course of a conversation the characters refer to something off screen: a building, an animal, a vehicle or, perhaps, a person. It is quite natural then, if the subject involved is really important, to splice a shot of it into the single take that covers the dialogue. That insertion is called a cut-away.

More than one cut-away shot can be introduced into a master shot to show the different points of interest that the players cover in the development of their dialogue. For example: two persons are standing on a hill talking, we see them in medium shot. One points off screen to the right. We insert a cut-away in which a far-off building is seen. We return to the master shot of the two players. After a moment the second performer turns and points to something off screen, left. We insert another cut-away showing a distant bridge. Then we return to the medium shot of the two actors where they conclude their conversation and turning, walk away to the background. Thus the sequence is neatly resolved, in a straightforward simple presentation.

In the example examined both cut-aways covered different subjects. Instead of two different cut-aways being inserted into the master shot, the subject matter of both inserts can be the same, but the second is a closer shot on the same visual axis as the first insert. Repeating our example, both players are standing on the hill, talking, facing us. (Fig. 8.4). They look up, off screen, to the sky. We insert the first cut-away, a tall tree with an eagle seen perched on a top branch. This is a full shot of the tree and the eagle.

We return to the master shot, and moments later insert the second cut-away, a closer view of the eagle on the branch.

The method can also be applied to silent scenes, where a group, or groups, witness some far off event, or are watched by another group.

144

FIGURE 8.4 Both inserts have a common visual axis, and are spliced into the master shot.

Case G

The next step is to insert more than two cut-aways in the same master shot—always covering the same subject. The formula is simple. The master is a full shot of the main performer or performers. The inserts progress from a full shot for the first, to medium shot for the second, to close shot for the third and close up for the fourth.

This formula can be applied to dialogues or silent situations. One can recall two examples from well known films. In Max Ophuls' *Lola Montez*, Peter Ustinov is seen as the circus master perched on a high scaffold, recounting the life of Lola Montez to the public. Down below in the arena Lola Montez (played by Martine Carol) turns on a merry-go-round where several groups of midgets represent stages of her life. The take covering Peter Ustinov is a static Full Shot, and is the main master take. On it are intercut a series of shots of Lola Montez beginning to recall a particularly painful event in her life. As a pounding sound increases in the sound track of the film, we get progressively closer views of her on the merry-go-round, intercut within the shot of Peter Ustinov.

The second example happens in Alfred Hitchcock's film *The Birds*. Melanie Daniels has stepped out of the school building and sits down close to the playground to smoke a cigarette. Unnoticed by her, several birds began to gather on the climbing bars located on the school playground.

The playground is framed in full shot, while a progressive succession of closer shots of the girl are spliced within that master shot. The scene is played completely in silence, and runs roughly like this:

Full shot. A lone bird arrives and lands on the climbing bars.
Full shot of Melanie Daniels smoking.
Full shot. Several birds on the bars. Another crow arrives.
Medium shot of the girl. She smokes.
Full shot. New birds arrive.
Close shot of girl. She smokes slowly.
Full shot. More birds join the crows already gathered in on the playground.
Close up of the girl. She stops smoking and turns her head to the left to look off screen.
A lone bird flying in the sky. The camera framing it in long

146

shot follows its flight from left to right, to show how the crow joins the ranks of birds now fully covering the metal construction on the playground.

Close up of the girl. She reacts frightened.

All the shots of Melanie Daniels seated on the bench, smoking, had the same visual axis.

Case H

Cut-aways can be tracking or panned shots, as well as static set-ups. For example: an actress is addressing a group. It is a long speech she is delivering.

We face her in medium shot.

The first cut-away inserted in a full shot of the group watching her silently.

Back again to her medium shot.

The second cut-away is a panning shot across the faces in the group.

We return to the master medium shot of the actress.

The third cut-away is a full shot similar to the first insert.

We close the sequence by returning again to the master medium shot where she finishes speaking.

Case I

A cut-away can evoke an event in the past. Akira Kurosawa and Alain Resnais are two film makers very adept at this sort of usage. The remembrance can be provoked by the subject that dominates in the master shot, or it may be a sudden visualization of the character's inner recollections.

In his film *Rashomon*, Akira Kurosawa has a scene in which the bandit (Toshiro Mifune) tells the court how he recalls the events on the day of the crime. There is a particular moment that is built like this:

The bandit says he remembers having covered a great distance with his horse that day.

Without interrupting the verbal narration of the bandit, a cut-away is introduced framing the horizon low on the screen, and on its edge the small figure of the bandit riding his horse is seen traversing the screen.

The bandit reappears as in the previous master shot, and continues his narration to the tribunal.

147

In this cut-away to a past event two different times co-exist briefly on the screen. The audience accepts this cut-away without difficulty because it is motivated by the performer's train of thought.

Alain Resnais specializes in the sudden intrusion of the past on the present, without warning and usually for a brief flash. His film *Hiroshima, Mon Amour* is full of such examples.

The French woman in the hotel room fixes her attention on the hand of her Japanese lover asleep on the bed.

Without warning, a brief take is inserted showing in close up the hand of another man wriggling in agony.

It is a brief pan shot that moves upwards over the prone body of the German.

The woman looks at her sleeping lover. There is no immediate explanation for that sudden, brief shot. It comes as a shock. It is only later, when the part recurrs several times more, that we understand that the hand belonged to her dead German lover, a soldier in World War II. It is a more difficult for the audience to grasp the point. Our first reaction is one of shock, we do not understand at all.

As the experience is repeated we learn to accept that appearance passively, waiting for the explanation that we are sure will later be provided by the author.

Case J

For how long should an insert or a cut-away be held on the screen?

It depends on the content.

If it frames a motion that is emphasized, it should begin with the start of the movement and finalize when it comes to an end. In fact, the length of the shot in such a case dictates itself. If the movement emphasized is part of a larger motion, the visual rapport between the master shot and the insert should be achieved by cutting on the action.

More of this, later.

If a static object is the one framed on the cut-away, or a silent close shot of a person with neutral expression, two seconds is enough, or sometimes even too long. But if the silent player giving a passive countenance to his screen interpretation is listening to a phrase, dialogue or a piece of music, this image can be easily held up to 10 seconds without seeming over-long.

148

Number contrast

What I have called 'number contrast' is one of the most useful recourses for covering long dialogues, since it masks the approaching and receding visual pattern of the film by featuring a different number of actors on the screen from shot to shot. Number contrast is obtained by parallel camera positions in groups of three and more actors, but more often mainly by opposing a reverse external position to an internal reverse camera site. This approach works with groups of two actors and more. Its most simple application would be a decreasing contrast in numbers, such as:

2 players to 2,
2 players to 1,
1 player to 1.

This would correspond to a visual pattern of medium shots, close shots, close ups, thus perhaps building to a peak moment in the dialogue. The pattern is reversed to return to the subdued curve of dialogue before mounting to the next peak.

A pair of reverse shots (in any of the five variants of the triangle principle) can be at different subject ranges for variety in the final edited result. If the apex of the triangular camera disposition (the establishing shot site) is a full shot, and the other two positions on the base of the triangle figure are close shots, the extreme differences in subject distance will provide a dramatic introduction and conclusion to the sequence.

Parallel editing of master shots

What is the main difference between the parallel editing of reverse master shots and the system outlined before, where inserts and cutaways were introduced into a single master take?

Fundamentally, it is a difference of concept. While with the first method the scene is covered in full from a single camera position, here the scene is divided in segments and each one of those pieces of scene is given a different visual treatment.

What the inserts and cut-aways did for the previous system, the parallel editing of pairs of camera positions does now.

Two major patterns can be outlined for this new technique:

1 An establishing camera site opens the sequence: a pair of external reverse shots cover part of the dialogue; a return is made to the re-establishing view of the group the editing pattern is changed into an internal-external camera opposition. The whole

group is re-established once more from a full shot, and a new editing pattern is employed (internal reverse shots). A re-establishing shot closes the sequence.

2   After establishing the scene from a full shot, the different pairs of reverse shots edited in parallel dovetail smoothly from pattern to pattern, using each last shot of a pattern as the hinge to begin the following editing pattern. Partial emphasis on a single line of interest or a change from north-south to east-west is achieved without resorting to a re-establishing take, whose use is more sparsely employed.

The order and nature of such editing patterns is decided by the director previous to shooting the scene, thereby limiting the role of the editor, whose creative labour is now channelled into controlling the screen time for the shots.

It is with this method that all the pairs of key camera positions outlined in previous chapters come into their own.

Variation A

With this technique inserts and cut-aways are employed for effect only, to stress an object, a spoken line or a facial expression within one or several of the editing patterns of the sequence.

The film maker need not be awed by the large number of pairs of key shots he has at his disposal. He selects and adapts for the needs of his story those types of combinations more suited to his purpose.

Variation B

Using shots at different distances for variety can be carried a step further (Fig. 8.5).

The four master camera sites shown could be edited in a simple pattern, such as the following:

Shots 1—4—1—4—2—3—2—3

progressing from close shots to close ups. To achieve that we group together the reverse shots of the same distance: 1 and 4 are close shots, 2 and 3 are close ups.

Yet, both distances can be contrasted, so that a close up follows a close shot, reversing the formula half-way through the sequence. The sequence will then become as follows:

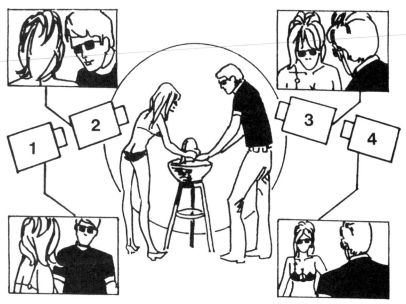

FIGURE 8.5 Four key master shots that can be used to obtain a dynamic visual presentation of a dialogued scene by contrasting distances on the reverse shots.

Shots 1—3—1—3—1—3—2—4—2—4—2—4—
This frequently used variation gives a flashy presentation to a brisk dialogue.

Variation C

Here is another widely used variation, applied to parallel editing of a two-player static dialogue. The system implies the use of two camera sites placed on a common visual axis to cover one of the players, while only one camera position is given to the other player. If you pick two key camera positions to cover a dialogue, and feel that the conversation is too long, you can move forward on the axis of one of the master takes to cover the second half of the conversation.

Fig. 8.6 illustrates two examples where two players are used as pivots in a group. If the dialogue is a short one the editing order of the sequence could be:

Shots 1—2—1—2—1—2
Since the dialogue is longer, halfway through it we move to a closer position on the same axis of one of the master shots (thus

emphasizing one of the players). The editing order now becomes:

Shots 1—2—1—2—1—2—3—2—3—2

Both examples illustrated have subtle differences in number contrast when the closer shot on one of the visual axes is introduced in the sequence.

Line of interest—changing sides

When a long dialogue between two persons seated at a table is covered from one side of the east-west line of interest flowing between them, and we risk monotony from the length of the dialogue itself, we can momentarily interrupt by switching to a north-south axis, then returning east-west but on the other side of the line. Fig. 8.7 shows the screen compositions and floor plan sites.

The shift in the line of interest can start in any one of the first three camera positions. In this case we have selected the central shot (2), where no player is dominant. The shift of attention is easily accomplished: the players stop looking at one another and turn their heads away from us towards a point off screen, left. We then cut to Shot 4, where performer C waves a hand to them. Cut to Shot 5 where both are looking to the left and react to the performer off-screen. Player C in Shot 4 moves away from the screen after breaking his visual rapport with the actors at the table. Shot 5 again, where players B and A stop looking off-screen left, and face one another again. We are now on the other side of the line of interest and a reverse angle coverage can be started again.

Our two main performers have exchanged areas on the screen and this change goes unnoticed due to the momentary polar shift. The editing order of this sequence can be as follows:

Shots 2-1-3-1-3-1-3-2-4-5-4-5-6-7-6-7-5-6-7

Pause between dialogues

Long static dialogues are difficult to sustain visually. They need continued peaks of attention. But such an accumulation, with brief passages of unimportant things said in between, are very difficult to write and to say convincingly, for two reasons: The effect obtained is too wordy, and a logical and natural transition between sections is quite difficult to secure every time.

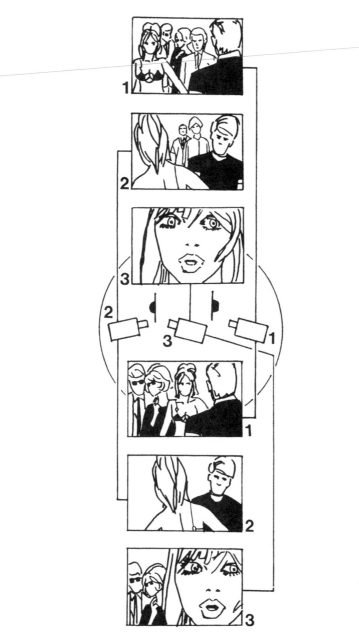

FIGURE 8.6   Three basic master shots can be used to cover a large group where two central players serve as pivots. Observe the differences in number contrast that distinguish both examples.

FIGURE 8.7 Crossing a triangular formation to the other side of the line of interest. A diversion, in this case a momentary crosswise change in the line of direction is used to achieve the shifting of the triangular camera placement scheme.

The solution is to do without these bridging phrases altogether, and replace them by visual pauses, thus obtaining a flow of only peak moments of dialogue on the screen.

The visual pause resorted to is one that portrays something relevant to the scene without interfering with the contents of the peak moments. Let us look at an example: David Lean, at the beginning of his film Doctor Zhivago, makes use of that technique:

1   The film begins with Yevgraf (Alec Guinness) looking through the window of his office.

2   Long rows of workers enter the hydroelectric plant early in the morning.

3   Yevgraf talks with his assistant remembering the hard times during the revolution.

4   A single shot of people coming to work at the hydroelectric plant.

5   Yevgraf states that he wants to find a particular girl among the workers.

6   A single shot of people coming to work.

7   The girl (Rita Tushingham) outside Yevgraf's office knocks and is received by him.

The sections numbered 3, 5 and 7 are part of a same continuous scene covering three important points in the dialogue. If they had been filmed as a continuous scene, the words separating the peak moments of attention would tend to distract the audience, defeating the purpose of relaying to them important facts about the story.

Visual pauses are therefore introduced: the workers coming into the plant, as seen in sections 4 and 6.

In this way *the peak moments of dialogue are isolated* and allowed to sink home. But to motivate the visual pause, and to prevent their being distracting digressions, their rapport to the main personage was established before in sections 1 and 2.

Sometimes the nature of the forthcoming visual pause is previously announced in a dialogue. Richard Brooks' film *The Professionals* has such an example:

Lee Marvin arrives for the train and is received by Mr. Grant himself, the owner of the railway. As they get on the train a worker points out to Mr. Grant that they will have to be moved into a siding to let an express go by. The train starts to move.

Inside Mr. Grant describes each of the three men he has gathered, thus informing the audience and the personages of their main traits and abilities.

The express passes Grant's wagon.

Inside the train once more, Mr. Grant explains his problem and his plan.

The visual pause used to isolate the peaks of dialogue looked natural because it was verbally planted beforehand during an otherwise neutral moment.

155

Everyday scenes can be covered easily with this technique:
Two people on the front seat of a moving car, talking. As a story point is made, cut to . . .
. . . an external shot of the car crossing the road from side to side of the screen. Cut again to . . .
. . . the interior of the moving car where both players indicate a new section of their dialogue.
The technique is simple and effective. Its proper use will ensure a clear and sharp development of the story on the screen.

Time compression

There are situations in which lengthy dialogue seems necessary to convey properly what is happening. And yet, we may still feel that the scene is too wordy, and slows down the rhythm of the film. There is a solution which is very cinematic in its results and is always an attention getter. Basically, what is done is to compress the time span of the dialogued sequence, specially in its central part.

The opening and closing parts of the sequence are treated normaly. Fig. 8.8 gives us a visual idea of the principle.

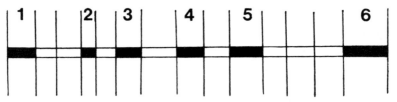

FIGURE 8.8 The line represents the total length of the scene, out of which key passages are selected and edited together, omitting other fragments considered not relevant to the spirit of the scene. Thus, time compression is achieved.

The line in the illustration represents the real length of the scene. The numbered segments are the ones portrayed on the screen. As can be seen, beginning and conclusion are respected, but in the centre significant fragments are selected (2-3-4-5-) and edited together by a simple cut. No optical transition joins the fragments.

Each fragment selected conveys a complete idea by itself, just that, and a cut is made to the next fragment. There is no change in background or location of the action, only a compression of time.

156

Case A

The selection of fragments presents the players in different body positions and parts of the location. Alain Resnais in *Hiroshima, Mon Amour* used this effect several times. We recall an instance concerning the Japanese lover, when he recounted some of his experiences to the French actress. Three shots containing his phrases were arranged roughly like this:

The man lying in bed, talking. As he completes a thought, cut to . . .

. . . same background, the man sitting in bed talking. His words continue the concept of the former phrases, cut to . . .

. . . same background. The man standing. He ends his exposition.

In this way the reactions of the woman who listened off-shot, were omitted (and with them her phrases and the resultant answers the man would have been compelled to give).

The scene gained in conciseness and impact by omitting unimportant time segments.

Case B

If this technique is applied to two people, each shot may contain only two phrases, a question and an answer perhaps and those phrases cover a complete thought or idea. The scenes are very brief giving a staccato rhythm on the screen, due to the direct cuts with which the takes have been joined. This mood is emphasized by the actors changing sites, body positions, and framing in the picture area.

A pause introduced in one shot would break the monotony of the staccato rhythm.

By presenting the scene with a contraction of real time, we have eliminated the hesitations, repetitions and verbal pauses between the peaks of dialogue, keeping on the screen only the important sectors of the scene.

Case C

The same technique can be taken a step further and one of the players can be periodically replaced in the sequence, as the conversation moves along a central theme.

In the French film *Without Apparent Motive*, J. L. Trintignant, playing the police inspector, interrogates a suspect. The inspector questions—the suspect answers, after a time this pattern is broken by having a second suspect unexpectedly answer a question, and then the first suspect answers the following question, and then the second, and then the first till the sequence concludes. What happens is that two different interrogations were held in the same room at different times. These scenes are edited in parallel to give the audience non-repetitive information, which would happen when the second suspect answers the same questions with the same results. With this approach only the information that differs as supplied by both is given to the audience.

The scene gained in clarity by a simple contraction of time.

In Milos Forman film *Taking Off*, a song called *Let's Get A Little Sentimental* is presented as sung in a fragmented jump-cut montage by a variety of girls at an audition. Each girl sings a single phrase or only a few words, and the lyrics are continued by the one that follows. Up to twenty girls are used to render the song on the screen.

Case D

Akira Kurosawa in his film *Ikiru* used the same technique but in a different context. The film begins with a group of women complaining in the municipal offices. The employee sends them to another section. By a series of swift wipes across the screen a succession of employees from different sectors of the establishment is presented, all saying in their own way that they are not involved and referring the women to the next office. At last, the whole thing comes full circle, and the women are returned to the first employee they saw.

One of the women suddenly gives vent to her indignation on the man and on the system he works for.

When the sequence begins we are shown the women and the employee, but after he directs them to the next office and the first wipe crosses the screen, the succeeding takes are a series of close shots of the employees, who, speaking directly into the camera lens, give their excuses in turn. The women are not seen or heard during the whole succession of faces, till the first employee reappears.

Kurosawa's social comment is put bluntly enough by this technique.

Case E

David Lean adopted this method of time contraction in *Doctor Zhivago*. But his variation is to use a narrator to express verbally the mood of the scene whose visual parts he contracts. Yevgraf finds Zhivago tearing pieces of wood from a fence. Yevgraf recognizes him as his half brother (so his interior voice informs us) and follows him home. There is a short scene between Zhivago and the two commissars who are removing his books from his room. The discussion is interrupted by the arrival of Yevgraf who snaps his fingers and disbands the group of neighbours.

Once more the internal voice of Yevgraf is heard on the sound track, while on the screen Zhivago embraces his step-brother, they eat together, and talk. But only the narrative voice of Yevgraf is heard. Suddenly there is a close shot of Zhivago where he says: 'Not liked? My poems are not liked? By whom?' And over a silent face of Yevgref his narrative voice on the screen gives the real answer he would have liked to have made but did not.

The scene progresses, with the players gesticulating and moving silently, until the narrative voice of Yevgraf is once more interrupted by Zhivago speaking.

Yevgraf's visit is visually reduced to a series of images compressing time and representing only the peak moments of their meeting.

Speeding dialogue tempo

There is a curious phenomenon for which I know not of a valid explanation. When you shoot a scene at a normal pace and project it later on a small screen, the pace reproduced on the screen equals that of the scene when it was photographed on film. But when this same strip of film is projected on a large screen to be viewed by a large audience, the pace of the scene slows down. This is a fact to which many film directors will attest.

With an action scene, the camera is undercranked, thus increasing the speed of the subject when, later, the film is projected at the normal rate. But how do we solve the same problem when dealing with a static dialogued scene? Speed up the tempo of the scene to about one-third of the normal pace.

This method should not be used when you want to convey mood, but when the dialogue is of an informative nature.

When a dialogue scene is speeded up, in this way actors tend to speak louder. If you instruct them to speak quietly their voice level will sound natural in the finished sequence.

9

THE NATURE OF SCREEN MOTION

If a film is to possess a smooth flow of parts, there must be control, organization and selection. For control, you must consider movement—movement of performers and of the camera. Both can describe circular, horizontal or vertical motions. The circular movement of a performer turning his body on one spot is equivalent to camera *panning*. The horizontally moving actor, walking, running or riding is paralleled by similar action of a camera mounted on a suitable mobile support. Obviously, an actor moves vertically when he rises from a lying position or seat, climbs steps, shins up a rope or is carried up by a machine. The camera can move likewise, and all three types of movement combined where necessary.

However, a sensation of movement can also be obtained solely by cinematic means—where a person sits in front of a projected moving background, as for interior shots of cars, trains, etc which are usually obtained by this method. Another case of implied movement is where we frame a person in close shot looking off screen and in the next shot cut to a view as seen from a moving vehicle.

The person will seem to be inside a vehicle which is in motion, though he is, in fact, static. (The illusion is reinforced if the actor moves his head appropriately.)

Film as a medium has a unique property: a continuous movement can be recorded by using only segments of the action shot from different angles. A significant movement glimpsed by sectors is often more livelier and more interesting than one recorded in a single take whole. But it is essential in this case that all the camera positions selected to cover it must be on the same side. See Fig. 9.1.

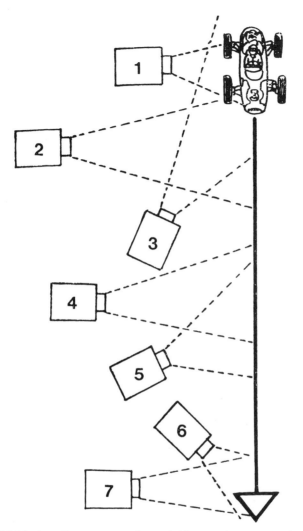

FIGURE 9.1 A continuous movement recorded by several cameras requires that these cameras be placed on the same side of the path travelled by the moving subject.

If the camera were placed on the other side of that line of movement for one shot, the subject would suddenly be moving in the opposite direction across the screen (see Fig. 9.2 placements 3 and 6), and these shots would not intercut properly.

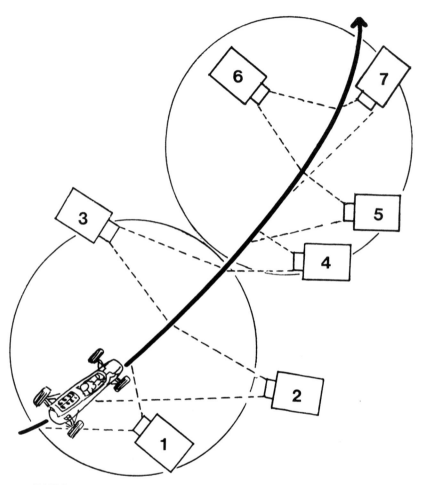

FIGURE 9.2 As in the triangle principle, one side of the line of movement must be chosen and adhered to. Any shots from the other side of the line of motion will not intercut properly with those previously used because the reversed direction of movement will confuse the audience.

Motion broken down

This sectionalized movement could be framed with the subject held in the same sector of the screen or entering and leaving the view covered by the camera (frequently such motions cover only a half-screen area, on opposed sectors), or by a combination of both.

Turning, sitting, standing, walking or running movements can be covered from two camera positions on the same visual axis, or by two or more on the triangular principle. Horizontal movement (the most common) can be across the screen, diagonally on the screen, from a neutral direction (coming straight towards us or going away) and in an arc. Any change in direction must be shown on the screen, so that the audience is not confused when a performer is suddenly seen moving in the opposite direction to that just shown.

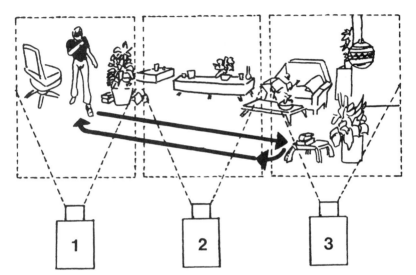

FIGURE 9.3 All changes in direction to movement on the screen must be shown to the audience to keep them properly oriented at all times. Shot 3 in this example accomplishes just that.

For example, if you move from your chair to your table to pick up a book (see Fig. 9.3), your rising movement would be shown with Shot 1, your walking movement to the table in Shot 2 and your arrival at the table in Shot 3. There you pick up the book and turn to go back to your chair. We see you turn and go out, returning to the previous camera position (2) on your way back, and your arrival at the chair seen from position 1.

Changing view with movement

Always keeping the camera on the same side of the line of motion is a limiting factor. Often you want to cross to the other side of moving subjects, because from there a more dynamic composition or a better view of the events is possible. You can do this by inserting cut-aways, by using a neutral direction of movement, by making a performer indicate the change or by contrasting motions in the same screen sector.

Using cut-aways

Cut-aways make the audience forget the sense of direction in the last movement shown, so that a new direction does not seem unnatural. An audience watching a film is always waiting for new shots. Their attention is so much involved that recent visual memory becomes very poor. They will rarely remember more than one or two shots preceding the one they are watching. A mind busy grasping story points, does not concentrate for long enough on screen directions to object to a change brought about by interposing cut-aways. A racetrack sequence, for example, where you want to cross to the other side of the track for a wider view could be planned as follows:

Cars cross screen from right to left; more cars, right to left, at a diagonal; other cars cross right to left in front of a crowded stand; close shot of a clock giving the time; a close shot of a board giving the positions; wide shot in which the cars move from left to right; closer shot in which other cars run from left to right.

Neutral direction

Another solution to the same problem is to use a neutral direction of motion, between changes of direction of movement across the screen. In the above case we would place ourselves on a bridge over the track and film the cars head on or from behind. These takes would be inserted between the changes of direction across the screen. The two neutral shots could be used together, so that the cars come straight at us and pass below out of the bottom of the frame and then appear from under us and race away into the distance.

Performer indicates the change

Where a performer indicates the change of direction, by turning his head or body he could be in a moving vehicle or on firm ground. The direction in which the performer looks in relation with the movement of the panorama across the screen as the camera travels past, indicates the true sense of direction of the vehicle.

Fig. 9.4 shows a typical case of a boat navigating a stream.

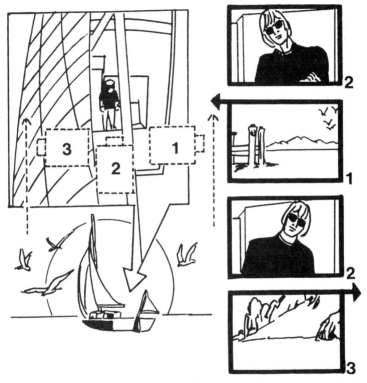

FIGURE 9.4 The opposed directions of tracking shots 1 and 3 can be properly related by interposing a shot of a person who indicates the change. This indication can be achieved by a simple turn of this person's head.

Let us show the forward motion of the boat on the screen by using only moving shots made from the sides—camera sites 1 and 3.

    Site 2 Close shot of a person facing us. He is looking off screen, right.

    Site 1 The river bank moves across the screen from left to right, as the boat apparently moves to the left.

Site 2 Close shot of the person. He turns his head from right to left.

Site 3 The river side moves across the screen from right to left, as the boat apparently moves to the right.

The boat is always moving forward. We do not lose that sense of direction in spite of the contradictory movements across the screen seen from positions 1 and 3. Shot 2, in which the person changes his side of interest, makes the opposition natural without disturbing our awareness of the real forward movement. The person who directs our attention blocks his background making it impossible for us to see the neutral direction in which the vehicle is moving.

In the sequence just described the person has his back to the prow of the boat, although that may not be apparent on the screen. His position in the boat is indicated by the order of movement direction seen on the screen. Using the same shots, we have only to alter the edited order to make the player seem to be facing the prow of the boat indeed (keeping his background blocked). Thus:

Site 2 Close shot of a person facing us. He is looking off screen, right.

Site 3 The river side moves across the screen from right to left, as the boat apparently moves to the right.

Site 2 Close shot of the person. He turns his head from right to left.

Site 1 The river bank moves across the screen, left to right, as the boat apparently moves to the left.

By blocking the background to the player, the shot could be made in the studio. Though placed on firm ground, it is possible to give the sensation that he is on the moving boat.

Two contrasting viewpoints of a static subject as seen from the same side of a moving vehicle can be 'joined' by interposing a person whose attention shifts from one side of the screen to the other. (Fig. 9.5).

With the camera at a three-quarter view to the front of the moving train (Shot 1) passing buildings are seen from a tangential path. Shot 2 (a studio shot) shows the person looking off-screen right and turning slowly to the left. Shot 3 shows the buildings from his new viewpoint, and we are now moving away from them as from a rearwards-looking three-quarter view.

In both moving shots, the static buildings moved from left

FIGURE 9.5 Two contrasting viewpoints from the same side of the moving vehicle record an advancing and a receding view of the panorama. They are related by a shot intercut between where a person turning his head from one side to the other motivates the change of viewpoint.

to right, thus confirming that the player's view was from the same side of the vehicle. This is not exactly a change of direction across the screen, but a change of viewpoint along the same line of Movement.

There are three other ways of moving to the other side of a line of motion or of interest. The first one involves using the horizontal action of a player, the second combines that horizontal motion of a subject with an accompanying panning displacement of the camera. The third approach uses the vertical motion of a person on the screen to mask the crossing of the camera to the other side.

FIGURE 9.6 The person indicating the change of direction from shot to shot can exit from the first and enter view in the other, thus relating two different places.

The three solutions to be explained are quite unobtrusive, and properly used will provide a smooth passage of which the audience is not conscious.

In the first situation a player watching a motion away from him, turns in the foreground and walks off one side of the screen, enters the next shot by the other side of the frame, and stops to look at a subject moving across the screen from right to left (Fig. 9.6).

The next figure shows the second variation.

A caravan moving from left to right: in the next shot a man walks from right to left. The camera pans with him and holds on him as he stops and looks to the far off caravan now moving from right to left. The diversionary motion of this player in the second shot was used to introduce a view from the other side of the caravan's line of motion see Fig. 9.6A.

The third variation begins by showing two players facing each other. The camera covers them from one side. Then one of them kneels down to pick something from the ground. As soon as the downward movement is completed there is a cut to the second

FIGURE 9.6A. The movement of a player at the start of the second shot masks a change in direction of the main subjects seen in the background.

shot, positioned on the other side of the players, but featuring only the static player at its beginning. Seconds later the kneeling player rises into frame. Both players have now reversed their positions on the screen, but the vertical movement of one of them masked the camera crossing.

In the last case covered, the players may be standing on the ground or floor of a building, or they stand on a moving vehicle. In this last case the same formula applies for the camera crossing to the other side of the players, regardless of the direction of movement of the vehicle.

Three additional ways of crossing the line of interest will be explained. They use contrasting movements to achieve the change. The last approach involves using the same half-screen area twice.

169

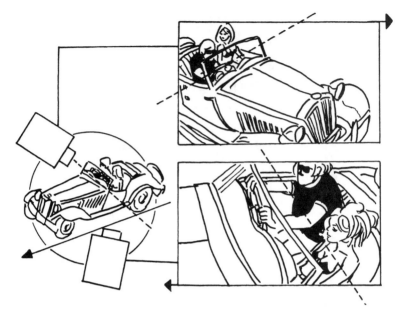

FIGURE 9.7 Opposed directions of movement are suggested when two tracking shots covering two central characters are intercut in parallel. These players either walk, or sit inside a vehicle.

A set of external reverse shots of two people in a moving vehicle, or walking with the camera, will present this opposition of screen directions. (See Fig. 9.7).

Alternating both master takes will produce the effect of contrasting movement without confusing the audience. Moreover, the screen position of both performers on the screen will always be the same.

The ruse of putting a static person between two shots to help convey the change of direction of a moving person or vehicle across the screen, works as well on firm ground as inside a moving vehicle. Fig. 9.8 shows a common example.

The rider moves from left to right in the first shot. In the second take, an onlooker moves his head from left to right looking towards the rider's off-screen passage.

In the third shot the rider is seen moving right to left. We accept this change of direction naturally, because the last shot represents the subjective viewpoint of the onlooker. Thus, opposed screen directions of a moving subject can be clearly presented.

170

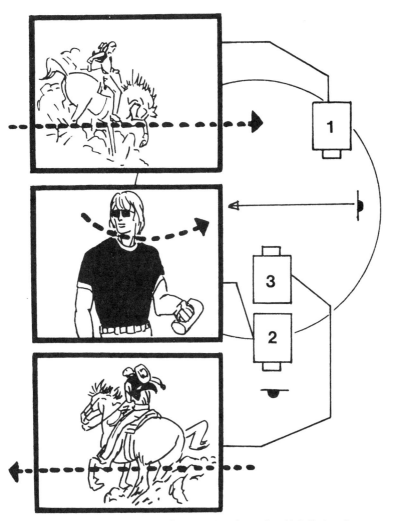

FIGURE 9.8   A stationary player on firm ground can be employed to indicate a change in direction of the main subject as it moves across the screen.

This static onlooker can be present in the background of the first shot, or not. Also, instead of using only one person turning his head from one side of the screen to the other, a group can be employed, provided that all turn their heads in unison and their eyes follow the same centre of attention (the rider) supposed to be passing off-screen behind the camera.

Contrasting motions in the same half screen

We come now to the last possible variation, where the moving person is always kept on the same side of the screen. The same half screen areas is used for both external reverse shots of the continuous motion.

Case A

Performer A is seen (static) in both shots, always on the left side of the screen in this case. He can easily be replaced by a static object, such as a parked car, a monument, a tree, etc. (See Fig. 9.9).

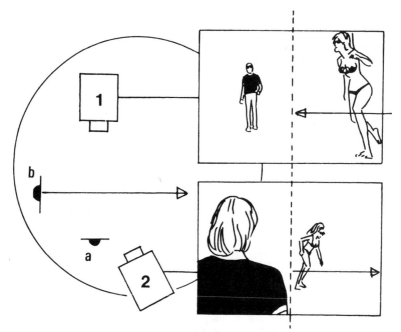

FIGURE 9.9 Contrasting movements of a subject, if remaining in the same half of the screen help to maintain a continuous sense of direction for the audience despite the change in camera angle.

Performer B moves from right to centre in the first take. As she arrives there, there is a cut to the second shot, where we see her move from the centre of the screen to the right. Thus, she was seen moving to the left in Shot 1 and to the right in reverse Shot 2.

Both subjects, the static and the moving one, have been positioned in the same screen area in both takes.

Case B

The movement in the previous example was continuous but a motion that has a pause in its middle can be presented using the same visual formula. Fig. 9.10 shows this.

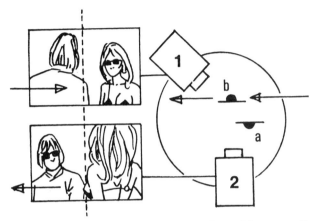

FIGURE 9.10 Opposed movements of a subject in a half area of the screen, will seem continuous to the audience, despite a pause in the movement introduced halfway through the scene.

Subject B enters from the left in Shot 1 and stops to talk to player A. We cut to Shot 2 where performer B ends talking to A, and exits left. Although performer B moved in opposite directions in the same screen sector, his sense of direction was continuous with respect to player A.

Case C

In the two examples just discussed, the camera occupied fixed positions in both external reverse shots. But it is possible to make one of those camera placements a moving one, keeping the contrast in movements on the screen. (Fig. 9.11).

Shot 1   Camera high, looking down on empty seats in a theatre.
         Our only performer walks along an aisle centre to right.
         As he nears the edge of the screen, out to . . .

173

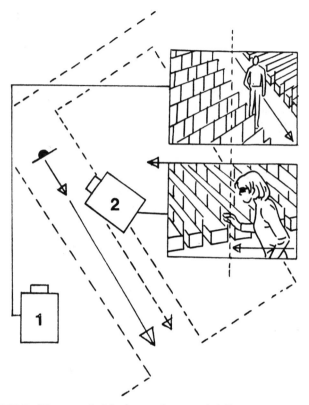

FIGURE 9.11   The same principle of opposed movements in the same screen sector is seen in action here. The variation is that the second shot is a track.

Shot 2   From the other side, the camera travels in medium shot from right to left, with our lone performer framed constantly on the right side of the screen.

The solution outlined works because the opposed movements happen on the same side of the screen in both shots.

Though it is important to maintain a constant screen direction, there is another factor which must be taken care of prior to shooting the film.

The disconnected film shots will have to be assembled later, and it is essential to know when to cut from take to take to obtain a smooth visual flow. To achieve that, certain conditions must be observed.

Conditions of the cut

The cut must afford continuity elements that prevent a confused presentation of the material shown to the audience.

Three basic rules must be observed when joining two strips of film that record segments of the same continuous movement. These three rules involve matching operations that can be defined as follows:

1 matching the position,
2 matching the movement, and
3 matching the look.

The first rule involves two types of position matching:

  a the physical position of the actors: their gesture, posture and place on the stage. Their clothing must, of course, be the same from shot to shot.

  b Their position in the film frame.

  c The movement of the people in the frame must be continuous as we move in closer or away from them by means of a cut.

  d The direction of their movements must be matched from shot to shot.

The third matching rule has only one requirement:

  e two persons or two groups addressing or facing each other look in opposed directions.

When two people or two groups move toward each other, we have opposed screen directions, and yet their individual movements maintain constant screen directions in respect of the camera.

One group always moves to the right, and the other to the left. Both opposed screen motions are intercut until the final reunion is achieved. This use of contrasted motion is the basis of conflicts— soldier moving against soldier, tank against tank, the Indian riders against the US cavalry, all moving to a pay-off, a take where both meet, always maintaining the same direction of movement.

Where to cut

At what stage of a movement should we cut? During, before, or after that movement takes place?

Let us see what happens in a cut. Take a simple example: a person stands facing the camera. We want to show a full shot of him where he is seen in relation to his environment, and then we would like to show him in medium shot (on the same visual axis) to highlight his facial expression. There is no movement in either. So we simply splice one shot after the other.

If these two edited shots are taken to a projector and watched on the screen, the transition from take to take is jerky. There is a visual jump on the screen and the transition from shot to shot is an attention-getter that disturbs us momentarily. Why? Because there is a change in volumes. That change is inevitable as we move closer to or farther away from a specific subject. There is no way to avoid it. Or is there? We need a distraction. That distraction must take place in the moment of the change of shot, that is, on the cut.

What sort of distraction is there so potent to shift our attention during a change? The answer is simple—movement, any movement. Hence it is best to either cut on the movement or cut after the movement. The more frequent cutting on the movement, is generally applied to two types of motion peculiar to the screen: movement *inside* the screen and movement *entering* and *exiting* the screen. These two types of coverage serve to present the three basic motions of a subject—circular, horizontal and vertical.

Cutting on action

Almost every shot begins recording movement of some kind. There are very few exceptions to this. The motion shown may be a cut matched with the movement at the end of the previous take. Or if it is a cut-away or a newly introduced shot, a movement of the person or thing shown must start it. It may even be a camera movement.

The reason for this is simple. Cutting on the movement will ease the cut to such an extent that the visual jar produced when changing the distance and placement of the camera with respect to the subjects, will pass unnoticed by the audience.

Even the big close shots that cover dialogue between static persons, start with movement. The performer may be just opening his mouth to talk, or might be making a facial expression previous to the delivery of his lines. Or one might see the attentive movement of his eyes as he reacts to what is said to him, or his head bending forward. There are, in fact, quite a number of small unconscious movements that an actor makes when concentrating —movements that are magnified by the camera in close shots.

Most matched cuts are made with the moving character placed

in the centre of the screen, particularly if only one subject is involved in the coverage. When two or more performers are shown, the screen is often divided in two halves, with the matched movement taking place in either half. Only the dominant movement is matched by cut. Background motions, and the direction of those movements, are also matched in addition to the main one in foreground, if they are conspicuous enough and if both shots are done on the same visual axis. Generally, that kind of multiple matching is avoided but in certain situations where movement is difficult to control, such as in a moving crowd, some special methods are applied to insure the smoothness of the cuts.

When actually filming scenes whose action must be matched, the main actor's final movement at the end of the first shot is repeated once more in full at the start of the next. Later, in the editing room, they can be matched. More often than not, about one-third of the first shot movement and two-thirds from the second are used.

10

CUTTING AFTER THE MOVEMENT

Although cutting on the movement is the most extensively used device for continuity cuts, let us first deal briefly with the technique of cutting after the movement. This type of cutting is often applied to approaches on the same visual axis.

The movement used may be where either the actor or the camera moves.

If the player moves, he is seen approaching in a neutral direction (in the centre of the screen, coming straight towards us), or he performs a vertical motion while staying in his place. Movements across the screen are not very good for this type of matched cut. If the camera is moving, it is either travelling sideways or vertically, or panning in either of those two directions. The cut is usually made from a full shot to a medium or close shot.

The technique is simple. Two or three frames after the motion in the first shot has been completed, you cut to the close shot on the same visual axis. This formula is used almost exclusively for a forward cut, it is seldom used to move back from a close shot to a full shot.

Here are some practical examples.

Case 1

Seen in full shot is the distant window of a small bungalow. Somebody inside raises the blind. As soon as it is fully opened, cut to a medium shot of that person, his arm still stretched upwards to the top of the window. He is standing still and looking out.

The first take contains all the movement. The second is a static shot. (Fig. 10.1).

FIGURE 10.1 After the completion of a vertical movement in the first shot there is a cut to a second where, to begin with, the subject is held stationary.

The rising motion contained on the long shot must be seen by the audience as it comes to its full completion. In fact, two or three frames of static picture must be left at the conclusion of this shot before cutting to the static closer view of the moving subject. The second take, if desired, can be a side view or a reverse shot of the motionless subject.

Case 2

Here is another example of a performer's vertical movement. In the previous example an upward motion was shown, now a downward movement is examined.

A young girl is seen on her knees in full shot. She is searching for something inside a bag.

Suddenly she picks out some loose clothes contained in it and throws them up, bending her body down and then after that remaining motionless.

As soon as she becomes static, there is a cut to a close shot of her on the same visual axis.

Fig. 10.2 shows the examples described.

179

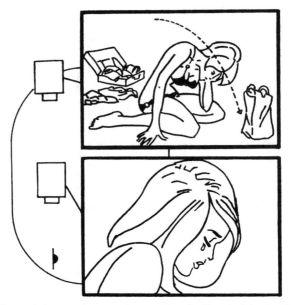

FIGURE 10.2 A downward movement covered by using the principle of cutting after the action.

If required, in the second shot you can cut back to a static long shot of the girl, seen small in the centre of the screen, her torso bent.

Case 3

The conclusion of a movement in a neutral direction, particularly a not too fast motion, may be treated in this way. Two people walk toward us. They stop, facing us, in full shot.

As soon as they stop we cut to a medium shot of them, standing still (Fig. 10.3).

No unpleasant jump should be visible in the transfer from one shot to the other if the change in image size is sufficiently great and the subjects do not move substantially.

Case 4

This technique can be used on the circular movement of a subject who turns and throws attention on a static performer standing behind him (Fig. 10.4).

180

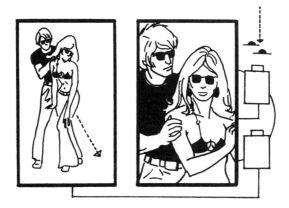

FIGURE 10.3 An action in a neutral direction can be subjected to the technique of cutting after the movement to advance the view to a closer shot.

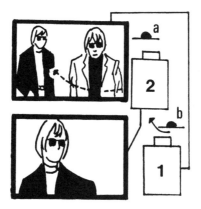

FIGURE 10.4 An actor turns and throws attention on the player positioned behind him. As soon as he concludes the turn, there is a cut to a close shot of the other performer.

The editing order would be like this:

Shot 1 Performers A and B facing the camera. Player B is in the foreground at the right side of the screen. He is talking. Player A in the background listens. Then B turns to face A. As soon as he stops turning, cut to ...

Shot 2 Close shot of player A on the same visual axis. He listens, as the voice of player B continues off screen.

Case 5

We said in Case 3 that the neutral motion of a player coming toward the camera could be used for a cut after the movement. The same applies to neutral motion going away from us.

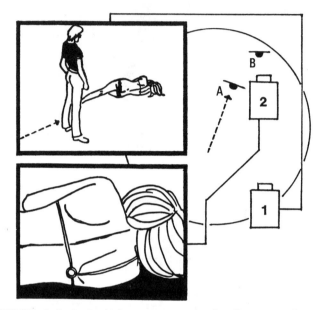

FIGURE 10.5   A situation in which a person moves away from the camera and towards another person or object in the background throws emphasis on that person or object. This lends itself to the technique of cutting after the movement. As soon as the moving player stops, cut to a closer view of the person in the background.

In the first shot shown in Fig. 10.5, player A is seen moving towards the prone body of B. Player A stops halfway in his path to B, and as he stops there is a cut to take 2, a close shot of B, shot on the same visual axis as before.

After the exact frame in which player A stops a cut is made to the forward camera position where he is excluded. Player B was completely static in both shots.

Case 6

A more conventional cut can be achieved with the same receding movement as shown in Fig. 10.6.

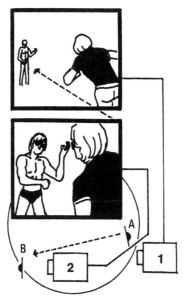

FIGURE 10.6 In this example both players are featured in the second shot, after the performer in motion has stopped near his partner.

In the first take, A walks away towards B (who is static) and stops in front of him. As soon as he stops you cut to the second take, which is an advance on the same visual axis. This solution is seldom used because normally, more dynamic approaches are employed for this type of scene as will be discussed later.

The same criterion of more dynamic solutions applies when motions across the screen must be dealt with. For the record, let us describe an example using a cut after the motion is completed.

Shot 1   A static player on the left, profiled to the camera, seen in Long Shot. The second player enters from the right, walks across the screen and stops, facing the static one. Cut.

Shot 2   A Medium Shot of both players profiled to the camera.

The cut made after the movement in the first shot had ceased, was achieved on a common visual axis. A reverse situation, in which the Medium Shot is used first, and the Long Shot afterwards, is a seldom used variant.

As pointed out above, more dynamic approaches to this kind of situation will be examined later when dealing into and out of the screen area.

Case 7

Sometimes a reverse camera position is resorted to immediately after the player has stopped in the first shot (Fig. 10.7).

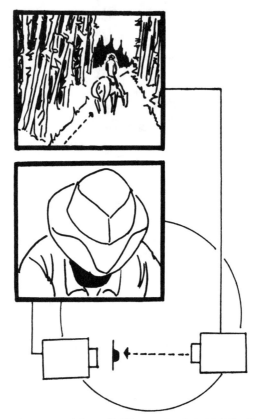

FIGURE 10.7 A reverse angle is used in this example, where a cut after the movement serves to join both shots.

From a height, we see a lonely road flanked by tall trees. A lone man on horseback rides slowly away from us. Then he stops. Cut.

Reverse close shot of the man. His eyes are closed, his head slightly bent down, he is asleep on the saddle.

Case 8

On some occasions the cut is made in the pause of the movement, (Fig. 10.8).

184

FIGURE 10.8 A pause in the middle of a continuous motion can be used for the technique of cutting after the movement to join both shots.

Player B in the first shot places a lamp on the table. For three or four frames his hand remains still on the lamp. Cut.

Side shot. B's hand in foreground moves out of the screen left. Thus the pause in the middle of a movement was used to change the shot and approach the main subject. This pause afforded an opportunity to introduce a cut after the movement.

The pause at the conclusion of the first shot can be longer if dramatically necessary, provided that you restart the movement from the first frame of the second shot.

Case 9

A walking movement can be treated in a similar manner. Player A goes to a control panel, stops and depresses a switch. He remains still for an instant. Cut. Side shot. He turns and comes back (Fig. 10.9).

The preceding examples dealt with fixed camera positions, where the performers executed the movements. The situation can be reversed.

185

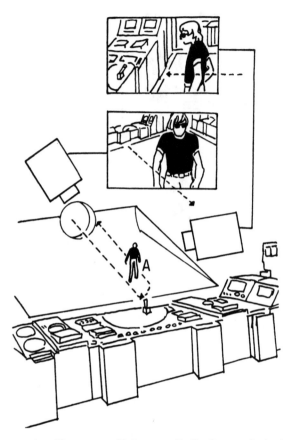

FIGURE 10.9 A walking movement in two opposite directions can be treated in the same manner as the preceding example. As soon as the man stops and before he begins to turn, cut to the second shot where he turns and changes direction on the screen. The cut takes place after the first part of the movement is complete, and a short pause precedes the change in direction.

Case 10

Our player is seated in the background. The camera tracks from right to left, showing an empty conference table. Through an archway we see a player, seated. The camera travels until it frames him centrally, then stops. Then, cut to a close shot on the same visual axis, showing the man slumped on the seat, sleeping peacefully.

FIGURE 10.10 The camera movement involved here is a vertical tilt. The camera pans up from subject A to performer B seen in the background. As soon as the camera ceases to pan upwards, cut to a closer view of player B.

Case 11

The technique is similar for a panning shot. The camera is tilted up from a subject in the foreground to frame the open window of a building in the background where a person is seen, in the centre of the screen. Cut to a closer shot on the same visual axis. (Fig. 10.10).

Although this technique of cutting after the movement is somehow a limited one, it is very useful when unemphatic visual approaches to a subject are desired. Since we cut as the movement concludes, we fulfil the natural unconscious desire of the audience to have a closer look at the subject to whom attention is drawn.

11

MOTION INSIDE THE SCREEN

The approach to screen presentation of a movement, whereby fragments of separate shots are cut together, creates a vitality peculiar to the film medium. On a practical level, it enables us to change our viewpoint smoothly around one or a group of characters. Where two whole shots of a single action are cut a good general principle is to use one-third of the movement (the start) at the end of the first shot and two-thirds of the movement (the conclusion) at the beginning of the second. This is not a strict rule but it might be a good starting point. The rigid rules that some film theorists have at one time set up and said cannot be broken have created a generation of film making habits that later had to be discarded as false or impractical. All rules can be broken if you know what you are breaking, and why. In the present case, the exact frame on which to cut from one shot to the other is determined by a visual comparison. The strips are moved up and down alongside each other, until two frames are found that closely match in position and direction of movement, where the cut is made. With practice you 'feel' where that cut should be.

Of course, the amounts of motion in the film strips may vary i.e. the complete movement in one may be longer, especially if shot in two separate shots. Hence, matching speed of movement when shooting should be sought for the two or more shots which are to be intercut.

If ill-matched, however, it is generally more satisfactory that the movement be faster in the second fragment. A two, three or four shot reconstruction can be shorter or longer than the actual movement. For example, if the first take is a full shot and the second a close shot, parts of the movement may be repeated or, in another case, some frames may be discarded with no loss of smoothness in transition from one shot to the next. Sometimes a matched cut will seem imperfect when done for the first time, because the motion was not precisely matched. It is easy to separate the strips of film and delete from one or both the few frames necessary to obtain a correct visual record. With some practice on the editing machine, the knack for judging correctly almost at first glance where to cut, will soon be obtained.

Turning

A person turning on the spot where he is standing, sitting or lying, moves on the central axis of his body in a right angle turn (90°), an about face (180°) or a full circle turn. The third possibility is the least interesting of the three for an action cut. All these turning movements can be covered by three of the five variants inherent in the triangle principle for camera placement (page 32). It can be readily understood that a set of internal reverse angles and a pair of parallel camera positions are unsuitable for shooting a continuous motion, due to the divergent coverage given by these camera set-ups. Let us take a look at the possibilities:

Case 1

A pair of external reverse shots can be used to photograph the turning motion of a player in a group. In the first shot both players face the camera, one located in foreground and the other further back. The player in front turns. His turning motion is completed on the second shot. Both players maintain the same screen positions in both shots (Fig. 11.1).

Case 2

A right angle turn with a right angle camera coverage is our next example. Figure 11.2 shows both camera sites and the pictorial composition they record. Only one player moves in the scene. The approach is quite simple as can be seen here.

Case 3

An advance on the same visual axis is one of the most commonly used devices for cutting on the action of a person who turns.

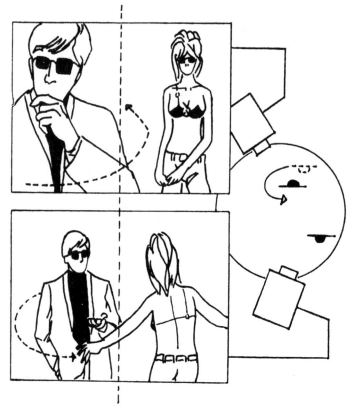

FIGURE 11.1 One player's single turning movement is divided into two shots. Both players maintain their screen areas. A reverse angle camera coverage is employed.

A player seen in medium shot in the first take, is profiled to a side of the screen. Then he starts to turn his head towards us. Cut to a close shot where he ends his turning motion. He now faces the camera. Both takes have the same visual axis, and the player is positioned in the same sector of the screen in both shots: either in the centre or in one of the three side areas into which the screen has been compositionally divided. Fig. 11.3 shows the most simple approach.

Case 4

Widening the group or narrowing it to one player as the second shot is introduced, as part of the matched movement, is the next

190

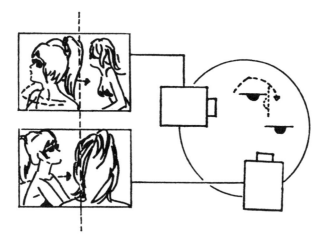

FIGURE 11.2 Right angle camera positions are used to cover this turning movement.

FIGURE 11.3 An advance on a common visual axis is used here to cover the turning movement.

possibility. Several examples will give an idea of the various treatments which are feasible.

The use of a right angle permits two approaches in the second shot. In the first shot, the dominant player is alone, facing the camera. As he turns 90° to one side, we cut to a right angle camera site where he is either in the centre of the screen or to one side of it. If he is in the centre the other players who have been introduced occupy the sides. If the dominant player is in a side area, the remaining screen area is occupied by the newly introduced performers. Fig. 11.4 shows both approaches.

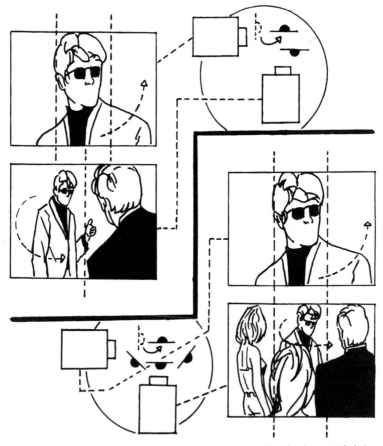

FIGURE 11.4 The examples shown here show two approaches for the second shot where the group is broadened to include one or several more players. The central player turns, covered by a right angle camera position which unites both shots.

Case 5

The same principle works when an advance on a common visual axis is employed to widen or narrow the group presented to the audience, using the dominant turning motion of one of the players as an excuse to introduce or exclude the group around this dominant player in the scene (Fig. 11.5).

FIGURE 11.5 Here the group is reduced from two persons to one by moving closer to the turning player. Emphasis is given to her and her movement.

Case 6

If a combination of external and internal reverse angle is used, the same effect of widening or reducing the group on the screen, can be obtained (Fig. 11.6).

All the examples quoted so far have involved groups of players placed on firm ground. But if they are located on a moving

FIGURE 11.6 An internal and external reverse camera position deployed around the turning player are used in this example to throw visual emphasis on the central performer.

vehicle, this turning motion will dominate the background movement. If the approach to the second shot is on the same visual axis, the background movement will always be in the same direction. If a reverse external combination is resorted to, the movement in the background will have opposed directions. If a right angle is used, one of the camera positions will register a background movement, while the other may have its background blocked by an obstruction. If the background can be seen, the direction of motion glimpsed there will be in a neutral direction, either forward or backwards.

In all instances, the foreground motion dominates, and is the one that must be precisely matched.

Case 7

There is a situation where opposed sense of direction in the two fragments of the same continuous motion occurs. This is where a lone performer is covered by a pair of external reverse angles on the extreme points of an 180 degree arc through which he turns (Fig. 11.7).

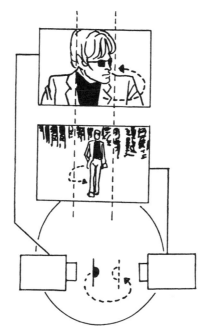

FIGURE 11.7 Opposed senses of direction are obtained when a lone player is shown turning as recorded from external reverse camera positions.

Shot 1   Player in close shot, facing the camera. He begins to turn about face and ends with his back to us.

Shot 2   Reverse full shot. Our player is in the centre of the picture with his back to us, and then turns to the camera and stops.

When editing these two shots, the first half of the turning motion is used from the first, and the complementary half begins the second. In the first the player moves from centre to one side; in the second from the opposite side to the centre. The conflicting directions are not confusing because the performer turning move-

195

ment is clear to us. He starts and concludes facing us. Sudden turns are often covered in this way.

Case 8

A sudden turn by two persons can be covered by the same procedure. Both players begin to turn away from us together, from the centre to a side of the screen, in the first shot, and end turning from the opposite side to the centre as seen from the second (Fig. 11.8).

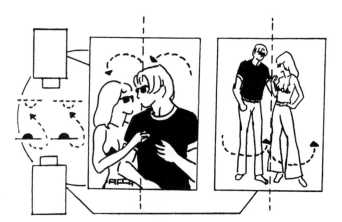

FIGURE 11.8 Two players who turn round simultaneously switch their screen positions in the second shot, if the movement is filmed from external reverse camera sites.

With external reverse angle camera sites, the players switch screen positions.

Case 9

Where an actor turns as he walks, the path of movement is an arc shaped figure. If we wish to stress the change of direction here a pair of reverse external sites or a right angle camera position will do it.

Not only must we cut on the action, but also locate the performer in the same screen sector in both shots. Fig. 11.9 shows an example involving external reverse angles.

196

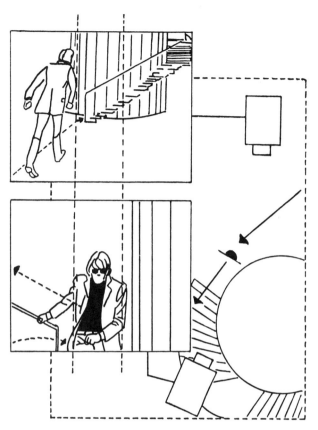

FIGURE 11.9 The turning movement of a single performer should occur in the same area of the screen for both shots into which the movement is divided.

Rising

This is a vertical motion. It does not matter by which combination of takes we record the rising movement (approach on the same visual axis, right angles or external reverse shots). The motion will always have the same direction—upwards.

Case 10

If we wish to keep the movement within the boundaries of the screen frame, it is best to cut from a medium shot to a backward full shot, or to a forward close shot.

197

Fig. 11.10 illustrates a rising movement that begins in medium shot and is completed in full shot. Both shots have a common visual axis.

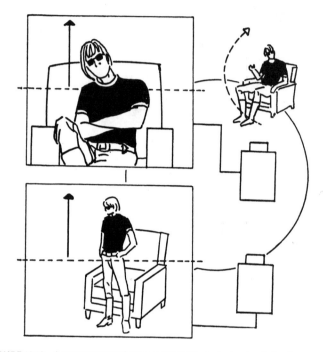

FIGURE 11.10 A common visual axis on which the camera retreats for the second shot is used here to record a player rising.

Case 11

In this example the motion begins in medium shot and concludes in close shot of the same subject. Again the second shot has the same visual axis as the first, where the movement originates (Fig. 11.11).

Case 12

Here a right angle camera position registers the upward motion of the rising player (Fig. 11.12).

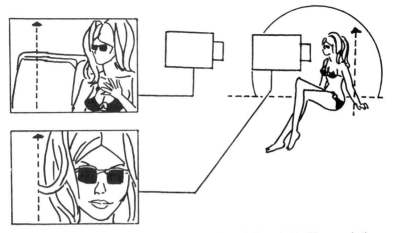

FIGURE 11.11   A common visual axis is used for both shots, but in this example the second camera position is forward of the first.

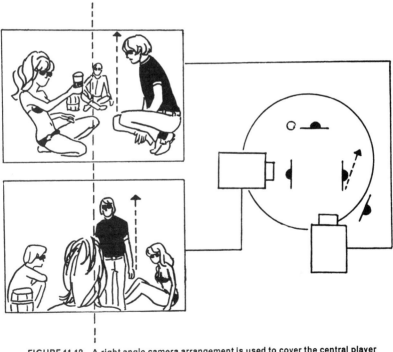

FIGURE 11.12   A right angle camera arrangement is used to cover the central player rising.

Case 13

A combination of an external and an internal reverse angle, provides number contrast (page 52) when dealing with a rising motion in the picture area (Fig. 11.13).

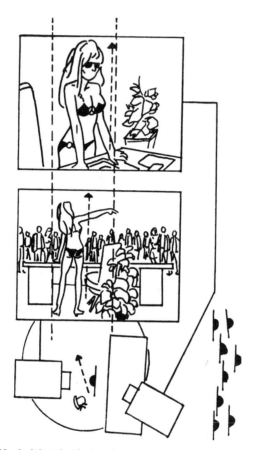

FIGURE 11.13 An internal and external reverse angle around the rising performer is employed in this example.

Sitting and reclining

Complete coverage for sitting and reclining movements filmed in two parts can be obtained by using the same sense of direction for both parts or, more irregularly, opposed directions.

200

Case 14

If the camera sites are on a common visual axis, the sitting motion of a player can be covered on the same sector of the screen in both shots. In the first shot the performer begins to sit down and finishes in the second, without leaving the screen boundaries (Fig. 11.14). We may cut from a full shot to a medium shot or vice versa.

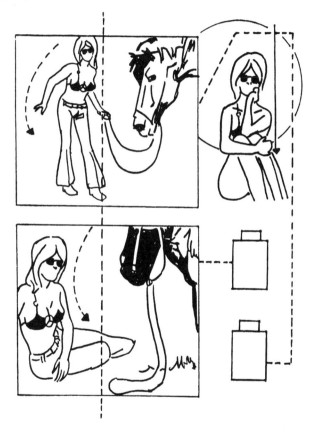

FIGURE 11.14 A common visual axis is used here to cover a player's downward movement.

Case 15

A lone performer sitting down, covered from external reverse angles is registered as two opposed arc movements on the screen.

The human body, due to its peculiar constitution, achieves a sitting position by bending its frame in an arc shape and travelling a curved path downwards.

The opposition of directions is obtained because the player has a profiled body position in both shots.

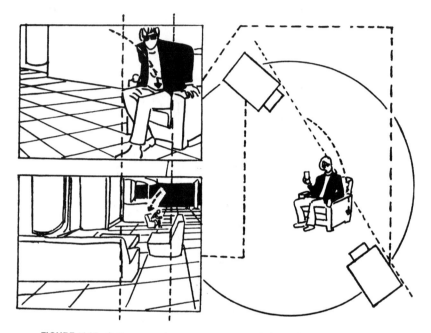

FIGURE 11.15 A reverse angle camera arrangement shows the actor sitting down. Opposed senses of downward directions (to the right first and to the left after) are obtained with this approach.

Figure 11.15 shows that a sitting movement that begins, right, is completed, left, in the reverse shot. For smoothness, the movement should be in the same sector of the screen, even if one shot is a medium shot and the reverse shot is a long shot, as shown here.

Case 16

Reclining movements done from the waist, are subject to the same rule of opposed direction in the two fragments into which the continuous motion might be broken.

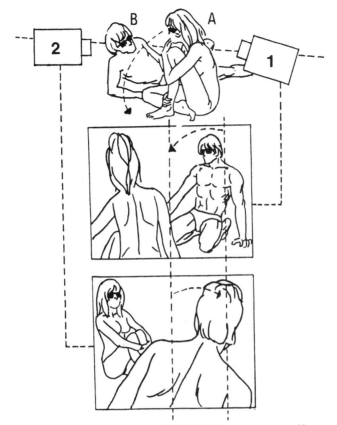

FIGURE 11.16 The reclining player on the right of the screen moves with opposed senses of direction in the change from one shot to another. In the first shot he moves from right to centre, and in the second from centre to right.

The example in Fig. 11.16 has an external reverse angle coverage, and only one player moves.

Shot 1 Player B is going to recline on his right elbow. His body moves from right to centre of the screen as he begins to recline.

Shot 2 Player B in the reverse shot finishes reclining but now moves centre to right.

The reclining player moves always in the same screen sector but with opposed movement directions in each shot, and the second part of the movement complemented the one shown in the first shot. Both players retained their screen areas on both shots.

Case 17

The juxtaposition of external and internal reverse camera positions around the reclining player produces opposed senses of motion in different sectors of the screen. Fig. 11.17 shows that the performer reclining to the left, as seen in Shot 1 (internal reverse), moves from centre to left. But he completes his motion framed in Shot 2 (external reverse) where he moves from centre to right. In Shot 1 he faced us, but in Shot 2 he has his back to the camera, which accounts for the opposed directions.

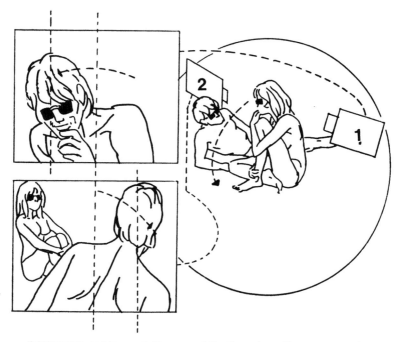

FIGURE 11.17 In this example the opposed directions of a continuous movement are stressed, because in the first shot player B moves from centre to left, and in the second from centre to right.

Case 18

In the two previous cases we cut from a front view of the subject in motion to a rear view. A reversal of the procedure can be used, covering with external and internal camera sites. Contrasting directions of movement in the same sector of the screen are obtained. Fig. 11.18 shows one player pushing the other across the screen, covered from an external reverse shot. The falling motion is completed using an internal camera position.

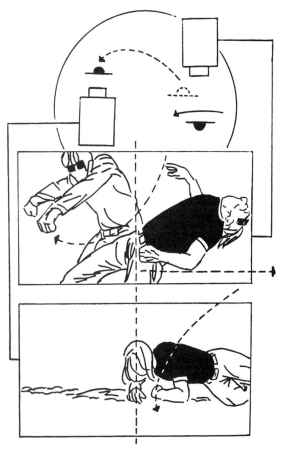

FIGURE 11.18 Opposed directions for a continuous movement are obtained by using an internal and an external reverse shot.

The external camera position is level with the players, but the internal coverage is from a low angle showing the end of the pushed man's fall.

Case 19

It is conceivable that both players might move together, reclining on one side. This movement is fragmented in two sections and the

205

players will have opposed directions of motion in the external reverse shots. They would move as a single unit. Their positions would be constant on the same areas of the screen from shot to shot. About one-third of the movement is seen from the first camera site, the remainder in the second (Fig. 11.19).

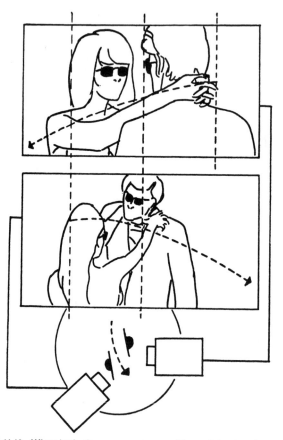

FIGURE 11.19 When both players move to one side, reclining together, a reverse angle camera coverage produces opposed senses of direction for both characters on the screen.

Case 20

In these two examples the actors maintained the same screen sectors but the following example introduces a variant—the moving performer in Shot 1 moves from side to centre of the screen and completes his motion in the second shot by moving from the opposite side of the screen to the centre (Fig. 11.20).

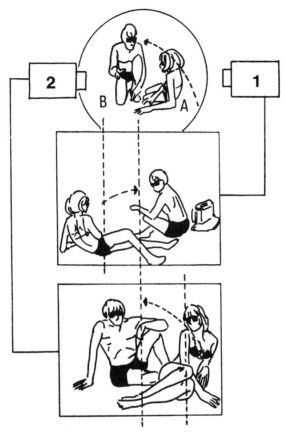

FIGURE 11.20 Opposed senses of direction and an exchange of screen areas is obtained by the method depicted here. In the first shot the reclining player moves from left to centre, and in the second she moves from right to centre. She is always kept in the centre of the screen. Her partner shifts sides.

Shot 1   Players A and B sitting with their backs to us. Performer A begins to recline towards B. She moves from the left to the centre of the screen.

Shot 2   Reverse external shot. Player A moves towards from B. She completes her motion by reclining from the right to the centre of the screen.

The first shot was a full shot of both players, and the second is a close shot of both facing the camera.

Walking and running

The movements examined in the previous sections concerned motion on a spot. It is time now to liberate our player and allow him to walk or run. Running and walking, whether continuous or interrupted, are among the most frequent movements that must be filmed.

Using external reverse shots

Case 21

An external reverse coverage of a walking or running movement records movement of the player in two neutral directions, going straight away from and towards the camera. These two directions can be alternated in their presentation to obtain two simple and basic variations. The operation is simple. In the first shot we see our main performer move away. In the second he comes towards us and stops. One-third of the movement was covered in the first shot and the remaining two-thirds in the second (Fig. 11.21).

Notice that both camera positions are on the same side of the line of movement. This becomes important if an object seen in the background in the first shot is included in foreground on the second. This object must be in the same sector of the screen in both shots.

The camera can be placed at the same or different height in the shots. Instead of walking towards an object, our player may walk to a waiting person, using the same technique. The amount of trajectory recorded in each shot can be reversed. Two-thirds of the motion in the first shot (going away), one-third in the second take (coming towards us).

Case 22

A reversal of the two basic shots is the next solution, as pointed out above. In the first shot the player comes towards us, and in the second he moves away. He does not go out of the screen in either shot. When he reaches a full shot or a medium shot moving straight towards us in the first shot, cut to the second shot where he is seen from behind moving away in a neutral direction, also framed in a full shot or medium shot (Fig. 11.22).

208

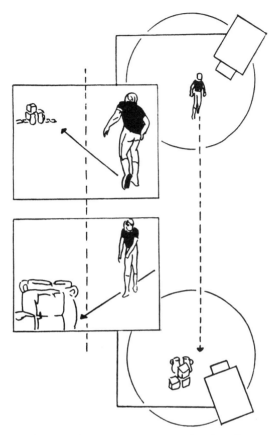

FIGURE 11.21 An external reverse camera coverage for a line of movement.

Case 23

The walking or running movement may be a continuous or discontinuous movement.

Now for the second variation. The motion is interrupted once near its middle. Our performer approaches, stops for a moment, and then goes away to his goal. Here is how the takes are edited as shown in Fig. 11.23.

Shot 1   Player A comes to us and stops in close shot, looking off-screen, right. He may remain silent or speak some lines.

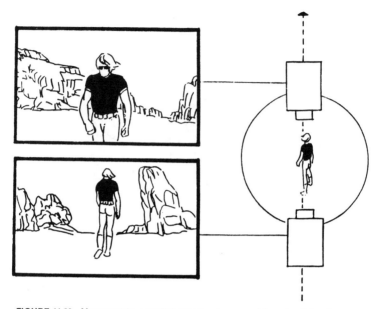

FIGURE 11.22 Movement in a neutral direction is covered by a frontal and a rear camera position, without letting the player go out of the screen on either shot.

FIGURE 11.23 A discontinuous walking movement can be covered with two shots.

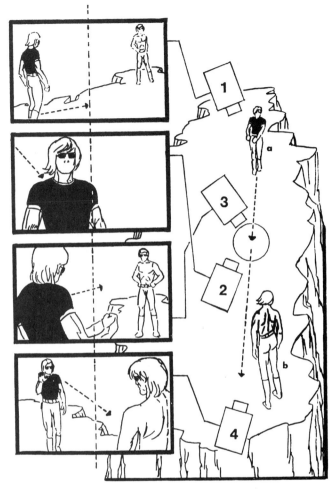

FIGURE 11.24 A player advancing towards an identifiable goal, in a discontinuous movement can be covered with four camera positions.

 Shot 2 Reverse. Player A starts moving away towards **B** in the background, who is waiting there.

Case 24

This continuous movement within the screen can also be recorded using four camera positions, as in Fig. 11.24.

Shot 1 Player A in foreground with his back to us. B in the background waiting. A starts to move. He walks away from us.

Shot 2 Reverse. Player A approaches and stops in close shot, looking off screen, right.

Shot 3 Reverse. Player A in foreground with his back to us. B seen beyond in the background. A again starts to walk towards the waiting performer.

Shot 4 Reverse. Player B in foreground with his back to us. He waits. A arrives and stops in front of B.

Both actors maintained constant sectors in all the shots into which the discontinuous motion of one player was fragmented.

Case 25

If the neutral motion of the walking or running player is filmed from two high camera positions, the player will ascend in one take and descend in the other (Fig. 11.25). As we cut from shot to shot,

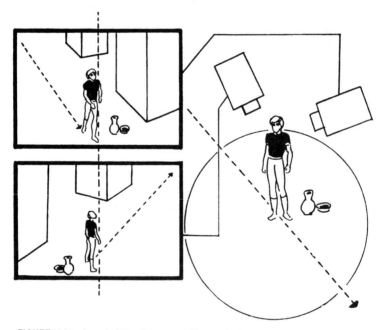

FIGURE 11.25 A neutral direction covered by two high camera positions set on reverse angles, records this movement as a descending one in the first shot and as an ascending movement in the second.

the objects or persons around the moving performer will change from one side of the screen to the other.

Case 26

The movement covered from two external reverse camera positions is not always in a neutral direction. Most of the time this motion has a diagonal path that extends from one side of the screen to its centre. The five preceding examples can be filmed with the walking or running player moving obliquely.

Sometimes the sense of direction of this oblique movement can be changed to make it appear continuous on the screen. That is what happens in our next example, as illustrated in Fig. 11.26. The real direction in which player C moves, is changed from shot 1 to shot 2, so that on the screen it appears to be the same continuous motion in both shots.

In the two shots into which the motion is fragmented, Player C moves in the same sector of the screen, from right to centre, in a diagonal path. In the first shot A and B have their backs to the camera. Player C is seen moving behind B and approaching the centre of the screen.

When we cut to the reverse shot, B and A reverse positions on the screen and face the camera. Player C, seen in foreground close to the right side of the screen, moves away from us to the centre and stops, facing the other players.

The second fragment of the motion is false because the reverse position of the second camera site changes the sense of direction of the moving player: she ought to move from left to centre.

To obtain smooth continuity her direction of movement is changed, giving this fragment the same direction as the first. The floor plan illustrated in Fig. 11.26 shows the situation clearly.

Using a common visual axis

Case 27

Now examine a walking or running movement from two camera sites on the same visual axis. These neutral movements away from or towards the camera straight or obliquely and in the same screen sector. Fig. 11.27 illustrates a simple approach to running movement. A player moves from foreground to a position far

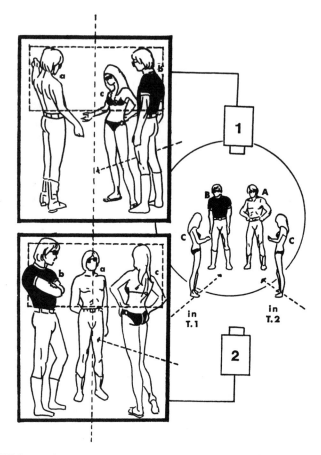

FIGURE 11.26 Sometimes the direction of movement is changed for the second shot to make it consistent with the direction shown in the first.

away. Two-thirds of the path are covered in the first shot. In the second, (forward, on the same visual axis) the player nearest the camera moves away to his goal and halts. The cut is made on the action with the remaining one-third of the path covered in the second shot. The player moved in the same sector of the screen in both shots: from the right to the centre.

Of course, we can reverse the direction of the oblique path so that it runs from left to centre in both shots. The same principle applies. It is the concept used that matters most—the execution is quite simple.

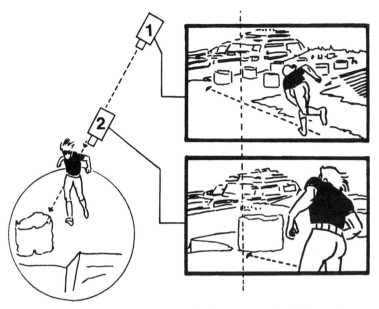

FIGURE 11.27 Two camera positions are placed on a common visual axis, used here to cover a running player.

To shoot this you let the performer run or walk from one point to the other in the first shot. Then, with the camera forward, and the actor in front and with his back to it, start the shot and instruct the player to run again along the remaining part of his path. Later, in editing you cut on the action, first removing the latter part of the first shot and the static section of the second.

Case 28

This same solution can be applied to two people moving together away from the camera. In the Fig. 11.28 example this is a short distance.

Shot 1   Full shot. Players A, B and C are talking. Then B and A turn and walk away together.

Shot 2   Medium shot. This position is an advance on a common visual axis. Players A and B, close to the camera, stop walking away from us and stop to talk.

215

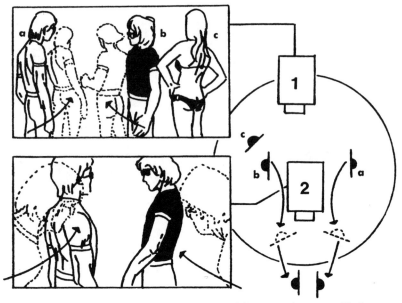

FIGURE 11.28 Two players move away in a neutral direction and are covered by two camera sites on a common visual axis.

No more than five steps were involved in the distance covered by the two performers. In the first shot three steps were walked, and two in the second, Number contrast has been added by excluding one actor (player C) from the second shot.

Case 29

In the previous examples the second camera position was forward on the common visual axis. It could have been further back (Fig. 11.29).

Shot 1 Medium shot. The player is facing the camera in the centre of the screen. He turns and walks away.

Shot 2 Long shot. The performer in the centre walks away.

Case 30

In the preceding case the first shot covered a short distance travelled by the player, the second a lengthy one. Reversed, but using the same visual solution is Fig. 11.30.

216

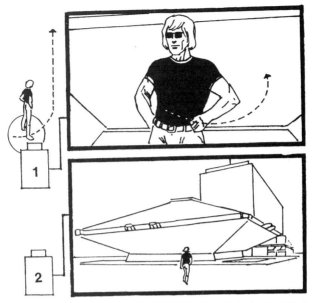

FIGURE 11.29 In this example the second camera position is further back, instead of forward as in the previous examples—on a common visual axis.

Shot 1   Medium shot. Player A standing nearby, back to the camera and on the right side of the screen, walks away in an oblique path towards B, who is waiting in the background, left. When A is close to B, cut to . . .

Shot 2   Same visual axis. Full shot. A (centre) walks two steps towards B and stops beside her.

The key to this technique consists in having the mobile subject conclude his movement at the beginning of the second shot, in the centre of the screen, by walking only one or two steps and stopping at that point.

The same principle can be applied to a full shot—medium shot camera coverage.

Case 31

Now consider some cases where the player moves, not away from but towards us.

In the first of these shots the man (or vehicle) is approaching in

217

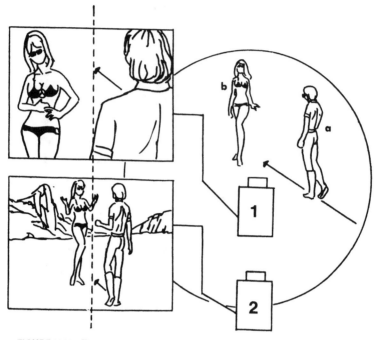

FIGURE 11.30 The moving player concludes his motion in the full shot.

full shot (centre). When he is crowding the film frame (and this does not mean that his body obscures our view completely, it suffices for instance to have his head reach the top boundary of the screen), cut to Shot 2. On the same visual axis this, too, is a full shot.

The man placed in the centre of the screen approaches once more and stops in foreground. The effect is to widen the view in the second take because the approaching motion of the player made him grow on the screen, and creates the visual need to cut back to relate him with his surroundings and show his final goal. The first fragment of this continuous movement served to identify the player to the audience as well as to show his intentions or feelings. Fig. 11.31 shows this situation.

There was almost equal movement in these shots but a higher or lower camera position could be used for the second to contrast with the (level) first.

218

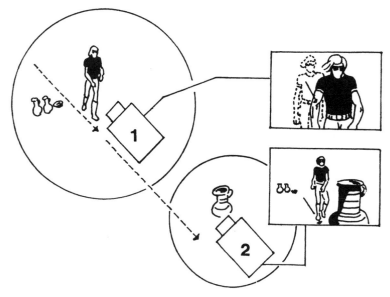

FIGURE 11.31 A neutral movement towards the camera in both shots can be covered with two camera positions on a common visual axis.

Case 32

The following example is widely used by film makers to show the beginning of a walking movement. It makes use of repetitive motion in the same zone of the screen (Fig. 11.32).

First, A is seen in close shot looking off-screen right. He then starts to move to that side. His head approaches in a diagonal from the centre to the right. When his face touches the edge of the screen, cut to the second shot. This new (full) shot is placed further back on a common visual axis with the player seen centrally, moving diagonally right.

Case 33

Now a static subject is seen in the shot of a rapidly approaching figure. Performer B in medium shot, back to the camera and on the right of the screen, waits for A who approaches in a straight line (left side of screen). The second shot is a close shot placed forward on the same visual axis as the first. Here B is seen in foreground on the right, with his back to the camera, and in a huge close shot.

219

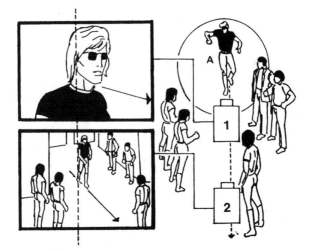

FIGURE 11.32 The beginning of a movement indicating departure can be initiated in a close shot and completed in a full shot placed on a common visual axis. There is screen sector repetition for the fragments of motion.

A on the left, seen closer too, stops walking and arrives in front of B. The first two-thirds of the movement are shown in the full shot, the remainder in the close shot (Fig. 11.33).

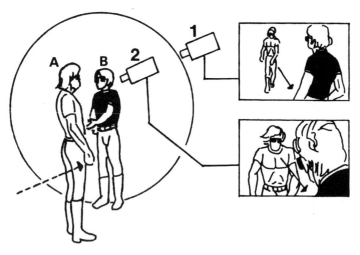

FIGURE 11.33 A motion indicating the arrival of a player at a destination in the foreground on both shots.

Two camera sites on a common visual axis can be used twice to film a discontinuous action such as that shown in Fig. 11.34.

Shot 1   The lone rider moves in the centre third of the screen in a full shot. He is seen small over the ridge moving obliquely left to centre.

Shot 2   Medium shot. The rider at the left screen edge approaches us and stops in mid-screen, looking to right.

Shot 3   Cut-away. Full shot. Herd of horses grazing on the plain. This shot represents what the rider is seeing.

Shot 2   Medium shot. The rider in the centre of the screen begins to move again, advancing until his figure is close to the right edge.

Shot 1   Full shot. The rider in the centre of the screen moves to the right, advancing towards us. His motion in this shot always takes place within the central screen area.

Shot 3   Reverse full shot. The herd of horses grazing on the plain, the rider in centre foreground moving away from us towards the herd.

Shots 1 and 2, on a common visual axis, were used twice, to cover the discontinuous motion of the rider. Notice how the first time those shots were employed, only the left area of the screen was used in both shots. After the cut-away, both takes showed rider moving from the centre to the right.

Thus the left and right screen areas were used in pairs, with repetitive motion in each sector before changing shot. The sequence was: left sector (twice)—cut-away—right sector (twice)—reverse shot (same site as cut-away). The rider was placed in foreground, descending the slope towards the valley, thus capping the sequence and reaffirming the value of the cut-away shown before, by the rider covering the same ground. In fact, this cut-away and reverse shot could have been shot on a different location from that of the player.

By intercutting these two shots the two locations appear to be the same place.

This time and place manipulation is quite frequent on the screen for practical reasons. It permits the film maker to make use of outstanding locations that are far apart geographically. If the situation being shot allows it, we should resort to this recourse.

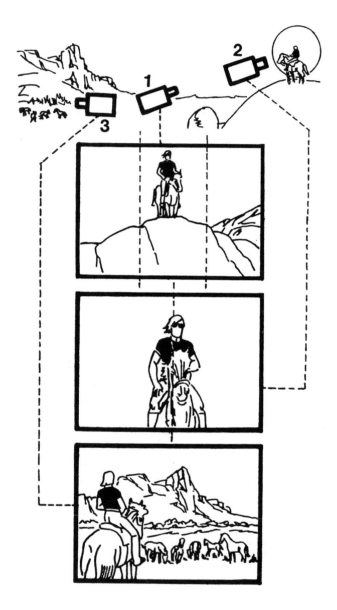

FIGURE 11.34 Each of the takes shown here is used twice to cover the discontinuous motion of an approaching player who stops to reconnoitre the terrain and advances again into new territory.

Case 35

In the diagonal motion across the screen, as depicted in Fig. 11.35, half screen areas are used for each shot.

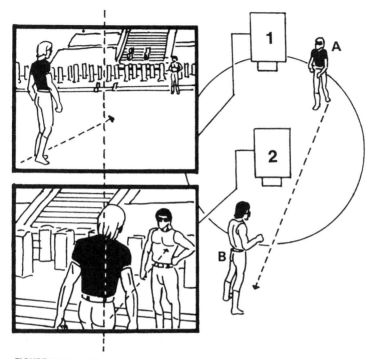

FIGURE 11.35 A diagonal movement across the screen is covered using half screen areas in each shot.

A in the foreground, in full shot, walks diagonally to B, seen in long shot in the background. When A reaches the centre of the screen cut to a medium shot. In this second shot framing A on the same visual axis and in the centre of the screen, he continues moving away from the camera diagonally from centre to right and stops, facing B, who remained at screen right in both shots.

Right angle camera sites

Motion inside the screen is enhanced by the use of right angle camera sites, because this method allows to cover motion over a larger span of terrain. A common visual axis for both camera emplacements limits the view for across the screen motion, circumscribing it to a narrow space. Right angle positions afford a combination of across-the-screen and diagonal motion, or across-the-screen and neutral direction movement.

Case 36

Motion by halves of screen space is employed in the following example, using positions with a right angle rapport. In the first shot the player walks across one half of the screen, while in the shot that follows he moves diagonally in the other half area of the picture frame (Fig. 11.36).

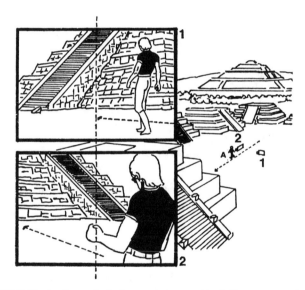

FIGURE 11.36 Another variant of movement covered by half screen areas in each shot. A right angle is used for the camera viewpoints.

Shot 1 Subject A on the right side of the screen, near the border, moves to the centre across the screen. When he arrives there, and is still moving, cut to . . .

224

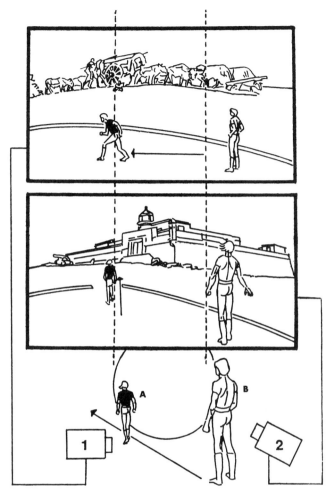

FIGURE 11.37 A ight angle camera disposition covers the departing player.

Shot 2 Close shot of A with his back to us, occupying the full half right side of the screen, moves away in a diagonal to the left side and stops in the background.

Case 37

A performer moving from one place to another without leaving the boundaries of the screen, may cover a long trajectory using two shots that have a right angle relationship, by applying a neutral

225

direction motion in the second shot. Fig. 11.37 illustrates a device frequently employed by film makers.

A crosses screen right to left. As he reaches the third sector, left, cut to a right angle camera position, where we see him move away from us. The end of Shot 1 and beginning of Shot 2 are on the same picture area—an important condition for this type of cut. If the moving figure is not precisely positioned the cut will not be smooth.

Case 38

Shot order can be reversed to cover an approaching movement, instead of a receding one as above (Fig. 11.38).

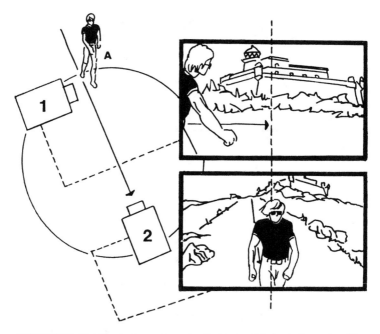

FIGURE 11.38 Right angle camera coverage of a movement that uses the centre of the screen as the centre for cutting between shots.

Player A, close to the left border of the screen in the first shot moves to the centre. There we cut to shot two, where A, centre, is seen in long shot, approaching in a neutral direction.

A reversal in which the player comes to the camera in a neutral

226

direction in the first shot, and upon reaching a medium shot, we cut to the second shot where he moves in medium shot from centre to side across the screen. This device is seldom used, although technically feasible.

The technique being discussed here requires that the player in motion has the same screen size on both shots at the moment of the cut, so that his second movement, either receding or approaching, enlarges or diminishes his figure. Discrepancies in the size of the subject on the cut will render it awkward.

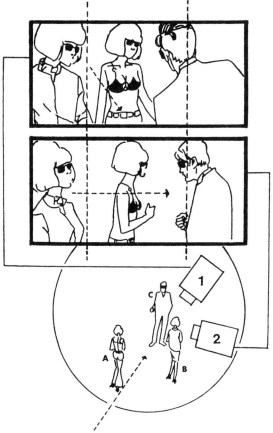

FIGURE 11.39 Right angle coverage for a movement that takes place in the centre of the screen in both shots.

Case 39

When a neutral movement in the first shot ends in a half-screen motion in the second shot, it is not necessary for the moving subject to enter the boundaries of the screen in the second. He may appear from behind one of the performers already located in foreground. Thus, his horizontal motion is shortened.

In Fig. 11.39 we see that in the first shot performer A moves towards us centrally on the screen. When she is near B, we cut to the second shot. Shot 2 is a side shot where A moves from behind B and walks across the picture area, stopping in the centre between the static B and C. To shoot A leaving, after speaking to C, we have only to reverse the shot order but using the same camera sites. When A disappears behind B (as seen from the second camera position) cut to the first camera site, where player A (centre) walks away in a neutral direction.

Case 40

The frame of an open door or any other type of fixed aperture seen in the first shot, can be used to frame the second part of the fragmented motion in the second shot (Fig. 11.40).

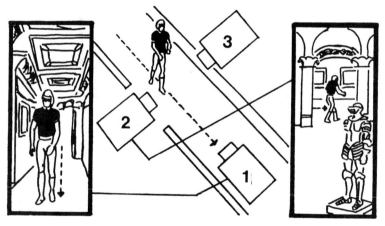

FIGURE 11.40 Another variant for right angle coverage of a movement that takes place in the centre of the screen in both shots.

Shot 1   A player advances down a corridor towards the camera in full shot. As he nears a door left, cut to . . .

Shot 2   Inside the room, looking through the door. He appears from the left in the doorway and stops to look in towards the camera.

228

Both fragments of motion were centrally placed in the picture and the player moved from left to centre in the second take, because the door was on the left side of the corridor. But if instead that door were on the right, the camera (site 3, Fig. 11.40) would see him appearing from the right. Shot 1 would remain the same because of the neutral movement.

Case 41

If the approach in the first shot is oblique the second shot must be placed on the same side of the line of motion (Fig. 11.41).

FIGURE 11.41 Right angle coverage that uses half screen movements in different sectors for each shot.

Shot 1 A moves on the right sector of the screen. He walks diagonally from background to centre. When he is between B and C, cut to . . .

Shot 2 Side shot. Player A in the centre walks to the left and stops there.

Both were full shots, and the centre of the screen was used to match the movement.

Case 42

Now consider a case where in the first take the motion is from the centre to one side and in the second shot from the opposite side to the centre of the screen (Fig. 11.42) i.e. the reverse of the above.

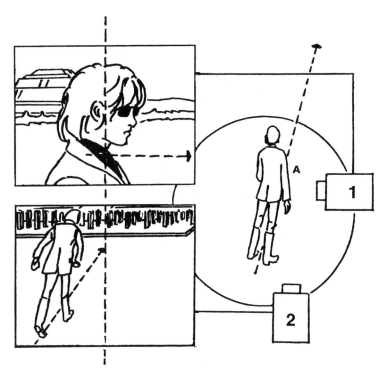

FIGURE 11.42 Another right angle variant to cover a departing player.

Player A, centre, looking right, moves right: as he reaches the right picture edge, cut to the second shot from behind, framing him left of centre walking away diagonally to the centre screen area.

Case 43

A right angle coverage of a walking or running performer can be used to relate two different areas of the set. Player A walks across the screen (centre to side) in the first shot, going away from C. In the second shot he is already in the centre (medium shot with his back to us, framed from the waist up) and walks away in a diagonal to the right towards B. Actor D on the left side of the screen, in the background, watches his movement (Fig. 11.43).

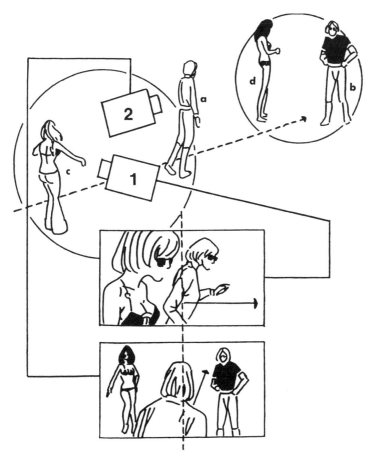

FIGURE 11.43 Two different zones on the set are linked by the movement of a player seen from right angled camera sites.

Case 44

Finally, a case where three takes (one at right angles to the others) cover a running man. The example has one peculiarity: movement is central in all three shots (Fig. 11.44).

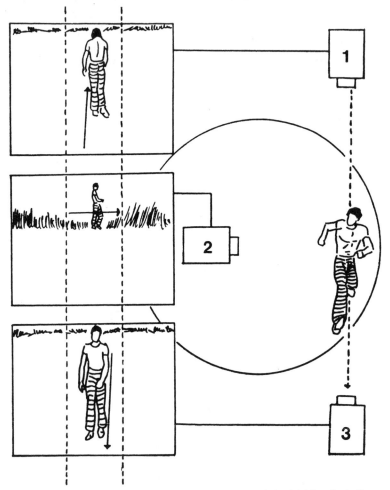

FIGURE 11.44 The second camera position in this example is at right angles to the other two camera sites. The motion of the player is recorded on the central sector of the screen in the three shots.

Shot 1 Full shot. An escaped convict in the centre of the screen runs away from us (neutral direction) on a bare marshy plain.

Shot 2 Long shot. Seen very small on the screen, the convict runs across left to right, within the central sector.

Shot 3 Full shot. He is seen small in the centre of the screen, comes up to the camera and stops in foreground (medium shot) to catch his breath.

Because the action is confined to the centre of the screen it is easy for the audience to follow the action even though the subject is sometimes seen in very small scale.

Movement across the screen

When joining two fragments of a continuous action within the boundaries of the picture, movement across the screen may be used to show the arrival or departure of a performer as follows:

Case 45

A simple situation; in the first shot the performer (centre) faces the camera and, turning round, he moves to the left. His face does not leave the screen in this shot but, on reaching the left margin, cut to the medium shot where the performer now in the centre moves out of frame left (Fig. 11.45).

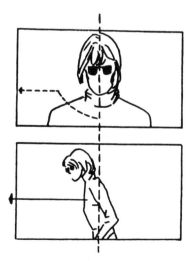

FIGURE 11.45 A movement across the screen seen from two camera sites on a common visual axis.

Case 46

The next example (Fig. 11.46) differs from the preceding one only in that the performer is already profiled on the screen in the first shot. His motion there is similar to the first shot in the previous example, while the second shot is the same.

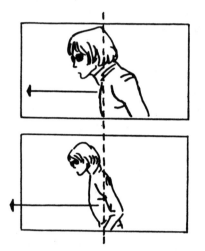

FIGURE 11.46 This example is similar to that preceding, with the difference that the player is already profiled to the camera in the first shot.

Case 47

The variation shown next (Fig. 11.47) uses a long shot for the second shot. The first shot is similar to the one in the preceding example; when his face reaches the side of the screen, cut to the long shot where the tiny figure of the player, right, walks slowly to the left where he stops.

Case 48

The technique of matching action in the same screen area in consecutive shots, serves also to unite a panning shot and a static camera shot that record an across-the-screen movement (Fig. 11.48). The player in the first shot runs from right to left framed in the right screen sector in a medium shot that pans with him. His body position is match cut at the end of this first shot with the beginning of the second, where he is framed in full shot with a

234

FIGURE 11.47 The difference between this example and the two preceding is that a long shot is used for the second shot. The player does not need to go out of the second shot as in the previous cases.

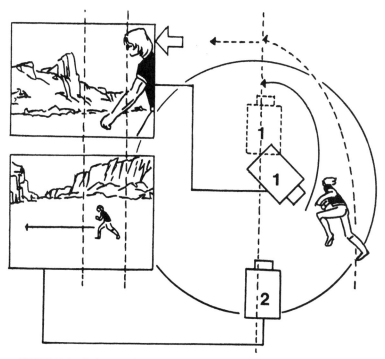

FIGURE 11.48 By keeping the player constantly in the same sector of the screen, a panning and a static shot can be joined smoothly.

235

static camera. In the second shot he runs from right to left, where he stops. Both takes have the same visual axis. This solution is often used to conclude a walking or running motion across the screen.

Case 49

Here a horizontal motion is filmed using opposed screen sectors but with the motion always having the same sense of direction. In the first shot (close shot) the moving player walks from centre to right, close to the screen edge. In the second (full shot) he walks from the left to centre and stops (Fig. 11.49).

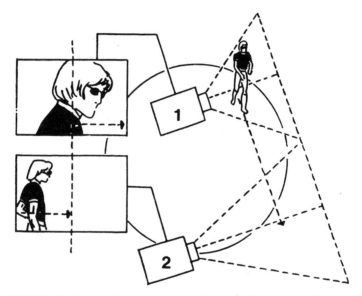

FIGURE 11.49   A horizontal movement covered by two parallel camera positions uses different areas of the screen for each shot. In the first, the player moves from centre to side, and in the second from the opposite side to the centre.

Case 50

Using cousecutive screen sectors side/centre, centre/other side, on a common visual axis, Fig. 11.50 shows someone in front of a group who starts to leave in the first medium shot profile view (screen right), and moves to the centre. Cut to a full shot of the group with him moving centre to left, and so out of the picture.

236

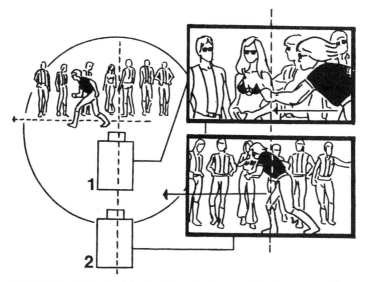

FIGURE 11.50 The horizontal action shown here is covered for the movement from one side to the centre in the first shot, and from the centre to the opposite side in the second shot. Both shots have a common visual axis line.

Case 51

Now the arrival of a character treated in the same way but in reversed order: he arrives (full shot) moving right to centre and in the second (medium or close) shot walks centre to left, which needs only one or two steps. A slight variation is obtained by repeating a movement across a small sector of the screen: the moving player enters the picture from one side and crosses say, two-thirds of the screen width (Fig. 11.51). Then cut to a close shot on the same visual axis, where he moves from centre to edge on the remaining sector.

The repetition in the second shot uses the central third of screen area.

Case 52

All cases of motion across the screen examined up to now have had cameras sited on the same visual axis and the same sense of direction in both shots. But two external reverse angles, or a combination of external-internal angles could be used instead. In Fig. 11.52 player A is departing. In the first shot he moves from centre to left. As he reaches the picture edge we cut to shot 2,

237

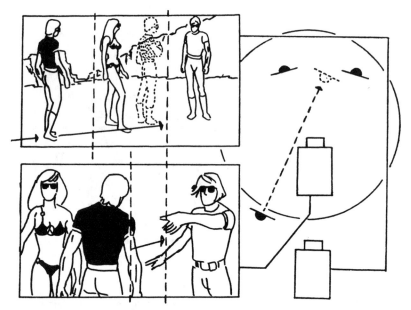

FIGURE 11.51 The movement is repeated in a small sector of the screen in the second shot to conclude the arrival of the walking actor.

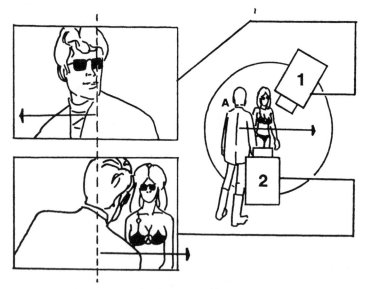

FIGURE 11.52 The departure of a player covered from reverse camera positions. His movement on the screen is in divergent directions.

a reverse view where A in the centre moves to the right and, so out of view.

An act of arrival reverses the situation. In Shot 1 he walks into shot and finishes the movement in shot 2 (Fig. 11.53).

FIGURE 11.53 A player arriving as shown by two contrasting movements on the screen. In the first shot he moves from one side to the centre, and in the second from the other side to the centre. The second shot is an internal reverse shot.

This formula presents a player with his back view in one shot and face-on in the other, so, if he is profiled, the suddenly opposed direction will not give a smooth effect in editing. This is because in profiled positions the centre of interest moves ahead, in front of the player, and by showing the motion in opposite halves of screen, that interest is shifted abruptly from one side to the other, thus breaking the principle of constant screen direction. But if the player in motion has his back to us in one half of the movement, and faces the camera in the other half, the centre of attention remains in the centre of the screen. So, for this formula with profiled positions either a neutral direction of motion (as in Fig. 11.54) or a pause (see p. 289) must be introduced between the shots.

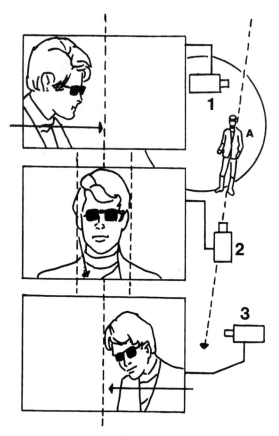

FIGURE 11.54 A neutral direction of movement is inserted between two conflicting shots to smooth the passage from one side view to the other. Thus, the action is seen as a continuous movement on the screen with a constant direction, despite the opposed directions of shots 1 and 3.

Case 53

A significant matching limb movement can sometimes serve to unite two otherwise incompatible reverse camera views of two players (Fig. 11.55).

The girl (right) slaps the man's face (left); as her hand reaches his face we cut to the second shot where the arm motion is completed.

Their positions are now reversed, yet the shots cut smoothly because the arm movement in the sequence has been in a continuous direction.

240

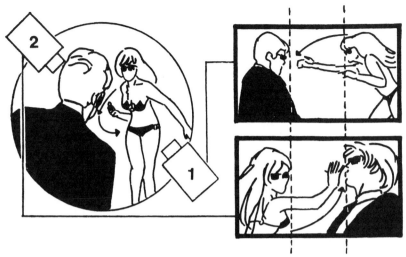

FIGURE 11.55 The continuous sense of direction of movement, in this case the swinging arc of the girl's arm as she proceeds to slap the man, masks a sudden switch of screen areas for both subjects in the cut from the first to the second shot.

Going through a doorway

Case 54

This is one of the most frequent movements in films. With a regular treatment, where the camera sites, inside and outside, remain on the same side of the line of movement, the result is as Fig. 11.56.

Case 55

If an irregular solution is consciously chosen, the fragments of action are in opposed directions, because the camera sites are on opposite sides of the line of action (Fig. 11.57).

This solution is more dynamic on the screen, especially if the motion is through an open door in both shots. If the door has to be opened, that movement is used to make the cut from shot to shot. The half circular motion will help mask a change of direction.

Case 56

Some film editors save time when showing a performer walking through a door that must be opened. Peter Hunt, film editor of

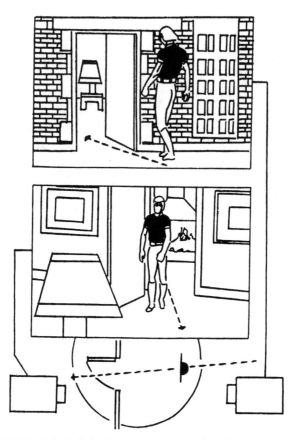

FIGURE 11.56 Method of showing an actor passing through a doorway uses the triangle principle for camera placement in the regular way. Both camera sites are on the same side of the line of movement.

Goldfinger, in the first sequence of the film shows James Bond, clad as a frogman kneeling at the base of a huge tank. Bond presses a hidden switch and a concealed door hinges open. Cut. Inside the tank James Bond closes the door behind him and comes forward (to lay plastic explosives over nitroglycerine drums). The actual motion of crossing the threshold was omitted, only the first part and the conclusion of the motion was shown, compressing time spent on a movement that had no dramatic value.

Conversely, should the opening of the door take place in a very dramatic situation, that could be stressed by delaying the opening as much as possible, without harming the effectiveness of the scene.

FIGURE 11.57 An irregular approach to crossing a threshold.

On other occasions, a pause at the beginning of the second shot is used, where the door is seen static for a few seconds, from the inside. Then it opens, and the player seen approaching it in the previous shot, enters.

Case 57

If two players are shown walking together in a neutral direction towards an open door, their screen positions will be reversed as we cut to the reverse shot for the second half of the action (Fig. 11.58).

Case 58

The same reversal happens if one of the performers stands close to the door waiting for the other to approach and enter the room. The movement of the walking player has a neutral direction in both shots. Whenever possible his position on the screen is matched (preferably in the centre), so that the waiting performer is seen first on one side of the screen and then on the other, while the moving player is kept in the centre of the frame.

243

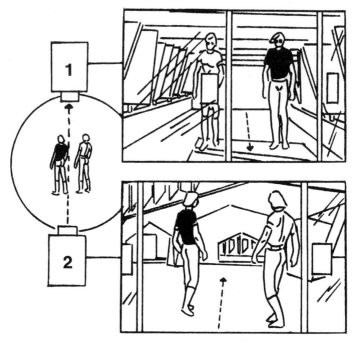

FIGURE 11.58 Two players walking away in a neutral direction exchange screen areas in the second shot as they approach the camera.

Case 59

A pause is sometimes used when a player enters a closed door. In the first shot we see him arriving outside the door and stopping to knock. After the knock we cut to the second shot—we see only the door, from the inside. Either somebody answers from off-screen telling the player outside to come in. or after a pause the player outside opens the door and enters. This pause at the beginning of the second shot serves to mask a change in the players direction of movement. The static view of the door from the inside, with no movement at all on the screen, held for one or two seconds before being opened, constitutes the visual pause.

Case 60

As we are dealing with cases involving a door, let us digress for a moment and return to the coverage of two static players placed one on each side of a closed opaque door. To obtain the feeling

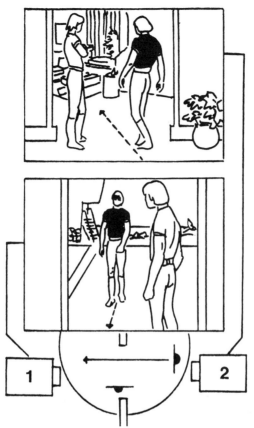

FIGURE 11.59 A reversal of the players' screen positions also occurs when one player moves close to a stationary player who watches him go by.

that they are communicating, the shots should be in opposed directions. Thus the feeling of rapport through a physical barrier is obtained in situations where two players have to speak to each other through a door that neither of them can open. Fig. 11.60 shows such an example. Notice that one player looks to the right while the other on the opposite side of the door looks to the left (the edge of the screen to which the other player has turned his back).

Brief summary

The most important factors dealt with above may be summarized as follows:

245

FIGURE 11.60 Opposed direction of looks where two players on different sides of a closed door must be presented to relate them visually on the screen.

1, a motion is broken into at least two fragments; 2, the cut from shot to shot is on the action itself; 3, a change of camera to (moving) subject distance is involved as we cut; 4, there are two basic types of motion—on the spot and along a path; 5, for on-the-spot motion, three variants of the triangle principle for camera placement are used to register a broken action—reverse shots, right angles and a common visual axis and all the variants (five) for motion along a path; 6, all the formulas presented can be reversed, changing from shot 1—shot 2 to shot 2—shot 1; 7, to film the fragments of action the screen is divided into two or three sectors; 8, the action filmed covers one sector per shot.

Three common rules may be said to apply to dynamic presentation of continuous movement split into two shots, each using half-screen areas:

The motion is repeated in the same sector of the screen, either in the same or opposed directions.

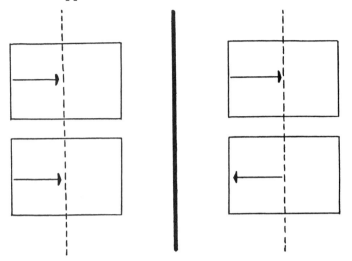

FIGURE 11.61 A motion is repeated in the same screen sector, either in the same direction or in opposed directions.

The movement begins and ends in the centre or starts on one side and finishes on the other.

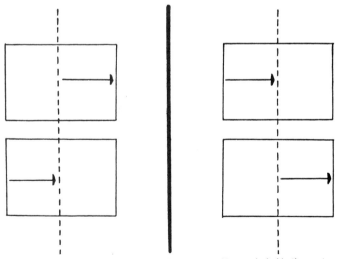

FIGURE 11.62 The movement begins in the centre and is concluded in the centre or it starts on one side and finishes on the opposite edge of the screen.

The motion converges towards the centre of the screen or diverges from it.

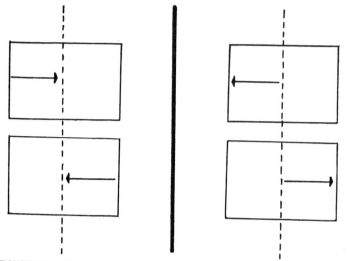

FIGURE 11.63 The movement converges on the centre of the screen or diverges from it.

A personal preference

Many film directors and editors prefer the economy of action offered by 'movement inside the screen'. The filmed movement is edited so that it does not go out of the screen in the first shot and enters in the second.

These film makers find that the suggestion of motion given by a subject moving from centre to border or vice versa, is more effective and economical than allowing him to really move out of the film frame. And it does not matter how fast the subject is moving. The standard chosen remains unchanged.

Using that criterion with the formulas and examples examined so far you will really obtain fast, economic and dynamic transitions from shot to shot that register a whole continuous motion of a performer, animal or vehicle.

Alternatively, the subject can enter and exit the picture—an approach discussed in the chapter following.

12

MOTION INTO AND OUT OF SHOT

With this technique the moving subject in the first shot leaves the shot totally or partially, and re-enters (or not) in the second shot. But there are two alternatives for the second shot: The subject re-enters shot by the opposite side to his exit, or, he is already in view in the second shot, either in the centre of the picture or placed to one side.

The three basic rules summarized at the end of the previous chapter are applicable here except for the modification implicit in prolonging the motion itself, so that it really enters or leaves the shot completely.

With a movement out of shot the cut would immediately follow the subject's exit:

1 The cut occurs when the subject is partially out of frame.
2 The shot is held for a few frames after the exit.

The techniques are reversed for subjects entering the screen. With the triangular camera coverage (p. 32) all its five variants are applicable here: external reverse angles, internal reverse angles, right angles, parallel camera sites, and a common visual axis for two or more consecutive shots.

Multiple fragments

If movement is short generally two visual fragments are enough to show the beginning and conclusion. With a long repetitive motion a single shot would usually be a very poor solution. Instead it could be broken into three or four fragments, or a cut-away could be inserted between the beginning and conclusion of the movement, thus shortening it without confusing the audience.

A repetitive motion can weaken a story by adding length without significant meaning or detail to the story. If the whole of a lengthy movement is to be retained it must be endowed with visual qualities that justify its use, although those might sometimes represent a forced, contrived *mise en scene*. A movement in which the subject goes out of the screen in one shot and comes into it in the next helps blend separate locations together more naturally and easier to accomplish as a convincing transition between two separate areas.

Fig. 12.1 shows a man walking in front of a building in the first shot and in front of a scenic mountain background in the second. The building and the mountain range might be oceans apart but on the screen the motion of the player will tend to confirm that they are close to one another. If the scene is shot in a studio the actor merely walks twice in front of the same back projection screen or blue backing for travelling matte process.

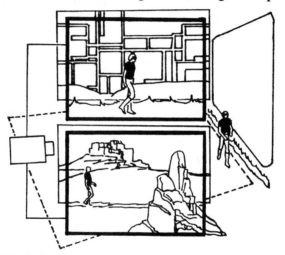

FIGURE 12.1   A player who crosses horizontally in front of two locations framed by the camera makes those places coexist side by side on the screen, notwithstanding the fact of their actual distance apart.

Motion in three fragments

Someone who begins to move from one area to another can be covered by three parallel camera sites that record distant fragments of a continuous movement. The subject exits from the area he occupies, travels through the space that mediates between his departure base and his arrival area, and finally stops at his destination. Figure 12.2 shows that case simply covered by three camera sites on a line parallel to the subject movement. Thus, the cameras register views that are framed at the same distance from the subject.

In the first shot there is a half screen motion from centre to side, where the player walks out of shot. In the second shot he enters from the opposite side, crosses the screen profiled to the camera and leaves by the other side; the whole screen is traversed. In the third the actor enters again from the opposite side and stops in the centre. Thus, a complete cross-screen motion placed between two half-screen movements, served to record the whole path travelled. A modification of this is to change camera-to-player distance. The most dramatic effect is obtained by selecting the centre camera position and moving it backwards so that a triangular camera disposition is formed with all three cameras pointing straight ahead.

The camera sites covering the extremes of the line of motion record the departure and arrival of the player, while the centre camera may frame:

1 The centre space between departure and arrival.
2 The intermediate space and the arrival area or departure zone.
3 The whole space, including in the shot the departure area, the intermediate space, and the arrival spot.

(The screen can be split into either two or three zones).

Case A

Figure 12.3 shows the first possibility described above. The first and last takes are close shots where the departure (beginning) and arrival (concluding) parts of the movement are recorded. The in-between take is a full shot where our performer is seen entering from one side and walking only to the centre of the screen. He and his destination are in opposed screen sectors.

In the example discussed we get screen sector motion repetition in the last two shots. The editing of these takes is quite simple. In the first take as soon as the performer is out of the screen completely (or almost) cut to the second shot where he re-enters from the opposite side and moves to the centre. On reaching the centre, cut to the third shot where he again enters into the screen and stops.

This combination of close shot—full shot—close shot, clearly shows a performer changing from zone to zone. The middle take

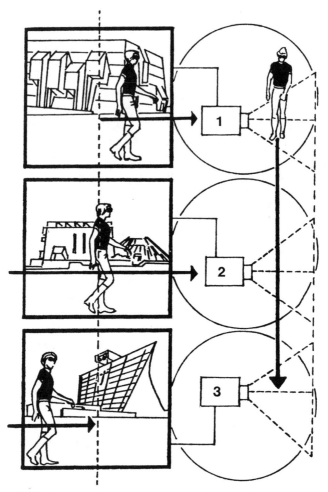

FIGURE 12.2 An horizontal movement covered by three parallel camera positions. All these are full shots.

acts as a sort of re-establishing shot (and is often used for that purpose) by showing the next zone towards which the performer is heading, or by showing both adjoining zones together.

Case B

When both adjoining zones are shown in the same take, the screen is divided into three sectors, and these zones are placed on the left

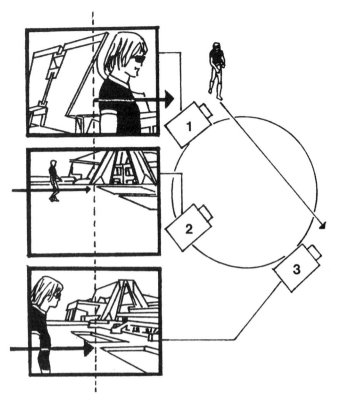

FIGURE 12.3 By placing the central camera position further back in a full shot the destination of the moving player is revealed before he reaches it.

and right, leaving the central area of the screen for the action of the main performer.

In such a case there is central movement only in the picture area (Fig. 12.4).

The shots are edited as follows:

Shot 1　Close shot. Player A hits B on the jaw, sending him out of screen, right.

Shot 2　Full shot. A is standing on the left. B staggers back in the centre. There is a wagon on the right.

Shot 3　Close shot. B enters from the left staggering back and his body slams against the wheel of the wagon, stopping violently.

The violence in the first and third shot is accentuated by the sudden cut to a far away viewpoint.

253

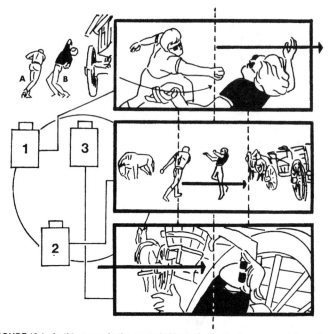

FIGURE 12.4 In this example the central shot includes the two zones of the set and the intermediate space between them re-establishing the whole locale for the audience. Shots 1 and 3 record departure and arrival respectively.

Case C

In the previous cases the three camera sites were parallel to the path of the performer, but can be placed in line with it. All viewpoints have a common visual axis, and the motion is recorded in fragments which move forward behind the walking or running player.

A further variation is obtained by combining movement inside the screen and motion that enters the screen. As shown in Fig. 12.5.

The first camera position is located on the stern of a sailing ship, pointing to the prow. Performer A in foreground begins to walk towards B in the background. When she is halfway, cut to 2, a site on the same visual axis as the preceding shot. A enters from right into the field of vision of the second camera position and continues walking towards B. When A is again halfway in her remaining path, cut to site 3, where A, close to the camera on her right, completes her trajectory and joins B.

254

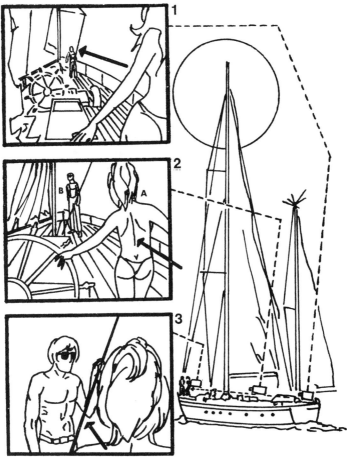

FIGURE 12.5 In the case shown here the three camera positions are located on the path of the movement itself, and advance as the walking player moves away to her destination.

Case D

In the example explained (Fig. 12.5) the subject in motion starts from one area close to the first camera site, and moves to B. A further variation can be obtained by placing his destination beyond player B. This motion can be either continuous, or with an interruption in the centre. The following example, illustrated in Fig. 12.6 makes use again of three fragments aligned on a common visual axis.

Shot 1   A moves from the right hand screen sector. Cut to . . .

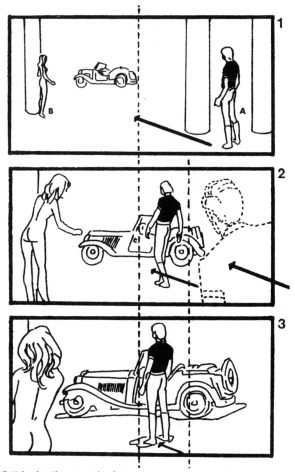

FIGURE 12.6 Another example of camera sites arranged on the line of movement itself. Here the moving player goes beyond the stationary one, and on into the background. Player B on the left side remains stationary but her figure grows in size as each new shot is introduced.

Shot 2 A enters from the right and stops in foreground with his back to us. After a moment he walks forward. He moves in the centre of the screen.

Shot 3 Player A in the centre of the screen takes two steps forward and stops.

In the example presented the performers have a common centre of interest—the car in the background.

The three shots progress spatially towards the car. Two methods were used to join the shots in sequence. From shot 1 to shot 2 repetition of screen zone movement was used—A moved in the right sector at the end of shot 1 and beginning of shot 2. To join shots 2 and 3 a different solution was applied. Action in the centre of the screen was matched precisely on that spot. B remained static in all shots and her figure came nearer from shot to shot, so that we see her in a long shot in shot 1, in a medium shot in take 2, and in a foreground close shot in shot 3.

Case E

An action fragmented in three shots may use screen sector repetition in all the shots, and can apply a right angle relationship between shots 1 and 2, and an advance on a common visual axis between shots 2 and 3.

The sequence of shots (Fig. 12.7) is easy to assemble:

Shot 1   A enters from right and moves across the screen to the centre. Cut to . . .

Shot 2   Reverse right angle position. B seen in the background, left. A, right, enters and moves away from us diagonally towards the centre. When he is near B, cut to . . .

Shot 3   Close shot of B. Same axis as preceding shot. B on the left of the screen. A enters by the right and stops facing B.

By piecing a motion in this way, two different locations can be shown as if spatially side by side. The illusion works perfectly on the screen.

The fragmentation of a continuous motion in more than four or five sections becomes annoying and defeats its own purpose. Where the distance is very great four shots could be used as shown in Fig. 12.8.

Movement can be confined to the same screen sector in the last three shots. But the aim is to find an editing formula that suggests the length of the path travelled without the full movement which tires the audience and slows down the story.

For that purpose only three shots would be necessary. In Fig.

257

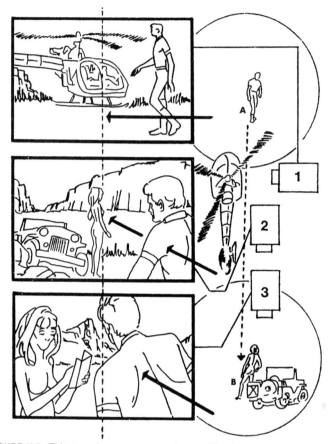

FIGURE 12.7 This example uses screen sector repetition in the three shots for the movement of player A. A combination of a right angle shot between shot 1 and 2 and an advance on a common visual axis between shots 2 and 3 allows this zone repetition of motion.

12.8 we would use only shots 1, 2 and 4. On the first, the moving player leaves his area. In shot 2, he is seen, small, traversing the space that separates him from his destination on the right, where the other performer waits. Shot 4 would begin by showing the waiting actor alone on the screen for several frames, and then the player in motion would enter the screen.

The length of time that the waiting player remains on the screen before the arrival of the other, suggests the length of the path travelled. A time contraction is usually resorted to when using this method. Motion of a repetitive nature (such as walking or

258

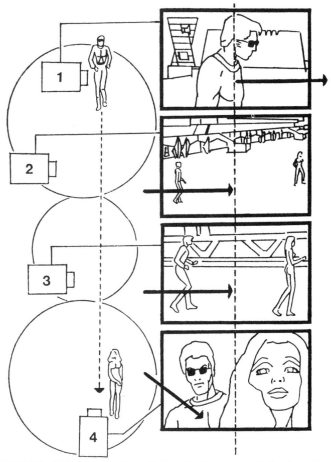

FIGURE 12.8 Multiple fragments applied to a lengthy movement of a player. Screen sector repetition is obtained in the last three shots.

running) is seldom of dramatic value in situations where the intention is to move a player from one place to another.

Fast, or violent motions can be fragmented into four or five pieces to stress visually the violence implicit in the movement itself. The case shown in Fig. 12.9 makes use of reverse angles.

In take 1 (a close shot) performer A lunges forward violently going out of the screen. In shot 2 (a full shot) he enters and runs to the background. Halfway along his path we cut to shot 3 where he is seen in medium shot on the centre of the screen. He moves quickly towards us going out of the screen.

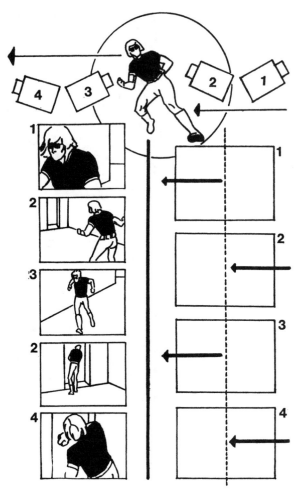

FIGURE 12.9 Multiple fragmentation of a movement to stress the violence of a person's movement.

The conclusion of this motion accepts three solutions:
1   We cut back to shot 2 (full shot) where the player ends his motion by arriving to the door and pounding his fists on it.
2   He arrives by entering close shot 4.
3   Both previous solutions are combined to conclude the motion, using shots 2 and 4 after the first three shots.
Solutions 1 and 2 involve four fragments, while approach 3 uses five sections to piece together the whole motion.

13

PLAYER *A* MOVES TOWARDS PLAYER *B*

The number of visual permutations possible for one player approaching another or a group are almost limitless. Those described below are only suggestions for basic situations that may be useful as a checklist for ideas.

Converging motion

The moving player comes forward on the screen in both takes, but in the first his movement is from right to centre on the right side of the screen, while in the second he moves from left to centre on the left side of the film frame. The movement of the approaching player converges towards the centre of the screen in both shots, using both right and left areas of the screen consecutively.

FIGURE 13.0 Converging directions of a single approaching motion towards a static player.

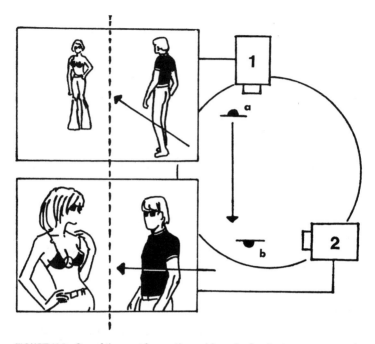

FIGURE 13.1 One of the most frequently used formulas for short range movements employed when only one player moves towards another. The camera positions are at right angles.

The presence of a mirror in the first shot allows the viewing of converging directions of the same single action by the approaching player, while the static performer is seen on the same side of the screen in both shots.

The inclusion of one or more mirrors in a shot has always fascinated film makers because of the opportunities they provide for unusual visual arrangements on the screen.

Right angle camera sites

Where the two main camera positions have a right angle relationship, the simplest solution is depicted in Fig. 13.1. A, with his back to the camera in shot 1, starts to walk away from us towards player B. Shot 1 is a full shot. Two-thirds of the movement are covered from this viewpoint. We then cut to shot 2, a medium shot, where A enters the screen and stops, facing B. B may be either standing, sitting or lying down.

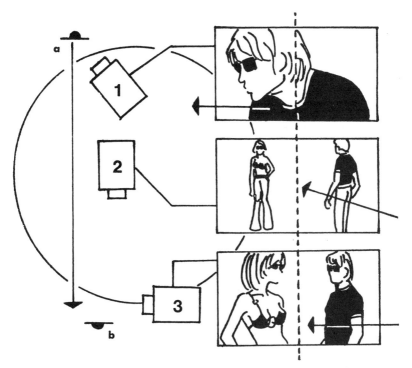

FIGURE 13.2　The first shot is an improvement on the previous example.

The difference in distance between the camera and the performer in both takes (FS to CS or MS) adds a visual variety. A always moves in the same sector of the screen. Although we showed movement from right to left, the reverse direction works in the same manner as in all the examples following.

An alternative, or addition to the above is where the beginning of the movement is first shown in a reverse close shot (Fig. 13.2).

Player A begins to move in close shot (1) where he goes out of the screen, entering into full shot (2) and concludes his motion by entering again in medium shot (3). Several of the following situations also open with a close shot.

Another solution is to make the first a panning shot. The actor walks in a straight path tangential to the panning arc of the first camera site (Fig. 13.3).

The illustration shows the 180° pan used in the first shot. It achieves the same as the two first shots in Fig. 13.2.

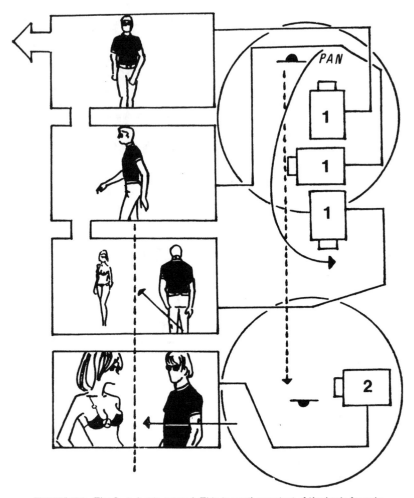

FIGURE 13.3 The first shot is panned. This is another variant of the basic formula shown in Fig. 13.1.

In the first case examined, and partially in the two variations following it, the moving player began his walk with his back to the camera and concluded by arriving at a profile position. Fig. 13.4 uses the right angle set-up to show the player starting the move from a profiled position and concluding it facing the camera. The performer in motion may come to the camera in either zone of the screen in the second shot.

264

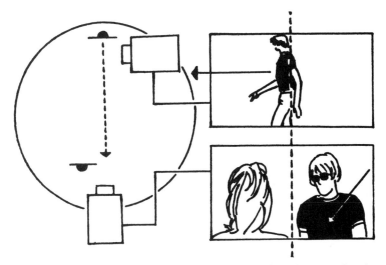

FIGURE 13.4 In this variant of the basic formula with a right angle relationship of camera sites, the moving player enters the second shot facing the camera instead of being profiled to it as in the previous examples.

Another possibility reverses the variation examined in the previous example. The moving actor comes up to the camera in the first shot and concludes by entering the screen in a profiled position. (Fig. 13.5).

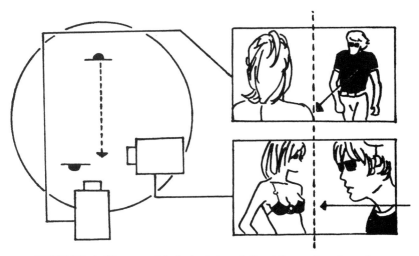

FIGURE 13.5 In this approach to the basic formula the stationary player is used as a pivot for the camera sites, keeping her in the foreground in both shots.

Fig. 13.6 shows the actor's movement profiled to the camera in the first shot, and with his back to it in the second.

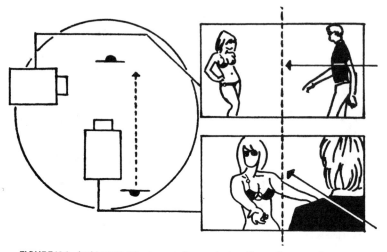

FIGURE 13.6 In this variant the camera sites are deployed in a pattern complementary to that shown in Fig. 13.5.

The case shown in Fig. 13.7 shows a camera pan applied to the second shot. In the first shot A is seen moving away from us towards B in the background. In the second shot A is in the centre of the screen (or entering it from the right) and being followed by a short panning movement that covers the conclusion of his motion as he comes to a stop facing performer B.

Reverse camera angles

Fig. 13.8 is the first (and most simple) of several variations using reverse camera angles to show the movement.

In the first shot the player walks up to the camera, and enter in the second shot with his back to us. With this formula we can also use a close shot where the beginning of the movement is recorded, as shown in Fig. 13.9.

So far we have shown both players in the two shots. Using internal reverse angles we can also cover the path traversed by the moving player.

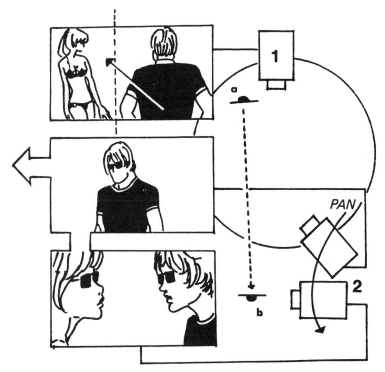

FIGURE 13.7 The change introduced to the basic formula in this example is in the second shot, where the camera is panned.

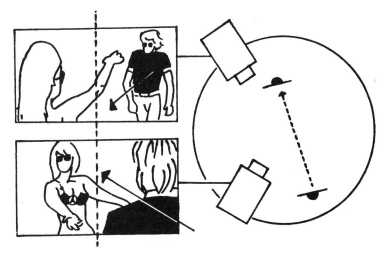

FIGURE 13.8 A simple approach using a set of external reverse camera angles.

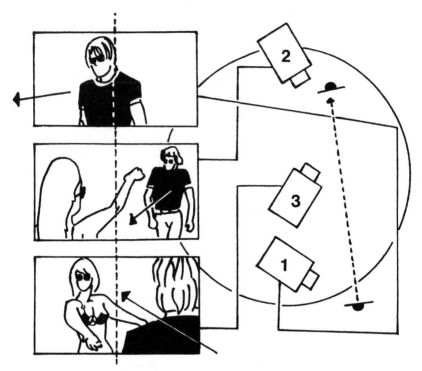

FIGURE 13.9 The first shot is an improvement added to the external reverse angle camera coverage in the previous example.

This variation was used before to show the beginning of the movement at the start of other formulas, but has sufficient value in itself to be employed alone. In the example shown in Fig. 13.10 both shots are at the same camera/subject distance, but this can be varied.

Parallel camera sites

Parallel camera positions have been extensively examined before to record movement of an actor across the screen, so it will suffice to include here only one example, the most simple (Fig. 13.11).

Common visual axis

Camera positions on a common visual axis are the key to the examples that follow. Fig. 13.12 shows a frequently used example.

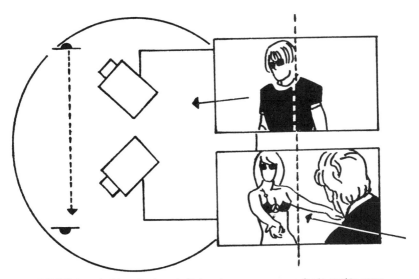

FIGURE 13.10 In this variant, a set of internal reverse camera angles is used to cover the player in motion.

The method shown in Fig. 13.12 is simple to execute and quite clear in the visual coverage that it affords. No wonder that it is used so often.

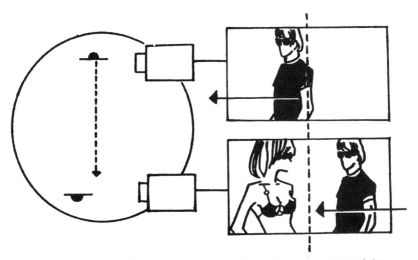

FIGURE 13.11 A parallel camera deployment used to register the movement of the player as he walks towards his stationary companion.

269

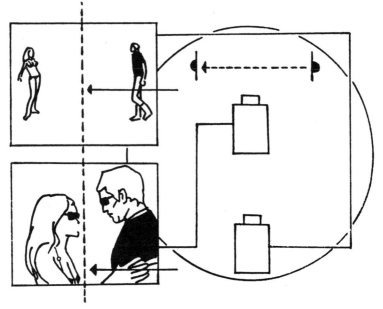

FIGURE 13.12   A common visual axis line for both camera sites is used here to show the player in motion.

Here (Fig. 13.13) the line of motion runs parallel to the axis line of the two camera sites for covering of the motion.

In the foregoing examples the arrival point (player B) was always visible in the two or three shots into which the movement of A was fragmented. In the following examples she appears only in the second shot. This is due to the fact that the motion covered is a diagonal across our field of vision (Fig. 13.14).

In the first shot player A moves away from the camera, in an oblique path, and leave the picture, left. He enters from the right in the second shot and stops, facing B. A is seen from behind in both shots.

In this case we reverse the situation in the preceding example. The moving player faces the camera in both shots (Fig. 13.15).

In shot 1, player A advances to the camera in a diagonal and passes out of shot, left. For shot 2 two solutions are available. B is included in foreground in both possibilities. A is either in the centre of the right sector moving towards us, or he enters from the right and comes to the foreground.

270

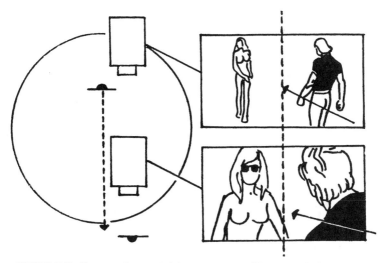

FIGURE 13.13 Movement in a neutral direction is covered by camera deployment on a common visual axis.

This frontal approach to an unseen destination in the first shot is the one most favoured by film makers. Coming forward is a more dynamic action than going away.

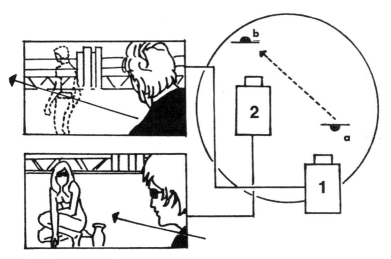

FIGURE 13.14 In the first shot A moves away obliquely from the camera and exits left. In the second shot he enters from the right, still seen from behind, and stops, facing B.

271

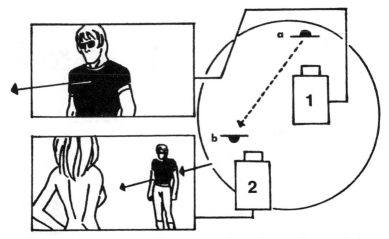

FIGURE 13.15 The difference between this example and that preceding it lies in the fact that here the moving player arrives facing us, whereas in the previous case he moved with his back to the camera.

A mirror can be present in the second shot, in the background, angled to the side where player A is still moving off screen. In this way, in the second shot, we first see her enter the screen (in the mirror) by the left, and as her figure goes out of the mirror right, her real figure enters the film frame from the left, and stops

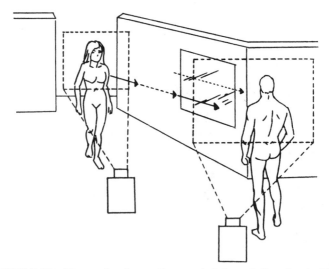

FIGURE 13.15A The use of a mirror on the second shot repeats the entrance of the moving player twice on the same section of the screen.

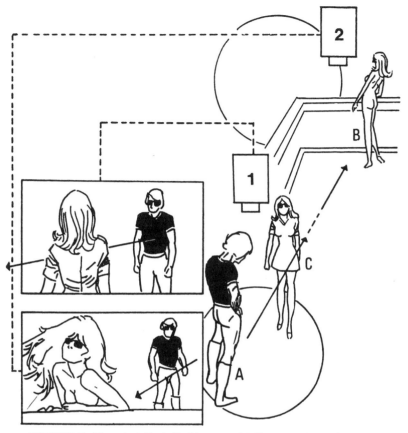

FIGURE 13.16 The variant afforded by this approach is that two stationary players are involved. The moving actor advances from one to the other in the two shots.

facing B. Thus, her entering motion in the second shot was seen twice, and in the same area of the screen (Fig. 13.15A).

As pointed out elsewhere, the use of mirrors affords the duplication of motion which gives startling and off-beat visual effects.

The same formula can be employed to show player A leaving C to arrive beside actor B in the second shot. (Fig. 13.16).

The motion follows an oblique path in both takes. C is excluded in the second shot. In the first take C and A are talking, then A moves diagonally crossing behind C and approaches, going out of shot, left.

273

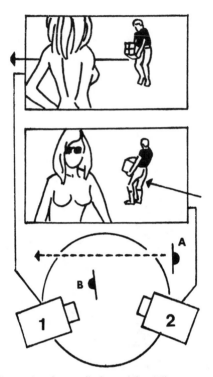

FIGURE 13.17 The moving player walks beyond the stationary one, who serves as a pivot for both camera positions, keeping him in the foreground in both shots.

In the second shot he is already on the screen in the centre of the right sector, and comes towards B who is framed in the foreground and then speaks to him.

A walks beyond B

A situation often found in a scene where the player in motion crosses beside the static one, and stops beyond him. This might be filmed as follows.

Player B, the static subject, can be used as pivot in both shots, thus relating visually both shots into which the movement has been split. As Fig. 13.17 shows, B has his back to us in the first shot and is facing the camera in the second. A goes out of the screen in the first shot and enters the second. His motion can be

274

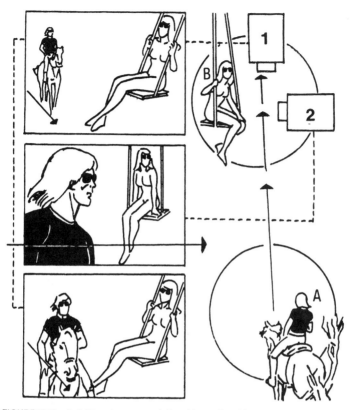

FIGURE 13.18 A right angle camera relationship employed for a movement where the walking player passes beyond his stationary companion. The first shot is used twice to show the beginning and conclusion of the movement. The second covers the central part of the movement.

motivated by giving him a significant piece of business, such as having him lift a heavy box in shot 1 and deposit it in shot 2. The second approach is shown in Fig. 13.18.

In shot 1, player A is seen in the background. He walks to us in a neutral direction. B is seated on the right side of the screen and seen in full shot. As A nears her, we cut to take 2, where A enters from the left and crosses our view passing in front of B and going out of shot, right.

Cut back to shot 1, where A having passed B already, moves towards us and stops in the foreground.

As mentioned at the beginning of this chapter the list of cases included here is not an exhaustive one.

14

USING MASTER SHOTS TO COVER MOTIONS ON THE SCREEN

Very few screen motions so far examined have allowed division and use of shots in two or more parts. Inserts or cut-aways in a master shot may provide a pause in the action recorded, serve to stress a situation or allow recognition of the characters involved.

In the following example the player pauses in front of a large building before moving on towards it. A reverse shot is inserted.

Master shot 1	Large building in the background. A enters view from the left and stops with his back to us, Looking towards the building. Cut to . . .
Insert 2	Reverse shot of A seen on the same side of the picture. He is looking off right. He advances and passes out of view right. Cut to . . .
Master shot 1	A, in the centre of the picture, moving away from us towards the building.

The combination is easy to execute. The master shot 1 is filmed without interruption. Player A enters, stops, then moves away towards the building. Cut.

The actor is brought back and positioned for the second shot. There we see his expression as he examines the building and then starts to walk towards it. In editing, a portion of the master shot 1, corresponding to the action seen in the insert, is removed and replaced by the insert 2. This reverse shot, being a frontal shot favouring the performer, shows the player's reaction much more clearly than if we stuck to shot 1 in its entirety.

In another case a subject seen moving in extreme long shot, generates in the audience the urge to identify him before becoming involved in his further actions. This can be handled as follows.

FIGURE 14.1 Player A, alone, faces the building. He enters shot, stops, then moves away (in the second shot) towards the building, again covered by the first camera position.

Master shot 1   A enters view from the left, running to the right. He is shown in very small scale, silhouetted against the sky, running across a beach. When

FIGURE 14.2 The first shot is used twice. The horizontal movement of the player is through thirds of the screen area—the first and third. The movement that should be in the central part of the screen in Shot 1 is substituted by the movement shown in Shot 2, which is from a right angled camera position, closer to the moving subject.

	he gets about one-third of the way across the picture, cut to . . .
Insert 2	A in the centre of the screen running towards us, exiting close to the camera, right. As he advances we are given a chance to recognise him.
Master shot 1	A runs the last third of the width of the screen seen in small scale against the horizon and leaves right.

Player A runs right across the picture in the master shot. A closer shot shows a segment of that motion. The division of his movement in thirds of screen space in the master shot, allows us to show the performer and his environment at the start and at the end, using segments 1 and 3. The motion performed in the central segment of the screen is taken out and replaced by the insert.

An improvement uses the preceding set-up but after cutting back to the master shot the sequence is concluded by adding a third shot to cap the action.

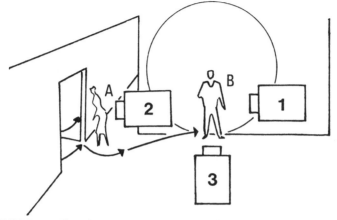

FIGURE 14.3 Floor plan showing the arrangement of the cameras to cover a simple movement of one player.

Full shot. The girl, A, enters through a door into the corridor. She is unaware of the man's presence, B. She closes the door with her back to us. He says quietly:

'Hello'!

Startled, she begins to turn to us, we cut on the movement, to a close shot on the same visual axis.

279

She ends turning towards us and looks off screen, right. She smiles as she recognizes him. Then she starts to move towards us, (right) and when her head is halfway out of the screen, cut to the full shot again.

The girl in the centre of the screen is walking towards us and towards B in the foreground. As she draws near, cut to a side close shot of B.

At the beginning of the shot, A enters from the left and stops. They talk.

An elaborate motion recorded in a single master shot can be enhanced by the introduction of two inserts. Fig. 14.4 gives the camera positions in such a case.

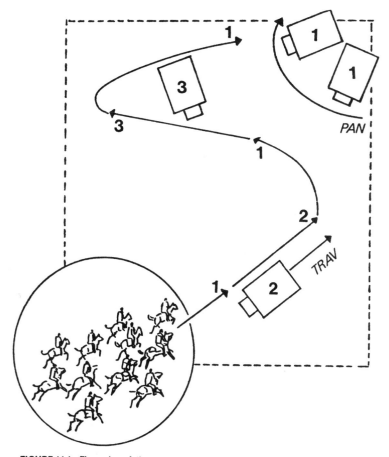

FIGURE 14.4 Floor plan of the camera sites that cover a simple movement with various camera viewpoints, one of them used as a master shot (1).

The scene takes place in a rocky desert where we see a mountain range behind. A path has been worn into the ground by constant use. The riders move in a line of three abreast, more or less equally spaced apart.

High long shot. Riders approach from left to centre.

Full shot. Camera on the road travels with them. They ride toward us.

High long shot again. Riders turn the bend to the right and move across the screen. Pan to the right with them.

Low full shot. Riders approach diagonally from left to right and exit the screen, right.

High long shot again. The riders turn the bend toward the camera, and move in a diagonal from right to left. Camera pans and tilts to follow them as they exit.

In this example the two inserts were used to inject dynamism into the master shot. This master is a panoramic view. Its value lies in showing the riders isolated in the large, wild terrain. The inserts provide violent motion that contrasts with the calmness of the master. An increase in sound level when the two inserts appear on the screen, and a sudden decrease when the master shot follows accentuates a feeling of impending menace.

Several master shots can be edited in parallel to cover a performer's movement in order to stress all the dramatic possibilities, and build a succession of images that create excitement, suspense or sheer action for the audience. Here is an example from an unfinished film entitled *El Señor del Este* (Lord of the East). The

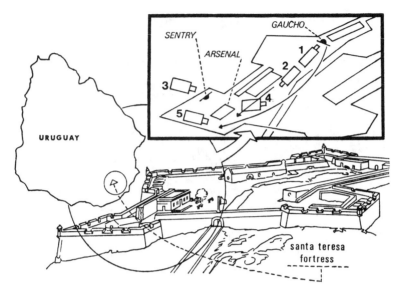

FIGURE 14.5 Sequence of shots edited in parallel as described in the text.

scene is Santa Teresa fortress, Uruguay. A gaucho, wearing the uniform of a Portuguese soldier he has overpowered, is about to cross the patio of the fortress toward the arsenal that he plans to sabotage. A soldier on the ramparts stands watch with his back to the courtyard. The gaucho starts to cross the patio (Fig. 14.5).

Shot 1 The gaucho moves from under the archway of the stone passage and walks out of shot, right.

284

Shot 2 Reverse shot. The gaucho enters from the left and moves towards the background. There we see his target: the arsenal.

Shot 3 From the fort's walls we see (foreground) the sentry standing with his back to the gaucho, who is seen in the background walking towards the arsenal.

Mood is important to this type of sequence. A far away male voice singing a song to the tune of a plaintive guitar, punctuated by the harsh sound of the sentry's boots scraping on the rampart's stones serve to highlight the sense of latent danger that can be suddenly unleashed.

Shot 4 Low angle. Camera moves back with the gaucho as he walks in medium shot.

Shot 3   Full shot of the walls. The gaucho moves in the back-
         ground.

Shot 4   Travelling low shot of the gaucho.

Shot 3   Full shot of the walls. The gaucho reaches the arsenal
         and disappears behind it.

Shot 5 The walls of the arsenal in foreground. The gaucho comes towards us from a neutral direction and kneels below the lighted window. He waits.

Shot 3 On the fort's walls the sentry changes position and looks towards the background.

Shot 5 The gaucho slowly rises and peeps through the slit window of the arsenal.

The whole sequence comprises ten fragments, taken from three master shots and two single shots. These single shots are used at the beginning of the sequence to show the two extreme zones between which the movement takes place. In take 1 we see the gaucho leaving his hiding place, and in shot 2 we show him heading for his target: the far away arsenal. Master shots 3 and 4 record his bold movement through the danger zone. Master 3 shows the sentry in foreground who might turn at any moment and challenge him. The movement of the gaucho is shown in this shot in three successive zones of the screen. They are intercut with master 4 that shows us the feelings of the gaucho as he moves across the open courtyard.

As our hero reaches the arsenal we cut to the master shot 5, where we show him coming to the window.

Then we intercut the pay-off of Master 3. We had toyed with the emotions of the audience by stating clearly (in a previous part of the story) that if the sentry turned, the plans of our hero would be ruined. (The audience already knows that there is a curfew enforced every night within the fortress walls). By showing the sentry turning now, we stress that the danger was as real as we had indicated, but our lucky hero saved himself on the nick of time. Then we return to master shot 5 where the gaucho starts the next phase of his operation, and the story moves on.

15

IRREGULAR CASES

Dramatic needs sometimes dictate visual presentations that violate the rules of motion already explained. The examples that follow fall within this category. Two solutions were applied to make them work—a pause, or use of a small screen sector. In many films a problem arises where a performer must move between two different zones of interest that have opposed dominant centres so that from a general camera position we face one centre of interest and see only the rear of the other. If this is to be avoided, a visual pause must be employed at the beginning of the second take. Imagine a case where two players are seen, one in motion, the other static, as in Fig. 15.1. Only two shots are used to cover the motion between both zones of interest.

Shot 1   Long shot. Player B is on the right, with his back to us. He faces the scenic background. A, on the left, walks across the screen towards B. When A reaches the centre of the screen, cut to . . .

Shot 2   Reverse medium shot. Player B is now on the left side of the screen, facing us. He remains alone for a moment and then A enters from the right and stops beside him. Both players now face the camera or look at each other.

The pause that masks the change of direction is introduced at the beginning of the second shot. The moving player is momentarily excluded from the shot, so that the static performer is briefly seen alone. This allows the audience time to adjust to the new camera position.

In a previous instance, when discussing opposed motion within the screen area, an example was examined where the moving player had his back to the camera in one half sector and faced it in the other (Chapter 11, Case 52). That condition was needed to achieve a coherent motion because in that case the centre of

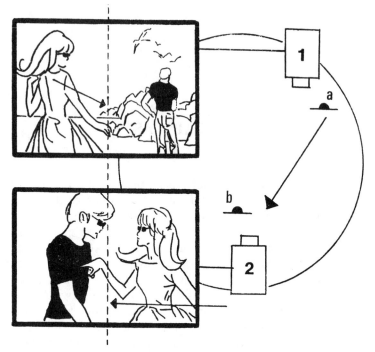

FIGURE 15.1 A visual pause is introduced at the beginning of the second shot to obtain a smooth change of direction in the movement of one player.

attention for the player, and the audience, remained in the centre of the screen.

With the present solution a pause is introduced at the beginning of the second shot and the moving player presents a profiled body position in both shots. The motion of the player or other moving subject can be either across the screen or diagonally.

Visual pause with larger groups

With a large static group the fragmentation of movement might be prefaced by the motion of another player (Fig. 15.2).

Shot 1   A and C are seen talking, B enters from the right passing behind C and stops (centre). B talks to A, who then moves towards B. As A crosses one-third of the picture area, the shot is cut to . . .

290

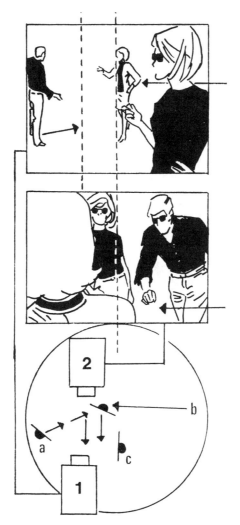

FIGURE 15.2 The people move, with a visual pause in the action of the second player.
The players interchange positions on the screen in the second shot.

Shot 2   Reverse medium shot. B, now on the left is profiled to
the right. (Fig. 15.2). Then A enters from the right and
stops, facing B. Later both turn away from us and walk
in a neutral direction to the background.
A reversal of screen zone position for both main players (B and A)
is unavoidable with this solution, but a pause at the beginning of

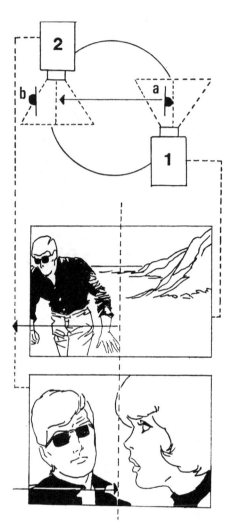

FIGURE 15.2A Opposed movement of a player in the same screen sector. A pause at the beginning of the second shot b ridges both movements.

the second take helps to create a momentary distraction for the audience, allowing their reorientation by breaking the direction on the dominant motion.

Instead of having the two subjects present in both shots, they can be shown together in only one shot. (Fig. 15.2A)

Player A goes out of shot by moving from the centre to the left, in the first shot. The second shot begins with B (static) on the right

sector. After a pause A enters from the left and stops in ths centre.
Motion was accomplished in the same screen sector (left) in opposed directions.

The pause is omitted

With a right angle camera coverage, the pause is sometimes omitted. A direct cut is used, and the player who moves does so on opposed halves of screen from shot to shot (Fig. 15.3). With a peculiarity. In one shot his movement is across a narrow central area. In Fig. 15.3 the second shot makes use of this short movement.

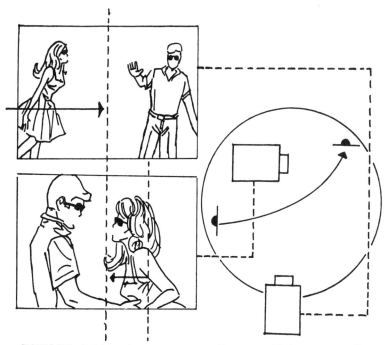

FIGURE 15.3 A right angle camera coverage with movement that converges on the centre of the screen In both shots.

Both fragments of the motion converge on the screen towards its centre. This visually interesting presentation works well not only where two persons meet, but also in cases where one performer, for instance, helps the other climb on to higher ground where the first player is already placed (Fig. 15.4).

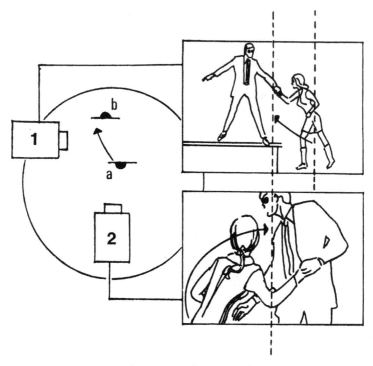

FIGURE 15.4 The pause at the beginning of the second shot has been omitted, and a direct cut is made. The movement in both shots converges on the centre of the screen.

A and B converge on the centre of the screen, A extends his hand to B. Cut on the action to the second camera position, right angles, where A's body enters from the left and joins B. Here the small movement was in the first shot.

Using reverse angles

Where one performer is seated, the other, standing, may feel compelled to move from one side to the other to stress a point or for some other reason. Once more, this motion is fragmented using opposed halves of screen (Fig. 15.5).

294

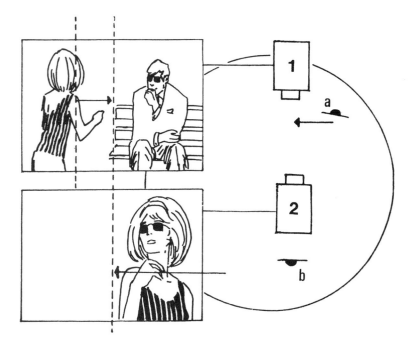

FIGURE 15.5 The stationary player is excluded from the second shot in this example.

The speed factor is thus very important and must be considered when planning this type of set up. In the example shown, the small sector motion was used in the first shot.

This solution is similar to the one presented in Chapter 13, Case 52 except that in the second shot the player enters rather than just moves from the side to the centre.

By using a close shot for the second take, the entrance of the player into the screen is made swifter, so that she traverses the half screen area faster than she took to cover the opposing half screen area on the previous shot.

As explained elsewhere, a single motion split in two parts should have both halves moving at similar speeds. But a close shot by increasing the size of the figure, also increases its speed of motion. Since the close shot is used for visual emphasis, this speed increase cuts well with the slower motion that preceded it. What will not work so successfully is a reversal, where speed from shot to shot decreases on the depiction of a continuous single motion.

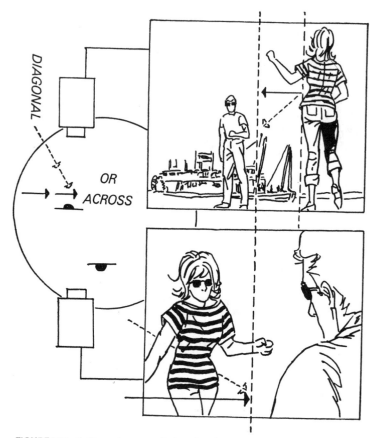

FIGURE 15.6 A diagonal movement where the players interchange screen positions from shot to shot; movement converges on the screen centre in both shots.

Although subject B was excluded from the second shot (which was his viewpoint), he can be present in that shot too—creating a reversal of players' screen sectors (Fig. 15.6).

As the illustration clearly shows, there are two alternatives for the sense of direction in which the moving performer travels. She may either displace her body horizontally across a half screen area in each shot, or she may move diagonally in a receding direction first, approaching in the shot that follows.

A player moving in a neutral direction can use the same formula (Fig. 15.7).

296

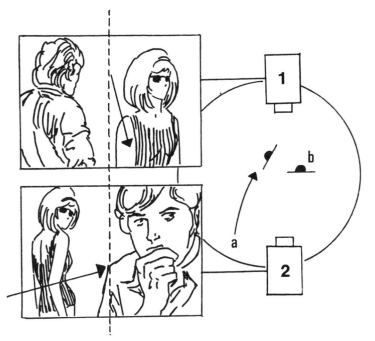

FIGURE 15.7 Movement in a neutral direction where the players exchange screen positions in the second shot as the moving person a, completes her action.

Shot 1   B in foreground, back to the camera. A (right) approaches us. When she is near B, cut to . . .

Shot 2   Reverse. B in foreground, right. A enters from the left. When she is behind B, she turns to him.

Instead of crossing the screen to the centre the neutral movement of coming and going away was performed in opposed sectors.

It is not necessary to show the player entering the screen from one side in the second shot. Although the use of that entrance helps in making the motion more dynamic, it will work if we only show the player with her back to the camera, standing beside B, and moving away to the background in the area of the screen that is opposite to that employed for the first shot. The use of close shot framings for both shots forces the screen reversal of both players in the film frame in a marked way. If the action is photographed in long shots, the same principle would apply, but the reversal of the players would be less noticeable, since both would be located in the

297

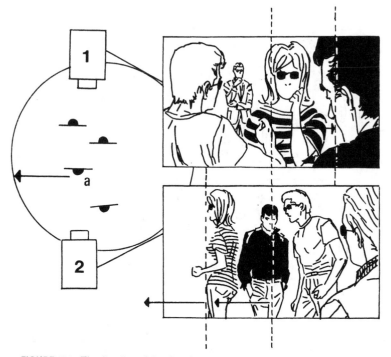

FIGURE 15.8 The direction of the player's movement diverges from centre to sides.

centre of the screen, seen in full figure. Their area reversal covers less screen space than the same action pictured in close shots.

Divergent motions

The performer may move away from the scene from the centre instead of coming into it.

First there is a medium shot of the group. A moves from the centre of the screen to the right, exiting by that side.

Secondly comes a reverse full shot. A (centre) completes her movement. She either exits by the left side or stops there and turns to face the group.

Constant screen position for one player

In some cases instead of exchanging sides of the picture one player may be kept to a constant screen area while the other crosses (Fig. 15.9).

298

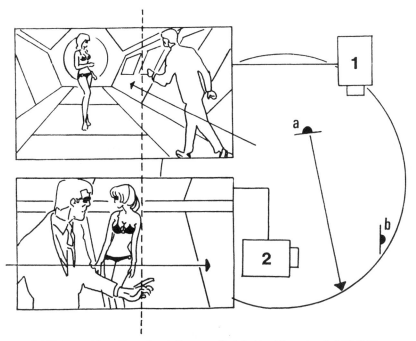

FIGURE 15.9 Player B remains stationary on the left side of the screen in both shots while the other player moves in a neutral direction in the first shot and across the screen in the second.

Shot 1 B (left, static). A (right) moves away in a neutral direction. Cut to . . .

Shot 2 Side shot. B (left, static). A enters from that side and crosses the screen, stopping in the right sector.

Both players move

A further irregular variation is introduced when both players move. The actors walk on parallel paths, but in opposite directions. They stop simultaneously and face each other (Fig. 15.10).

Shot 1 Actors enter shot from opposite sides and walk towards the centre framed in medium shot. As their figures are about to overlap, cut to . . .

Shot 2 Reverse. Both players enter view in close shot, again from opposite sides, and stop, facing each other.

The positions of the actors in the second shot are reversed. But

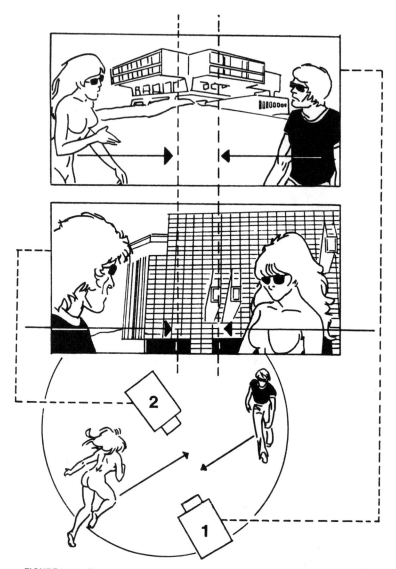

FIGURE 15.10 The players move in opposed directions towards a meeting point. The second camera position transposes them on the screen but the cut works smoothly because the converging movements in both shots are equal.

their converging motions in each sector of the screen are identical, although performed by a different player in each screen section from shot to shot.

16

PLAYER *A* MOVES AWAY
FROM PLAYER *B*

Shots in which one character moves away from another in similar circumstances to those previously examined, only of course, requires a reversal of the procedure. It would suffice only to reverse the order of shots and direction of movement, to obtain smooth and varied coverage for all these. As in chapter 13 where player A moves towards player B the triangular camera placement principle still applies.

Before going into the most used and classical approaches for this type of motion, let us record an oddity. By including on the screen image two mirrors angled to each other, it is possible to show the departing player beginning his motion by leaving one mirror and entering the other to record the second half of his movement. The mirrors act as two mini screens for his movement, while the static player is ever present on the large screen itself.

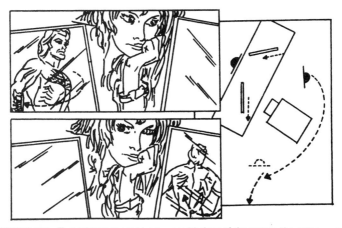

FIGURE 16.0   Two mirrors record on opposed halves of the screen the going away motion of a player.

301

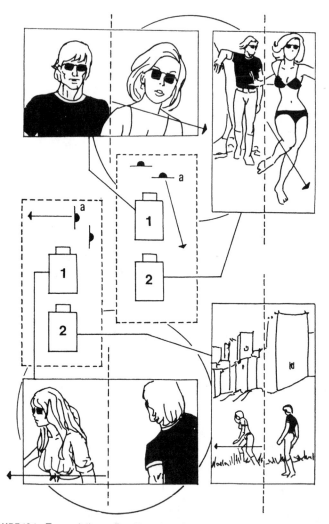

FIGURE 16.1 Two variations offered to cover a departing movement. The first covers movement in a neutral direction and the second, movement across the screen.

Two camera positions placed on a common visual axis can be used to film a motion of departure either across the screen or diagonally towards the camera in both shots (Fig. 16.1).

The fragments of motion are recorded on only one half of the screen, and in the same sector for both shots. A exits by the side in the first shot and moves from the centre to the same side in the

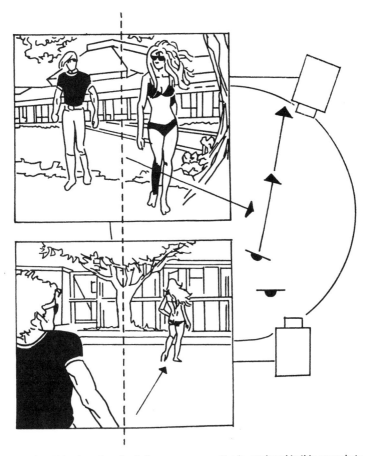

FIGURE 16.2 An external set of reverse camera sites is employed in this example to cover the departure of one player.

second. An external reverse camera coverage would look like that shown in Fig. 16.2.

A right angle camera placement used to cover the departure of a performer would show both players in the first shot and only the moving one in the second (Fig. 16.3).

A moves out of view in the first shot but in the second she is already in the centre of the screen, and walks away from us in a neutral direction.

303

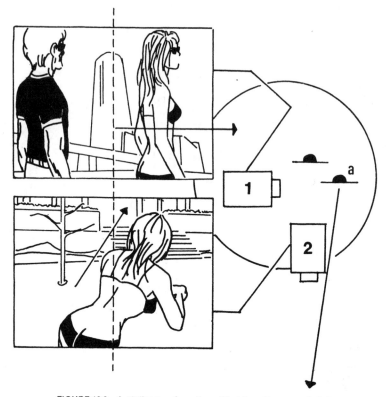

FIGURE 16.3 A stationary player is omitted from the second shot.

This second shot becomes, in fact, the point of view of the player who remains in the place. The distance at which the moving player is seen in this second shot, corresponds to the personal point of view of the static player. If both were seen in full shot in the first shot, the moving player can be seen in a full shot moving away in the second shot, since the distance travelled across the screen to its edge, is longer than if this action were witnessed by the audience in a medium shot. In that last case the departing player is seen closer to the camera in the second shot, to correspond with the shorter distance travelled in the first shot.

By seeing the player in motion, first close to the camera, then far away, and then close again, a dynamic visual rhythm is conferred on the fragmentation of the continuous motion.

304

FIGURE 16.4 The camera is panned in the second shot to follow a player who walks away from her stationary companion.

A further development when using a right angle coverage is to make the second shot a pan (Fig. 16.4).

First, (close shot) A in foreground turns and goes out of view, right. Cut to a full shot where A (centre) continues to walk to the right. The camera pans with her.

The effect obtained is similar to that outlined in Fig. 16.3, except that now the second shot is not the point of view of the excluded player, but an impersonal point of view that stresses the motion of the departing player. That is the subtle difference between the two similar modes of covering such a scene. The first one is emphatic, the other is less so. The film maker chooses the one most appropriate to the narrative needs of his scene.

FIGURE 16.5 The departing player's movement is divided into three shots.

The movement may sometimes be covered with several camera angles, especially for lengthy movements. Fig. 16.5 shows an example using three fragments.

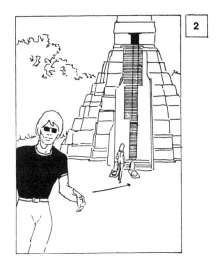

Shot 1 A in foreground turns and exits right.
Shot 2 Reverse. B in foreground. A in the centre background, moves away to the right. She does not exit from the screen in this shot.
Shot 3 Low close shot. A enters from the left and crosses our view, leaving by the right (or alternatively stops in the centre).
Two people face each other and are covered by two external

reverse camera sites. The dominant person (seen beyond the one in foreground) moves away from his companion. If that motion in the first shot is directed towards the camera, the continuation of the movement in the second shot will happen within the boundaries of the screen (Fig. 16.6).

The solution is similar to the one shown on page 297 Fig. 15.7 except that now the moving player does not re-enter the screen.

FIGURE 16.6 The moving player comes towards us in a neutral direction. As she approaches the stationary person we cut to a reverse shot behind her, where she moves away from the camera, passes the stationary player and continues on her path to the background. Due to the external reverse angle coverage employed, the positions of the players on the screen are transposed.

In the first shot the player starts to move; in the second she completes the motion passing the static player, and irregular case where they exchange screen areas. But if the departing performer moves to the background in the first shot, he moves out of view in the second. In practice, two master shots are edited in parallel, alternating between angles (Fig. 16.7).

Shot 1 Medium shot of A and B. They enter shot from the right and stop, facing each other. She has her back to us, and he dominates. He says: 'When shall I see you again?'

Shot 2 Reverse close shot of both. She replies: 'After vespers, in church.' She begins to turn away from us.

Shot 1 Medium shot. She ends her turning movement and walks towards us and out of shot, left.

Shot 2 From this reverse position we see her in the left sector of the screen walking away towards the background.

Shot 1 Close shot. He remains alone for an instant looking off screen left. Then he turns and crosses the screen exiting left.

The movement of the girl was recorded in the same half of the screen in both shots. A farewell scene treated visually as we have described, acquires a dynamic quality of motion on the screen due to the use of the same sector of the screen for all shots of movement and because of the repetitive editing pattern from intercut master shots. Juxtaposed close and medium shots add a contrast in distances.

Movement must flow smoothly into movement. A departure motion, though only a small part, may be integrated within the general design of movement to a sequence (Fig. (16.8).

Shot 1 B in foreground rings off, turns to the right. Camera pans with him, framing B, left, and A beyond. A is packing a suitcase. B speaks to her.

Shot 2 Medium shot of A. She raises her head at the beginning of the shot, reacting to B off-screen. She replies, and then closing the suitcase, takes it and exits view, right.

Shot 3 B in foreground, right. A enters from left and walks to the door, centre background. She opens it and exits.

Shot 4 Reverse. Close shot of B bending and picking up phone again, he dials a number, puts the receiver to his ear, waits for a moment and speaks.

FIGURE 16.7 Simple reverse camera coverage for a departing movement fragmented into several pieces using only two master shots obtained from the camera positions shown.

310

FIGURE 16.8 Departure integrated into a more complex pattern of movement that precedes and continues the central action shown here.

Numerous variants to shot 4 are possible. After she exits in shot 3, the next shot might show her walking down the corridor of the hotel, with the action of the story staying with her. If, instead, the story details what happens to player B, an incident that develops a relevant story point can be staged following shot 3. Movement flows into movement.

Note the curious way in which the camera was moved from the right to the left side of player A.

In the first shot at the conclusion of the panning movement he is seen framed on the left side of the screen, with his back to us. Shot 2, featuring player B, is an advance on a common visual axis. She is looking left, which ties this shot visually with the preceding one. Then she moves out of shot by the right. In shot 3, she enters left, and goes to the background. But now we are on the other side of player A, who is seen on the right side of the screen. And yet the action plays smoothly, because her dominant exit-entrance motion played on opposite sides of the screen, overrides the fact that player A has been shifted to a new area of the screen on the re-establishing shot 3. The dominant motion of player B made this smooth transition possible.

311

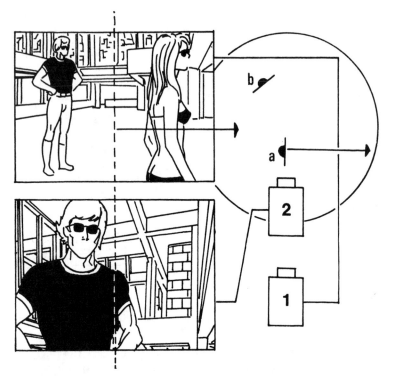

FIGURE 16.9 The moving player is excluded from the second shot, thus emphasizing the stationary one, who remains in shot seen from close by.

The method used in this example to visually move over to the other side of a performer, without seeming to violate the triangle principle for camera placement can be added to the collection of methods outlined in Chapter 9, employed to achieve the crossing of the line of interest or of motion.

If a performer moves out of shot, the next shot need not continue his movement. It might be more effective to cut to the facial reactions of the remaining static performer.

In Fig. 16.9, as soon as A leaves the screen in shot 1, cut to a close shot of B on the same visual axis. If applied to the departure of a vehicle passing out of the full shot, cut to a close shot of the hero who was previously seen in the background.

This mode emphasizes the player who remains on the screen, making him the key figure. Cutting to a close shot of him stresses any movement he might then make.

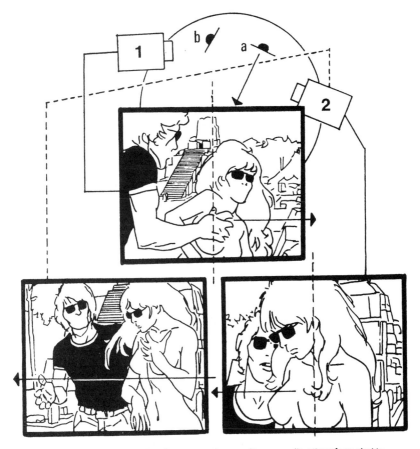

FIGURE 16.10 The departing player moves in opposite screen directions from shot to another. A external reverse camera coverage is used here.

A reversal of the shot order is not as emphatic. For instance, we cut from the Close Shot of the static player, back on the same visual axis to the player that starts to move and goes out of the screen by a side, leaving the lone static performer a small figure in the scene. In this way both players are de-emphasized: the going away player because she is so little time on screen on the last shot, and the static one because he is framed far away from our position.

Contrasting directions of continuous retreating movement are possible with two external reverse camera sites that cover motion across the screen (Fig. 16.10).

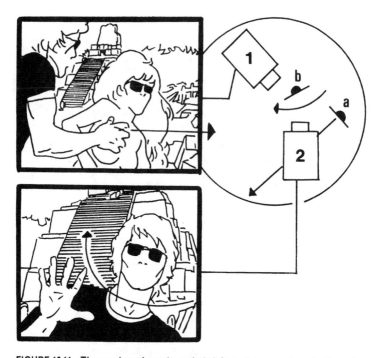

FIGURE 16.11 The moving player is excluded from the second shot. The stationary player turning his head in the second shot suggests the direction of movement of the player who is now out of camera range.

First, a close shot of both performers; A exits the screen, right. Cut to reverse shot 2, also a close shot. Two approaches are possible. In one, A is in the centre of the screen hiding player B with her body. A moves from centre to left and exits.

Alternatively, A enters the foreground from the right, with her back to us, and crosses between B and the camera, exiting left. B turns his head right to left.

With external and internal reverse camera positions, the subject's departure is not shown but only suggested by the turning head of the other performer (Fig. 16.11).

When A exits the first shot, cut to the second where B follows the implied movement of A.

A screen exit from one side to the centre is also possible (Fig. 16.12).

314

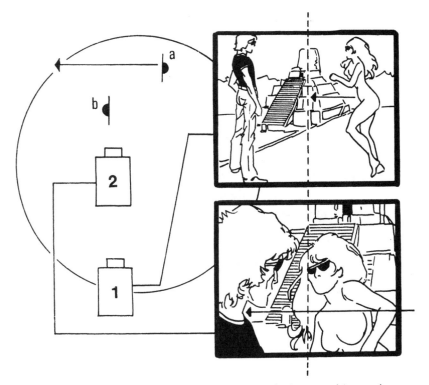

FIGURE 16.12 Two camera sites on a common visual axis are used to record a person who passes behind the stationary player as she leaves.

Shot 1   B and A are talking. A decides to leave and walks to the left, reaching the centre of the screen. Cut to . . .

Shot 2   Close shot of B (an advance on the visual axis of the preceding shot). A enters from right and crosses behind B and exits left.

In the first shot A's short movement to the left covers half the screen width very quickly. In the second she crosses the whole picture width behind the static player who dominates the scene from his central position.

A variation of the above is to frame both players in separate shots. Starting with an establishing shot showing them together, move to single shots of each, edited in parallel. One player then moves away. Fig. 16.13 shows this simple variation.

FIGURE 16.13 The stationary person is excluded from the first shot. The moving player passes behind him in the second.

Shot 1   Close shot. A moves out of shot centre to left.
Shot 2   Close shot of B. Behind him, and out of focus, A crosses right to left.

This is a very usual way of relating such individual shots without reverting to an earlier establishing shot which would also create a digression for the audience by emphasizing the wrong player. By showing A moving in the background out of focus of the second shot her role is de-emphasized without loss of sense.

Departure can be presented in such a manner that it discloses the remaining subject at the beginning of the second shot, giving us a frontal view of this player (Fig. 16.14).

The camera sites are at right angles to one another. In the first shot, player A turns to move away. In the second, with the camera behind her, she finishes turning as she leaves the shot—disclosing the static player in front view. By this simple dynamic visual presentation, attention is thrown on to the other player. In the example shown, A turns away from us, but the same principle applies if she turns towards the camera to leave (Fig. 16.15).

In Fig. 16.14 the departure is from the same screen sector in both shots, whereas in Fig. 16.15 it is from centre to sides of opposing halves of the screen. The stationary player remains in the centre.

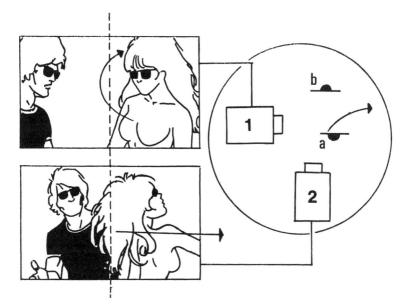

FIGURE 16.14   Right angle coverage of a departing player. In the first shot the person starts to move away from the camera. In the second shot as she completes the movement she discloses a frontal view of the stationary player.

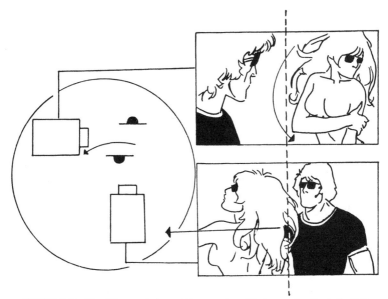

FIGURE 16.15   The difference between this example and that preceding lies in the fact that in this case the departing player begins her movement towards the camera in the first shot instead of away from it.

317

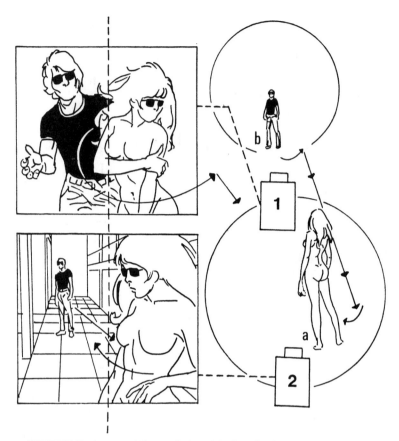

FIGURE 16.16 A pause at the conclusion of the first shot (remaining with the stationary player) serves to shorten the repetitive motion on a lengthy path.

A departure involving much movement need not show more than the two extremes of the movement—a reversion to the time shortening principle explained elsewhere. Fig. 16.16 shows the present set up.

Shot 1 Close shot. A and B talk, then A turns and approaches us exiting right. The camera stays on B for a moment as he continues to speak, then cuts to . . .

Shot 2 Full shot. A in foreground walks towards the camera, stops and turns to face B in the background.

Once more, this action is in the same half of the picture area and on the same visual axis. The difference in procedure lies in the fact

318

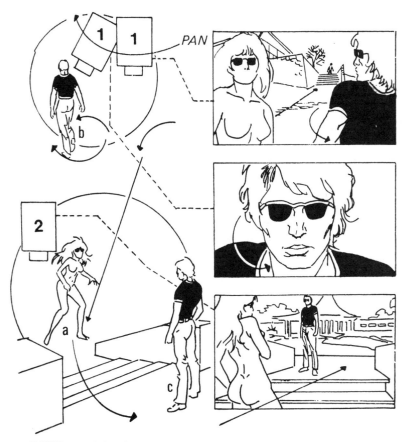

FIGURE 16.17 A diverting movement is introduced at the conclusion of the first shot to omit the long movement of the player towards the other in the background.

that when A *goes to* B the pause is at the beginning of the second shot, but when A *goes away from* B the pause is made at the end of the first.

A similar solution is made possible by supplementing the pause with a visual distraction. Such a problem arises when the departing player moves directly to the background where his destination can be seen. The distraction is aimed at making us lose interest momentarily in the moving subject and his destination and concentrate on the character who remains in foreground (Fig. 16.17).

Shot 1   A and B talk in the foreground. C, seen in long shot at the top of a short flight of stairs, waits in the background. Then A starts to walk away from us towards C. B, in the foreground, moves to the right and the camera pans with him, excluding the others. The camera stays on B momentarily for a reaction or for him to speak and advance the story.

Shot 2   Medium shot of C. A enters from left reaching the top of the stairs and turns to look with C off-screen right to B.

Here the combined movement of camera and foreground player is visually distracting. A camera movement alone could have been used by tilting to a detail in the foreground visually indicated by the remaining player. The camera movement, although safer, can be avoided if the foreground player walks towards the camera, thus blocking our view of the background, and forcing us into a close shot of his face.

Instead of a pause, a cut-away may be inserted to shorten the distance between departure and arrival.

This cut-away must be related to the main action of the story. Fig. 16.18 illustrates an example of this type taken from a well known film.

FIGURE 16.18   An example taken from Alfred Hitchcock's film *North by Northwest*, where a cutway is used to shorten the path that must be traversed by the moving player.

Shot 1   Cary Grant comes out of the corn plantation and starts to run to the highway in the background, where a truck is approaching at full speed.

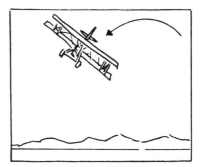

Shot 2 Long shot. A biplane turns towards us and begins to fly straight towards the camera.

Shot 3 Full shot. The camera in the centre of the highway. Cary Grant enters right with his back to us and stops in foreground, waving his arms to stop the truck driver.

The scene will be found in Alfred Hitchcock's film *North by Northwest*, and belongs to the now famous sequence in which a plane chases Gary Grant in broad daylight through plain open country.

The cut-away in the example given is relevant to the story, since it informs the audience of the whereabouts and intentions of the pilot in the biplane. This cut-away is used to shorten the length of ground travelled by Cary Grant from the corn plantation to the highway, and concentrates on the important points of the action.

17

PLAYERS MOVE TOGETHER

We have analysed screen movement where one performer, the dominant one, enters and exits. But both players may move at the same time and, in that event, three types of movement are available to them:
1 both move in the same direction
2 they move towards each other
3 they move apart.
Each one of these approaches will be examined separately and several examples within each variant will be offered.

Case 1

When both players walk in the same direction, i.e. one behind the other, a dynamic presentation can be obtained by editing the pair of external reverse shots as described below, and in Fig. 17.1.

Shot 1 Full shot. B moves from the centre of the screen to the right and exits. Cut to . . .

Shot 2 Reverse full shot. A enters shot from the left and moves away behind B.

In shot 1, A moves from left to centre and B from centre to right. In shot 2 both execute similar movements in the same areas of the screen. But in shot 1 performer B exits the screen, whereas in shot 2, A enters from the opposite side. B, in the second shot, is already in the centre of the screen moving away into the background.

Case 2

If three people are moving in a single line, a somewhat similar solution is available (Fig. 17.2).

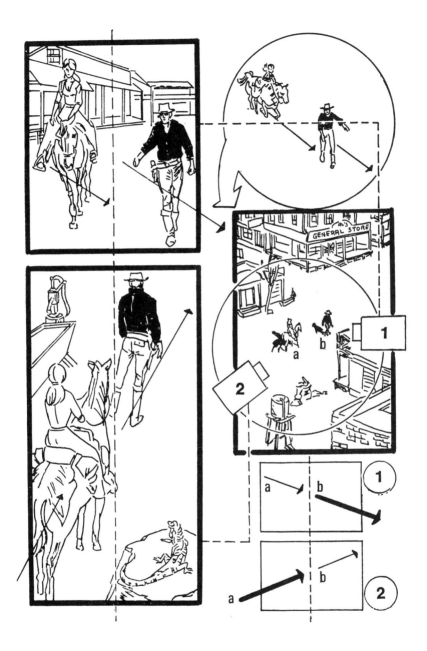

FIGURE 17.1 Movement through halves of the screen area for each player in each shot.

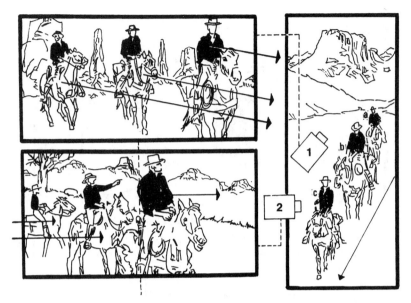

FIGURE 17.2 Movement that begins in the centre of the screen for the second is employed here to unite the shots visually.

There is an almost right angle relationship between the two camera sites employed for this dynamic cut approach. The principle at work is the same.

Shot 1   A, B and C move diagonally and in single file out of the shot, right. As the last leaves, cut to . . .

Shot 2   C in the centre of the screen, moving to the right. He stops; B and A enter from left and stop.

As can be seen, the entrance of C into shot was omitted. By allowing him to move from the centre outwards, a more dynamic effect is achieved.

Case 3

A right angle coverage is also possible as shown in Fig. 17.3.

In the first shot four persons are standing, profiled to the camera, watching something off-screen left and then begin to move to the left. A exits screen, B (centre) moves to left screen edge; C and D reach the centre. Cut to the second shot, at right angles. A and B are already in shot, right, and walk away to the burning plane in the background followed by others who enter shot from the right.

FIGURE 17.3 A right angle camera coverage for the departure of several players, moving one behind the other.

Screen areas repetition for C and D is obtained, while A and B move in one half of the screen first, and in the other in the next shot.

Case 4

Two players approaching each other suggest a right angle camera coverage (Fig. 17.4).

In the first shot both players, moving in a neutral direction, walk towards each other. Cut to shot 2, where both enter shot from their own sides and stop near the centre.

Case 5

Cameras placed on a common visual axis will also record this converging motion well (Fig. 17.5).

The first shot is divided in three vertical compositional segments. Both performers are placed at the extremes, and are allowed to move up to the inner boundaries of the segments. Then we cut to a close shot, advancing on a common visual axis, where each player is seen from his own sides, and coming to a stop.

325

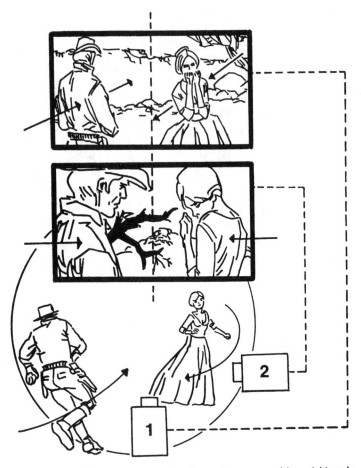

FIGURE 17.4 The converging movement of two players covered by a right angle camera arrangement.

It is perhaps unnecessary to point out that both players should move at approximately the same speed, so that their motion on the screen would allow them to arrive on cue to their allotted screen areas. If one performer moves more slowly than the other, he or she would have to delay his or her entrance into the screen in the second shot. The visual presentation would be weaker.

Yet it is possible to cheat, if such a discrepancy is present in the first shot, by making both enter the second shot at the same time.

FIGURE 17.5 Converging players seen from two camera positions on a common visual axis.

Case 6

The players might approach one another at right angles, as in Fig. 17.6.

The editing procedure would be similar to those in the preceding case.

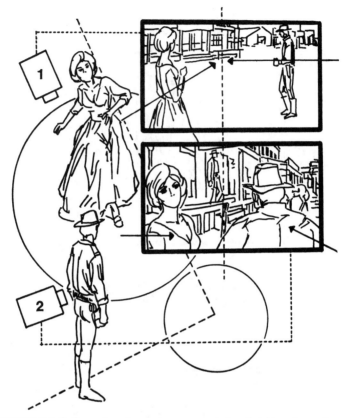

FIGURE 17.6 Both moving players converge on paths at right angles and are covered by a right angle camera arrangement.

Here the right angle camera deployment coincides with the right angle movement of the players themselves. Neutral and transverse motions are attenuated in half-areas of the screen from shot to shot.

Case 7

This meeting of two performers whose movements converge on a central point, can be extended to two groups. In editing, one could alternate between movements or present them in the same shot. For example: an Indian chieftain and a cavalry commander agree to meet in neutral ground to talk over their differences. Both come with armed escorts who remain up in the hills as the chiefs descend

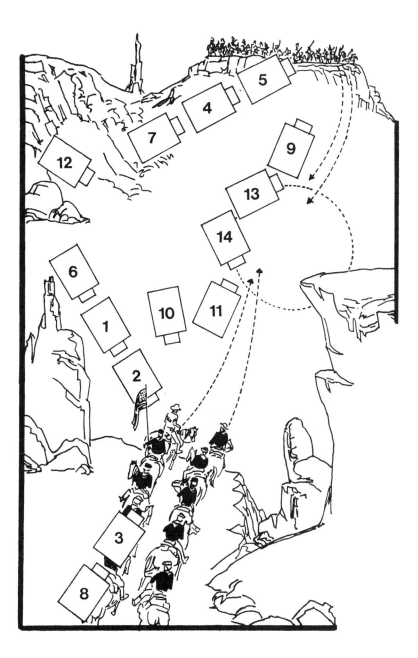

FIGURE 17.7 The movements of characters who converge on a central point can be extended to two groups.

to their meeting point in the valley. Here is how the sequence is developed.

Shot 1   Low full shot. The group of cavalry men appear over the rim of the hill and stop. They moved from right to left. As they stop cut to . . .

Shot 2   Low close shot of three cavalry men. An officer, an Indian scout and the commanding officer. They look and wait.

Shot 3   Reverse full shot. From behind the group of mounted soldiers we see the other hill. Faint sounds of hooves are heard.

Shot 4   Low full shot. Indians appear on the ridge of their hill and stop. (They moved from left to right).

Shot 2 Close shot of three cavalry men. The commanding officer waves his arm.

Shot 5 Low close shot of three Indians. The centre one is the chieftain.

Shot 2 Low close shot of the three cavalry men. They wait.

Shot 5 Low close shot of the three Indians. The chief raises his arm and then lowers it.

Shot 2 Low close shot of three cavalry men. The Indian scout and the commanding officer move to the left and go out of shot. They begin to descend.

Shot 6 Full shot. Both cavalry men (the Indian Scout and the commanding officer) descend to the left and go out of shot. The other soldiers wait at the top of the hill.

Shot 5 Low close shot of the three Indians. The chief and his son move right and descend out of shot on that side.

Shot 7   Full shot. Both Indians descend left to right and pass
out of shot right. They ride slowly. The other Indians
spread out along the top of their hill.

Shot 8   Full shot. Several soldiers on horseback in foreground.
Beyond, in the valley, the two cavalry men and the two
Indians ride down toward each other. On the hill be-
yond, the row of Indians watch.

Shot 9   Full shot. On the same visual axis as the preceding shot
with the row of Indians on top of the hill. The Indian
chief and his son ride towards us, descending the slope
and passing out of shot below.

Shot 10 Medium shot. The Indian scout and commanding officer enter shot, right, cross the view diagonally descending to the left and out of shot.

Shot 11 Reverse full shot. Both pairs of riders move towards each other.

Shot 12 Full shot (side). The two Indians enter left and two cavalry men from the right, converging at the centre of the screen.

Shot 13 Close shot of the Indian chief. His face dignified but inscrutable. He waits in silence.

Shot 14 Close shot of the commanding officer. He is the first to speak.

Shot 13 Close shot of the Indian chief. He replies.

Shot 14 Close shot of the commanding officer. He speaks again.

The whole sequence has a slow rhythm that confers a measure of tension to the total event. There is mistrust in both groups, and they approach each other cautiously. The construction of the sequence, from a story viewpoint, is simple and explicit:

The soldiers and Indians arrive and the agreed signal is exchanged. Both leaders descend to the valley to talk.

The filmic language applied to the scene is simple too:

The first group (the soldiers) is identified. Then the whole locale is established. The second group (the Indians) arrive. The ritual of exchanging signals is performed. It is covered in single shots of each group.

A delay is created when the Indians take their time in answering back.

When both parties descend, they are first shown individually with two shots for each group, widening the view on the second shots to include the terrain in which they move. Now a re-establishing shot is introduced. Both groups are seen in that shot.

Afterwards, attention is centered on the two chiefs and their companions slowly riding to the bottom of the valley. From now on their respective armed escorts are excluded from the sequence.

Two full shots show us how they stop, facing each other. The faces of the two leaders are now seen in close shot. These two people dominate the sequence from now on. When both parties later return to their armed escorts, their movements will be more vivid.

With the conference over, there is no need to return so slowly. It would be an anticlimax if they did.

Case 8

For the third possibility, mentioned at the beginning of the chapter, where two players move away from each other we have only to use in reverse the formulas described for the players who walk towards each other. A visual emphasis will suffice to give the idea, as shown in Fig. 17.8.

Duellists, back to back, and seen in close view in the first shot. They receive the order from off screen and start to move away from each other. As soon as both leave the screen, we cut to a second shot where we see them walking and widening the distance between them. Finally they stop.

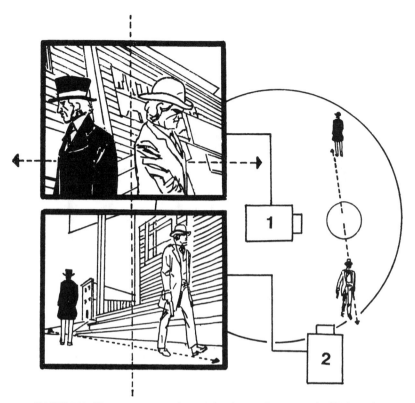

FIGURE 17.8 Players move away from each other on divergent paths. Right angle camera coverage registers the movement.

Case 9

A group of players moving away from each other may sometimes serve to disclose a goal hidden by their presence—a motion similar effect to where theatre curtains part to reveal the stage. The following case makes use of this effect:

In a sumptuous hall of a large palace, the nobles are gathered to dance. Suddenly a lackey enters and in a pompous voice loudly announces: His Highness, Prince Charles!

The music fades and the dancers break up and begin to clear a path to reveal the lords at the end of the hall. The Prince advances through the crowd, towards the owners of the castle. Here we are only interested in showing that parting movement of the crowd.

337

Shot 1 Long shot. The people in the first rows of the crowd begin to move to the sides of the screen and exit view at either side.

Shot 2 Full shot. Closer to the crowd. Those in the foreground move out of view at either side.

Shot 3 Medium shot. The last few people move away out of shot disclosing the three owners of the castle.

Each shot lasts about two to three seconds. All shots have a common visual axis, and we progress into the crowd with the introduction of each new shot. The courtesans move from near the centre to the sides. The movement is identical in all the shots.

FIGURE 17.9 A parting curtain effect that reveals the stationary players at the back of the group.

Intermittent motion

Looking back on our examination of horizontal movement in and out of shots, we realize that we have covered only continuous movement of one or two performers. But intermittent motion, i.e. where the performers move in turn, is very common in films. It happens in most dialogue scenes where players shift position. This will be examined later when we discuss shots edited within the film frame and the construction of sequences.

18

SOLVING DIFFICULT EDITING SITUATIONS

Two difficulties in editing film shots concern those extremes for which there is often some dramatic need—namely the total lack, or, over-abundance, of movement. This chapter presents a selection of approaches to cover such difficult situations clearly yet interestingly.

Movement between camera and static subject

Case 1

Let us first examine a case of lack of movement in the central performer of the scene.

Our player is seated at a lone table in a night club. Empty tables around him emphasize his loneliness as we see him in a long shot of the room. Now we wish to cut to a medium shot of him, so that the audience can identify the player and see the expression on his face: tired, disenchanted, eyes lowered, fixed on an empty glass.

The man does not move. It is not necessary. In fact it would be a dramatic error to give the performer any type of motion. But how do we cut from a static long shot to a static medium shot yet avoid a visual jump on the screen? One way is to introduce a distracting movement performed by a passer-by and cut using this movement (Fig. 18.1).

Shot 1　Long shot of A. After a moment a passer-by enters from one side and walks across the screen. When her figure, in the centre of the screen, hides A completely, cut to . . .

Shot 2　The camera's view completely blocked by the body of the passer-by who continues moving to disclose A in

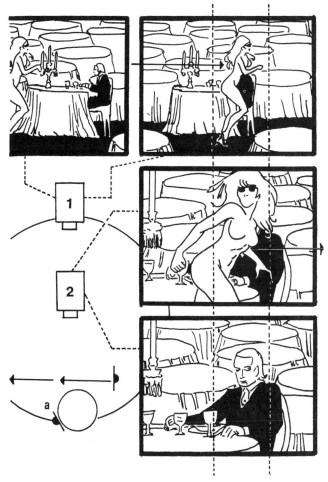

FIGURE 18.1 A smooth cut is obtained by hiding the stationary player in the centre of the screen and cutting on the movement of the passing player across the screen.

medium shot. The passer-by exits. This shot is on the same visual axis as before.

What matters is that a smooth passage from shot to shot be obtained.

It is not necessary for the passing figure to fill the screen completely, either in the first or second shot. But he should hide completely, or almost completely, the person to be shown in closer view.

341

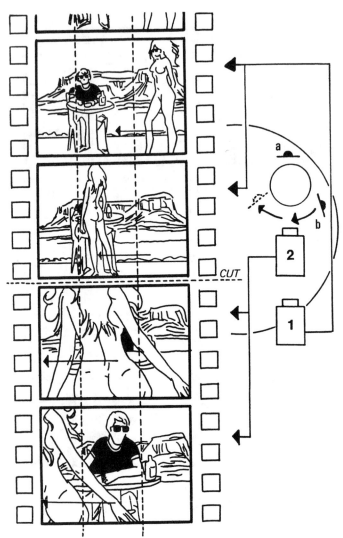

FIGURE 18.2 The player who produces a hiding effect by moving across the frame need not leave the shot in either of the two shots into which the movement is divided.

Case 2

The person who is used on the screen to facilitate a smooth cut might already be on the screen, say, also in a static position. He has only to cross our view to effect the above result (Fig. 18.2).

Shot 1 A seen in medium shot seated at the table. In fore-

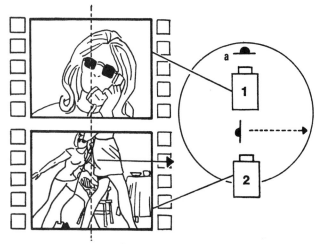

FIGURE 18.3 A player moving from centre to side of the screen can unite the shot with a previous one without movement. The stationary player is seen beyond the moving person in the second shot.

ground, right, B stands talking to him. Moments later B moves to the left. As soon as she hides A in the centre of the screen, cut to . . .

Shot 2 B, in the centre of the screen, discloses A and stops moving. A is now in close shot.

Motion at the beginning of the second shot

Case 3

The above situation can be reversed so that we move back from a close shot of the static performer (Fig. 18.3).

Shot 1 Close shot of A. She is sitting still, talking on the phone. Cut to . . .

Shot 2 Full shot. A person in the centre of the screen moves to one side disclosing A in the background.

In the first shot there was no movement at all. But motion is sharply introduced at the beginning of the second shot. Background movement can be introduced behind the static player and continue during the second shot. It would not interfere with the cut because movement which is closer to the camera is sharper and dominant.

For this key movement, any natural character that can be part

343

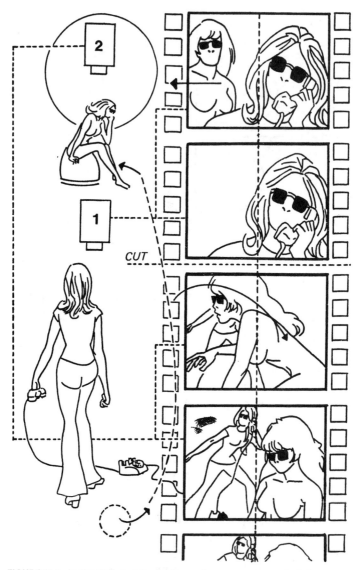

FIGURE 18.4 In the first shot the background woman moves out of view. In the second shot the moving woman, blocking our view, sits down and reveals the woman on the phone behind her. The seated woman is seen in profile. The movement of this woman affords smooth continuity and reestablishes the scene.

of the scene would be suitable—a waiter, for example, if the scene takes place in a restaurant.

Case 4

Instead of an incidental person, an important player can be used. He might be someone who is reintroduced to the audience, while at the same time his movement helps to smooth the cut which repositions the static player (Fig. 18.4).

In the first shot a girl is on the phone, standing. Another woman close to her pauses for a moment and then moves away out of shot, left. After a while we cut to the second shot where our view is blocked by the second woman, who is sitting down near the camera. As she sits she reveals the first woman, still speaking. The shot now frames the second woman close by and in the foreground, profiled with the first woman seen in the background in full shot, on the other side of the screen. Thus, both purposes were neatly accomplished: the second character was reintroduced into the scene and was visually related to her friend whose new position on the film frame is clarified for the audience.

Motion beyond the static players

Case 5

In the examples examined, the movement was between the camera and our main subject, and the emphasis was placed on the static performer. But if this player is in motion, and moves behind the

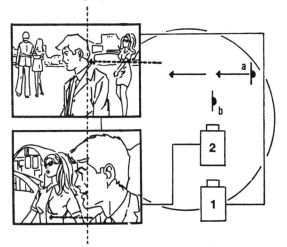

FIGURE 18.5 When the moving player is hidden behind the stationary subject in the first shot, the cut is made to the second shot where the moving player emerges from behind the other.

static subject, it is he who becomes important while the other acquires a subordinate role (Fig. 18.5).

Shot 1   Medium shot. B stands in the centre. A enters from right moving left. As she passes behind B, and is hidden by him, cut to . . .

Shot 2   Close shot of B on the right. From behind him appears A who moves to the left and stops in that area of the film frame.

There can be several static persons in the first take, but only one is in motion: A. B must be on the centre of the screen in the first take to get an effective cut from shot to shot.

Case 6

A panning shot and a static one can be related using this technique of blocking the character or vehicle in motion as it passes behind a static subject (Fig. 18.6).

In the first shot a person stands in the road at left waving his hands at an approaching car. The car crosses the screen right to left in long shot. When the car begins to pass behind the static person (both framed now in the centre of the screen) we cut to the second shot at right angles to the preceding camera position, and frame a medium shot of the static player with his back to us. From behind him emerges the car crossing the screen and exiting left. The static player turns to us to watch the receding car (off screen) with a disappointed expression on his face. This second shot is a fixed camera set-up. (This example belongs to Alfred Hitchcock's film *North by Northwest* and happens in the sequence where a biplane chases Cary Grant on a lonely country road.) The other noticeable variation made on this example was the introduction of a right angle relationship for both camera sites, instead of an advance on a common visual axis as happened in all the previous examples. The movement recorded in the first shot lasts longer than that in the second where the subject moves out of shot quickly due to its increase in size, thus creating a dynamic visual emphasis for the motion itself.

Using right angle camera sites

Case 7

Where two static players are featured separately, one in each shot

346

(at right angles), they can be linked by the movement of a subordinate subject (Fig. 18.7).

In the first shot of A, a waiter in the foreground stands for a moment with his back to us, then turns and exits left. Cut. In the second shot, at right angles, the waiter (centre) moves out of shot left, revealing B. Thus we dispose of the establishing shot where both main players (A and B) would be shown together, giving the audience their true physical positions on the set.

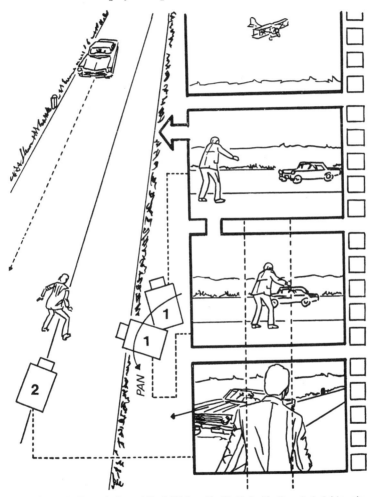

FIGURE 18.6 Example from Alfred Hitchcock's *North by Northwest*. A right angle camera set up is used for a cut where the moving subject (the car) passes behind the static subject in the foreground.

By resorting instead to the formula just described, the introduction of player B is more dramatic and clear for the audience due to the movement of the subordinate subject, the waiter, whose relation to the first player (A) had already been established for the

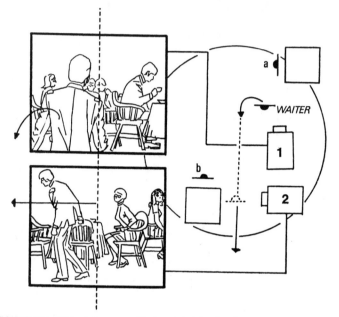

FIGURE 18.7 Two stationary subjects related by the departure of a secondary person. A right angle camera arrangement is used.

audience in shot 1. Also with this method both main players may have their individual centres of interest (food they are eating, for instance) without the need for opposed glances to relate them from shot to shot. Such a requirement may, in fact, work against the good of the scene.

Both players move

Case 8

Both players might be in motion, crossing each other. The same formula can be applied. (Fig. 18.8.).

In the first shot, a full shot, A walks obliquely from left to centre, while B moves across from right to centre. As they cross, and B is hidden by A, we cut. Medium or close shot of the players (same

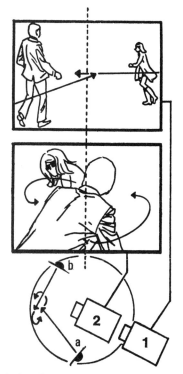

FIGURE 18.8 When both performers cross in the centre of the screen, the cut can be made on this crossing using two camera sites on a common axis.

visual axis). B emerges from behind A and, finally, the players stop at the sides of the screen.

Hiding a moving subject in the first shot

Case 9

If a subject is moving in a neutral direction in the centre of the screen, we can rarely cut directly to a closer shot on the same visual axis. As a figure recedes it also diminishes in size. A forward cut would increase its size suddenly, and then it would decrease again. Naturally the effect is visually jarring. It is not the same with a cross-screen motion, because there the subject remains the same size. So, for an advance on the same axis towards a subject moving in neutral direction, a distraction must be introduced (Fig. 18.9).

349

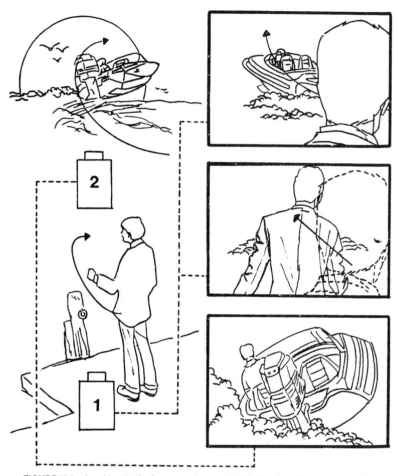

FIGURE 18.9 A subject in the foreground moves to hide the departing person in the centre of the screen. As soon as this main performer is hidden we may cut forward to a closer shot of him, obtaining a smooth cut.

Shot 1 A man, his back to us, is seen on the right side of the screen looking towards a lake. A motorboat appears right, turns, and moves away from us in the centre of the screen. The man moves forward, blocks our view of the boat. Cut to . . .

Shot 2 Close shot of the boat (same axis). The boat moves away.

A simple solution where movement in a neutral direction is hidden by a distracting stronger movement for a smooth cut.

Using a strong foreground motion

Case 10

Abundance of movement is the other extreme that presents difficulties for a precisely matched cut when two shots are on the same visual axis. This motion, usually found in crowd scenes, is of a conflicting nature. Several movements with opposed directions are present in disorganized crowds. One or two central performers moving or standing against such a busy background, could be difficult to edit without some very noticeable visual jumps.

The principle of using a distracting movement on which the cut is to be made, is also applied to solve this multiple motion problem.

Case 11

A right angle camera change can use the same technique of employing two different persons to momentarily mask the player to be emphasized by a cut with a busy background (Fig. 18.10).

A stands alone in the centre of a crowd. For the cut a person enters the foreground and obscures him. A second person in the foreground (and approximately same scale) moves in the same direction and we see A not only closer but in side view.

Case 12

Two crowd shots can be filmed on the same visual axis with this type of solution. First we have a medium shot of several couples girating on the dance floor. To move back to a position where the dance hall is seen in full, if two characters cross the foreground the momentary distraction is so strong that mismatches in the background will go unnoticed.

Substitution of the static subject

Case 13

Movement of a player who hides our centre of interest previous to a shot change on the screen, can also be used for time transition. David Lean in his film *Doctor Zhivago* employed the device in a

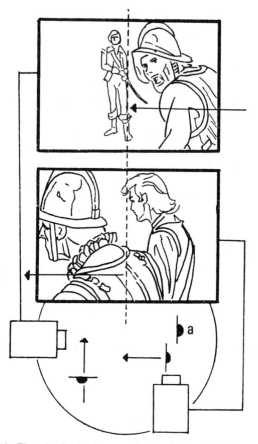

FIGURE 18.10 The subordinate players moving in a right angle relative to each other provide a smooth cut from shot to shot on a main stationary subject who stands beyond the others.

sequence where Yevgraf (Alec Guinness) visits his half-brother Zhivago (Omar Sharif). Yevgraf finds Zhivago tearing down a fence to obtain wood for his stove. Later in Zhivago's room he meets his family and they talk. This scene is narrated on the sound track by Yevgraf. Almost in the centre of this sequence the effect that interests us takes place.

Zhivago stands in medium shot, against a bare wall. Yevgraf enters, right, and crosses to the centre hiding Zhivago. There is a cut to the second shot, on the same visual axis, with a foreground figure moving away to disclose Yevgraf in close shot standing still against the wall. The effect is startling. This 'reversal of roles' suggests a change in time as well (Fig. 18.11).

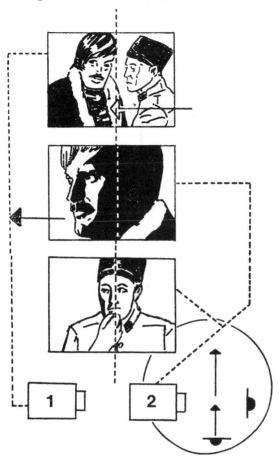

FIGURE 18.11 The players' positions are transposed, the moving person is rendered static and vice versa to obtain a transition in time using a cut on the centre of the screen which hides the stationary subject.

Redirecting attention

Case 14

When cutting back from a close shot to a long shot of a person moving in a neutral direction, the problem of size is very acute in the second shot, because the distance involved minimizes and

353

weakens movement. So a dominant action should be introduced at the beginning of the second shot. One approach might be as shown in Fig. 18.12.

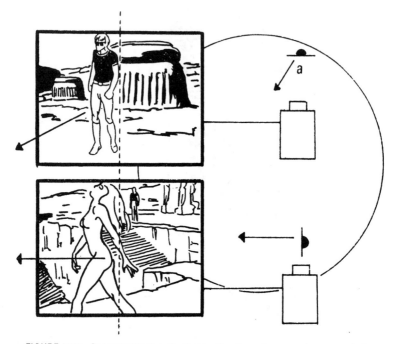

FIGURE 18.12 Our attention is redirected by the strong foreground movement of a second player at the beginning of the second shot. The main player in the background comes forward.

A comes forward and exits left. In the second shot a secondary figure moves from centre to exit left, revealing the small figure of A approaching from the background. Alternatively, the subordinate character enters view from the side by which A left (Fig. 18.13).

The movement of this subordinate subject redirects the audience's attention towards the central performer. Her entrance close to the camera is a strong one and the direction of her motion will be followed by the audience.

As A again becomes the centre of our attention, the passer-by loses herself in the scene by stopping in front of a window or going into a store or disappearing through a side street.

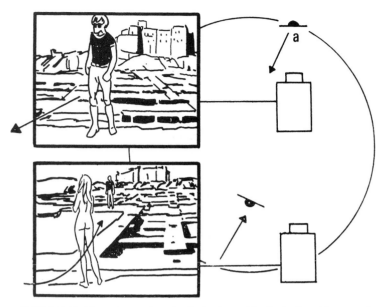

FIGURE 18.13 The entrance of a subordinate player at the beginning of the second shot redirects our attention towards the diminutive main character in the background.

Case 15

A similar solution is applied when dealing with a crowd placed behind and to the sides of the moving main subjects (Fig. 18.14).

In the first shot A and B walk to us from a moving crowd beyond and occasionally in front of them, too. A and B approach head-on and exit left. We cut (same visual axis) to where an onlooker, C, enters, right, crosses diagonally and stops at the left, together with other members of the crowd. From the central background come A and B. C, crossing close to the camera, helped to disguise all the mismatches in the background crowd. When A and B pass C and reach the foreground, they might stop or perhaps the camera may begin to track back with them depending how the scene is to continue.

Case 16

A variation is where the scene is totally blocked at the beginning of the second shot (Fig. 18.15).

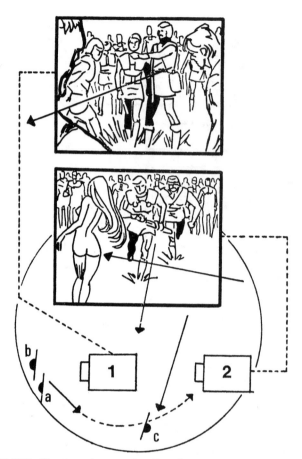

FIGURE 18.14 The strong foreground motion of a subordinate subject (C) at the beginning of the second shot is used to minimize the mismatches that a crowd scene creates from shot to shot.

Shot 1 A and C face us. A is talking. He advances and exits left.

Shot 2 (Same visual axis) B in foreground, back to the camera, blocking our view. He moves away to the left and stops, revealing A advancing toward the camera. He stops to talk to B. C remains in the background.

The screen was blocked at the beginning of the second shot, because when player B crosses in front of C, the cut comes before he leaves the screen completely. That crossing motion takes place in the left hand sector, and to match it properly should be con-

356

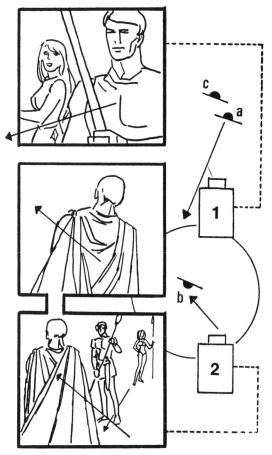

FIGURE 18.15 A player who blocks the camera lens at the beginning of the second shot is used to provide a strong motion that hides any mismatches in the motion of the second player (A) as he comes forward, seen on the same visual axis as in the preceding shot.

cluded in that area in the second shot. Instead, they are seen on the right, hence the foreground distraction.

Using non-human movement

Case 17

The lens of the camera need not be blocked by a player. Such natural phenomena as water, sand, dust or smoke can serve the

FIGURE 18.16 The vigorous movement of the group of players in the foreground towards the sides revealing the scene beyond, serves to mask many incomplete movements of the player disclosed. In this case the fall from the horse was suggested in the first shot and not shown in the second, where it was substituted by the strong movement in the foreground. When the main player is revealed he feigns the final part of the fall without actually carrying it out, because it could be dangerous.

358

same purpose. They fall or pass between the camera and the player and reveal a closer shot of the emphasized player when they cease or thin out. A flash of light flaring in the camera lens can be used to obtain a similar effect. The next shot would also begin with a flash of light and then regain normal exposure, revealing a closer shot of a character, or a new angle on him or a different player. The shots would be cut on the flash. Franklin Schaffner used a shadow crossing the screen to obtain the same effect in his film *Papillon*.

Parting curtain effect

Case 18

Sometimes a player's movements must be faked to avoid a dangerous stunt. This rules out the possibility of cutting on the action of the main player. A distraction must be introduced at the beginning of the second shot to hide the omitted full action. This distraction is a motion that begins in the centre of the screen and parts to the sides like curtains. In Fig. 18.16 the two extremes of a dangerous motion, falling off a horse, are faked.

In the first shot the central player simulates the beginning of a fall from the horse. In fact he only bends down. In the second shot the crowd in the foreground, with their backs to the camera, part to reveal the player slumping to the ground with exhaustion. The crowd momentarily obscured the supposed fall. This can be done with vehicles or other objects relevant to the scene.

19

OTHER TYPES OF MOTION

Although straight line action is by far the most usual, circular and vertical motion, passing out of and entering view are the further variants that make screen action more vigorous and interesting. Again a number of cases are given here.

Circular movement

Case 1

With circular movement, the performer's action must be visually clear to avoid conflicting sense of direction (Fig. 19.1).

Shot 1   High shot. A enters the background from the left, running in an arc toward the right and then left, close to the camera. Exit lower left side.

Shot 2   Reverse. A enters at the lower right corner and runs in an arc to the left, turns right and exits.

Shot 3   A enters left and stops in the centre.

The circular movement is tangential to the two first camera positions, placed outside the periphery of the circle. The third camera position is located inside the circle. Change of screen direction by reason of the circular path of A is clearly visible in the first two shots.

If the third camera position is placed outside the circular path travelled by the running player, the motion depicted in Shot 1 would be repeated.

The use of the two first shots can be applied to record a person turning round a street corner. Even if high camera angles, eye level, or low angles are used to record this motion, recording it by using halves of the screen remains unchanged to convey the circular path.

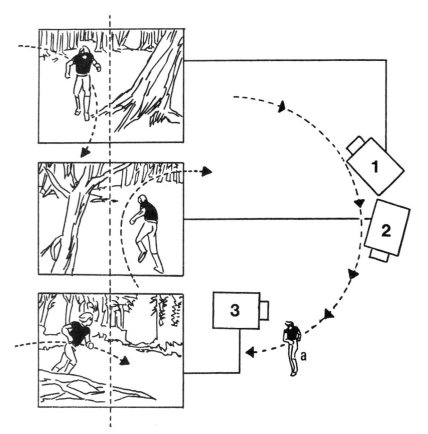

FIGURE 19.1 A player's circular movement is covered using half screen sections of motion. The two first camera sites are tangential to the circular path of the player, while the third is inside the circle itself.

Since the approach described for the first two shots involves a pair of back to back reverse camera positions, the device can be used to link two different locations by a motion that becomes continuous on the screen. It suffices to have the same actor present on both locations, carrying out the movement.

Case 2

Coverage from inside the circular path is also possible. The camera positions may be back to back (Fig. 19.2).

In the first shot A exits right, and in the second enters left. He stops there facing B who waits for him. In the first shot A looks

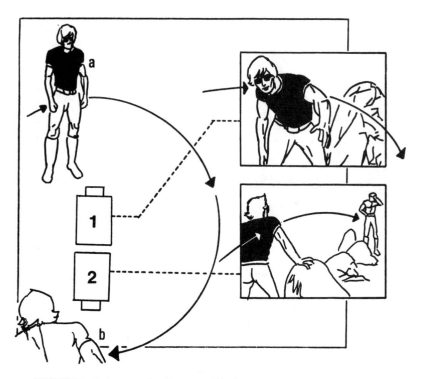

FIGURE 19.2 Both camera locations are within the circular figure formed by the path traversed by the player in motion.

off screen left while going out by the right, thus stressing the circular nature of his path.

Case 3

If one camera position is outside the circular path and the other inside, the respective position of the players on the screen will be reversed from shot to shot (Fig. 19.3).

B holding A by her hand pulls her to him. This forces her to accomplish a circular movement pivoting on B's right arm. She exits screen left, in the first shot and re-enters right in the reverse shot. The movement of A is recorded on opposite sides of the screen, but always moving in the same direction.

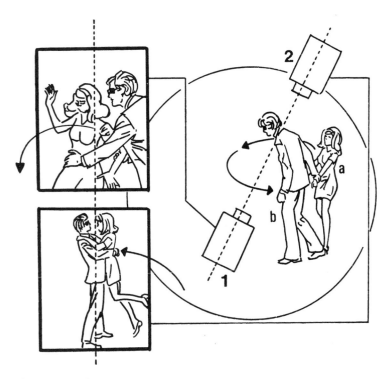

FIGURE 19.3 The players are transposed on the screen in this exterior reverse camera angle on a circular motion.

Case 4

A circular movement covered by tangential external reverse camera positions, featuring two performers, transposes their positions. Only one of the players moves, and both have the same centre of interest in the middle of the screen. This is implied in one of the shots and visible in the other (Fig. 19.4).

Shot 1   Medium shot. A, in foreground moves in a half-circular path towards the window where B is looking out. As he nears his companion, cut to . . .

Shot 2   Close shot from outside the window. B in foreground at right. A enters left, completing his movement, and stops.

A's movements in these shots are in opposed directions; both converge towards the centre of the screen. In this and the previous

363

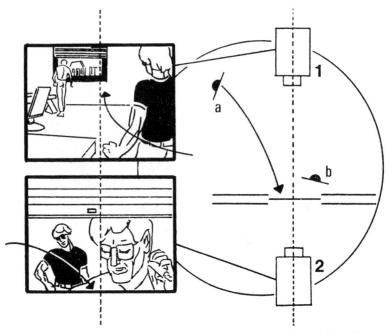

FIGURE 19.4 Tangential external reverse camera sites produce a transposition of the screen areas occupied by the players.

examples the fragments into which the circular motion was broken were executed using only half-screen areas in each shot.

Case 5

A performer moving around a large group can be covered by two reverse camera sites, one inside and the other outside the circle.

Fig. 19.5 shows the floor plan of the scene. Players B, C and D are all seated and therefore static. A executes the circular motion around them.

In the first shot we see B in the foreground. Behind him A enters from the right and crosses to the left. As soon as she is out of shot cut to the reverse second shot.

B has his back to us and players D and C are seen. A enters in foreground left and crosses rapidly to the right. For a few moments we see only B, D and C then A re-enters in the background, right, and stops among the group. She has a tray with drinks on it that she begins to distribute to the other players. Leaving and then re-

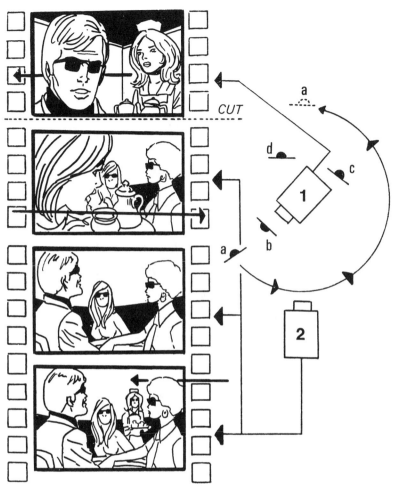

FIGURE 19.5 An internal and external camera location used to cover a circular movement. This moving player exits at one side and re-enters shot from the same side (instead of the opposite) in the second shot.

entering the shot on the same side in shot 2 clarifies A's movement as circular.

Case 6

A similar impression is given in this case except that the movement takes place in the background in the first shot and in the foreground in the second (Fig. 19.6).

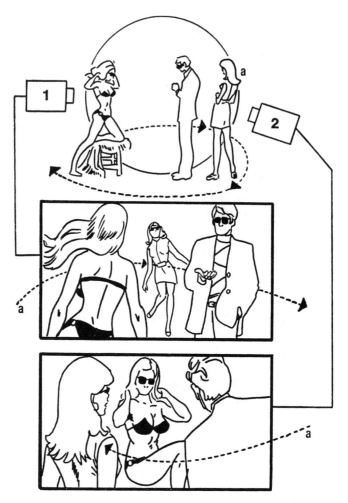

FIGURE 19.6 A circular movement registered in the background of the first shot and in the foreground on the second.

Both camera sites provide an external angle coverage around the static players in the scene. In the first A moves and exits right. In reverse shot 2, where A enters from right (foreground) and moves to the left. A pause at the end of shot 1 is necessary to account for the path travelled by player A out of shot before re-entering.

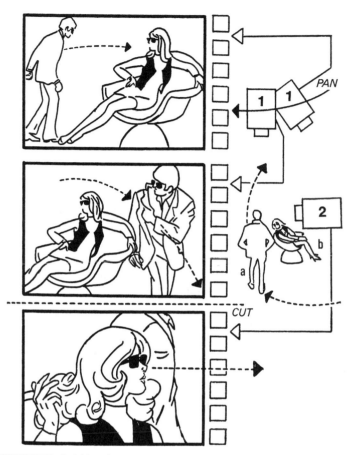

FIGURE 19.7 A right angle camera positioning to cover the circular movement of a player behind a stationary companion. The first shot is a panning camera movement.

Case 7

A right angle camera placement where a moving and a static player are present can be used to emphasize the static player in the second shot (Fig. 19.7).

The change in angle maintains the travel of the player across the screen—the direction which maximises screen activity.

Shot 1 Medium shot. A, left, and B, right. They talk. After a moment A walks behind B and turns towards the camera. The camera, having followed A, is now framing both performers in the centre of the screen. When A is directly behind B, cut to . . .

Shot 2 Close shot of B. Behind her A moves out from the centre of the screen to the right. B remains alone in the shot.

The main part of the circular motion is covered in the first shot, while the concluding portion is fleetingly shown at the beginning of the second.

Case 8

If the subject exits by the left, leaving an empty screen (and the shot continues) he cannot re-enter into the screen from the other side.

The audience would be conscious that a trick had been used on them. But if a second subject remains in the shot after the first has left and moves his head as if following the movement of the other player behind the camera, that player can then re-enter the shot from the opposite side.

Head movements of this kind can indicate to the audience that a circular change in direction is taking place behind his viewing position (Fig. 19.8).

By placing a mirror behind the static player the one leaving in the foreground would be seen in the mirror moving in the background, so that his reflected image is followed by the film audience, while the player with his back to the mirror watches him going. When the moving player later re-enters physically into the screen from the other side, the audience is in no confusion as to his whereabouts. Such a shot offers only one problem: how to conceal the camera from the mirror. In this instance the static player remaining in shot blocks the reflection of the camera in the mirror with his body.

A further variant, is to introduce a forward zoom, as the moving player goes out of the screen, so that the composition is tightened on the screen by framing a closer view of the static player and the reflected image of the moving performer on the left. Then the moving player crosses behind the static one to the right of the mirror. Later as his image turns and begins to walk forward, as seen in the mirror, the camera lens zooms back giving him space to re-enter the screen from the other side, and stop in foreground, left.

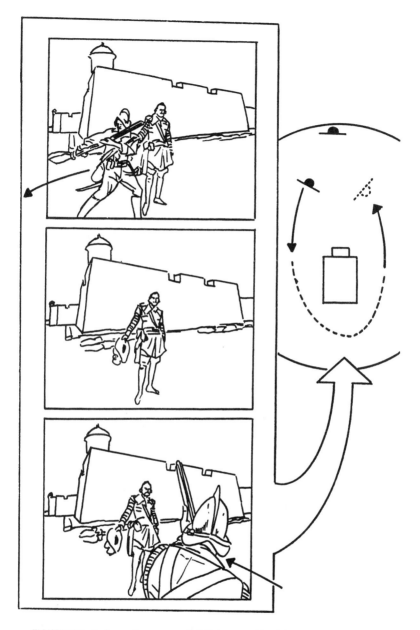

FIGURE 19.8 A player who passes out of shot on one side of the screen and re-enters by the other in the same shot, calls for a stationary player who indicates the path of the absent player by turning his head or following him with his eyes. This justifies his reappearance from the other side to the audience.

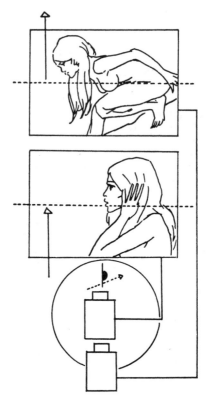

FIGURE 19.9 A vertical movement covered by two shots with a common visual axis. We cut forward to the second shot.

Vertical movement

Vertical movement in and out of shot can be up or down. The triangular camera placement principle applies here.

Case 9

An advance on the same visual axis is simple to execute. A raises her body, the upper part passing out of shot and in the (closer) second shot rises into the frame. It is a strong entrance that clearly punctuates the vertical motion performed (Fig. 19.9).

The effect can be obtained without the rising player moving out of the first shot (as when she is seen in long shot) using entrance motion on the second shot only. If more people are present in the

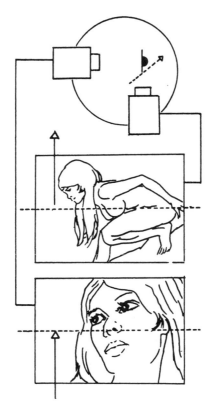

FIGURE 19.10 A right angle camera coverage of vertical movement.

first shot, they can be excluded as we cut in to the closer shot, or the order of shots can be reversed for different situations.

Case 10

A right angle coverage makes use of the same rules outlined for preceding example, as shown in Fig. 19.10.

She rises inside the shot as seen from a side view and concludes her motion by entering the second shot from below, but with a frontal camera position.

In this and the preceding case the second camera position occupies a higher level than the site that precedes it. This is in order to accompany the upward movement of the rising player.

371

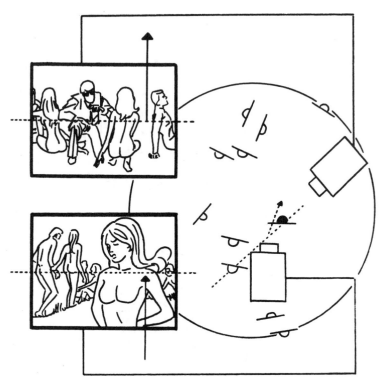

FIGURE 19.11 Reverse angle coverage of a vertical movement where the rising player is used as pivot in the scene.

Case 11

A reverse camera coverage, using external angles, obeys the same rules as in the two former cases. In the case depicted in Fig. 19.11 the rising player is used as a pivot in the scene.

Case 12

Sometimes a horizontal movement performed in a neutral direction becomes a vertical motion on the screen in the second shot because for this shot the camera is placed high over the players pointing down towards them (Fig. 19.12).

The description of such a scene would run as follows:

Shot 1 Low shot. In foreground two people enter from the right, turn and walk away into the background.

FIGURE 19.12 A high camera angle gives rise to a movement of the players upwards through the field of view.

Shot 2 High shot. They enter from below and walk into the background (either out of shot or with camera following).

If, in the second shot the camera follows the players from above in a vertical upward tilt, they will remain in the same screen sector, until the camera stops the upward movement, and then the players will ascend the screen as they continue moving to the background.

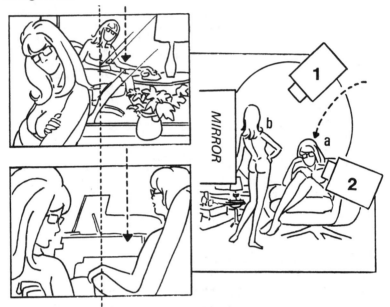

FIGURE 19.13 The vertical movement in this case occurs first in a mirror and then with the real player present in the shot.

Case 13

An imaginative film maker will always look for new approaches to the known and common event. A curious way of editing a downwards motion can be obtained by using a mirror (Fig. 19.13).

    Shot 1   Close shot of B, foreground, left. A, right, reflected in a mirror (located behind B) begins to sit down.

    Shot 2   Medium shot. B, left. A, right, sits down. Both performers are now seen in profile.

The reflected and the real vertical action took place in the same picture sector.

Case 14

In the act of sitting down the body normally moves through an arc. An interesting effect arises with a right angle camera position.

In the first shot (Fig. 19.14) A begins to sit. Cut. Side shot of A blocking the screen and sitting down in an arc to one side revealing B beyond.

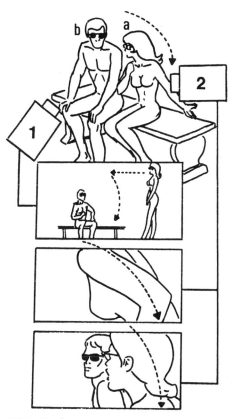

FIGURE 19.14 Right angle camera placement. At the beginning of the second shot the player seated in the foreground blocks the screen to disclose his companion in the background.

Case 15

Human limbs often describe an arch as we move about. A woman lowering an object above her head down to waist level might be presented in two shots. The second shows details of the object lowered.

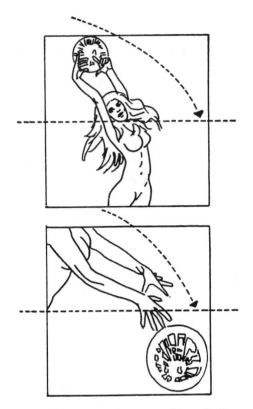

FIGURE 19.15 A vertical movement with screen repetition using the upper area of the screen for both shots.

In the first shot (Fig. 19.15) the player brings the object down to the central horizontal line of the picture area. We cut to a close shot on the same visual axis. The object enters from above and is lowered into the scene.

Sometimes a reverse angle is used for the second shot, contrasting the arc paths travelled while keeping the motion constantly in a vertical direction (Fig. 19.16).

Dynamic stops

Case 16

An actor's movement may be intended to end abruptly, particularly if he is running and suddenly stops or if he interrupts his walking

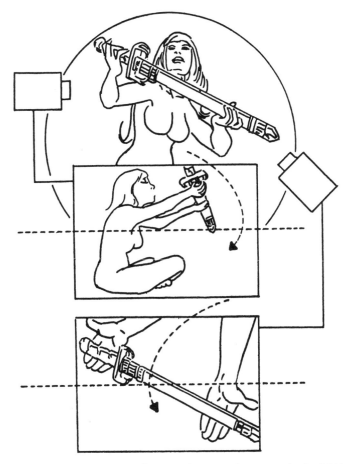

FIGURE 19.16 Opposed senses of direction for a vertical movement (to the right in the first shot, to the left in the second). The upper area of the screen is used for both shots.

movement. A dynamic presentation stresses the violence of the force that is brought to a halt. Two camera sites placed on a common visual axis are most apt here (Fig. 19.17).

Shot 1 A runs head-on to the camera at full speed. He exits shot (almost) close by the camera.

Shot 2 A, in the centre of the picture, runs only two steps towards us and stops abruptly (same visual axis for both shots).

The stop comes as a slight shock because the preceding shot

377

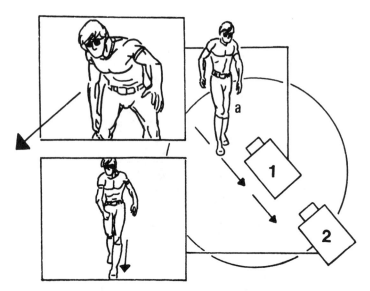

FIGURE 19.17 A dynamic stop is achieved by showing the player moving at full speed in the first shot and coming to a halt with only a couple of steps forward in the second.

implied the opposite. If the running player in the second shot moves only one step forward and then jumps down into a trench, a pit, or down a small flight of stairs, his abrupt descent will look stronger on the screen, especially if a natural obstacle is suddenly revealed when the second camera is moved backward.

Case 17

The same technique can be applied if one or both performers rolls almost out of shot and comes to rest in the centre of the picture area in the second shot. This second shot is behind but on the same visual axis as the first camera site as if made to compensate for the inadequate coverage of the first.

If, for instance, we have two men in a fight, struggling on the ground, we can show them rolling forward almost out of view and in the second shot in the centre of the screen, near the camera coming to a halt. The man on top raises his knife and stabs his opponent.

The action gains dramatically if presented with the second shot emphasized in this way.

378

Case 18

The formula also works if the action is covered from above in the first shot and from a level camera position in the second (Fig. 19.18)

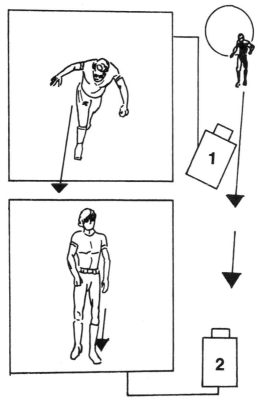

FIGURE 19.18 A shot from above and a level view of the player can be combined to obtain a dynamic stop.

Since the player is walking, only one step forward in the second shot, will suffice to bring him to a halt. Had he been running, two or three steps would have been necessary.

In the example in Fig. 19.18 only one person is involved, but a group of six or seven moving in the same direction can be brought to a stop using the same technique and camera coverage.

20

TWENTY BASIC RULES
FOR CAMERA MOVEMENT

The moving camera brought to film a new dimension, a new freedom, but in the process it also became a dangerous weapon. It can so easily destroy illusion. Unjudicious use of a moving camera quickly develops into an annoyance that conflicts with the pace and even the meaning of the story. John Ford is credited with the dictum 'Nail down your camera and depend on the cutting'. Such a drastic viewpoint was not made without reason although, like all condensations, it contains a measure of exaggeration.

Movement and the camera

Roughly, there are three types of movement that can be put on film:
1 People or objects move in front of the camera.
2 The camera moves towards, across or away from static persons or objects.
3 These movements take place at the same time.
The camera itself can provide three different movements: panning, travelling or zooming (during the shot). The speed at which the film travels inside the camera would also affect the speed of a motion seen on the screen, adjusting it, perhaps, to above or below the norm.

Successful screen movement lies in knowing not only how to create it but when and why.

Basic guidelines for camera movement

The following list will help you to control camera movement properly.

380

1 A moving camera can give the audience the heightened physical sensation felt by a character in the story, by introducing his point of view when involved in a violent motion. The driver in a car suddenly feels that he has no control on the brakes. We see his face react with fear as he looks at the road ahead. The next shot is made from his point of view. The camera hurtles down a winding road towards a dangerous curve seen straight ahead.

2 The camera behaves as if it is the eyes of an actor. This is the so-called subjective technique. It provides a greater involvement with the feeling of a character. In the preceding example we occupied the place of a performer only momentarily, cutting back immediately to exterior shots of him or the vehicle. If the shot is longer the camera more convincingly becomes one of the performers. It lurches, staggers and moves forward or backwards, just as a player would do. All the other players in the scene treat the camera as a performer and look and react directly into the camera lens when addressing it.

It is, however, rather difficult to obtain successful shots using this technique because the audience is aware that a trick is being played on them.

The film *Requiem for a Heavyweight*, directed by Ralph Nelson, had a good scene at the beginning that made use of this technique. Robert Montgomery's *Lady in the Lake*, a film made in the forties, explored this technique to the full, revealing its limitations as well as its possibilities. It is probably the only full length feature film to employ this technique from beginning to end. Other film makers have used the technique more sparingly; Kadar and Klos in *Death is Called Engelchen*, Delmer Daves in *Dark Passage* for the first twenty minutes, John Guillermin for the German commando raid sequence of *I Was Monty's Double*.

3 Panning or tracking (travelling) can be used to present the scene either directly or through a player's eyes. The information is usually presented directly in a documentary style film. A series of objects is presented without being related to a previous or following shot where a player is seen watching. If a person in a police station is told to look at the line of suspects, the panning or travelling shot across their faces becomes his subjective view, because this shot is preceded and followed by others showing him making the inspection.

4 Panning or tracking shots can disclose an expected or unexpected situation at the end of the movement. For example, the

camera first shows an over-turned chair, then a lamp lying on the floor, a pair of shoes abandoned in awkward positions, a broken flower-pot, and finally a dead body. What to expect at the end of this panning or travelling shot was gradually suggested to the audience as the shot progressed.

An unexpected conclusion would be achieved if at the end of the shot a goat was seen chewing on the rug. For the audience, conditioned to expect a definite result, the pay-off comes as a surprise.

5 A straight cut is faster than a moving shot because it establishes the new point immediately. If we pan or track to a new point of interest instead of cutting, we expend a lot of useless footage photographing irrelevant things, simply to travel there. Significant action or objects must be photographed during the pan or track to justify its use or the sequence may drag.

6 A pan or tracking shot from one point of interest to another can move with a secondary subject that might come into view at the beginning and leave as the camera stops on the new centre of interest.

For example, the beginning of a shot might be an exuberant floor show in a crowded nightclub. A waiter carrying a tray with drinks comes into camera range, and we pan or track with him as he moves along the tables. The camera stops on two central characters in the story seated at a table in the foreground and the waiter goes on out of shot.

7 A panning or tracking shot that moves from one point of interest to another has three parts: a beginning, where the camera is static, a moving centre section and a conclusion, where the camera again becomes static. We cannot cut from a moving to a static shot of the same static person or object as a visual jump would occur. But after the camera has come to a standstill in the first shot we may successfully cut to a static shot of the same subject in the following shot.

8 Combined panning and tracking are often used to follow a subject or vehicle moving in front of the camera. We travel along with a man in a wheelchair going down a corridor. As the man reaches a corner he turns away from us. The camera stops tracking and pans with him as he moves into a crowded auditorium where his presence is awaited.

9 A tracking or wide panning shot following a subject performing a repetitive action, can be cut to any desired length, as necessary, in editing. A tracking shot of a moving car, constitutes repetitive

motion, so that ten seconds or two seconds of the shot can be used as needed. In fact, the shot may be broken into two or three fragments, and intercut in parallel with another series of moving or static shots that cover different, or the same subject matter.

10 When cutting from a pan or track to a static shot where a moving person or object is shown, it helps to keep the subject framed in the same sector of the screen. Direction of movement on the screen must be constant too. For example:

A man swims in the river. Seen in static long shot. He moves approximately in the centre of the frame from right to left.

Close shot. Pan with the swimming man from right to left. He is framed constantly in the centre.

Long shot, from another part of the river. The man is seen small in the centre of the screen swimming from right to left.

Tracking medium shot. From a boat accompanying the man as he swims from right to left. He is framed centrally.

11 Camera motion, either panning or tracking can be used selectively to exclude undesired material and introduce new persons, objects or backgrounds, into the scene, all the while moving with a central action.

12 Panning or tracking must be executed in a secure, precise manner. You must be sure of the movement you want. Jerky panning, or undecisive pivoting of the camera first to one side, then to the other, reveals an amateur, inexperienced conception and execution.

13 Subject movement draws attention away from camera motion. Let your subject move first before following him with the camera, and stop the motion of the camera before your subject stops too, to allow him to move a little further on the screen.

14 When executing continuous pans or tracks, move the camera along simple paths. Let the actors or the vehicle do all the complicated motions within the frame area.

15 Pan or tracking shots should start and conclude in pictorially balanced visual compositions.

16 The useful length of a static shot for editing purposes is based on the action it contains, while the length of a moving shot depends upon the duration of the camera motion. The timing of a panning or tracking shot must be just right. Too short or too long a movement will work against the story being told.

17 Panning or tracking shots are often used to re-establish pictorial balance. When a subject leaves the shot, the remaining

performer of group becomes visually unbalanced in the picture area. A slight pan or track forward may re-establish balance quite simply. The same thing happens when a new player enters into the scene. These camera movements are slow, and only involve small displacements.

18 The illusion of motion can be obtained by seating the subject in front of a back, or front, projection screen or blue screen for the travelling matte process. Although the subject is static, the background motion will supply the illusion that he is on a moving vehicle. If we actually want to show the player walking in front of the process screen, a 'treadmill' is installed out of camera range on the floor of the studio, and the performer walks on it. The treadmill will make his movements look natural while keeping him in the same position.

19 Tracking shots are frequently used to obtain a static screen composition that is held for the whole duration of the shot. A camera moving back in front of a walking subject always frames him from the same distance while his background changes continuously.

20 Frequently the motion of a vehicle where the players are located is merely suggested.

An establishing shot shows a car going down a street at night. Next we cut to the actors inside. For practical and economical reasons these shots are filmed in the studio. It is not necessary to set up a back projection screen behind the car mock-up. A play of lights falling first from one side and then the other (suggesting the street corners being crossed as well as the areas of light and shadow found on any street or road at night) will be enough to complete the illusion of movement. If the sequence is capped with a shot where the car is seen moving along the road, the illusion will be strengthened.

Solid dramatic motivation

Camera movement must have justification at all times. Your decision to use a moving camera must be in terms of results obtained. These reults must contribute to a clearer, dynamic, and precise story telling.

21

THE PANNING CAMERA

A panning shot can scan a subject horizontally or follow a moving subject. In the second instance the camera and subject might move continuously or intermittently.

Scanning panoramically

Case 1

A continuous horizontal pan reveals a collection of static subjects, such as people, machines, objects or distant views. These scanning pans cover wide sectors, up to a half circle at a medium-paced scanning rate. (Full circle pans are more difficult to perform and look less natural). Too fast or too slow a pan defeats the purpose by dwelling too long on the subject for the visual reporting involved, or hurrying across it without allowing the time necessary to grasp the details. These shots are often preceded or followed by another where one or several people are shown looking around and are, in fact, the subjective view of the onlooker. Short pans are sometimes used to move across from one centre of interest to another. With only two centres of interest, the panning motion serves only to link two subjects visually.

Case 2

In the previous case the reaction of the player as he begins to look around is seen in the shot that precedes the pan. But it is possible to integrate both motivation and reaction in the same shot. In

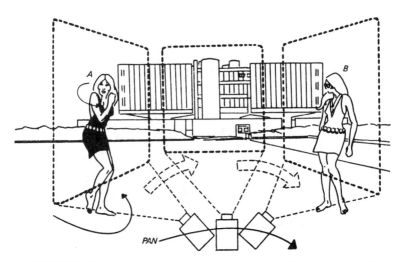

FIGURE 21.1 The turning player motivates a camera pan at the end of which is disclosed the subject which caused the person's reaction.

Fig. 21.1, the shot begins with the camera framing player A looking left. She hears a sound off-camera and, as she turns her head to the right to look, the camera begins to pan to that side with her and, leaving her, continues until it reaches player B who attracted A's attention.

Thus action and reaction are contained in a single shot. This procedure can also be applied to a performer who begins to move to a new zone of the set. The shot begins with the player static in the first zone, then, as he starts to move to one side, the camera begins to pan with him. But instead of staying with him, it pans faster, reaching the second zone before him. So the audience has a view of the second zone with its own centre of interest (which may be static or in motion, and with its own pictorial composition) before the actor re-enters.

Chase sequences

Case 3

Chase scenes frequently make use of repetitive pans that follow pursuer and pursued either individually or together. Several combinations are employed. One involves making a pair of panned shots from the same place, before moving to another site where, again, a pair of panning shots are made from the same camera position. Here is an example:

Shot 1 Full shot. Two cavalry men run towards us. We pan with them through a half circle from right to left, and see them.

Shot 2 Full shot. Same place. Four Indians approach at full gallop. We pan with them in a half circle right to left. They follow into the distance.

The same technique is applied at the next camera position where the action is in a different terrain. Pursued and pursuer are shown in different shots.

Case 4

Another technique uses parallel editing of pursuer and pursued moving in individual panning shots that pan continuously. Each player is framed centrally in half-circle pans.

In the previous case the actors' path was tangential to the camera movement (Fig. 21.2).

Now the players are made to run in a circular path and equidistant from the camera. If a long focus lens is used at close range the shallow depth of field will keep only the players in focus, while foreground and background appear blurred. (Fig. 21.3).

This helps to disguise the fact that the path traversed by the players is not a straight one. If obstacles are placed between the camera and the players in motion, the effect obtained in these panning shots will be very dynamic, as the players are constantly seen through a succession of intermittent clear spaces. But if these obstacles are a series of vertical bars, such as a fence, a disturbing stroboscopic effect will be obtained. Irregular shapes are therefore preferred.

Case 5

Pursuer and pursued will be seen alternately in the centre of the screen, as shot follows shot. If, instead of two persons, five or six run in the same direction, each photographed individually with long lenses, and with progressively shorter pans, tension is built up as each player is substituted by another in a seemingly continuous panning shot.

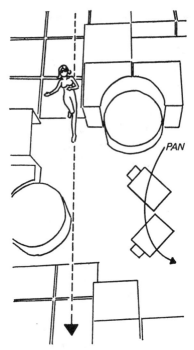

FIGURE 21.2 The moving subject runs along a path tangential to the panning movement of the camera.

Case 6

This same technique can be applied to a running person. Seen in close shot (using a long focus lens) the player moves behind obstacles in a circular path around the camera. If, each time the camera is blocked *in full* by a foreground obstruction the cut is made to the next shot that also starts on a fully blocked frame, a path impossible to cover with a travelling camera can be obtained, and all these shots cut into one another will seem to be one continuous take, of remarkable length and precision in framing.

The variation in distance from camera to subject in each cut should not be too great. If too large a disparity comes after each fleeting black screen (during the blocking of the camera lens in the panning motion) the shots would not seem continuous, but a receding and approaching pattern would be achieved instead, which is also an interesting visual variant.

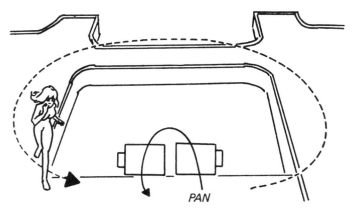

FIGURE 21.3 The subject runs in a circular path around the camera keeping at a constant distance, which makes it easier to pan.

If the background and lighting of each panning shot, as well as costumes are changed, the passage of time is suggested.

Case 7

Akira Kurosawa, that extraordinary Japanese master of film language, has used the preceding effects extensively in his films. But he improved the crude technique of alternating panning shots to cover a chase sequence, by cutting from a panning shot of the pursuer to a static take of the pursued, thus generating a visual contrast particularly well suited to the violence of the scene.

As we shall see in the example that follows he was not content with the simple juxtaposition described, but improved on it with a subtle variation introduced in the second part of the sequence. Thus his visual treatment of the scene was enriched.

His film *The Hidden Fortress* contains a famous sequence where Toshiro Mifune, on horseback, pursues two soldiers armed with spears who fled on their horses. The action takes place in a narrow road through a dense forest.

We quote a section of the sequence to illustrate the editing technique used by Kurosawa.

Shot 1   The first soldier in the centre of the screen rides away from us. A second rider enters, left, and moves away. The camera is in a fixed position and movement is from left to centre.

389

Shot 2 Mifune rides from left to right. The panning shot keeps him in the centre of the screen, the background blurred, foreground empty. Mifune raises his sword. The panning movement covers only a right angle.

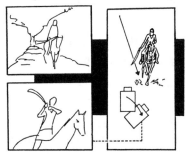

Shot 3 The two soldiers enter by the left and ride towards the centre of the screen. They are looking back over their shoulders. Static camera.

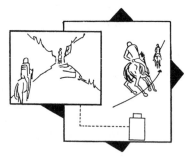

Shot 4 Mifune on horseback seen in medium shot (framed from the knees of the horse's front legs). Mifune is holding his sword high, and is standing on stirrups. Pan from left to right (90°).

Shot 5 Static camera. The first soldier in the centre of the screen in full shot. He rides away looking back over his shoulder. Second soldier enters, left, and when he reaches the centre of the screen in medium shot, cut to . . .

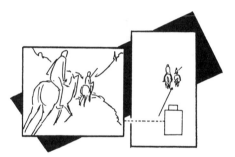

Shot 6 Big trees in the background. Mifune rides from left to right. Almost a right angle pan.

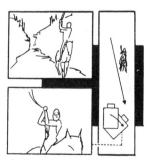

Shot 7 Camera low. Static. The first rider (centre) moves away. Second soldier enters left and as he reaches the centre cut to . . .

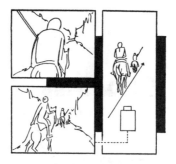

Shot 8 Pan left to right. Mifune in medium shot crosses in front of the camera until framed from behind pursuing the second soldier. The pan is almost a half circle.

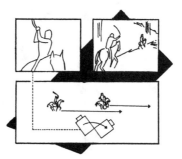

Shot 9 Mifune in medium shot. He rides left to right. A near-right angle pan.

Shot 10 Close shot of the second soldier. Pan to the right to see him move away. The first rider is seen in the background Mifune enters, left, and catches up with the second rider. He begins to strike down with his sword. Cut on the downward stroke. (Right angle pan.)

392

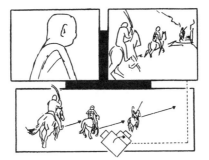

Shot 11 Low shot. Pan left to right. The second soldier, foreground, right. Left, Mifune ends the downward movement of his sword. The second rider begins to fall during the pan. At the end of it he hits the ground in a cloud of dust. The first soldier is glimpsed in the background, right. When Mifune and the riderless horse cross the centre of the screen, cut to . . .

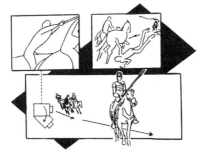

Shot 12 Low shot. Static. The first soldier at the left rides to the centre, looking back over his shoulder as he moves away· As soon as he is at the centre, cut to . . .

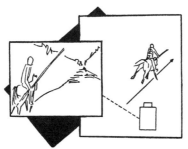

Shot 13 Mifune, centre, full shot, runs to the right. On the left we see the other lone horse galloping behind. Pan almost 90° right. Low shot.

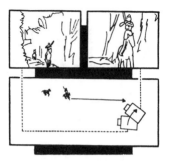

Shot 14 Low shot. Pan left to right. The shot begins with a medium shot of the first soldier leaving right. Mifune enters left. The first rider turns back on his saddle and prepares his spear to repel the attack. The camera stops panning and sees how both ride away along the road.

Shot 15 Low shot. Panning left to right framing only the legs of the two horses. The swift pan covers a half circle.

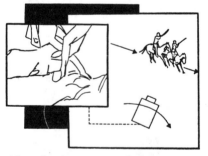

Shot 16 Both riders in the centre of the screen seen in full shot. Mifune, behind, strikes some sword blows that the first soldier blocks with his spear. The pan covers a right angle.

Shot 17 Low shot. Half circle pan following the legs of the two running horses moving left to right. The shot has 24 film frames.

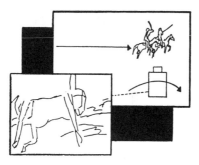

Shot 18 Both riders in the centre of the screen move towards us, ride close to the camera and pass into the background (half circle pan). The men exchange blows.

Shot 19 Low shot. A half circle pan, left to right, following the legs of the horses as they run past the camera. The shot consists of 29 film frames.

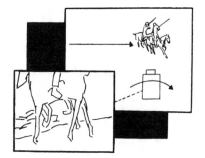

Shot 20 Medium shot of both riders (framed from the knees of the horses upwards). The animals run side by side. The men exchange blows. A panning movement catches them close to the camera as they approach and is cut as soon as they have their backs to us.

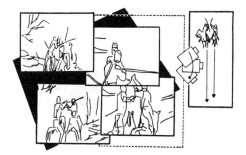

Shot 21 Low shot. A half circle pan, left to right, following the legs of the horses as they run (27 frames).

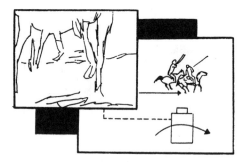

Shot 22 Camera high. Horses side by side. The men still fighting. Short pan from left to right.

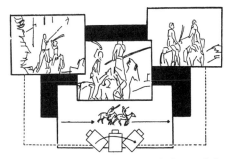

Shot 23 Low shot. A half circle pan, left to right, following the legs of the horses as they run (25 frames).

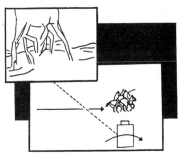

Shot 24 Full shot. Both riders in the centre of the screen. **Pan from left to right through right angle. When both riders reach a close shot, Mifune lunges at the back of the first soldier. At the conclusion of the pan the soldier begins to fall forward out of shot, right.**

Shot 25 Low shot. Static camera. Both horses enter close to the camera and the wounded soldier falls in foreground. Mifune and the horses move into the background. Then he turns to the left and disappears among the bushes.

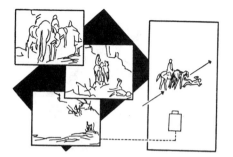

The technique used by Kurosawa in this sequence is simple and rich. Shots 1, 3, 5 and 7 show the pursued soldiers *moving away*. Their actions take place on the left side of the screen only, and are filmed from fixed camera sites. The pursuer, Toshiro Mifune, is shown in shots 2, 4 and 6 *moving forward* in right angle pans, left to centre. Having established a violent rhythm for the chase, the director disposes of the first pursued man in four shots.

Shots 8 to 11 document how Mifune reaches his first opponent and kills him. Shot 8 establishes the distance between these two men, shot 9 shows Mifune gaining ground, and shots 10 and 11 portray the death of the soldier.

The establishing shot 8 is a half circle pan; shot 9 only a right angle pan of Mifune, left to centre. Shots 10 to 11 move from centre to right and there is a cut on the downward stroke of Mifune's sword. In shot 12 (static camera) the remaining soldier is re-established. He moves on the left side of the screen. Shot 13 shows Mifune riding ahead of the lone horse of the soldier he has killed. In shot 14 Mifune reaches his second opponent. Shots 13 and 14 are right angle pan shots, but the first is from left to centre and the second from centre to right.

Now Kurosawa changes his visual tactics. He intercuts shots of the two men on horseback exchanging blows with close shots of the legs of the horses galloping side by side. Shots 15, 17, 19, 21 and 23 show swift panning shots of the legs running on the road. Each of these shots lasts only one second on the screen. Shots 16, 18, 20 and 22 show the men fighting. With the exception of the first (a right angle pan shot) all are half-circle pans. One long, wide pan (shot 18) and two faster, close pans (shots 20 and 22). The director needs only two shots to end the sequence. Shot 24 shows how Mifune wounds his opponent in a right angle pan from left to centre. The wounded soldier begins to fall.

398

The last (static low) shot of the sequence shows both horses entering, close to the camera, and the soldier falling in foreground. Mifune and the riderless horse continue down the road and away.

The construction of the sequence is a model of economy. All irrelevant details are omitted. For example, shot 12 not only re-establishes the excluded soldier, but masks Mifune's advance along the road who, in the next shot, is shown far ahead of the riderless horse. In shot 14 Mifune has reached his other opponent. Out of twenty-five shots, six use a static camera while the remaining nineteen are all panning shots.

Intermittent panning

Case 8

Intermittent activity by various groups can be covered by a continuous pan (Fig. 21.5).

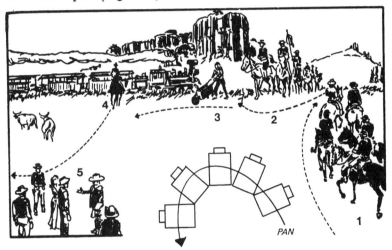

FIGURE 21.5 A continuous pan covers overlapping actions of several groups who move around the camera in the same general direction.

A group of soldiers move in double line (1) from right to left. The camera begins to pan with them. As they move away they meet an onlooking group turning to the left (2). The camera follows them. The soldiers stop in front of a gardener (3) pushing a wheelbarrow. The camera follows him. The gardener stops as a man on horseback (4) passes in front of him. The camera moves with the rider. As he exits screen left, the camera stops in the foreground.

Camera movement was slow and continuous throughout. The end of the shot was static. The intermittent, overlapping actions gave a sense of place while at the end the two central characters (5) were introduced naturally as part of the whole ensemble.

Case 9

If a panning shot must cover several points of interest in its path, it is wise to provide pauses in the movement, which allow the audience a better view of them (Fig. 21.6).

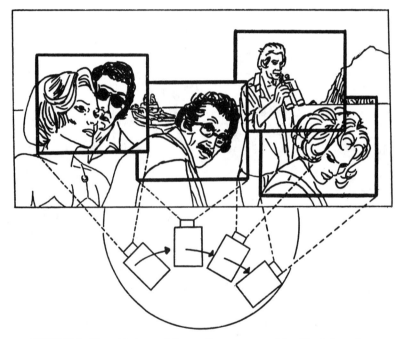

FIGURE 21.6   The subjects are stationary, the camera pans intermittently from player to player as they interrelate with one another.

The players are given bits of business appropriate to the situation and which move the action on to the next player or group, thus justifying further camera movement. This way, results on the screen look more natural. A succession of short pans that cover stationary subjects will need stronger dramatic motivation than if the players themselves provide that motivation with their own actions. In the second case the movement of the camera complements that of the players.

Full circle panning

Case 10

Panning by degrees need not be supplied only to covering stationary players. Performers who, in turn, move within a circle, the camera panning with them as they move to new positions, suggest coverage by a full circle camera pan which can record a whole scene. Michelangelo Antonioni used such a set-up in his film *Cronaca di un Amore*. Fig. 21.7 gives a schematic diagram of the movements executed in that shot.

FIGURE 21.7 Movements for a 360 degree pan in Michelangelo Antonioni's film *Cronaca di un Amore*. The continuous scene runs for 132 metres of film (about 5 min) and takes place on a bridge.

401

The scene took place in the centre of a bridge and was acted out by the two main characters. The multiple pauses used paced the shot so completely that you have to pay extra attention to notice that a full circle panning movement is involved.

Such a shot must have strong plotted action in front of it to be successful.

Case 11

Fast circular panning is sometimes used to cover a dance routine, as if taken from the viewpoint of one of the dancers. The dance partner may remain in the foreground but behind, the scene spins swiftly round. The usual way to film this scene is to tie the cameraman and the actor with a short rope round their waists. This will ensure some accuracy in framing as both persons girate.

Unless a strong dramatic reason motivates its use, this type of shot should be used sparingly. It is just a form of camera acrobatics and one that has been overdone.

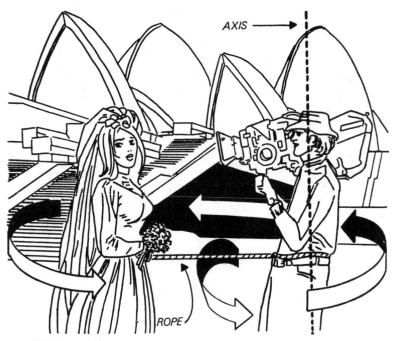

FIGURE 21.7A Maintaining a constant camera to subject distance in a scene involving a rapidly rotating pan.

402

Case 12

An actor walking slowly in a circular path followed by a panning camera will cover the total surrounding background while keeping the player constantly framed in the foreground and on the same side of the screen. If there is a crowd in the background, the idea that the player is completely surrounded will be very graphically conveyed. (Fig. 21.8). Harry Andrews in the prison riot scene in Sidney Lumet's *The Hill*, and Burt Lancaster and his group surrounded by the Mexicans in Robert Aldrich's *Vera Cruz* are two films where the technique described was used quite effectively.

FIGURE 21.8 A circular camera movement which keeps a player constantly in the foreground throughout the shot.

Fast panning

Case 13

A very fast circular pan is called swish pan. It connects two points of interest and provide a short blurred image of the scene en route.

It is used to link two adjoining scenes spatially. At the end of the first shot a swish pan is initiated. The second shot begins with a swish pan and then stops, framing a new scene. If both blurred parts of the two shots are joined a fast linking device is obtained.

Nowadays, some film makers use swish pans of pure blurred movement sandwiched between two static shots to accomplish the same effect. Changes in time or locale are indicated by the use of such pans.

David Lean in his film *Doctor Zhivago* uses a swish pan to relate two scenes that take place on the same set. Komarovsky and Lara are dancing. The music ends and the couple come to a stop on the dance floor. There is a swish pan to the right and we see Komarovsky helping Lara to a seat at the table on the edge of the dance floor. The swish pan serves to omit their walk across the room which would add nothing to the scene and might even tend to slow it down. Thus the swish pan bridges two parts of the set disposing of dead time.

Case 14

A swish pan can be used to relate two different vehicles visually, conveying the idea that some time has elapsed and the player is now travelling at a different place and time. Richard Brooks, in his film *In Cold Blood*, uses this effect. A bus is seen approaching. The camera begins to pan with the vehicle to the right. When the bus passes close by the camera as it pans, a blurred view of the body of the bus is obtained. A cut is made on this blur. The next shot starts with the blurred motion of a train passing the camera. The instrument pans in the same direction as the preceding shot and stops, framing the train going into the distance (Fig. 21.9).

Case 15

A swish pan is sometimes used in the middle of a shot in a chase sequence. The shot starts framing player A running from left to right. The camera pans almost a half circle with him. Suddenly the camera swish pans back to the left in a swift blurred motion, to frame player B, the pursuer, coming into camera range. The camera now pans with this new player, to the right again, following him until he leaves the shot.

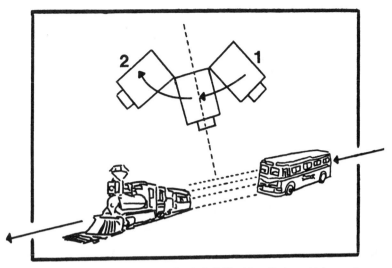

FIGURE 21.9 The blurred pan is used in *In Cold Blood*, to unite two vehicles moving in the same direction across the screen.

Case 16

Sometimes a panning shot starts by framing the main subject on one side of the screen and ends with that subject on the other side. That is to say, in the panning the camera moves faster than the subject it covers. This is sometimes required to keep well balanced pictorial compositions at the extremes where the camera is fixed. (Fig. 21.10.). This recourse is also employed to give the performer screen space in front of them through which to move out of the screen when the camera stops panning.

In two directions

Case 17

The camera may pan in opposite directions in the same shot, provided that there is a pause in between. Here is a simple example. B and A are standing together. A walks to the right and stops during which movement the camera pans to the right framing him alone. After a moment A returns to B. The camera now pans to the left again framing both performers.

405

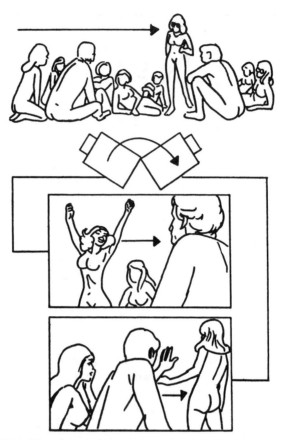

FIGURE 21.10 The camera pans faster than the subject being covered so that at the end of the shot she is on the opposite side of the screen.

Vertical tilts

A vertical pan is known as a tilt. Tilt movements are not used as frequently as horizontal pans. A camera tilt, up or down, is easier to execute since, in general, it is used only to cover vertical movements of a performer or object.

Case 18

A continuous vertical pan may connect different points of interest placed one above the other. The camera is usually tilted slowly to allow the audience time to take in the changing view properly.

Here is an example: It is night. Fireworks explode in a dark sky. As they finish the camera begins to tilt down, it passes a group of musicians, placed on the flat roof of a house, who begin to play a gay melody. The camera continues downwards to frame an open patio where people in evening dress have assembled around long tables for a banquet which is being brought in by waiters. The camera moves down further to frame an elaborate cake on a table in the foreground. There is an inscription on it: 'To Tish'.

Case 19

A discontinuous vertical pan serves to connect centres of interest placed vertically but the players or objects suggesting that coverage need not themselves necessarily move vertically as the example chosen from John Huston's film *The Unforgiven* illustrates here. A door opens through a rectangle of light on the floor. We see in the foreground a painted animal skin, stretched on the ground.

Two pairs of boots walk into the room through the door and stop in front of the skin.

The person on the left walks away to the background. The camera tilts up following him. He opens a window and more light comes in. The player on the right turns towards us. We see the centre section of his body and a gun in his right hand.

407

The player on the left comes back to the foreground. The camera tilts up again and frames the faces of both men. They look down at the skin (now off-screen).

The player on the right bends down out of view to pick up the skin and then re-enters from below holding the skin.

Now both players turn and move away to a table in the background where they spread the skin out. The camera tilts down to frame them in medium shot.

As the example shows the shot is a continuous one where the camera moves from one centre of interest to another and remains on each before tilting up or down again.

Case 20

Tilt shots move either up or down in right angle arcs relative to the horizon. If a tilt starting at the horizon moves through a half circle the whole scene will be upside down at the end. Some chase sequences may sometimes profit by the use of this property of a tilt shot. For example: a tank pursues a man. They run towards us. The camera is high up, framing them from above, and continues the tilting movement after they pass below us. Now the scene is upside down and man and tank seem to defy gravity by clinging to the face of the earth as they run towards the inverted horizon. A well known Russian film, *Ballad of a Soldier*, used such a shot. (Fig. 21.12).

Side tilts

Case 21

Sometimes the upside down framing at the end of a tilt is used to comment on the disrupted mental balance of the central character in the scene. But a sideways camera tilt is favoured by other film makers. The camera leans partially to one side as the mental breakdown takes place, and is kept tilted in the following shots until the character's condition is normal again. Tilted reverse shots have an opposed direction from shot to shot (Fig. 21.13).

A right-angle sideways tilt is used only for very strong dramatic reasons since it brings the horizon into a vertical position.

Tilts first to one side and then to the other, are applied to a camera held inside a set of a ship's cabin or of a submarine, to simulate an explosion by rocking the camera rather than the set sideways. The actors move, to assist the illusion.

Joining a static and a panning shot

Case 22

A static and a moving shot can be joined together, covering horizontal or vertical motion, by making the second take a hori-

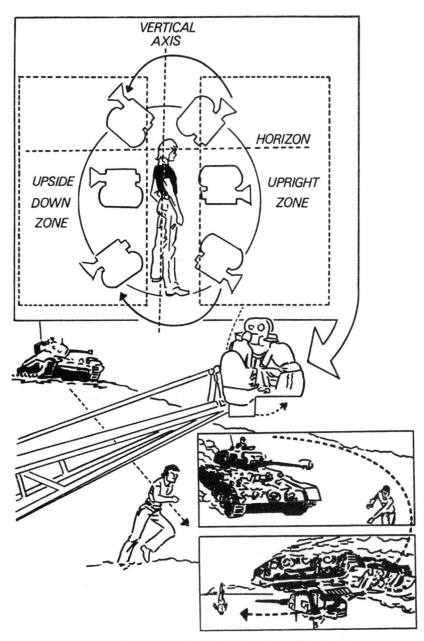

FIGURE 21.12 A shot used in the Russian film *Ballad of a Soldier*, where the camera is tilted down through an arc of 180 degrees thus giving an inverted view of events in the final part of the shot.

410

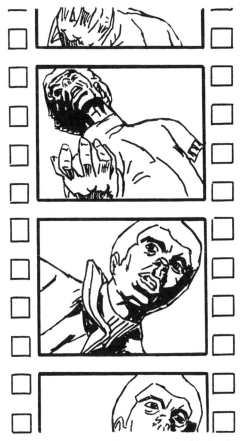

FIGURE 21.13 Tilted compositions on the screen are used to denote an abnormality in the situation or in the characters portrayed—and with opposed senses of direction provide a visual contrast from shot to shot.

zontal pan or a vertical tilt. The procedure is simple enough. In the first shot A goes out of one side of the frame. (He either moves across the screen or, coming towards us, he exits close to the camera In the second shot he enters from the opposite side and the camera pans with him. When he has reached his destination in the background, the camera stops. (Fig. 21.14).

Case 23

With two performers in the shot, one moving and the other stationary, the same combination can be applied (Fig. 21.15).

411

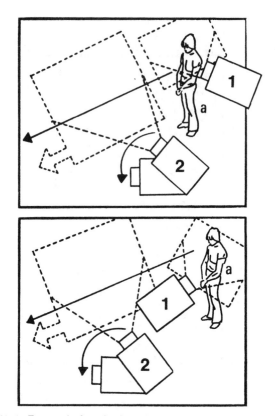

FIGURE 21.14 Two similar formulas for joining a stationary and a panning shot to cover an actor's movement. In the first case the player exits parallel to the camera in shot 1, while in the second case the player in shot 1 comes diagonally towards the camera.

In the first shot A comes from the background, passes B and exits right, close to the camera. At the start of the second shot, both players are seen in profile. In the centre of the screen A moves to the right. The camera pans with him excluding B left.

Case 24

An advance on the same visual axis to record the movement of A crossing behind stationary B, showing how B stops on the other side, can be easily achieved using a static full shot followed by a panning close shot (Fig. 21.16).

412

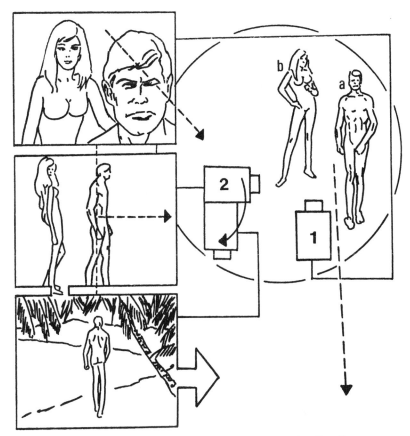

Fig. 21.15 Another variant for joining a static and a panning shot. Here the camera sites are at right angles to each other.

Here is a description of the scene:

Shot 1 Full shot. B stands on the left side of the screen. A, right, starts to move left. When she reaches the centre of the screen, and is close to B, cut to . . .

Shot 2 Close shot. B, left, and A, right. At the start of the shot the camera is already panning to the left with A who now crosses behind B and stops on the other side. Final screen composition is A on the left and B on the right.

The cut on the action is with the moving player in the same screen area in both shots.

413

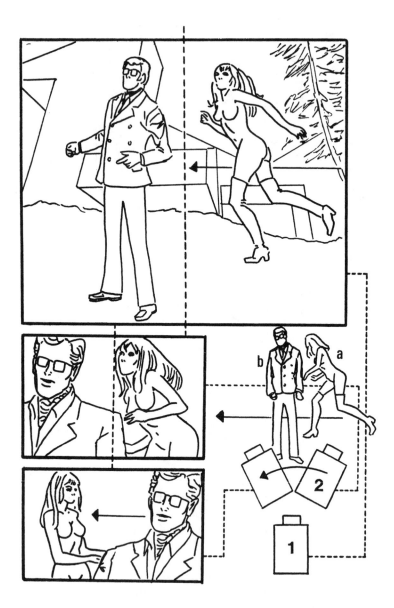

FIGURE 21.16 A further variant for joining a static and a panning shot (see text).

Case 25

In our survey of the uses of panning movements we find that a further possibility is to have the moving player go out of one shot and enter a second (Fig. 21.17).

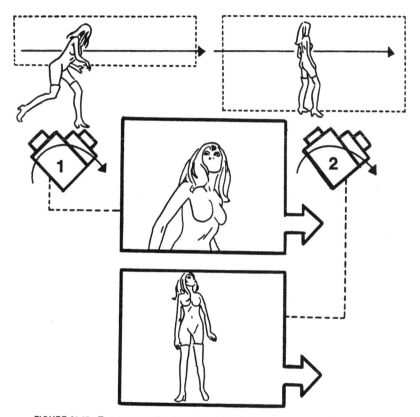

FIGURE 21.17 Two consecutive panning shots of the same moving character are joined by letting the moving figure leave the screen in the first shot and enter in the second.

From the first position, the camera frames the moving player in close shot. At the end of the pan she exits. She enters the next from the opposite side. This new take is a full shot, and we continue panning in the same direction as in the previous take following the moving player.

FIGURE 21.18 Foreground obstacles at the conclusion of the first shot and beginning of the second are used to join two consecutive panning shots.

Case 26

Two consecutive panning shots where the player never leaves the screen can be edited together if a foreground obstruction is used to achieve the cut (Fig. 21.18).

Here is a description of the scene.

Shot 1   A walks through a crowd. There are people in front of and behind her. She is framed in full shot. Panning with her, we frame a person so close to the camera that our main player is hidden behind. Cut to . . .

Shot 2   A person in close shot on the right. From behind appears A in close shot and moves in the same direction as before. The camera pans with her. There are now no obstacles between her and the camera, although the crowd continues to move behind her. At the end of the pan, A stops. People continue to cross the screen from side to side.

Case 27

Two shots that pan in opposite directions can be joined together if the actor's movements is in a diagonal across the screen (Fig. 21.19).

In the first shot the actor moves off round a corner and into a street, the camera panning with him left to right. Cut. The player, still on the right, approaches walking left and we pan with him right to left.

In order to achieve a successful cut, the player's position and size must be identical on the screen at the moment of the cut. As shown in Fig. 21.19, the performer is seen on the right side at the same distance from the right edge, and with approximately the same vertical height in both takes. Minor mismatches will be accepted by the audience. Panning speeds are important. The camera is slowing down on its horizontal pan at the end of the first shot and begins to increase its speed in the opposite direction on the next shot.

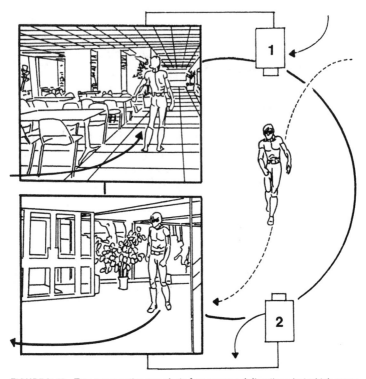

FIGURE 21.19 Two consecutive pan shots from opposed directions but which cover the same subject can be joined if the cut is made with the player located in the same screen sector.

Case 28

Positioning the player in the centre of the screen allows two panning shots of him to be edited consecutively. The shots have a common visual axis (Fig. 21.20).

The first shot here is a close shot and the second a full shot but the order can, of course, be reversed. If the player is located on one side of the screen in both shots a reverse angle coverage can be obtained, with both shots panning in the same direction (Fig. 21.21).

With this formula the second shot can be in a totally different place. Thus a transition in time is obtained using a continuous movement by the same player.

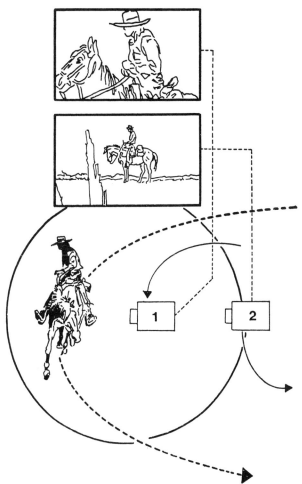

FIGURE 21.20 The consecutive shots of the same subject where the camera positions are on a common visual axis at the moment of the cut.

Case 29

Interrupted movement in one direction can be covered with a panning shot on the first phase of the movement and a static reverse shot for the second part (Fig. 21.22).

Here is a description of the scene.

Shot 1   Low shot. A car approaches. It then turns to the left and the camera pans with it. The car stops several yards away in a full shot, now seen from behind. As soon as the car stops, cut to . . .

419

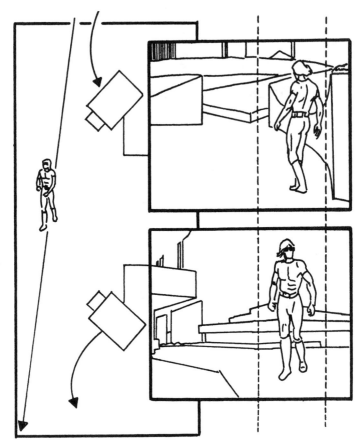

FIGURE 21.21 Two consecutive external reverse panning shots of the same player who moves in the same direction in both shots.

Shot 2   Reverse low shot of the car. Its doors open and people jump out and run forward out of shot, left.

Case 30

Vertical tilt shots can be joined to static shots using the formulas described.

Those panning shots suggested here can be reversed with the static shot used first and the pan second extending even further the possibilities for covering action.

FIGURE 21.22 The first shot is a pan while the second is static.

Acrobatic pans

The two examples that follow depict panning shots that are visually stunning.

For this purpose the camera has to pass through some sort of aerial loop.

Case 31

A horizontal pan is made with the subject coming towards the camera and passing *in front* of the camera operator, who follows it with his camera.

But what happens if the subject in motion passes *behind* the camera operator during a horizontal pan?

In order to keep him framed on the screen the camera operator will be forced to bend his body backwards. This motion demands that the camera should be placed upside down during a sector of

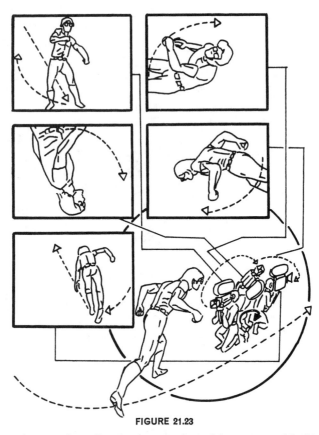

FIGURE 21.23

the panning motion. On the screen the subject covered behaves as follows: he is seen upright approaching toward us, then his body turns sideways as he begins to travel around three edges of the screen; first on one side till he reaches the top edge, at which time he is seen completely inverted on the screen; and descends by the opposite side or edge to attain a normal standing position and moves away from the camera.

This visual somersault was used quite extensively by the cameramen in the TV series *Mission Impossible*.

Fig. 21.23 illustrates the case described.

Case 32

When the camera is pointed straight down to record an across the screen motion, a startling effect is obtained by rotating the

422

camera 180 degrees on its vertical axis. In the film *The Strawberry Statement* such an occurrence took place. A slim rowing boat seen from above entered the screen from the right. As it reached the centre of the screen, the camera was turned a half circle on its vertical axis, so that the boat reversed direction and went out of the screen by the right, the same side from which it had entered (Fig. 21.24).

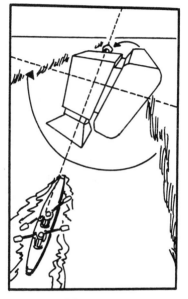

FIGURE 21.24

It does not matter if the turn is done to the left or the right, the final result will be the same, as long as you keep to a 180 degree arc.

22

THE TRAVELLING CAMERA

On the screen, movement has direction, strength, speed, duration and timing. In general, a large number of movements create a feeling of energy, hurry, excitement or violence. Little or no movement suggests dullness, quietness, depression, solemnity or, at the other extreme, depending upon the context of the scene, an emotional tension so great that all activity is suspended.

Movement often coincides with the line spoken. If the movement precedes the line, the line is emphasized. If the line precedes the movement, the movement is emphasized.

Many of the methods used for panning shots are equally applicable to tracking shots. Here are some suggestions:

1   The most pleasing moving shots are obtained when the camera tracks smoothly, without bumps, at a constant speed. If an increase in speed or a slowing down are required, these must never be sudden movements.

2   Trackings that cover subjects framed in long shot or full shot are enhanced if static objects are placed between the paths of subject and camera. Better pictorial compositions are obtained by providing planal contrasts so avoiding an appearance of flatness.

3   Tracking shots with pauses where the camera and the subjects momentarily stop can add variety or even break the monotony of a continuous repetitive movement.

4   If the player and camera are to pause during a tracking shot, it is generally better to avoid stopping where there are objects in the foreground unless they have some special significance in the story, because they will certainly be emphasized very strongly. If they are only obstructive they are better avoided.

Intermittent action covered by a continuous tracking

A continuous tracking shot need not follow a single person or group from beginning to end. It can, for example, begin with a medium sized group that halts in stages, while the camera continues tracking in a constant direction.

Suppose we track with a group of soldiers and their officer, taking some condemned prisoners to the execution ground. A priest walks with them. First we travel with the full group. Then the soldiers stop. The priest, the stretcher bearers and the officer continue walking. The stretcher bearers kneel down to attend a wounded prisoner. The officer and the priest go on. The officer stops. The priest continues and joins one of the prisoners. The camera stops. Stanley Kubrick employed such a shot in his film *Paths of Glory*. (Fig. 22.1).

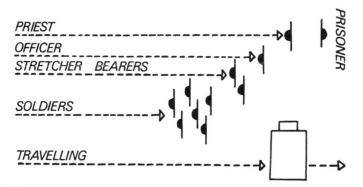

FIGURE 22.1 A simple case of intermittent movement covered by continuous tracking. The group decrease in number as they stop along the way. Only one reaches the final destination.

In the example given, camera and players were moving on parallel paths. But the same principle can be applied to a group which is followed from behind by the camera. (Fig. 22.2).

A approaches along a corridor. E enters from behind the camera, right, and walks away past A who turns a corner into another corridor and the camera, panning with him (left) begins to track behind A. F comes down the corridor. He greets A and continues to walk towards us, going out of shot, left. As A reaches the phone booth where C is talking into the phone, we see B enter from a nearby door and cross in front of A, walking to the left into another corridor. The camera turns left, following B. At that moment C leaves the phone booth and walks behind B. The camera travels in the new corridor behind both B and C. Halfway along the corridor B enters by a door on the left and we continue to track behind C who joins a noisy group of four men. At that

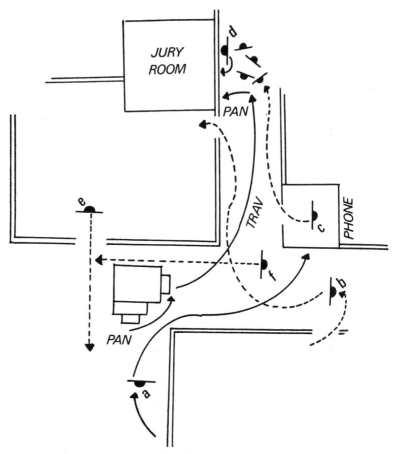

FIGURE 22.2 Another example of overlapping action covered by a tracking camera which moves behind the players in action.

instant an usher, D, asks for silence and points to a door on the left. The camera stops and pans to the left with the gesture of the usher, to a door with the words *Jury Room* on the glass.

The continuous tracking had, at all times, overlapping movements that led the audience's interest to the culmination of the shot. The movements were carefully integrated with each other as if in a ballet designed exclusively for the camera.

Joining a static and a tracking shot
Where a camera tracks with walking or running people it is not easy to slow it down when they stop, the framing at the end of

426

such a shot is critical, thorough rehearsals and a good camera crew are required to synchronize movements. It is easier to achieve that stop by simply cutting to a static camera position.

Case 1

If the performer walks towards us and the camera tracks back with him for the latter part of the walk, we can cut to a fixed camera position on the same visual axis but at full shot distance (Fig. 22.3), where the player is centrally placed.

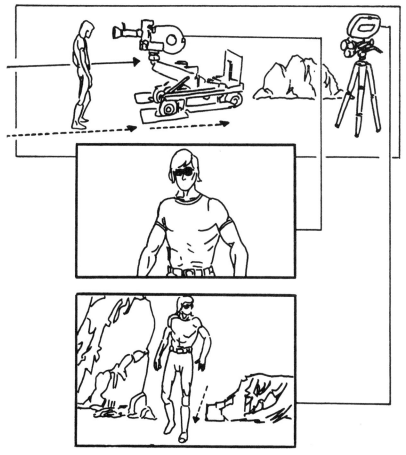

FIGURE 22.3 Motion on a common visual axis is used to join a tracking and a static camera shot of the same moving subject.

Case 2

With quick movement in the first shot, such as where the actor runs towards a back-tracking camera he can increase speed at the end of the shot and move forward out of shot. In the second shot the player (centre) runs forward two or three steps and halts (Fig. 22.4).

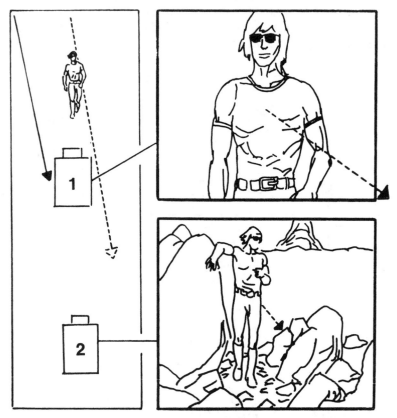

FIGURE 22.4 It is easier to join a fast tracking shot to a static camera position if the moving subject is allowed to go out of the screen in the tracking shot.

Case 3

If we track back with a player who then changes direction it is better to show the change in the second static shot (Fig. 22.5).

The first shot corresponds to those in the previous examples. The player walks in close shot and we track back with him. We

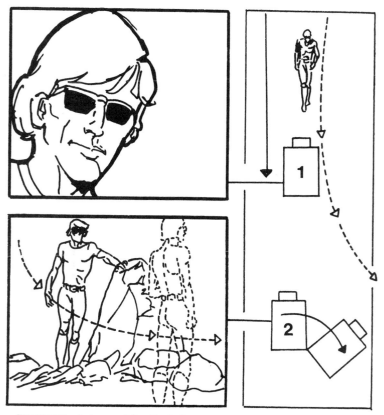

FIGURE 22.5 A change of direction in the subject's movement is best shown in the second, static camera position.

then cut to him in full shot, centre. He takes a couple of steps towards us and then turns and walks out of shot possibly followed by a camera pan.

Case 4

A shot tracking parallel to the player can make use of other solutions. In the first, close, shot, we track with the player profiled or in three-quarters view. We cut to a static full shot. The player enters from the side opposite to his direction of movement and stops in the centre (Fig. 22.6).

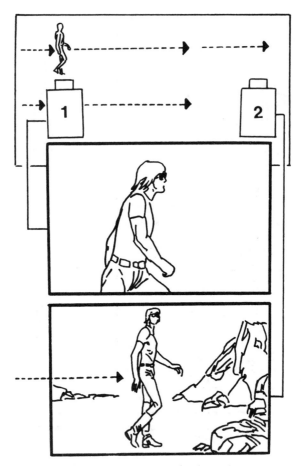

FIGURE 22.6 A parallel camera arrangement for the static camera site is used in the formula depicted here.

Case 5

A panning shot can be used as the second shot, thus slowing down with the performer as he stops walking or running (Fig. 22.7).

In the first shot he moves with the tracking camera. We cut to a full shot.

The player, centre, moves in the same direction; the camera pans with him till he stops.

As pointed out in previous cases, the size of the figure in both shots and the position on the same screen area, are critical for the

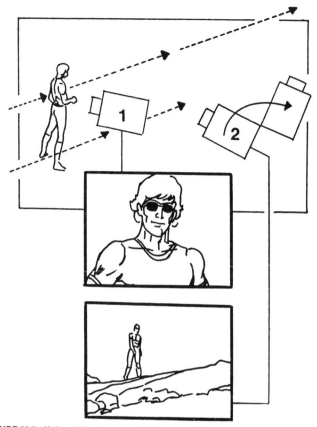

FIGURE 22.7 If the subject movement is too rapid, the second shot with this right angle arrangement, can be a pan.

success of the transition on the moment of the cut. Particularly here, where the actor's figure begins to decrease rapidly in size as he moves away on the second shot.

Case 6

A static right angle camera site can be used as the second shot to cover a running person. In the first shot the player is portrayed centrally in a medium shot. The camera moves with him along the same line. Near the end of the shot the camera pans slightly to one side leaving a half screen empty in front of the player. In the next, fixed, shot the player in the same screen position runs away from us to the centre of the picture area (Fig. 22.8).

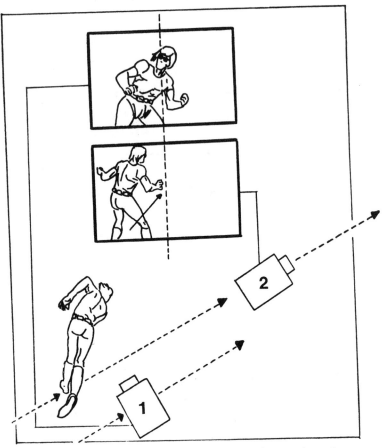

FIGURE 22.8 In this right angle arrangement, the moving player remains on the same side of the screen in both shots. The static shot frames him from behind going away in a neutral direction.

Case 7

A reverse angle camera position can be used to show a group of players halting in a place (Fig. 22.9).

In the first shot the camera tracks with the group seen in full shot.

Cut to a reverse medium shot. Static camera. The players enter shot moving in the opposite direction, and stop.

The fixed camera position is placed on the other side of the line of action, thus obtaining a very dynamic visual conclusion to walking or running movements.

FIGURE 22.9 An external reverse camera set-up using a tracking and a static shot to cover a group in motion who come to a halt in the second shot.

Intermittent camera tracking

Case 8

For most tracking shots the camera is mounted on a dolly running on some form of suitable tracks assembled for the particular shot. The camera may travel continuously or intermittently or reverse its direction of movement at any point. Fig. 22.10 is a floor plan view of a scene using a tracking camera.

Two soldiers, A and B, are walking through a battlefield. The camera travels sideways with them. When they reach position 1,

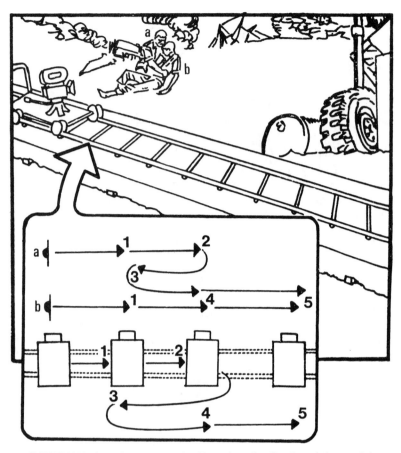

FIGURE 22.10 Intermittent camera tracking, where the direction of the march is reversed once and then resumed.

both lie down and wait. The camera stops tracking. The soldiers get up again but only A continues to position 2, where he stops, followed by the tracking camera. Realizing that he is alone, A turns and goes back to B. The camera reverses to the other side with A, returning to position 1—the third camera stop. B is wounded. A helps him to his feet and puts one of B's arms over his shoulder. Both walk laboriously to position 2—the fourth camera stop.

The camera resumes the original direction of movement. Both soldiers rest, then continue to position 5, where, again, they stop with the camera. B says he cannot go on. He wants to be left there, to die.

The actors can move behind various obstacles between stops—for example, barbed wire, upturned cannon and tall grass.

Case 9

The camera might track the whole length of the long run, stop and then return to the first position. In Fig. 22.11 the actors move intermittently.

FIGURE 22.11 Intermittent movement of both camera and players is used in this example.

The shot begins from a static camera position framing A in the centre of a group. When A starts to walk through the parting crowd, the camera tracks right. He reaches B, stops, and B walks to the right and stops beside C. The camera stops framing B and C among the group. C then comes forward and stops in the foreground. The camera is still static. C walks to the left through the crowd. The camera starts to track back (left). C stops in front of D and gives him a key. D moves to the left and inserts it in a machine. The camera stops framing D in the foreground operating the machine. Other players are seen beyond.

Using both sides of the track

Case 10

The camera may reverse its direction of travel on the screen though moving in only one direction, by merely panning through a half circle to the other side of the track. The movement is continuous and the audience can accept the contrasting directions without difficulty (Fig. 22.12).

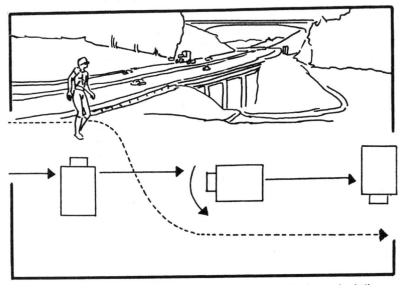

FIGURE 22.12 Both sides of the track are used in the same shot by panning in the middle of the tracking shot.

Case 11

A shot might track down the entire length and use both sides (Fig. 22.13).

A approaches B and both run a short way to point 1 where they stop. They start to run to the left again and the camera tracks with them to that side passing in front of a fence briefly seen in the foreground of the previous shot. The camera stops at point 2 and pans from 2 to 3 following the actors.

The camera faces the other side of the tracks and starts to move again, tracking with both players from 3 to 4. Camera and players halt for a moment, and then run back to point 5 where they fall. The camera follows to point 5 to conclude the shot.

436

FIGURE 22.13 Another example in which both sides of the track are used for a continuous travelling shot which keeps reversing its sense of direction periodically to accompany the action.

A half circle pan at one end of the track turns the camera from one side of the tracks to the other. While the motion of the camera from points 1 to 4 was continuous, the movement of the dolly was not. The fence was included to add visual variety to the shot at intervals.

Winding paths

Case 12

An actor who appears in a tracking shot does not have to be confined to a straight line; he could approach or move away from the camera by following a sinuous path but with the camera moving in a straight line. With this kind of action, static objects between the camera and the actor are essential to give the illusion of depth and planal contrast. If he is supposed to give the illusion of struggling to find a path through a difficult medium (a crowd or a forest, for example), it is much more convincing if he weaves in and out and perhaps is occasionally engulfed. He adds to the realism of the situation by pushing people or bushes aside, as if they offer some resistance.

The camera may track parallel or diagonally to the crowd or forest. Camera movement is as in Fig. 22.14.

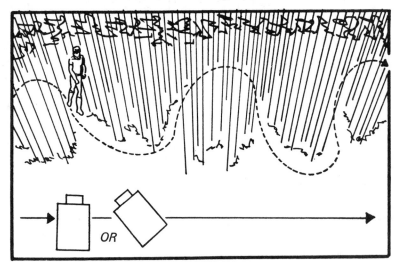

FIGURE 22.14   The sinuous path of a player is covered from a straight camera track.

Case 13

In a further variant, the camera tracks back in a straight line, while the subject moves on in front following a winding path. The camera pans from side to side to keep him in view. This formula can be used to show a character pushing through a thin crowd waiting for some event (Fig. 22.15).

Case 14

The same straight camera path with the camera panning from side to side can be applied to a static group placed in semi-circle. The

438

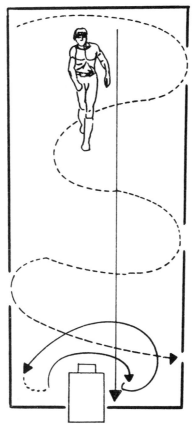

FIGURE 22.15 When the player advances in a winding path this can be covered by a straight camera movement retreating in front of the player.

camera starts with a long shot and tracks in, panning from side to side as it goes and finally comes to rest framing the central player (Fig. 22.16). Such a movement requires strong dramatic motivation. This same approach can be applied to a zoom shot.

Case 15

Intermittent camera tracking following a person who moves from zone to zone in effect turns the winding path into a series of triangles (Fig. 22.17).

From position 1 we frame A in close shot. When he moves to zone 1, the camera tracks with him to position 2. He is seen now

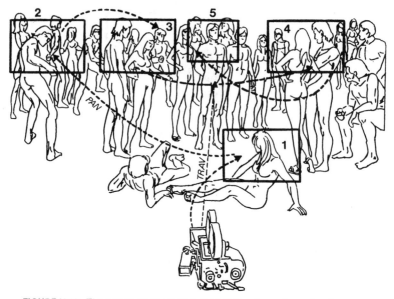

FIGURE 22.16 The camera advances on a straight line forward, panning from one side to another until it stops, framing the central character in the semicircular group.

in full shot. He pours himself a drink. B crosses in the foreground. Then A comes forward and stops in close shot in position 2. Behind him B crosses the screen from one side to the other in the opposite direction. Now A moves back to zone 3. The camera tracks from position 2 to 3. A sips his drink as he looks out of the window, then turns and advances to zone 4. The camera tracks from position 3 to 4 to frame A in close shot again. The horizontal movement of B was introduced to break the back and forth motion of the main performer, thus adding variety to the screen presentation.

Case 16

The winding paths of two actors may cross in front of a continuously moving camera (Fig. 22.18).

This allows some contrast in the number of figures appearing on the screen. Player A in foreground slows down and is excluded by the tracking camera which now concentrates on B as he comes forward. When B is nearby, A re-enters the background from the side where she passed out of view and crosses behind B to place herself on the right side of the screen. Composition B-A is main-

440

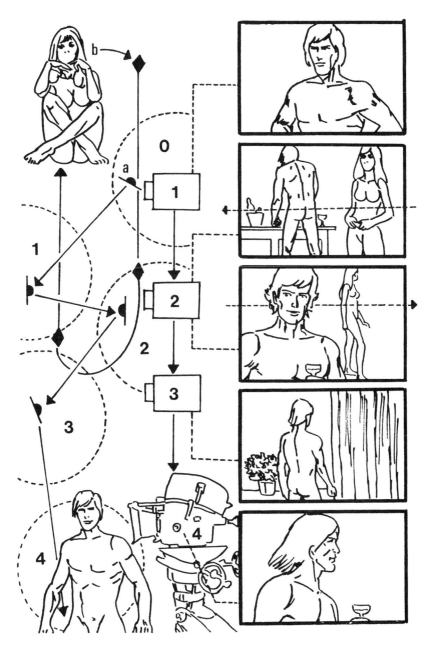

FIGURE 22.17 Intermittent camera movement covers intermittent player's movement which assumes an irregular shape or arrangement, forming triangles.

441

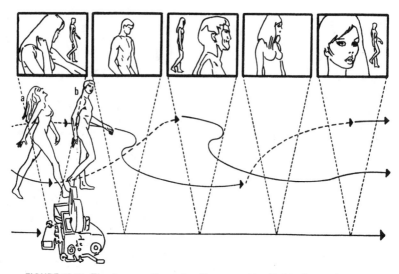

FIGURE 22.18 The sinuous patterns of motion are combined in this shot, so that each of the two players appears alternately on the screen.

tained for a moment, then B slows down and A is framed in close shot once more. Later B re-appears in the background. The dotted lines in Fig. 22.18 correspond to the paths of the performers not recorded by the camera.

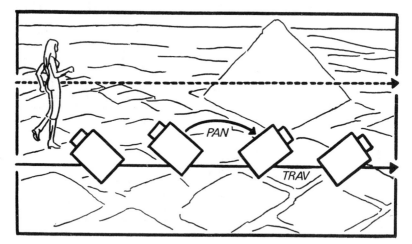

FIGURE 22.19 A panning movement in the middle of a tracking shot changes the framing of the subject from a front to a rear view.

Case 17

A half circle can, of course, be executed in the middle of a tracking shot as well as at the end. Two variations are possible. If the shot starts with the camera framing the front of the player, after the pan the camera will be framing her from behind (Fig. 22.19).

The reverse effect will be obtained if the camera starts the shot framing the players from behind. They will face the camera at the conclusion of the shot with their positions reversed (Fig. 22.20).

In these two examples the camera tracks along a straight path and the distance between the actors and the camera remains constant.

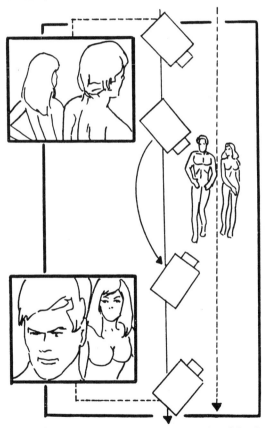

FIGURE 22.20 If the camera starts tracking with the rear view of the players, a pan in the middle changes that relationship to a frontal coverage. The camera must move faster than the characters during the pan to be able to frame them from the front. In the previous case the camera slowed down during the pan.

Case 18

The camera may track in a straight path that then moves round through a right angle turn if, say, the actor abruptly turns a corner. If the player walks in front of the camera as it tracks back, the shot is simple to execute (Fig. 22.21).

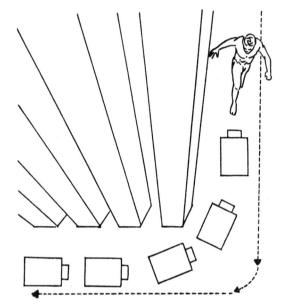

FIGURE 22.21 A player's right angle path of movement is repeated for the camera movement that precedes him.

In a more elaborate set-up the players might move along a right angle path, opposed to the one followed by the camera (Fig. 22.22).

The camera tracks behind two soldiers who run through a deserted street. When they reach a corner, the two players move off towards a wrecked trolley bus which has been abandoned in the middle of the street. Distant machine-gun fire is heard. The two soldiers stop beside the trolley and check their whereabouts. The camera continues tracking all the time, panning to keep the actors framed and turns into the new street. The soldiers then start to run toward the camera and then keep pace with it as it tracks.

The changing subject distances here give the take added pictorial value. When the actors pause but the camera continues to

444

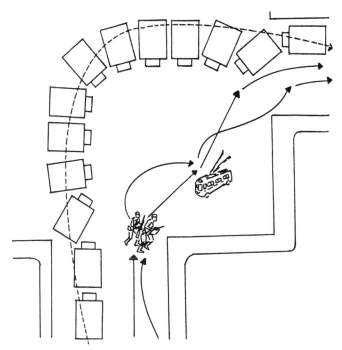

FIGURE 22.22 A right angle camera turn on a continuous tracking shot to cover an intermittent movement of the players in the scene.

move, a suggestion of doom is introduced, derived from the contrast of motion and quietness and the context of the scene—the isolation of a deserted street, menacing sounds from an unknown place, a war going on.

Case 19

A pan in the middle of a tracking shot can be used when covering two static players as in Fig. 22.23.

The camera begins framing a close shot of A and B. Then it tracks forward to B. When the camera reaches her it begins to pan to the side, the direction opposite to that in which it is travelling. The panning movement uses player B as a pivot. The camera continues tracking but now recedes from A and B until it stops, framing them in medium shot.

445

FIGURE 22.23 A player is used as a pivot for the panning shot as the camera tracks. Both subjects are stationary.

Camera and performers move in opposite directions

Occasionally, a shot is arranged in which camera and performers move in opposite directions. Several variations are available.

446

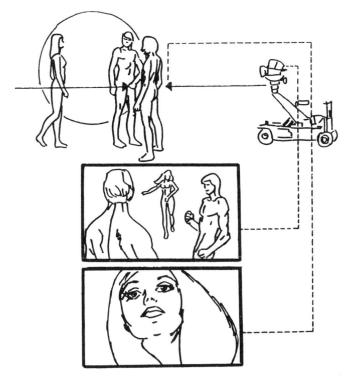

FIGURE 22.24 Player and camera, both in motion, converge toward each other in a neutral direction.

Case 20

Player and camera travel towards each other and stop face to face. If foreground players are involved, they are excluded at the end of the shot (Fig. 22.24).

As can be readily appreciated, the solution outlined has good potential for stressing a performer or a situation. The opposed movements of camera and players are equally emphatic if a departing player moves away as the camera recedes. By moving away from the scene as the main player goes away, a break in the mood of the play is underlined by visual means on the screen. Several movements of this type in succession, either all converging or diverging featuring different players will stress the situation that follows after those movements are completed. It is enough to involve two or three players for visual stress.

447

Cas

If the camera and the actress have converging oblique paths, the take will start also in a full shot and conclude in a close shot (Fig. 22.25).

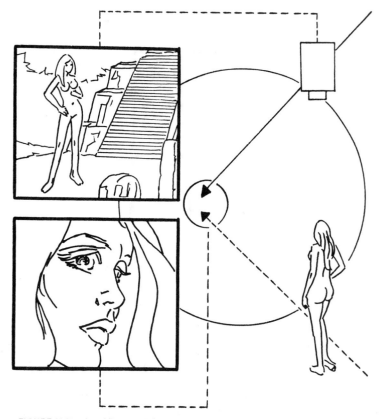

FIGURE 22.25 An oblique path for the camera and player are used in this example.

Case 22

Another set up has the camera and subject cross on parallel paths, the camera panning to follow the subject as she passes. She appears to approach and then move away from the camera (Fig. 22.26).

448

FIGURE 22.26 Camera and player move in opposite directions. When they cross, the camera pans with the player as it continues to move away from her.

Both camera and subject move at similar speeds in opposite directions. She may stop first, momentarily before the camera does.

Case 23

A further variation is obtained if a central static player is included in the shot. The player in motion, and the camera, converge towards the static player but the moving player stops before the camera does. The camera halts only after obtaining a reverse view of its initial position (Fig. 22.27).

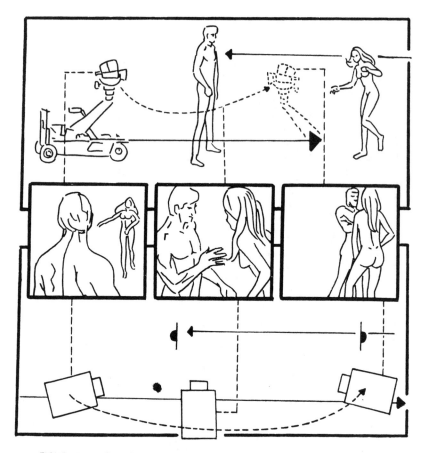

FIGURE 22.27 One of the players and the camera move in opposite directions. The stationary character is used as a visual pivot in the scene.

Case 24

If the camera moves in the opposite direction to that of an oncoming group and does not pan to follow it, it is wise to have the camera angled forward in a three-quarter position. (Fig. 22.28).

This camera position allows us to watch the players comfortably, as they approach from the background and move out of shot. If the camera is placed parallel to the players, it gives a profile view and they will appear to cross the screen more quickly. But the speed is too great for comfortable viewing and the fast repetitive motion quickly becomes annoying.

FIGURE 22.28 A large group moves in the opposite direction to the camera, which observes them from a three-quarter view.

Case 25

This case involved a quarter circle pan on a tracking shot (Fig. 22.29).

Here the camera moves in the opposite direction to the walking player, A, using the static subject, B, as a pivot.

Case 26

If player A walks towards B, the last camera position is a side shot of both (Fig. 22.30).

The difference is that at the end of A's movement, she remains facing B in profile, while in case 25, both players adopted an L relationship in their bodies' 'rapport'. A stood beyond B, in a frontal view, while B was profiled to the audience.

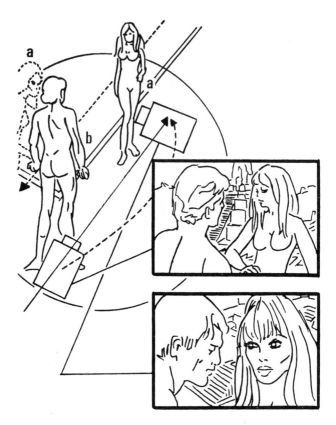

FIGURE 22.29 A track is used to move the camera from one static zone to another at right angles to the first.

Case 27

An inversion of the position of the players on the screen is obtained if the moving actor walks between the static player and the moving camera (Fig. 22.31).

More involved track and pan movements can be obtained by reversing the track and pan in the second part of the shot. A girl talks to her man, then she walks to the left. The camera travels with her left and pans to that side to pick up her image and that of her companion on a mirror. She stops, facing the mirror, and the camera stops tracking and panning—framing her on the right, her reflection in the centre and the reflection of the man on the left.

452

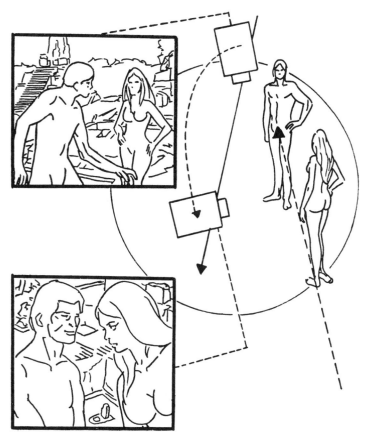

FIGURE 22.30 The procedure here is similar to that used in the previous example except that at the end the players face each other.

She turns to face the camera. In the mirror the man advances to her and stops closer but without physically entering the screen. She starts to come forward to the right, and the camera tracks back and pans to the right with her. She crosses beyond the man and the camera tracks with her alone. She stops; so does the camera. She turns to face the man off screen, left. As she completes her turn, the man enters the picture from the left, and both remain in profile to the camera. Camera and players moved in a choreography for the screen, which is the basis of editing shots 'in the camera' to be explained later on.

453

FIGURE 22.31 Here the camera movement is similar to that used in the previous examples, but the players cross over and exchange their position on the screen.

Case 28

A panning movement can be used at the opening of a shot, followed by a track as a continuation of the pan—capping the shot, in effect, with another pan when the dolly has stopped moving (Fig. 22.32).

It is a simple formula for introducing the players (in the first pan), travelling with them as they speak, and seeing them head for their destination (in the second pan). In this way the tracking is used only for the most important part of the shot. In the pan at the end of shot 1, the destination of players A, B and C may be seen in the background (actors D and E).

Shot 2 would cover the approach of the main players, by means of a quarter circle pan, and frame the whole group when they meet.

Single file formations

When players move in single file, a camera which tracks with them may move faster or slower than they do.

454

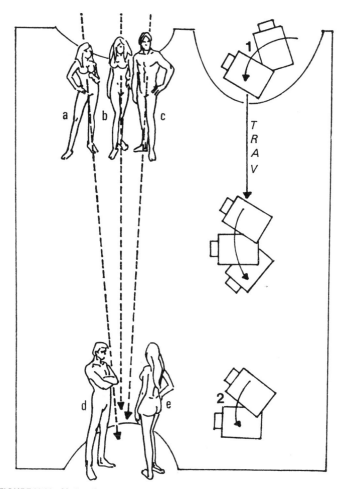

FIGURE 22.32 Motion flows into motion as both shots feature camera movement that dovetails smoothly to cover a group walking to a waiting twosome.

If the camera moves faster, the actors can be revealed one by one and swiftly left behind. But if the camera maintains a constant speed, the actors may come into range one by one, slow down to keep pace with the camera, then increase their speed and advance out of shot while the person behind takes his place. The cycle is repeated with as many people in the line as desired.

Another variant is to have one person out of line moving with the camera faster than the others so that he gradually passes each other player.

He can walk either between the camera and the row of people, or beyond the line. In the first case he is in foreground, in the second, the background.

A further refinement is to have the line of people move in the opposite direction to the main actor and the camera so that he remains in the centre of view either in the foreground or background, while the line of people cross on the other side. This gives a very dynamic shot.

But to be effective in this, and the previous cases, the camera should be angled three-quarters towards the line, never parallel to it (Fig. 22.33).

FIGURE 22.33 A three-quarter view to cover a moving group from a tracking camera shows the action in a much clearer way than would a parallel moving camera.

Tracking speed

Tracking speed for a camera is almost always dictated by the speed of the subject being covered. If the camera moves towards or away from a static subject or group, the speed with which it does it will, in effect, comment upon the scene.

A typical change from a full shot to a close shot of a player can be used to stress any facial expression or body movement of the player on the terminal sector of the tracking motion.

A swift departure movement can be used to reveal new information in foreground that has caused a reaction in the player seen in close shot.

Slow tracking provides an intimate mood, creeping in quietly to the player.

Slow and steady tracking in movements towards a speaking or silent player, makes the audience identify with him more fully. His problems become ours, our sympathy for him flows out more freely.

Slow, backward tracking can stress a feeling of sadness or loneliness. It isolates the stationary player from the audience.

When repetitive tracking movements are used, either moving sideways across the landscape of different locations, or accompanying different subjects covered separately in each shot, the speed of tracking should match. Likewise, when repetitive forward movements are used towards different subjects (or repetitive receding movements) the speed should be the same. When you intercut receding tracking shots between forward tracking takes, to comment on static subjects or objects, the same requirement applies. Different speeds from shot to shot will mar the effect.

Subject approaches tracking camera

Subjects covered by a camera tracking frontally need not start from a close position. A car moving along an avenue is seen in full shot with the camera moving back in front of it. The car gains speed and approaches. When it is almost parallel, the camera pans slightly to one side with it and frames a medium shot of a passenger on the back seat. Car and camera now move at the same speed (Fig. 22.34).

The shot could begin with only the subject moving towards the camera which only begins to move with her when she is nearby (Fig. 22.35).

When the camera begins to move, a slow start which gradually gains speed will avoid the camera drawing attention to itself. Yet, it is wiser to have the player pause in front of the camera and, as she moves on again, start the camera moving with her. In this way the new motion of the player motivates the movement of the camera.

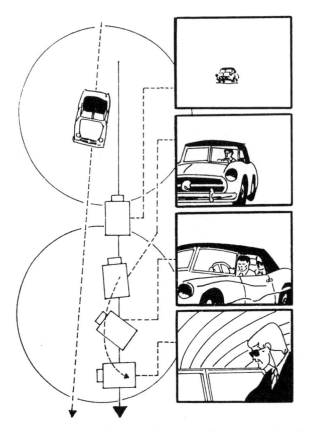

FIGURE 22.34 The car moves faster than the camera as it comes towards us, then the car slows down to the same pace.

Motivated action is accepted naturally by an audience because it does not draw attention to itself emphatically. It fulfils their subconscious desire to move with the scene.

Editing consecutive tracking shots

A long tracking shot of a player can be broken to intercut with reverse tracking shots of what the performer is looking at when he moves. The direction of the movement is reversed. Such a shot in fact becomes the player's subjective view (Fig. 22.36).

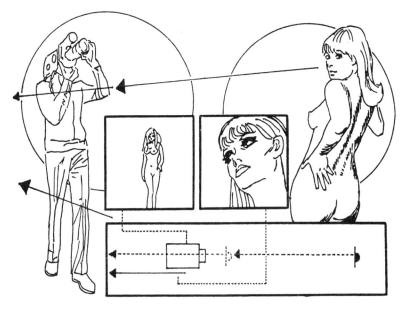

FIGURE 22.35 The camera waits in a stationary position as the player approaches. When she is close enough, the camera begins to track backwards with her.

The viewpoint of the moving player is thus visually stressed, as the audience alternately becomes the player advancing to a target.

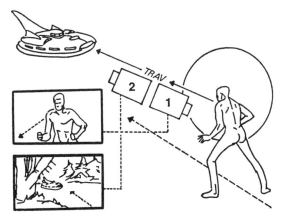

FIGURE 22.36 The second camera position is the subjective point of view of the moving player. Here a neutral direction is used.

If we are tracking sideways with a player, he will remain in the same screen sector with the background revealed at one side of the screen and hidden on the other. This is reversed in a travelling reverse shot (Fig. 22.37) that represents this point of view.

FIGURE 22.37   The second camera position is again a subjective viewpoint, but here a horizontal camera movement is used for both shots.

If the camera tracks behind a subject, going forward after him, in the reverse shot the camera tracks back with the player who is coming towards it (Fig. 22.38).

Here is such a case:

Shot 1   On the lower patio. Camera follows the actor from behind; he then climbs the stairs. As the camera reaches the first step we cut to . . .

Shot 2   Camera above on the edge of the stairs, facing the actor. It pulls back with him as he comes to the top and travels back with the performer down the corridor.

A more simple movement, where the actor walks on a plain ground, can be covered using the same formula.

460

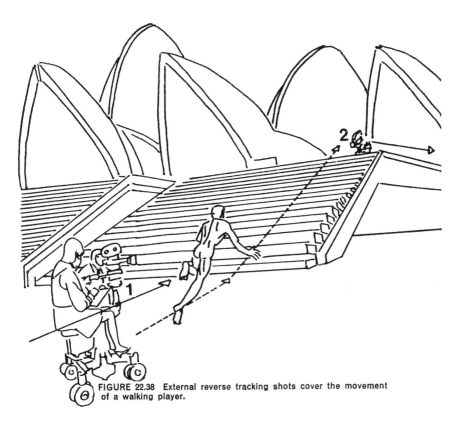

FIGURE 22.38 External reverse tracking shots cover the movement of a walking player.

Static shots intercut within a tracking master shot

Case A

A frontal tracking shot will allow intercutting of static cut-aways. The movement of camera and the player is kept constant in the master tracking shot. Related shots, that comment on or stress the story point, are intercut.

Here is a sample sequence:

Shot 1   Medium shot of A. Camera, low, moves back with the player as he walks towards us. He has a set of head-phones clamped over his head and a small microphone in front of his face. He holds a board with a check list, and moves in the middle of a crowded underground control room.

A: 'All right. Let's hear your final reports.'

461

Shot 2 Close shot of B. He is sitting profiled left in front of a large control panel. He presses some switches.
B: 'Computer ready, sir.'

Shot 1 Medium shot of A. Camera tracks back with him.
A: 'O.K., Burke?'

Shot 3 Close shot of C. He is standing in front of a bank of instrument panels, profiled right.
C: Tracking station is locked on the signal.

Shot 1 Medium shot of A. Camera tracks back with him. He checks his list with a pencil.
A: 'Ignition systems ready?'

Shot 4 Close shot of D. He has his back to us, and is seated in front of two monitoring TV screens, where a rocket on a launch pad is seen.
D: 'Yes, sir. Green lights all around.'

Shot 1 Medium shot of A. He walks towards us and stops. Camera stops too, keeping the medium shot distance.
A: 'All right. Control. Two minutes to go.'

22.38A

As the example shows, the interplay of questions and answers gives the visuals greater coherence, even when as in this case none of the players are related visually by lines of interest between them. The four players involved have all their backs to each other.

462

Case B

A common noise held on the sound track will help give coherence to a similar editing situation, where a master tracking shot is intercut with stationary shots. Here is an example:

Shot 1   On the torn, ravaged street, among the debris and the wrecked buildings, a heavy armoured tank moves forward. A group of armed soldiers advanced behind it, continuously on the lookout for snipers. The camera travels sideways to the subject, with the group framed in full shot.

Shot 2   A sniper with a rifle takes up position behind a wrecked window frame on the first floor of an abandoned house. He aims in a diagonal towards the lower right corner.

Shot 1   The tank and the group of soldiers move with the camera

Shot 3   Two men near a door frame, behind a pile of debris are ready with a machine gun. They aim left.

Shot 1   The tank and group of soldiers move with the camera on the street littered with burnt objects and chunks of cement.

Shot 4   Two civilians prepare a bazooka, and point the gaping mouth of the weapon towards us.

Shot 1   The tank and the group of soldiers advance along the street followed by the camera.

Shot 5   In the foreground, the men holding the bazooka have their backs to us and are aiming it towards the tank and the soldiers, seen in the background coming towards us.

Shot 4   Reverse viewpoint. The two civilians face us. They fire the weapon left of the camera.

Shot 1   The tank and the group of soldiers. The camera travels with them. The shell suddenly explodes on the street under the front of the tank. A geyser of smoke and flame billows up.

Shot 2   The sniper behind the wrecked window begins firing his rifle.

Shot 3   The two men by the door frame, fire their machine gun. The tank engine and tracks shaking the pavement make an impressive noise used throughout the sequence. Shots 2 and 3 are intercut into the master shot to show how the resistance movement is preparing its surprise attack. Although no precise reference to

22.38B

their whereabouts in relation to the tank is given, they are related by intercutting and the all-pervading noise of the advancing tank.

The last part of the sequence introduces shots 4 and 5. Shot 4 when first shown has the same vague relationship to the main event as shots 2 and 3. But when shot 5 is introduced, relating both elements visually in the same take, then significance is clarified. The master tracking shot, being continuous and of repetitive action, allowed frequent intercutting.

Circular tracking

Circular camera movement is tricky and must be used with restraint and only when strong dramatic reasons demand it. A continuous tracking circular shot tends to eclipse the story point by calling attention to the camera acrobatics.

Circular tracking around two people is often used to convey an emotional experience so overwhelming that it becomes a key point in their relationship—for example, a couple kissing after an unexpected revelation has restored their faith in each other (Fig. 22.39).

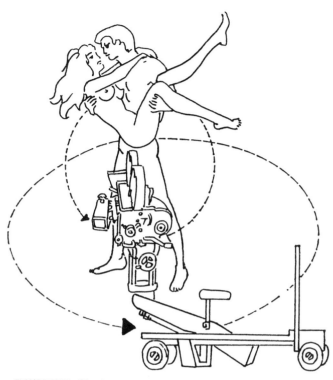

FIGURE 22.39 Circular camera movement around two stationary players.

Some variation is obtained if the camera moves with one of the players in a circle around a stationary central performer. The moving player remains facing the camera, the other is seen from a constantly changing viewpoint (Fig. 22.40).

Sometimes only a half circle is enough to convey a specific mood in a shot.

For example, a leader is addressing the peasants. The camera moves in a half circle behind them keeping the leader framed in the centre of the background (Fig. 22.41).

A feeling of dependence on a central figure or force is stressed because attention, even during the movement, conveys on the leader as a pivot. A half-circle camera movement can involve panning for the shot at the extremes. Thus the internal part of the

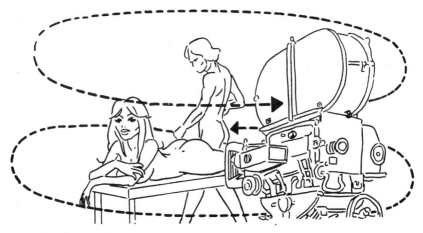

FIGURE 22.40 Player A walks around his stationary partner and is followed by the camera.

FIGURE 22.41 Half circular camera movement around a stationary group of players.

circle is covered frontally at the beginning or conclusion of the shot. Such an arrangement was used by Laurence Olivier in his film version of *Hamlet*.

During the presentation of the play in the castle, arranged by Hamlet to prove the guilt of his stepfather, the King, and the key figures in the drama are distributed in three groups in front of a stage (Fig. 22.42).

22.42A

Here is a description of this unique shot.

    The shot begins by showing Polonius, King Claudius
and Queen Gertrude (1) seen in full shot from one side.
The king is visibly disturbed and Polonius is watching
him. He walks one step forward to observe the king
better. The camera pans to the left (2) to show Horatio
on the other side of the central pit. Horatio is looking
at the king too. The camera continues panning left
(3) to show the woman on stage entering and discover-
ing the body of the other player. Hamlet is seen in the
foreground looking right towards the king, off-screen.
Behind him the actress kneels beyond the other player
on the stage miming. Now the camera travels right in a
half circle passing behind the players as the play continues. The camera (4) passes behind the Queen, the
king and Polonius. At that moment the murderer in the
play comes onto the stage and comforts the weeping
woman. Two hooded men enter and take the dead man
away. The camera stops (5) behind Horatio. He is seen
in the foreground, right, the players behind on the left.
Horatio now looks to the left and steps that way. The
camera pans with him (6). Hamlet and Ophelia are seen
in the background left, Horatio still in the foreground,
right. Then he walks again to the left, the camera pans
with him to that side. Claudius and Gertrude are

467

framed left (7). Horatio still in the foreground, right, turns his head to the right towards the stage and the camera tracks in a half circle to the left, panning to the right as it begins to move (8). It frames the miming players in their reconciliation. The camera passes behind Polonuis, the king and the queen and in the background we can see the two players on the stage moving away. As the camera tracks left, past the queen in the foreground, it pans right (9) framing Horatio in the background, the courtesans lined around the central pit, and stops in a medium shot of the king and queen profiled, left. The king stands up, visibly disturbed, and raises his hands to his eyes.

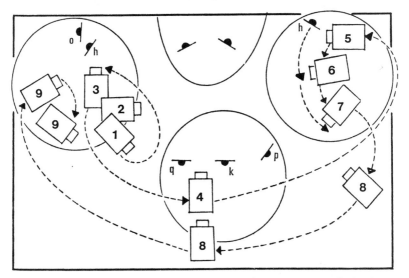

FIGURE 22.42B   Diagram that shows the movements of the camera, using a half circle path, during the mime played for the king and his court in the film version of Shakespeare's *Hamlet* directed by Laurence Olivier.

As the description clearly shows, the half-circle camera path was used twice in the same take, and at the end of each half circle pans reveal frontal views of the central characters (queen-king) scrutinised by the other two groups (Hamlet and Horatio). The action in the centre of the stage continued uninterrupted during the whole shot, but this activity was glimpsed at intervals and only at peak moments of action that were significant for the reactions of the other three central groups.

23

THE CAMERA CRANE
AND THE ZOOM LENS

With the aid of a camera crane the camera with its crew can be raised vertically or in an arc. For the most part, the crane is not used to provide camera movements but simply for stationary shots from angles that would otherwise be difficult or impossible and certainly time consuming to obtain.

Following action

A crane is used to execute simple and usually gentle movements. Its most obvious application is to follow actors who move up or down from one level to another. Such is the case with a player ascending a staircase. The camera on a crane keeps him in medium shot for example, throughout. Crane movements allow visual 'punctuation' shots or to move from a tight group in the foreground to a large group in the background. Or, again, to comment emotionally on the mood of a scene by using slow vertical movements. Sometimes an unexpected aerial view of a scene, perhaps tracking, gives the audience a detached viewpoint suggesting an impartial frame of mind.

Foreground props stress height

If an object with some vertical height is kept in the foreground when executing an upward crane movement, an increased sensation of height will be conveyed to the audience, because of the illusion of depth. Downward crane movements may profit from the same formula.

In Fig. 23.1, a group of riders, framed in long shot, advance towards us. The camera, high on the crane, captures them in the

FIGURE 23.1 A vertical prop in the foreground stresses the sensation of height on a crane shot.

background. In foreground the naked branches of a tree are seen jutting up from below. As the riders approach, the camera pans down in an arc with them.

It passes behind the branches of the tree in foreground and frames the riders stopping close by the building at the entrance to the street.

To visually unite two or more story points

Crane movements are often used to describe visually complicated sets, by starting from above showing, say, the whole group of players and paraphernalia involved in a ceremony. The camera then descends from the general to the particular, or *vice versa*, going from one point of interest to another.

Crane shots should be adapted to patterns of action and not the other way about. The action is first designed to suit the dramatic purposes of the scene. Once this has been decided the camera movement is designed to contribute with patterns that achieve the fullest visual effect. Misuse of crane motion is easy—in particular there is a temptation to swing the camera. This can ruin a film. Crane movements should be used sparsely and only when they contribute something of value to the scene.

To inject movement into static situations

Crane movements combined with tracking shots serve to describe visually a static group or situation. Sidney Lumet, in his film *The Hill*, used the following shots to describe a group of soldiers in formation on their parade ground awaiting the arrival of the commanding officer.

It was a hot day and the point was to show their discipline, while enduring physical discomfort. Fig. 23.2 gives a plan view of the set-up.

Shot 1   Full shot of the lines of men. The mast with their flag is seen in the foreground. The camera gradually rises.

FIGURE 23.2 A stationary group is covered by four moving camera set ups, two of which are crane shots.

471

Shot 2 Side tracking shot. The camera is at a three-quarter angle to the men and at shoulder height. It tracks across the lines of men.

Shot 3 From behind the group, the camera descends. As it comes down it picks out the side of a building in the left foreground.

Shot 4 Side shot tracking to the left, the camera very low, parallel to the men. Some men are seen kneeling and cleaning other soldiers' shoes. When the camera stops tracking it frames (in the foreground) two hands shining a pair of shoes of a man standing at attention.

Shot 5 View from below with the camera tilted up, close to the mast where the flag hangs limply in the still air.

Shot 6 Close up of a sweating face. He looks right.

Shot 7 Close up of another sweating face. Profiled right.

Shot 8 Close up of a third sweating face. Profiled left. Two flies on the soldier's cheek. The camera pulls back and swings up to the left to frame the lines of men from behind, facing the door of the fort, where the commanding officer enters in a Jeep.

The crane shots, effective as they were, served to highlight the mood pervading the scene—human beings under stress, mental and physical.

The only movements in the sequence were executed by the camera and not the actors. If they had been photographed from static camera positions, a series of jump cuts would have resulted.

Static rows of players and static camera set-ups hardly go together. The antithesis is visually stronger.

To single out a story point in a panoramic movement

A combined down-pan up-crane movement is often used to cover slow-moving bucolic scenes or to stress very fast action. Fig. 23.3 depicts the first possibility.

The camera in a high position frames a couple walking towards us. The camera descends slowly, tilting up gradually to keep the players framed centrally. When both performers are nearby, the camera pans with them and, at the same time, swings on the crane arm. The actors are now seen from behind, and, as they walk

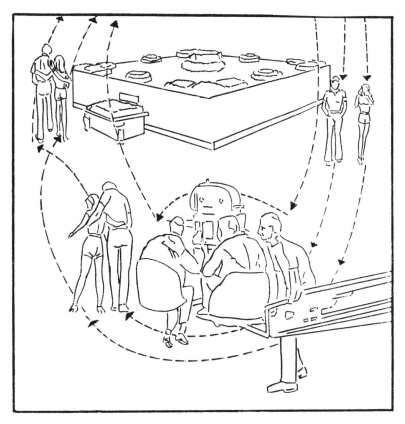

FIGURE 23.3 The crane movement in this example is used to stress a point in the scene, coming from the general to the particular.

away, the camera rises, gradually tilting down to keep them in shot, with a pause if required while the camera is level with them. This gives the players time to make a story point before moving on. If the camera remained level on the crane platform, it would begin and conclude the shot by only showing the distant view and the actors would be revealed halfway through the vertical movement, Faster subjects, such as a car coming towards the camera, can be covered with a more rapid crane movement. In such a case the arm of the crane practically swings in an arc, coming down and going up while moving in the direction of the vehicle.

The key to this formula is to move from the general to the particular and back to a majestic view of the proceedings. In this

473

way, halfway through the shot a selected event is stressed and its protagonists are then moved into the mass motion once more.

To provide strong movement for cutting on action

When covering a crowd from a height, it is difficult to cut to a reverse shot if strong movement (such as people walking through the crowd) is lacking in the scene. We are now concerned with the motion of a disorganized crowd moving in conflicting directions. As no clear cut pattern of motion is available on which to hinge our cut, a crane movement will help (Fig. 23.4).

FIGURE 23.4 Disorganized patterns of action are made coherent for the camera by introducing a crane movement.

Shot 1 Long shot. Camera static, high on a platform, tilted down. We see the colourful crowd moving in the market place.

Shot 2 A fruit stand in close shot. The camera rises to reveal the crowd from a reverse angle.

By cutting from a static long shot to a moving close shot, the problem of cutting on action is solved, because the movement shown in front of the camera at the beginning of the second shot is quite strong due to its closeness. Furthermore, the rising camera movement allows a smooth cut between shots. The upward camera movement can be combined with a track. If the first shot is a track also (moving in an opposite direction) the camera movement alone will give visual cohesion to the disorganized motions that it covers.

Zooming

The principal difference between tracking the camera towards the subject and operating a zoom lens from wide angle to telephoto settings is that with tracking shots the perspective of the scene changes (foreground features grow in size more rapidly than those in the background) whereas in an equivalent zoom shot, all parts of the scene are magnified equally.

When the zoom is on the telephoto lens setting, it acquires the characteristics of this lens: the planes of depth in the picture are, in effect, 'flattened' and the background appears to be pulled in toward the subjects in foreground.

Like the camera crane, the zoom has basic applications where its capacity for movement is not used at all. The crane has a platform that can be quickly set to any height. The zoom, combining a wide variety of focal lengths, provides a quick means of selecting a suitable one for the particular scene.

Some zoom lenses have a greater range of focal length than others. There are three basic ways in which a zoom is employed:

1 The lens zooms towards or away from a static subject.
2 The zoom covers a moving subject.
3 The camera moves while zooming.

The first two possibilities involve a static camera. The zoom effect is the only movement visible. But the third possibility adds camera movement which might be a pan or track or the two combined with a zoom.

Zooming speeds

Slow zooms usually have a constant rate of visual advance or recession. A fast zoom is used for shock effect. But a zoom can start slowly and gradually increase in speed. A sudden halt will be obtained when it stops. A fast start and a slow conclusion will be more pleasing to the eye but the start will be quite sharp and disturbing.

A slow-fast-slow combination seems to be the ideal when using a zoom that goes from one extreme to the other of the range available. It is not essential to use the full range of focal lengths afforded by the zoom lens. Zooming in short sections is generally more effective. Zooming towards a static subject draws attention to the zoom itself. A fast zoom provides visual punctuation that pinpoints the chosen subject, sharply excluding all surrounding matter. Thus it can stress a player's reaction, such as a shout or scream, or an object partially hidden by his clothes, or the barrel of a gun blazing towards the camera, or a silent witness in the background whom the zoom pulls forward to stress.

A slow zoom, quietly creeping forward towards tear-filled eyes can lend an intimate mood to a scene by suggesting participation.

The zoom is better motivated and thus better integrated with the shot if the player in a zoom shot moves with the optical change.

A zoom shot might be called for where a body is seen in motion (Fig. 23.5).

FIGURE 23.5 The movement of the player motivates the zooming of the camera lens. This may either magnify or diminish the image size.

When the shot begins, A is seen profiled left. He is obviously looking for something. As he turns his head towards us, we zoom back to reveal the object in the foreground.

A zoom shot can be suggested by a body movement:

A man walks towards the camera. The zoom lens on its tele position frames him in close shot. The zoom gradually pulls back with the advancing man, keeping him in a close shot. This backward optical movement simulates a physical travelling but the results are different.

Another possibility is opposed directions of motion—the camera zooms in towards a player who walks straight towards us. The zoom stops with the actor.

Zooming and panning combined

A zoom might be combined with a pan or tilt. For example, a short pan accompanying a player who walks towards another, may start by framing a medium shot of the first player and conclude on a zoom close shot of both performers.

FIGURE 23.6   Zooming can be done on a pan. A very smooth result is thus obtained

477

In the example in Fig. 23.6, the distance covered by the moving actor was very short, and the zoom used only a part of the focal range available.

A head turn in close shot can motivate an exploratory panning to which a zooming motion is added.

In the situation in Fig. 23.7, player A is hidden behind a column in a dimly lit oriental garden, framed in close shot. He is looking left. Suddenly he reacts to a noise heard off screen and turns his

FIGURE 23.7 A turning or walking player motivates a panning and zooming camera movement in which it leaves the first player to come to rest on the second.

478

head to the right. The camera begins to pan with the movement of his head and continues panning to the right across the garden. As it pans it slowly zooms in, to stop framing a medium shot of player B hidden behind a statue, with a weapon in his hand.

The slow exploratory pan combined with a zoom motion gave the illusion of smooth travelling through the garden between both points of interest, while the camera rotated on its horizontal axis.

A half-circle pan combined with a zoom forward or backward will provide a sweeping arc exploratory movement that scans a landscape, a building or the interior of a house. The movement of a lone player who walks from one zone to another can be covered with this pan-zoom technique.

In the previous chapter an instance was given in which a combined pan and zoom follow a meandering path (Fig. 22.16), as the camera pans alternately between two subjects. Michelangelo Antonioni, in his film *Blow Up*, used this effect as the subjective point of view of the main player examining two photographs. The camera framed one of the pictures for a moment, then panned to one side to a second, zoomed in and held a static view of this photograph. Then it panned back to the previous picture and zoomed in too, stopping on a much closer view. When the camera once more panned to the second picture, the zoom was resumed and an extreme close up of the second photograph capped the shot. Mario Camus, in a film made in Argentina, *Digan Lo Que Digan*, starring the Spanish crooner Raphael, used the same effect to stage one of the songs (*Cierro mis Ojos*) zooming alternately from the player to his reflections in five mirrors placed behind.

Tilt shots using zoom effects

A tilt and backward zoom out to wide angle is often used for establishing shots. A close shot of the rippling surface of a river shifts to a full shot of a bridge spanning it combined with an upward tilt.

Camera tracks as it zooms

A camera tracking in a straight line with the lens moving *across* the scene, can employ a combination of several patterns of motion provided by the camera, the zoom lens and the performers. Such is the case of the example in Fig. 23.8.

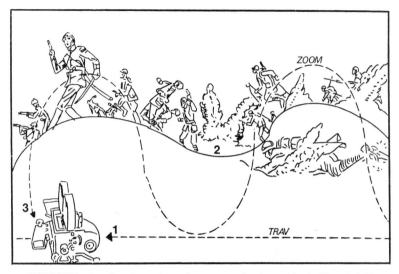

FIGURE 23.8 An advancing and receding zoom motion is combined with a straight tracking movement which covers an undulating actor movement. Three patterns of motion are thus combined.

The scene covers a battlefield—undulating terrain, full of natural crevices and barbed wire fences. The soldiers advance from right to left. Grenades and shells explode among them and casualties are heavy. The leader urges them on and the camera tracks left at a steady rate, always level. The scene is framed in long shot.

While tracking, the camera zooms in on the leader bringing him to a close medium shot. The camera holds on him for a while then zooms back to the previous long shot view of the battlefield. It keeps the long shot (wide angle extreme of the zoom range) for a while longer and again zooms in on the leader, repeating this process several times.

The men and the camera have been moving continuously to the left, amid explosions, people running, falling and crossing each other. Three definite patterns of movement may be seen here: a straight, horizontal camera track; an undulating path for the soldiers; an approaching and receding zoom pattern from a moving camera.

This combination was successfully used by Stanley Kubrick in his film *Paths of Glory.*

A camera that tracks and pans while it zooms gives the illusion of moving unhampered and without physical barriers. Tracking and panning masks the zooming and can render it almost imperceptible if the zoom is slow enough.

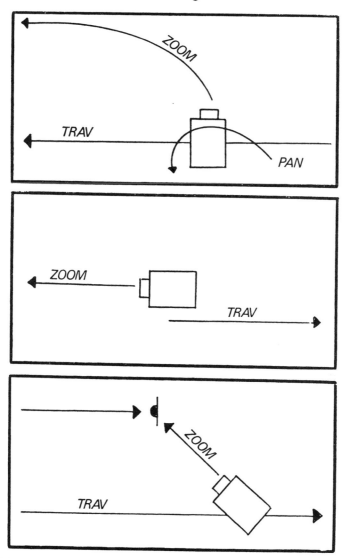

FIGURE 23.9 Zooming while panning and tracking. Zooming forward as the camera tracks back. Optical distortion is obtained. Subject and camera travel in the same direction, and the zoom is effected diagonally.

481

A combined track and zoom can provide a startling visual effect if their movements are suitably opposed. If the camera travels backwards and the zoom moves forward, especially in a corridor, there is a peculiar distortion of distances and object sizes. Alfred Hitchcock used the effect in his film *Vertigo* to convey precisely that sensation when James Stewart looks down the staircase in the church bell tower. Another type of distortion, but not as blunt, is also obtained when a camera, angled three-quarters to a group, moves backward in front of the ensemble, at full speed, and then zooms in obliquely towards the players. In *Doctor Zhivago*, David Lean uses the effect in several cavalry charge scenes where the camera rides with the group of soldiers over a frozen river. Fig. 23.9 shows each of the effects discussed.

Zooming through foreground obstacles

Objects of irregular shape, such as the struts at the back of a chair, or a series of rings, or any other obstacle, might be framed in the foreground of a zoom shot. When the zoom lens is set on wide angle, the foreground and background will be in focus but when moved to telephoto objects in the foreground will gradually pass out of focus until they are only a blur of colour through which the main action can be seen in sharp focus.

Interesting effects are obtained if the object or objects in foreground have movement themselves, preferably a repetitive movement. The film *The Ipcress File*, directed by Sidney Furie, explored the possibilities of the zoom motion used in the way just described.

24

ACTION SCENES

Without 'action scenes' film making would not have developed into the major commercial activity that it is now. The effectiveness of such sequences is due to a basic premise of film language, action and reaction, and parallel film editing is the key.

The action shown in such a sequence must be clear at all times to the audience—not a series of haphazardly built snatches of action but a solidly constructed story. For that, there must be clarity of motivation and care with detail. The story development depends on a series of incidents usually of four types—the chase, the physical fight or battle, the fight against a mechanism, and the accident. Any of these become more dramatic if they involve a fight against time.

The chase can assume several forms. The protagonist is pursued by the evildoer or villains of the story. The main player may be holding something that the other party wants or he (she) is the prize coveted by the opposition. The situation can be reversed and the protagonist chases the villains. The forces that each group brings into play can be equalized or a strong difference is present in favour of either one.

When any of the two groups falls into a seemingly inescapable situation, they must be able to extricate themselves from it not by a coincidence or by an accident, but by their own strength or ingenuity. They must solve the problem themselves in a logical way and within their possibilities, or with the help of a logically acquired element, either human or material. A chase can be conducted on foot, riding an animal (horse, camel, elephant), on a land or water vehicle or with an airborne machine, and all the combinations that these four elements allow.

There are several varieties of physical fight. The opponents may fight each other with bare hands or weapons, ancient or modern. A human being may be fighting a beast or mechanism. The fight can spread to a group and become a brawl. A full battle might be staged where large forces are in conflict.

A cardinal rule governs each of the above categories: the fight must be designed blow by blow. Every situation in the action scene must be carefully planned beforehand. The plot should never be given away prematurely or interest is quickly destroyed.

A mechanism that is about to produce a catastrophe if not put out of action, or that may blow off by a mistake or a wrongmove, has been effectively presented on the screen countless times. The transference of a dangerous element from place to place, where accidents can happen, is the second variety. Mechanisms that will trigger an alarm is the third variation. The addition of a time limit increases the apparent danger and intensifies audience interest.

Accidents on the screen can be real or staged. They usually involve high speed vehicles such as racing cars, motorcycles or planes. Real crashes and nerve racking spills have been filmed by cameramen on the spot when they actually happened and incorporated into the action sequence of many films. These accidents are usually recorded in a single shot since there is no pre-planning of any kind, and so they are the product of chance.

Staged accidents are more cinematic because they can be broken into several shots, thus affording a multiple vision of the event with certain aspects stressed quite forcibly. Specialised stuntmen can wreck vehicles spectacularly, but a simple camera trick can overturn any vehicle. A racing car, or a motor boat speeds on a diagonal path towards the camera, which pans to follow it. As it fills the frame of the screen the camera is suddenly turned over on to its side. The effect obtained is that the vehicle overturns. Two factors must be taken in account when carrying out this effect: Firstly the horizon line must not be visible on the screen, or the effect will be ruined. If the horizon line is missing the audience will accept the sudden swift movement as belonging to the vehicle and not to the camera. Secondly the camera must be tilted in a direction contrary to that of the moving vehicle. This changes the direction of the vehicle to a sudden vertical movement up the screen.

Standard formulas

The following rules, briefly enunciated, have proved successful in action scenes over the years.

Dialogue impedes action. Audiences must be shown, not told what is going on. Brief and terse commands uttered by the combatants are the exception.

Dialogue can be used as a pause in the action to give audiences a rest. Continuous action soon saturates emotion, and this must be renewed by pauses where verbal explanations can be used to clarify story points.

The pause in the action can be a physical one. It gives the combatants time to regain their breath before the final showdown. After a tense fight the combatants separate to regain strength and measure the opponent's condition. Suddenly they lunge and a brief exchange of blows concludes the fight.

Combat sequences can be built slowly and resolved quickly.

When a mechanism is defied, the obstacles must be first established. Then the identity of those who are going to try to conquer it is given. Some of the artifacts to be used must be presented visually but no explanation (or only partial ones) of how they will be employed are provided. Then the plan to overcome the mechanism is seen in action. Several interruptions take place where the situation nears complete disaster, but they are averted by the participants. Finally success or failure crowns the efforts of the defying party.

Credibility must not be strained except for humorous purposes.

The outcome of a chase must not be predictable to the audience. The diversity of obstacles faced by both pursuers and hunted must keep the outcome uncertain.

The double chase is a further variant. The hunter pursues his victim, and both are pursued by a third party interested in either of them. If the first two ignore the presence of the third the conclusion of the chase depends on the behaviour of this last one.

If two groups of pursuers chase the protagonist of the story, the peril doubles. Intricate buildings offer the best possibilities for this variation. Open ground nullifies it.

Some fight sequences use a gimmick to cap the action. A special weapon concealed in an outlandish place has been repeatedly resorted to in spy films.

Action sequences should not extend beyond their resolution point for too long. A humorous scene can be used to release tension.

The subjective point of view

Physical conflicts can be presented from multiple impersonal points of view or from localized focal points. For an impersonal point of view the camera examines each of the players and each of the situations without singling out an outstanding character whose point of view is imposed on the audience. All the facts are presented from the outside. The audience is kept as a spectator and not asked to participate emotionally.

On the other hand, action can be presented through the viewpoints of the central players of a film. A series of reaction shots taken from the emphasized player's position on the set accomplishes the trick. The technique tends to present in a frontal close shot the images of the central character, and in long shots the views of the action he is watching. His involvement in the action can be passive or active.

The attitude of the player is taken to be passive when he merely witnesses the event from afar, and reacts to it without going away. Such is the case of the role played by James Stewart in Alfred Hitchcock's film *Rear Window*. The action across the inner courtyard of the apartment building is always seen by the audience from this player's point of view.

The situation where the player engages in the action itself, is, in effect, active. In these scenes, as the action is being established, the parallel editing of the shots adheres to the limitation of emphasizing in frontal close shots and close ups the figure of the central player, while showing distant views of his opponent.

When both engage in physical combat they are framed in full shots that cover both (impersonal points of view) going back to the former subjective point of view as soon as they separate. Thus visual emphasis is thrown back on the main player. This player is seldom seen in the foreground of the reaction shots, since these represent his subjective point of view and therefore exclude him. The central character is never seen from his opponent's point of view.

The subjective approach by firmly adhering to the point of view of the central character forces the audience to see the action as this player sees it. Since we are treated to a series of action and reaction shots, we are not aware that we are being forced to observe the events from a chosen and fixed point of view. This technique is not only efficient in action scenes but is in its own right a good approach to heighten the emotion of a dramatic scene where dialogue is predominant. The main player speaks to another while concentrating on a different task that the subjective camera approach emphasizes visually. The director can also communicate feelings that are not implied in the dialogue being spoken. Thus the scene is enriched by cinematic means.

An important detail for this technique is to preserve emotion if the main player moves. In our previous discussion of the subjective point of view we had assumed that the main player through whose eyes we saw the action was standing or seated. If he must move to another part of the set, *do not cut back to give him space to move.* This would destroy the mood of the scene. Use the same static shot in which the player is framed to pan or travel with him as he moves to another part of the set. Emotion is thus preserved. Do not be tempted to cut back to a full shot because there is room to do so. If you do, your view is no longer subjective, but objective and the approach changes.

The subjective point of view is quite adaptable and can be applied to small groups that have different locations on the terrain or movie set. Here is an example taken from David Lean's film *The Bridge on the River Kwai*. In the last reel of the film, a group of imprisoned British soldiers cross the bridge leaving the detention camp for a new destination. They are watched from three different locations by the group planning to blow up the bridge. Figure 24.1 gives the positions of the players and the cameras.

Shot 17 Low medium shot of Warden (Jack Hawkins) by a rock looking off screen right. A young Thai girl beyond on the right. Warden rises his binoculars and looks through them (92 frames).

Shot 18 The screen is darkened by a round matte, representing the view through the binoculars. We see the bridge from above. The prisoners are approaching the bridge. (189 frames).

Shot 19 Medium shot of Shears (William Holden) and Yay (M B Chakrabandhu) behind some rocks. They have sub-machine guns and are looking off screen right (57 frames).

Shot 20 Long shot of the bridge as seen from the position of these two men. The prisoners are reaching the first support of the bridge (141 frames).

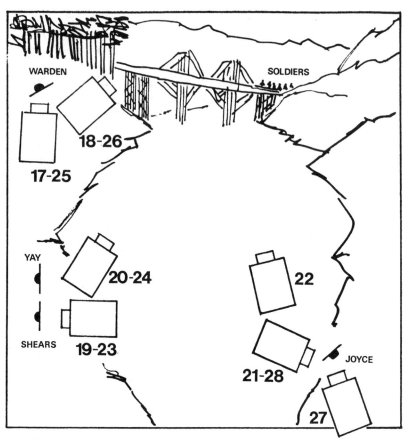

FIGURE 24.1 The subjective point of view can be applied to small groups with different locations on the set. An example from *The Bridge on the River Kwai.*

Shot 21 Medium shot of Joyce (Geoffrey Horne). He is crouched behind a rock and looks off screen left. He moves to the right and the camera pans with him (130 frames).

Shot 22 From his point of view we see a long shot of the bridge. The British soldiers reach the centre (164 frames).

Shot 23 Close shot of Shears and Yay. Some visual axis of shot 19 (71 frames).

Shot 24 This shot is the continuation of shot 20. The British soldiers now cover the bridge (139 frames).

Shot 25 Medium shot of Warden as in shot 17. He has the binoculars in his hand and does not use them to look off screen right. (96 frames).

488

Shot 26 Full shot of the bridge from above. Some trees in foreground. The British soldiers still crossing, whistling *Colonel Bogey* (99 frames).

Shot 27 Full shot. Joyce in foreground with his back to us. The dry river bed and the bridge seen beyond. The prisoners still crossing (90 frames).

Shot 28 Medium shot of Joyce as in shot 21. He rises and moves to the left. The camera pans with him left (156 frames).

The technique used is simple. The first site is presented in close shot. Then follows a shot of what the player located there sees. This is a long shot of the main event. The second and third sites are successively presented using the same technique. Thus the central action is seen on the screen from varying angles.

There is a further variation. The central action that is being observed from several emphasized points of view suddenly becomes dominant. We move closer to this main action and relate it to its own centre of interest. This approach can be used as a visual pattern in the sequence. Here is an example:

A man with a gun is hiding in a forest. He is seen in close shot.

A leopard moves slowly along a trail seen in long shot. Closer to the foreground is a goat tied to a post.

A second man with a rifle. He is hiding in the top of a tree, and is seen in close shot, from slightly below.

From his point of view the leopard is seen down below coming forward in a long shot. The goat is in the lower right corner.

Close shot of the leopard. The camera is level with it as it comes closer and stops, looking ahead.

From the leopard's point of view the goat is seen in long shot, tied to a post in the centre of the trail.

The first hunter seen in close shot, looking on.

From his point of view we see the leopard in long shot moving again along the trail towards the goat.

The second hunter seen in close shot. He looks down.

From his high point of view the leopard comes along the trail towards its prey.

Medium shot, level with its subject. The leopard comes to the camera and stops.

From the leopard's point of view the goat is seen in full shot.

The leopard suddenly runs forward out of screen, right.

Reverse. The leopard enters left and runs towards the goat in the background.

View from above, from the second hunter's point of view. The leopard rushes towards the prey, steps over a pit hidden by branches and falls into it spectacularly.

Observe how the leopard, seen first from the point of view of the two hunters, became intermittently emphasized in the sequence to relate it with its own centre of interest, the goat. The pattern was repeated twice in this sequence until the payoff in the action was reached.

Random shifting subjective points of view are the next development. Instead of adhering to an ordered pattern that is repeated (the two previous examples) the focal viewpoints follow the emotional line of the event they record. The sequence that follows, taken from David Lean's film *Doctor Zhivago*, uses three subjective points of view alternated through the sequence. Figure 24.2 gives a floor plan view of the camera positions used.

Shot 1   Line of cavalrymen, their backs to us, looking towards the long empty street ahead of them. Music is heard from round the corner at the end of the street.

Shot 2   Close shot of the commanding officer, looking right.

Shot 3   The empty street from his point of view. A moment later the crowd begins to turn the corner.

Shot 2   Close shot of the officer, impassive.

Shot 4   Zhivago appears on the balcony of his house and comes towards us. He stops, looking off screen left.

Shot 5   From his high point of view we see the crowd below turning the corner and moving away towards the higher side of the street.

Shot 4   Close shot of Zhivago.

Shot 5   From his high point of view. The crowd moves away with the noise of the band.

Shot 6   Pasha comes towards us directing the musicians.

Shot 2   Medium shot of the officer. He says, 'Draw sabers!' Pan left to the soldiers on horseback who unsheath their sabres, present arms and keep them at the ready.

Shot 6   Pasha at the head of the crowd advances and stops in close shot. He looks up the street to the left.

Shot 7   Long shot. The line of cavalrymen is coming forward blocking the whole width of the street.

Shot 6   Pasha in close shot. The music dies behind him and people move nervously to one side.

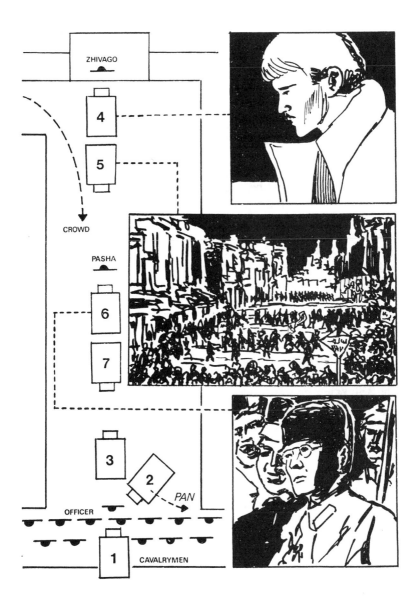

FIGURE 24.2 With randomly shifting subjective points of view, instead of adhering to an ordered pattern that is repeated the focal viewpoints can follow the emotional line of the event.

Shot 7 Long shot of the cavalrymen, they increase speed as they run towards us.

Shot 6 Close shot of Pasha. The people behind him panic and begin to disperse.

Shot 7 Long shot. The line of cavalrymen is approaching at speed.

Shot 6 Close shot of Pasha. People run and he is shoved aside.

Shot 4 Close shot of Zhivago. He is still astounded.

Shot 5 From his high point of view we see a full shot of the crowd scattering to all sides as the cavalrymen charge them.

Shot 4 Close shot of Zhivago.

Shot 5 The impending clash seen from above.

Three key characters are used in the sequence to develop it and gain our emotional complicity. The cavalry officer is first used to show us, through his eyes, the crowd entering the street before the massacre. Next, Zhivago is presented occupying a reverse position. Through his eyes a wider perspective is acquired. Then Pasha, within the crowd (he is the only identifiable person there) allows us to see through his eyes the brutal beginning of the cavalry charge. As hysteria grows among the crowd, Zhivago's point of view gives us again a larger perspective of it.

Five ways of enhancing visual action

The following concepts have proved effective in increasing the visual excitement of an action scene.

1 A combination of static and moving camera viewpoints will confer more visual impact to a chase scene or to a group of running people. The closer views of the subjects are made with a moving camera, while the long shots are filmed from fixed camera positions. A static shot is followed by a tracking one, and the formula is constantly repeated with occasional pauses in the action. Here is an example:

Long shot of a street from above. A fleeing couple runs in an arc from the upper left to the lower left and so off screen.

Meidum shot of the couple. The camera tracks back with them.

Long shot. The couple, small in the centre of the street, run towards us.

Medium shot of the couple. We track back in front of them again.

High full shot. The couple comes towards us and stop in the foreground. They look around and then separate, running in different directions.

The moving camera shots may sometimes be jerky (hand-held camera). They must be of short duration (no more than 5 sec perhaps) to avoid annoying the audience. This uneven movement will often add excitement to a chase.

2 Planned cumulative action within a static shot can be very exciting. The many planes of depth in front of the camera can be used in patterns of action that recede from or approach the camera. Action can be staged on them progressively or simultaneously.

Here is an example. An American Indian half kneeling in the left foreground seen in full shot, shoots an arrow towards a mounted soldier who enters the screen from the right in the background. The soldier falls while his horse continues onwards, leaving the screen left. A second soldier on foot enters from the right and runs his sword into the archer's midriff. The Indian falls. Between the soldier on foot and the camera a second Indian enters on horseback and jabs a lance into the soldier. The Indian exits screen right as the second soldier collapses. In the foreground right a third soldier and Indian roll in, in hand to hand combat. The Indian manages to roll on top and stabs the soldier repeatedly with his knife. All these actions overlap swiftly so that the rhythm of the scene does not slacken as the action progresses from background to foreground. The scene quoted comes from Raoul Walsh's film *They Died With Their Boots On*.

3 The violence of a blow can be stressed on the screen by dividing it into two shots. A bare fisted knock or a leg kick can be split into two takes to obtain a more violent presentation. The first part of the motion is recorded in a medium shot and the concluding swing in a close shot on the same visual axis. When shooting such a scene two complete blows are photographed and later edited as described. In the second shot we can keep a static camera position (in that case the performer being hit stumbles out of the screen) or we may pan with the person who suffered the blow as he falls.

A vehicle smashing an obstacle can be treated in the same way:

A truck speeds along a road towards the wooden doors of the courtyard gate. The action is seen in long shot. The vehicle moves left to right.

Full shot of the doors. The truck enters screen left and crashes into the door which begins to give way.

Reverse full shot. From inside the courtyard we see the other side of the gate. The truck crashes through and exits screen right at full speed.

Three cameras running simultaneously are required to record that situation, for obvious reasons.

4   Action running between the camera and the fighting group will provide intermitent glimpses of the main event. This heightens our interest as we strive to follow the action beyond. If the fighting persons are part of a larger group engaged in a full scale battle, we can introduce other combatants moving in front of the central group and crossing the screen between them and the camera (if a long focal lens is used the foreground combatants can be thrown out of focus). These crossing parties can move on foot, on horseback or on a vehicle. They must not stay long in foreground and should exit to be replaced by other groups. Movement need not be in one direction only; the crossing can be from both lateral sides.

If the quarrel is between two people only, witnesses can be introduced who move before the camera, crossing in front of the combatants. A variant to this is to present a group of animals instead of people, moving in front of the camera between it and the main action. Low camera angles will visually stress these continued interruptions. A moving machine in the foreground (a huge rapidly turning wheel for instance) can be resorted to for the foreground action in place of persons or animals. Static objects of irregular shape can be placed in the foreground and the camera pan or track with the fighting group beyond, so that these static objects cross the screen as the camera moves.

5   In a full scale battle, crowd scenes where the action runs wild should be alternated with action scenes where the hero or heroes are engaged in personal combat. It is an expanding-contracting pattern applied to coverage of the action, that keeps the audience shifting from the general to the particular and vice versa. In that way the main characters are integrated into the spectacle and their relationship to the whole can be appreciated with a stronger sense of identification. These crowd scenes, as well as those where the protagonists are singled out, should not be loose ones where the action lacks a central purpose.

Minor story sub-plots should be developed, so that each of these sequences presents in itself well rounded sketches that advance the story.

All actions where a violent conclusion is imminent, and the audience is aware of this possibility, can be built with a succession of short shots that carry the action swiftly to its pay-off. They can be organized in two ways; 1, by a random shortening of the shots previous to the disaster, or 2, by a progressive shortening of the shots capped by the climax itself.

The several narrative lines involved should be edited in parallel presenting the reactions previous to the disaster. A random shortening will be shown in a fragment of a sequence taken from Robert Aldrich's *Four for Texas*.

Shot 102   Medium shot of Frank Sinatra on the driver's seat of the stagecoach. He faces the camera, and pulls at the reins with force. With his right foot he presses the brake lever (21 frames).

Shot 103   Close up of his right foot pressing on the brake lever (22 frames).

Shot 104   Close up of the brake pressing against the turning wheel of the stagecoach (32 frames).

Shot 105   The camera tracks back in front of the vehicle, framing in close shot the two front horses of the team. Between them we see Sinatra beyond on the driver's seat (32 frames).

Shot 106   Medium shot of Sinatra's hands pulling the reins back with force (31 frames).

Shot 107   Side shot of the heads of the first team of horses. The camera frames them in medium shot and tracks left with them (36 frames).

Shot 108   Low shot of the horses legs kicking up some dust as they run left. The camera tracks with them (46 frames).

Shot 109   High shot. Fixed camera site. The stagecoach seen in full shot approaches in a diagonal to the left (33 frames).

Shot 110   Medium shot inside the stagecoach. Dean Martin on the left side of the screen turns and grabs a handle near the centre window. The dead fat man is slumped on the right. (35 frames).

Shot 111   Close shot of the window, from the inside. The panorama flies past outside (10 frames).

Shot 112   Close shot of the dead fat man (12 frames).

Shot 113   Close shot of Dean Martin inside clutching the handle of the vehicle. The coach begins to tilt to the left. The screen is blackened as the floor rises into view (14 frames).

Shot 114   Front close shot of Sinatra as in shot 102. The carriage begins to tilt to the right, taking him to that side and going out of the screen. (10 frames).

Shot 115   Full shot. The stagecoach overturns in front of the camera. The driver is thrown into the air and lands in front of the camera. A cloud of dust rolls towards the camera obscuring the screen. As the dust settles the first titles of the credits appear. Very long shot.

The construction of the scene reveals a careful arrangement of the shots. First, the driver is seen pulling the reins and stepping on the brake. Their effect is observed, there is no reduction of speed as the coach reaches a turn of the road, where a full re-establishing view of the vehicle is intercut. Then the reactions of those inside the stage are observed. Finally the vehicle begins to overturn (shots 113–114). The last take documents the catastrophe.

The shots are quite short, many are less than one second long. Their lengths are also arbitrary: 29–22–32–32–21–36–46–33–35–10–12–14–10 frames. The last four shots are the shorter ones and accelerate the tempo of the sequence before the climax is reached. The duration of these four shots is roughly half that of the shots preceding them.

An example from Alfred Hitchcock's *The Birds* will illustrate the other possibility: a progressively diminishing length of the shots prior to the visual climax.

Shot 29   Full shot of the parking lot from Melanie's viewpoint. A car in the foreground is burning fiercely. A second car behind catches fire and explodes. Some men in the background rush in to fight the fire. A third car explodes on the right. Dense smoke covers the scene. (73 film frames).

Shot 30   Close shot of Melanie at the window of the cafe. She is profiled left, looking down. Two men behind her look up to the right (20 frames).

Shot 31   Close shot of the stream of petrol leading back to the filling station. Flames advance from right to left on the stream in the middle of the street. (18 frames).

Shot 32 Close shot of Melanie as in shot 30. She reacts (16 frames).

Shot 33 Close shot of the flames as in shot 31. Camera pans left with the advancing flames (14 frames).

Shot 34 Close shot of Melanie as in shot 30. She is looking to the right now, fear on her face (12 frames).

Shot 35 Long shot of the filling station. The stream of fire on the right is advancing towards the gas tanks. A policeman, the wounded station attendant and Mitch, run away to the left (10 frames).

Shot 36 Close shot of Melanie as in shot 30, looking right (8 frames).

Shot 37 Long shot of the station as in shot 35. The tank explodes in a roaring inferno. Big tongues of fire rise higher than the buildings. (34 frames).

By substracting two frames progressively the editor, George Tomasini, created a mounting crescendo leading to the explosion. The editor used only three shots that were intercut in parallel. With seven fragments he quickened the tempo of the film. Each shot lasts for less than a second: 20–18–16–14–12–10–8 frames. The last shot is on the screen for only a third of a second. Notice also that the subjective point of view principle is at work on the sequence. Melanie is the key character, and it is through her eyes that the catastrophe is witnessed.

The acceleration of the tempo prior to the climax creates a brief tension in the audience that finds its relief in the outburst itself.

Breaking the climatic action into several shots

When there is no surprise in the climatic action because the audience is expecting it as a logical conclusion, a detailed account of the catastrophe can be shown from its inception to its aftermath, intercut with the reactions of the players that provoke the event, and those who suffer the consequences. The most exciting shots, where the violent action takes place, are divided into at least two fragments. If the destruction is slow and massive, the action can be divided into several shots. The following example belongs to Michael McCarthy's film *Operation Amsterdam.*

Shot 1 Seen in full shot, Peter Finch throws a pack of dynamite. Eva Bartok stands behind him in the street.

Shot 2 The package slides under the truck blocking the street. Close shot.

Shot 1 Eva Bartok and Peter Finch turn to go inside the shop. Full shot.

Shot 2 Close shot under the truck. A soldier crawls in and extends his hand to grab the sticks of dynamite.

Shot 3 Medium shot. The couple enters the screen by the right. They are inside the shop.

Shot 4 Full shot. The truck blows up fiercely.

Shot 5 Long shot. Same visual axis as that preceding. The cloud of dense smoke climbs to the sky.

Shot 3 The man and the girl press themselves together.

Shot 5 Remains of the truck begin to fall.

Shot 3 The couple huddled together, the camera tracks into them and stops, framing them in close shot.

The director did not hesitate to divide an exciting event into three shots—the truck explosion, achieving a dynamic result by editing in parallel with the action of the couple taking cover inside the shop. Notice also the refinement in suspense: a soldier is introduced prior to the explosion, trying to retrieve the dynamite when the couple have already turned their backs on the situation.

An amateur would perhaps hesitate in cutting what he considers a valuable shot. By presenting the event in its entirety without interruptions, he would be lessening its dramatic impact and limiting the pleasure of the audience.

An action broken in two is stretched in time, so that the visual pleasure of witnessing a spectacular action is doubled for the audience.

Here is a case taken from David Lean's *The Bridge on the River Kwai*—the final scene where the bridge is blown up as the train crosses it.

Shot 133 From above. The locomotive enters shot from the right travels to the bridge seen beyond in the background (2 seconds 11 frames).

Shot 134 Close shot of Nicholson (Alec Guinness) from below. He takes a few steps towards us. He is mortally wounded. He raises his head to the sky and falls down, out of shot (3 seconds 6 frames).

Shot 135 Medium shot. Nicholson's body enters, left and falls across the lever of the detonator, pressing it down (26 frames).

Shot 136   Long shot. In the foreground lie the dead bodies of Shears, Saito, Joyce and Nicholson. Beyond is the bridge. The train is seen moving along the upper right part of it. The first pillar of the bridge explodes spectacularly and the centre part of the bridge collapses. The train continues until it reaches the edge of the gap (4 seconds 4 frames).

Shot 137   Medium shot of Warden and his group of Thai girls. Some of the girls are standing. They all look down to the right. They begin to rise (2 seconds 9 frames).

Shot 138   Long shot of the bridge from the side of the river formerly occupied by Yay and Shears. The locomotive and some wagons plunge into the river. (5 seconds 11 frames).

Shot 139   Medium shot of Warden and his group. As in shot 137. Pan up with Warden rising to his feet and leaning on his crutch. They look down, right. (1 second 11 frames).

Shot 140   Long shot. From the point of view of the preceding group. Some wagons from the train plummet into the river (3 seconds 5 frames).

Shot 141   From below as in shot 138. The two last wagons of the train fall into the river. The second pillar exploded completing the destruction of the bridge (3 seconds 10 frames).

Shot 142   Medium shot of Nicholson lying beside the detonator box. Composition as in shot 135 (4 seconds 7 frames).

Shot 143   From the same point of view as shot 136. The last pieces of the bridge collapse into the river (7 seconds 20 frames).

Shot 144   Medium shot of Clipton (James Donald). He is looking off to the left. He walks to that side and the camera pans with him as he walks downhill. He stops and says, 'Madness!' (4 seconds 7 frames).

Shot 145   High angle. Full shot of the four dead bodies lying on the sand bar, near the water: Nicholson, Saito, Joyce and Shears. (3 seconds 1 frame).

Shot 146   Medium shot of Warden standing in front of the camera. He looks off screen right, then turns to the Thai girls in the background and says: 'I had to do it! I had to! . . .' 'They would have been taken alive!'

He again turns to us and looks off right once more (16 seconds 18 frames).

Shot 147 From the same point of view as shot 140. The aftermath of the explosion as seen from above, from Warden's position (3 seconds 14 frames).

Observe that the blowing up of the train was filmed from three points of view. Each of these shots was used only twice in the whole sequence to cover the catastrophe from beginning to conclusion. The destruction of the bridge itself takes 28 seconds on the screen to complete (the length of the six fragments employed) yet the sequence from shot 136 to shot 147 runs for 60 seconds and 6 frames of film. The length of the event was stretched by including the reaction shots of Warden and his group of Thai girls, and the lone medic Clipton up on the opposite side of the river. By presenting the event in this way a richer version of it was obtained.

High speed and slow motion for action sequences

In the silent era of the cinema it was discovered that by undercranking the camera a dynamic effect was imparted to chase or action sequences. That discovery is still valid today. The normal filming speed is 24 frames per second, and a moving subject is photographed at 16 frames per second the resultant film, projected at normal speed, the apparent velocity of the subject photographed will be increased.

Motor boats, cars, riders on horseback, crowds running on foot, will all will appear more dramatic if this subterfuge is applied during an action scene. Care must be taken not to overdo this effect, or the movement will become so jerky that it will produce laughter.

If laughter is the effect you are after, be sure to work at speeds close to 8 frames per second. Subject movement will be tremendously increased.

Slow motion is used to impart majesty to a movement. A diver jumping from a high point down to the sea, an object falling away from us to the ground below, acquire in slow motion a grace of movement (even as they desintegrate or splash) that normal speed would not reveal. Climaxes in which somebody jumps from a high cliff, a vehicle plunges into the sea, or a huge explosion destroys a large prop, can be filmed at slightly higher speeds to be projected at the normal rate of 24 frames per second, obtaining an imposing effect that enhances the scene.

500

Death scenes have been filmed in slow motion on the screen. Akira Kurosawa with his *Seven Samurai* started the fad, and some very interesting and disturbing effects have been obtained on the screen, such as Sam Peckinpah did in *The Wild Bunch* where in the middle of a frantic shooting deaths took place in slow motion.

Follow focus technique

As a camera tracks, pans or tilts, or as actors move up to or away from the camera, or pass by at different ranges, points of interest in the view as seen by the camera shift position. This makes it necessary to adjust focus to keep the subject sharply defined. This can be done in two ways: manually or automatically. With the first method, a focus puller stands by the camera and adjust the focus ring as required. But the ring can, alternatively, be controlled remotely by either a mechanical or remote control device.

There are four basic situations requiring follow-focus control. 1. The camera moves about the set and films either stationary or moving subjects. The camera may track towards or away from the subject or it can move alongside, framing the moving subject from a fixed distance. 2. The camera remains stationary while the subject moves up to, or away from it during the shot. 3. The camera remains stationary but is panned or tilted, or both, during the shot, switching from one subject to another at different distances. 4. The stationary camera films two or more static subjects in the scene, shifting focus from one to the other. Visible guides are established on the floor of the set to help the focus puller to set to the correct distance on the lens at predetermined positions—the beginning and end points of the tracking as well as particular intermediate distances. These marks are either chalked lines or strips of tape on the ground. When there is some difficulty in keeping one or more players at a fixed distance while the camera tracks backward, a wooden T-shaped assembly can be attached to the front of the camera dolly. It is only necessary for the actors to keep in line with this device to maintain the correct distance and stay in sharp focus.

In some shots the focus may deliberately be switched to the background and perhaps returned to the foreground again. Many dramatic effects can be obtained by selective focus used in this way.

25

EDITING IN THE CAMERA

Modern film makers have rescued the long master shot from the oblivion that followed the abandonment of the old theatrical front-only camera set up and endowed it with techniques developed for editing in the camera, or in other words, within the film frame! This approach needs no visual cuts to achieve its effects but relies on camera and subject movement. Experimentation with this technique has been extensive and has even led to the extreme of making a full length feature film using only ten shots edited in the camera—Alfred Hitchcock's film *Rope*.

Pre-planning is required

Shots suitable for editing in this way cannot be made haphazardly or with the inspiration of the moment. They require careful pre-planning, with a studied integration of player and camera movement, like a choreography that must be precisely executed by the actors and the camera crew. When well executed, results are very pleasing. The scene flows smoothly, the audience is not aware of the technique and the actors have a better chance to drop into their characters, since the scene is played continuously as in the theatre.

Mistakes when making this type of shot can be quite expensive, especially for limited budget productions. The amount of film expended in retakes is quite considerable. Thus, thorough rehearsals are vital before attempting a shot. But if a mistake is made, a good director should be able to find a way of partially using the shot by resorting to a cut-away at that point and returning to the master shot again afterwards.

With a well trained cast and camera crew, the speed in shooting surpasses by far the cumbersome efforts needed to cover the same scene using the fragmentation technique of piecing it together in several shots. Television serials, which have a limited number of production days, have greatly profited from this technique. But an integration of both techniques, ordinary physical editing and editing within the frame, is the most sensible way of benefiting from the best of both. In themselves, the two systems have limitations. A film maker who knows screen language thoroughly, however, will surmount them by blending these techniques for his expressive purposes.

There are seven basic techniques governing shots edited within the film frame:

1 A pause between movements;
2 A change of zone;
3 Approaching or receding from the camera;
4 Change of body positions;
5 Substitition by sectors;
6 Switching of screen sectors;
7 Numerical contrast.

Several of these techniques are usually combined in any such shot, rather than being used alone.

The pause between movements

The player or the camera moves from one zone to another, remains there for a while, and then moves to a third area and stops. If the movement is continuous (unbroken by pauses) it will become just a following shot because no matter how many pictorial variations are involved along the shot, the audience simply would not have time to appreciate them. Each new player or camera position presented has to be held on the screen and so established before moving on to the next.

The change of zone

The screen position in a cinema theatre is always fixed. We see things on it as if we were looking through an opening. If that opening remains stationary (fixed camera) the background we glimpse will be always the same and seen from a constant point of view.

In shots to be edited in the camera, this would constitute a limitation and, in practice, becomes annoying in a very short time. The background must vary to give the impression of space wherein the actors move. The change of zone required to obviate this can be achieved 1, by a stationary camera, 2, by a panning camera or 3, by a tracking camera.

Case 1

With a stationary camera, the zones are arranged in depth towards the background (Fig. 25.1), i.e. a foreground zone, a middle zone and a background one.

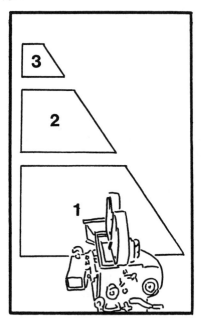

FIGURE 25.1   Three action zones can be arranged in depth in front of a stationary camera.

Case 2

If a panning camera is used, the relationship between the zones of action can vary, as shown in Fig. 25.2.

For pans of less than half a circle the Fig. 25.2 examples should provide adequate variety. In the first case, the three zones are deployed in an arc around the camera, so that movement from one to the other will keep the framing distance equal for the three zones. The second, third and fourth examples suggest two zones equidistant from the camera and the third either closer or further away.

504

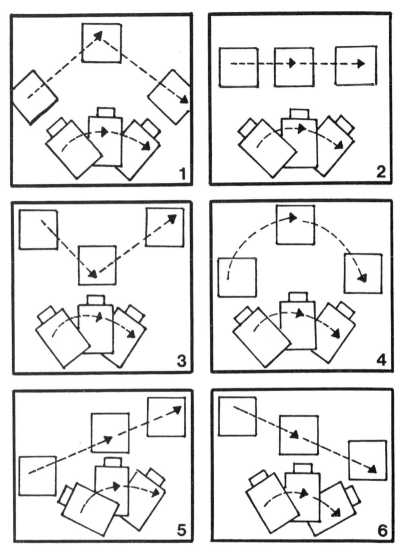

FIGURE 25.2 When the camera pans the relationship between zones of action can vary.

The fifth and sixth examples show the zones at different distances from the camera.

If a completely circular camera movement is involved, panning

505

from zone to zone will cover as many or as few zones as wished to complete the circle (Fig. 25.3).

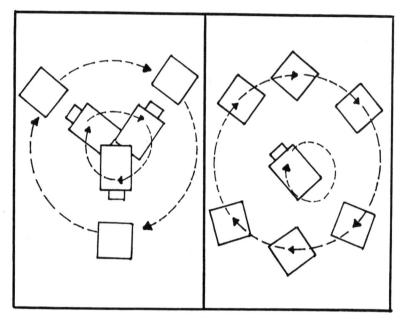

FIGURE 25.3 Several action zones can be arranged around a panning camera.

Case 3

If the camera tracks from zone to zone, these areas might be along a straight path. Or an irregular arrangement can be chosen. If a horizontal path is used, three approaches are possible. (Fig. 25.4).

In the first case the camera tracks backwards or forwards over the three zones. In this example all the zones are shown either at the beginning or conclusion of the take, depending whether the camera is advancing into or receding from the scene.

In the second and third examples the zones are placed parallel to the camera path and equidistant from the camera. A triangular arrangement of the zones in relation to the camera path provides further variants for internal visual coverage (Fig. 25.5).

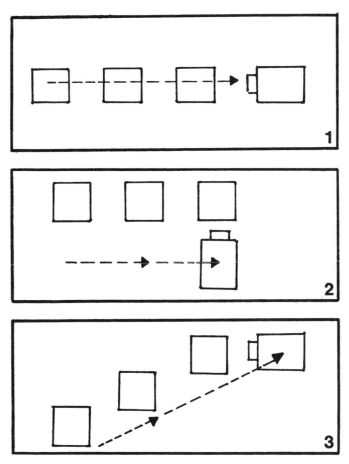

FIGURE 25.4   A moving camera can travel over the action zones themselves, or parallel to them in a horizontal or oblique line.

A single player can be moved in depth, using a static camera position, but the variations to be encountered are quite limited. As Fig. 25.6A shows, geometric figures are best suited to this technique: oval shapes, triangular, U figures.

The actors in the scene will move in triangular paths approaching the camera or going away from it. Should the camera move diagonally to a straight subject-path through the zones the distance will shift (Fig. 25.6).

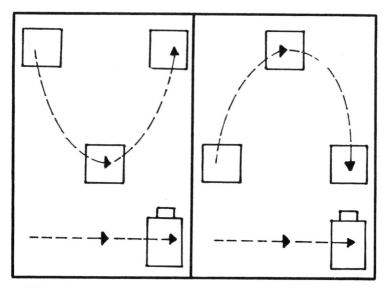

FIGURE 25.5 Action zones could be arranged in triangular form for scanning by a tracking camera which moves as shown.

These zones of action can be placed at height too, covered by a camera that tilts up or down or from a crane, perhaps panning or tracking also. A further possibility is to reverse the movement of the camera within the shot, thus, in effect, using one or two zones twice.

Approaching or receding from the camera

Motion in depth is the key to this simple technique. Variations are achieved by moving from foreground to background or vice versa, and recording this movement by using:

1 a stationary camera,
2 a panning camera, or
3 a tracking camera (forward or backwards).

Action zones might be in a line running straight to the background or tangential to the camera. But it is important that only one player at a time moves from zone to zone no matter if the group is large or small. The others remain in their places, thus ensuring clear changes of action zones which are easy to execute, simple to understand and unobtrusive for the audience who will follow the dominant motion naturally.

508

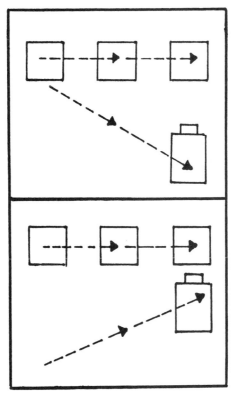

FIGURE 25.6 Action zones are arranged in a straight line, and the camera tracks in an oblique line that approaches or recedes from the action zones.

Case 4

Stationary camera positions offer a wide variety of approaches for movement in depth. Several visual combinations are available. Here are some simple ones, with two players.

Both players (A and B) in foreground. B moves to the background. A remains in foreground (Fig. 25.7).

Both actors in foreground. B moves to the background and, moments later, returns to the foreground (Fig. 25.8).

Both players in foreground. B moves to the background. Then A joins him (Fig. 25.9).

Both actors in foreground. B moves to the background, remains for a moment and then returns to foreground. Now A moves to the background, while B remains in the foreground. Later, A returns to the foreground (Fig. 25.10).

509

FIGURE 25.6A   A single player moves in depth, going to the background and coming back towards the camera. She travels a "U" path.

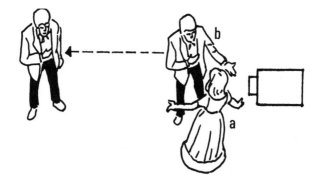

FIGURE 25.7   Movement in depth: Both players are in the foreground, B moves to the background.

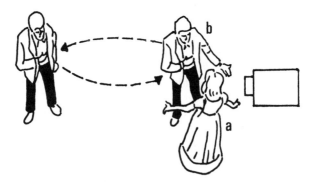

FIGURE 25.8   Both actors are in the foreground. B moves to the background and then returns.

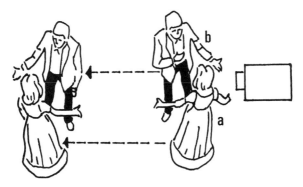

FIGURE 25.9 Both actors in foreground. One moves to the background, the other then follows.

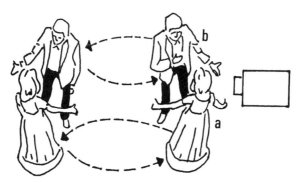

FIGURE 25.10 Both actors are in the foreground. Each in turn moves into the background and return.

Case 5

A panning camera will easily unite two action zones placed on a line that runs at a tangent to its location. The player closest to the camera moves to the background, followed by the panning camera. The movement can be reversed in the same shot, having the actor return to the foreground in which case the camera pans in the opposite direction (Fig. 25.11).

Case 6

A camera tracking forward or backwards with a moving player, will increase the number of possible visual combinations. Here are some examples:

511

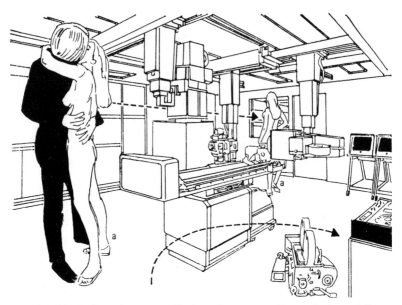

FIGURE 25.11 A panning camera unites two action zones on a line running tangentially to its location.

The stationary player is placed between the camera and the other performer in the background. The background actor comes forward to the static player in the mid-distance, while the camera tracks in towards him (Fig. 25.12).

The moving player is placed between the camera and the stationary person in the background. The foreground player and the camera move together towards the background, approaching the static player (Fig. 25.13).

The camera need not be moved during the whole shot, but only for a section of it to provide emphasis where desired (Fig. 25.14). The shot begins with both players framed in medium shot, talking to each other. B then comes forward and the composition of the screen becomes A—B², when player B turns and goes back to A, the camera travels with him and stops framing a close shot of both (A—B³). B then walks to the background and the pictorial composition changes on the screen to A—B⁴. A lateral camera movement tracking to either side will exclude the static player (Fig. 25.15).

512

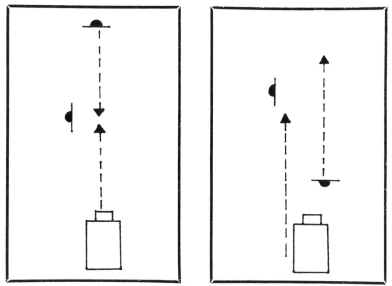

FIGURE 25.12 A stationary actor stands between the camera and the other person, in the background. The background actor moves up to the other as the camera moves in on them.

FIGURE 25.13 The moving person is placed between the camera and the stationary background figure. The camera follows the foreground figure as he approaches the other actor.

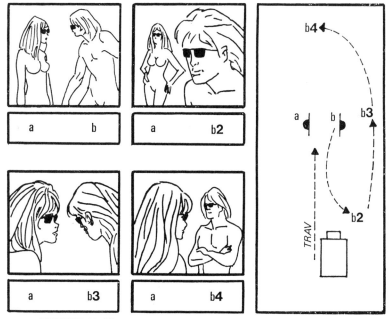

FIGURE 25.14 The camera can move to emphasize only a part of the shot.

513

FIGURE 25.15 A lateral camera track following the moving player will exclude the stationary subject, in this example, the car.

Further possibilities are, of course, possible with more than two players. Instead of following the player in action, the camera may be used selectively with a stationary group. The tracking camera will pinpoint each member by approaching or receding from him.

Changing the body position

As in the theatre, on a cinema screen the body position of a performer can be either dominant or subordinate (Fig. 25.16).

A frontal view of the body, facing the camera, is known as an *open* position. A side view is a *neutral* view. If the performer has his back to the camera, this is a *closed* position.

Open, frontal positions are the strongest, dramatically speaking. Closed or rear views of a player are the weakest. (This concept

514

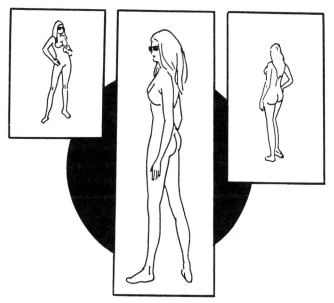

FIGURE 25.16 The three basic body positions are covered by the camera.

is subordinate to the context of the scene because, for instance, a player introduced to the action showing only his back will become the centre of attention by keeping his identity unknown).

Changes in body attitude are more effective when combined with changes in position on the stage or set. The change in body position is marked by integrating it with walking. A feeling of naturalness is preserved and the audience is unaware that their centre of interest is being consciously manipulated by the film maker.

Sometimes both players in a scene move in depth and so change the pictorial composition (Fig. 25.17). The dominant player moves first.

Instead of resorting to a cut to obtain an external reverse coverage of both players, that reversal comes about by their movement in mid shot. A change of body position might mean a change of direction and level—he can move from a lying to a reclining, kneeling, sitting or standing position. These levels can be successfully combined with those of his partner (or partners) to form visually pleasant combinations of vertical movement (Fig. 25.18).

515

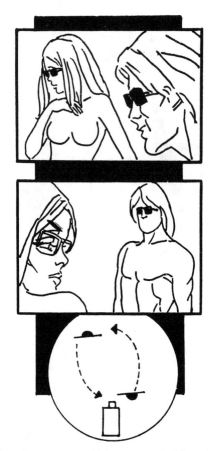

FIGURE 25.17 A stationary camera obtains a reversal of the actor's positions by having them move from foreground to background and vice versa.

The shot begins with both players (A and B). B rises and the camera tilts up framing her alone. A now rises and enters the screen from below. Both players are now standing. B then kneels down, going out of shot. A remains in shot.

Substitution by sectors

This technique implies use of a fixed camera location. The trick is in substituting an actor placed in a particular sector of the screen by another, without moving the others also seen in the shot.

516

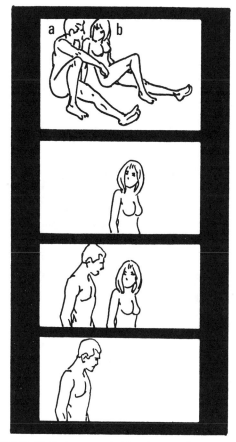

FIGURE 25.18 Vertical movement of the players with number contrast.

As we already know, the screen can be 'divided' into two or three vertical sectors and the movement can be in foreground or background planes. Substitution uses these factors for its effects.

Case 7

A and B are seen in the foreground, profiled to each other. B turns and exits right. C then enters from that side and occupies the sector of the screen vacated by B. A remains in the same sector of the screen (Fig. 25.19).

517

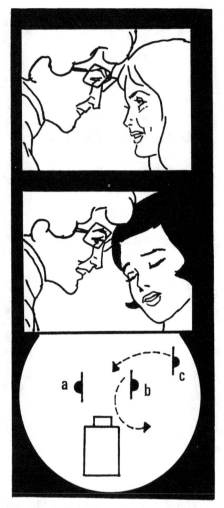

FIGURE 25.19 A simple substitution by sectors. One player goes out of shot and is replaced by another.

Case 8

A substitution in depth is the next variant, and simple to accomplish (Fig. 25.20).

At the beginning of the shot, A and B are seen in the foreground facing the camera. When A exits shot left, he discloses C in the background. C either remains in the background or comes forward to a close shot beside B.

FIGURE 25.20 Here the substitution by sectors is achieved in depth.

Case 9

A composition in which the screen is divided into three sectors is ideal to portray situations where a leader gives commands to subordinates.

The leader is framed centrally and the players at his either side exit and enter, replacing each other (Fig. 25.21).

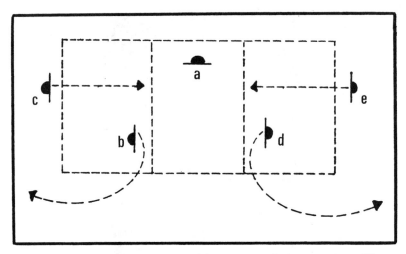

FIGURE 25.21   The actors on one side of the screen are substituted by others, while the centre one remains still throughout the shot.

Case 10

Alternate changes of sector, using only two screen areas, is a more elaborate solution (Fig. 25.22).

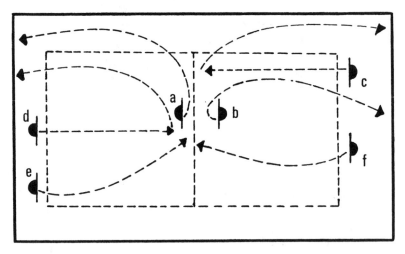

FIGURE 25.22   In this example all the players are substituted up to the last two.

A and B are on the screen at the beginning of the shot. B leaves and is substituted by C. Then A leaves and is substituted by D. Now, D leaves and is, in turn, substituted by E. E remains while C is replaced by F.

Case 11

There are times when the substitution by sectors is accomplished using only two players. One remains in shot while the other enters and exits. This is repeated and then inverted. Another variant is to have one player enter, right, stop in the centre of the picture and then exit right. The second player enters left, stops in the centre and then leaves left. The first player then re-enters right and the whole formula is repeated. To obtain variation, the three depth planes into which a scene can be broken are used in combination with one another. An example will illustrate the technique. Fig. 25.23 shows the set in which the scene will take place.

The whole action is shown in a single shot, with a static camera and the techniques used are explained below.

FIGURE 25.23 Three planes of depth in the scene are used in combination.

At the beginning of the shot the set appears as follows: in the foreground is a desk with papers and other paraphernalia. Above. in the foreground is a light, turned off at present; in the background is a raised catwalk with a vertical stair on the left, descending behind a block construction placed in the middle ground. In the background on the right is a closed door.

The action in the scene is as follows. The camera is in a fixed position.

1 The light in the foreground is switched on.

2 Player A then enters from the right (foreground) and gets busy sorting some papers on the table.

3 Unknown to him, B enters the catwalk from the left in the background and crouches to look down.

4 A exits shot right.

5 In the background B rises, goes to the stairs and descends, disappearing behind the block construction.

6 A re-enters from the right with a small leather bag. He picks up some papers and puts them into the bag, and then exits right of picture.

7 Nothing moves for an instant, then the light in the foreground goes off, obviously switched off by A out of shot.

8 B appears from behind the block in the middle ground and calmly walks towards us, keeping to the left side of the screen. When he reaches a close shot position, his figure is silhouetted against the background which is lit. He takes a pocket torch from his coat, scans the papers on the table with a slender beam of light.

9 Suddenly, in the right sector of the screen in the background, a door opens and two armed guards appear.

10 B, in the left foreground, quickly switches off the torch and kneels down, moving out of shot by the lower side.

11 On the right, in the background, the two armed guards shine a strong lamp up to the catwalk at the left and turn flashing the light into the camera lens and, switching it off, move to the right, walking out of shot in the background.

12 B rises and re-appears in the foreground, left. He picks some papers from the table and exits shot left.

Notice how the scene was played in depth using foreground and background action.

Note also that A moved only in the right sector of the screen and B on the left, at all times.

In this scene twelve different bits of action took place by means of four elements:

1 The light; this was switched on at the beginning of the take and turned off midway through it.

2 Player A: he entered and exited from the screen twice, each time moving in the foreground righthand sector.

3 Player B: he entered the background, descended from a height, hid behind an obstacle, reappeared (still on the left side of the screen) advanced to the foreground, exited the screen by the lower side, re-entered and finally exited left.

4 The guards: they moved only in the background righthand sector.

In the first half of the shot the foreground actions of A were contrasted with the background movement of B. But when the latter came to the foreground, the same technique was employed in his relationship with the guards in the background. Both areas of the screen, left and right, were used in depth in an alternating way.

Switching the light on and off in foreground added a pictorial variation that reinforced the mood of the scene.

Switching screen sectors

Pictorial compositions cannot remain constant for long unless there is a special reason for it. Variations within a group recorded on a long master shot edited in the camera, must be introduced if monotony is to be avoided. Fixed compositions allow a limited number of ways by which important moments, actions or pieces of dialogue are stressed.

Both actor and camera movement are essential if the expressive possibilities are to be widened.

The most simple variation is a switch of sectors. The player on the right moves to the left and the other vice versa. This switch can be obtained with the simultaneous movement of both players or by moving only one of them. The second case involves camera movement.

When both players move to exchange screen sectors, they cross over.

As in the old theatrical convention, the dominant player is almost always placed slightly upstage of the other (Fig. 25.24).

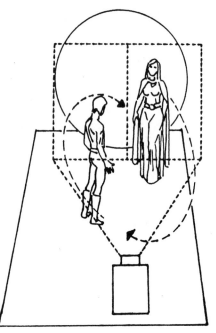

FIGURE 25.24 Players cross over and exchange screen sectors and the dominant player upstages the other.

The player placed upstage faces the audience, the other has his back to it. Substitute a camera for the audience and you have the same situation on the screen. The dominant aspect can be modified by opening or closing the body position (Fig. 25.25).

This works well on the screen, with a fixed camera position, but one of the players could move out of shot so that the remaining one becomes the dominant party. If the camera follows the actor who leaves, then he is emphasized. When the dominant player crosses another person on the stage, he is more likely to pass in front of the other than behind him unless he is sitting down. The reason is easy to see. When the dominant player passes behind the other person, the eyes of the audience, which have followed him to this point, tend to remain with the stationary player.

With a close shot, however, the dominant player can cross behind the other person, who has a closed body position, without this happening (Fig. 25.26).

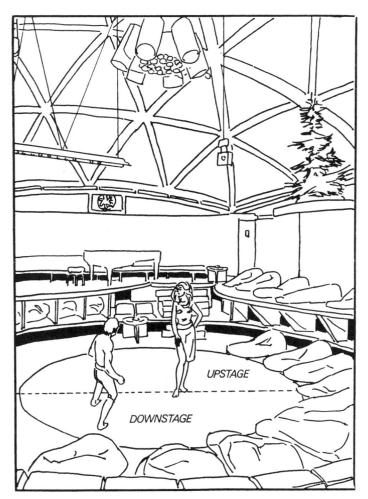

FIGURE 25.25 The 'upstage' actor faces the camera, the other has his back to it, the dominant aspect is modified by opening and closing the body positions.

Another old stage convention is the compensatory movement made by a performer who has been crossed, to re-establish stage balance. He moves a short distance in the opposite direction beginning at the moment he is cut across when he is hidden from the audience by the moving player.

With stationary camera coverage this method can be applied on the screen (Fig. 25.27).

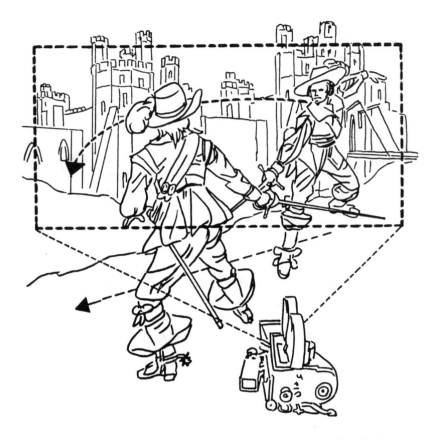

FIGURE 25.26 The moving player crosses beyond the static actor (seen in close shot).

A couple stands in front of the Watergate Building. He is on the left and she in the centre, further back. Later he begins to move across the screen towards the right. When his figure hides the woman's body, by passing in front of her, she begins to move to the left in a compensatory motion. As the man reaches the right side of the screen and stops, she also stops in her new position on the left side of the film frame.

The camera remained stationary, while a neat area transposition was achieved by the players.

Another old theatrical device applicable to screen movement involves that described above except that audience attention in-

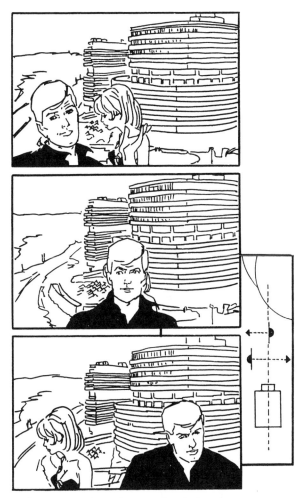

FIGURE 25.27 A simple cross where both performers move.

stead of being fixed on the dominant player, is shifted from the dominant to the other player and then back to the dominant actor again (Fig. 25.28).

Player A begins to move upstage crossing *behind* B. At that moment B describes a half circle movement in the opposite direction, carrying the eyes of the audience with him. B stops (with

527

FIGURE 25.28 The circle 'dress' a subtle way of crossing the players on the stage.

a partially closed body position) and throws attention on to the other performer by looking at him. A then concludes by turning to the audience opening his body position.

All movement must be motivated, or must be made to appear so. This is the oldest axiom for stage presentation, either if viewed by an audience in the theatre or a film camera on a movie stage. The most natural reasons for movement are found in the dialogue itself.

Movement that is the result of emotion is the most effective. If there is no emotional reason for moving, a practical one can be found.

Knowledge of the laws of film language gives us technique, and technique is one of the film-maker's most precious assets. It serves us constantly to sustain our work even when the most essential element, imagination, fails us. If we rely on technique and dispense with imagination, we become mechanical. If we rely on imagination alone and ignore technique, our work will be chaotic. We must know our film medium and respect craftmanship.

This is the only way to make the transition from competent craftsman to artist.

If the camera is close to the players, the stationary performer need not move to re-establish screen balance. The camera simply pans with the moving player and a smooth switch of screen sectors is obtained (Fig. 25.29).

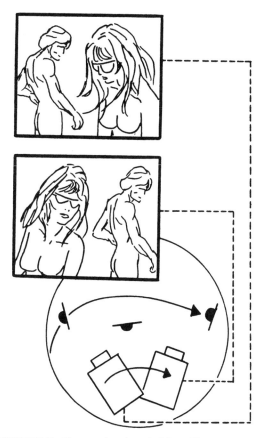

FIGURE 25.29   The crossing player is followed by a camera pan.

The actors do not need to be close to the camera to achieve this switch. By moving one person in depth, from background to foreground and vice versa, a simple panning movement will achieve the same result (Fig. 25.30).

The shot begins by framing A in the foreground and B behind.

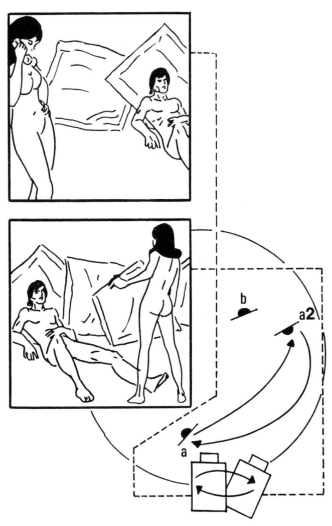

FIGURE 25.30 The main player moves in depth, thus changing zone.

As A moves to her new position, the camera pans to the right with her framing B–A². She then returns to her former position in the foreground and the camera moves back to the left with her and the first pictorial composition is repeated. A tracking camera may be used to obtain the same effect. In such a case there is also a change of zone (Fig. 25.31).

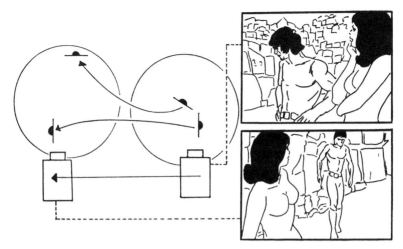

FIGURE 25.31 A tracking camera causes the players to switch positions on the screen as they move with the camera.

The actors exchange screen sectors during the track, with static screen compositions at both ends of the track. The following examples are applied to three people exchanging sectors during an intermittent pan and tracking movement.

Case 12

Three players exchanging screen sectors follow the same principle. But it is easier and more dynamic if they also change zones. The camera may pan as in Fig. 25.32.

This shot involves an 180 degree pan. The shot begins by showing players A, B and C talking in medium shot. A then moves to the left. The camera pans with her. She stops at her new position. B enters from the right and stops in his new position. C enters from the right, behind them, and crosses to the left and moves out of shot by that side. The camera remains framing the others. Now A moves to the left to the other side of B. The camera pans again with her to the new composition. B starts to move to the left and as he crosses A, she too begins to move in the same direction. The camera pans left with them, picking up C in the background. When the camera stops we see the three players moving away from us as shown. During the shot the actors exchange screen sectors from zone to zone.

531

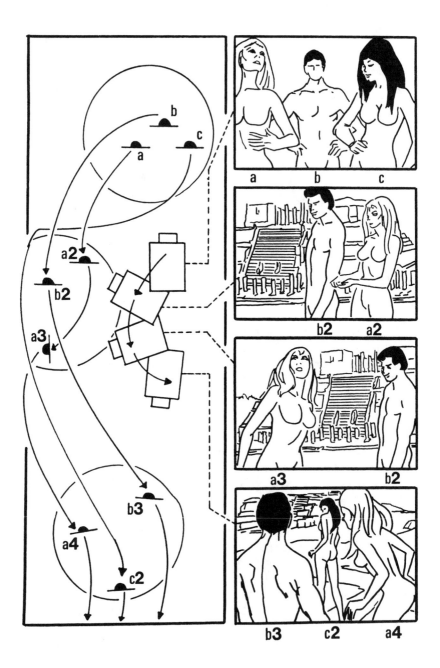

FIGURE 25.32 A simple case of editing in the camera using three action zones.

Case 13

A tracking shot with three people can be planned with a large number of variants.

In the following simple example there is a change of screen sector and action zones (Fig. 25.33).

When the shot begins, A and B are seen talking to each other. They start to walk and the camera moves with them. A moves first, crossing behind B so that during the track the compositions is B–A.

When they stop, C enters right. They talk. The composition is B^2-A^2-C. B exits shot, right. The camera having stopped with the players, pans right to frame A^2-C alone. Both players start to walk and the camera tracks with them once more in an A–C composition. When they stop, composition on the screen becomes C^2-A^3.

Although there were only three stationary camera positions (the two extremes and a pause in the middle of the track) there were five pictorial variations.

Changing screen sectors is a useful device for shots edited in the camera. It is not employed alone, but integrated with other techniques, so that the result is richer, and more expressive and serves the scene better.

Numerical contrast

The confrontation of one person by a group, or a small group by a large one, has dramatic significance in itself. Such numerical contrast emphasizes by isolation. These results can be applied to master shots which are designed to be edited within the film frame.

There are three basic ways of achieving numerical contrast for such shots.

One of the performers exits shot leaving his companion alone in it. Later, he re-enters—a 2–1–2 contrast (Fig. 25.34).

When a performer moves, the camera pans or tracks with him. If he moves to a zone where he remains alone before returning to his companion, the patterns of contrast are simple—2–1–2 or 3–1–3.

If he moves to a zone where other players are present, the number combinations possible increase (Fig. 25.35).

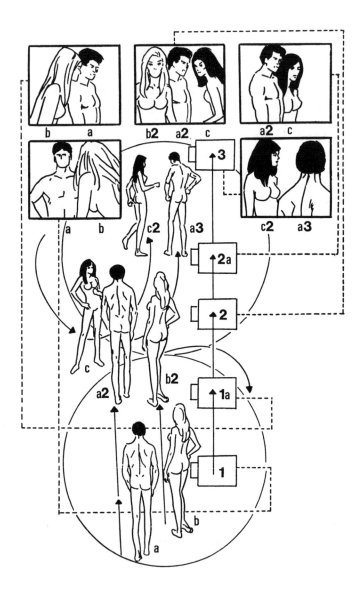

FIGURE 25.33 Editing in the camera using three stationary camera positions and five pictorial compositions to put the scene across.

534

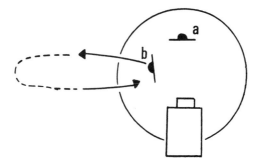

FIGURE 25.34 One actor exits shot while the other remains; the first then re-enters —a number contrast.

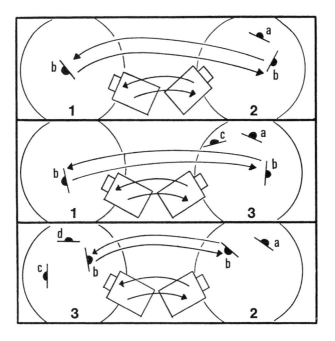

FIGURE 25.35 The camera follows the departing performer whose movement alters the number contrast.

If the camera tracks into or back from a group, the number of players covered can be decreased or increased, according to dramatic needs (Fig. 25.36).

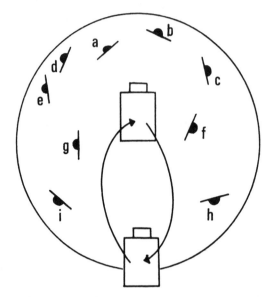

FIGURE 25.36 The camera tracks towards or away from the group, which may be covered as a whole or in part.

Fig. 25.37 shows numerical contrast in combination with other techniques.

A and B are seen in medium shot. B exits and the camera remains, framing A alone. Afterwards she moves from zone 1 to zone 2. The camera pans with her. She stops in zone 3 facing B. Then B moves to zone 3. The camera pans with him. He remains for some seconds and is then joined by A.

Notice the different techniques employed in this simple shot:

1 Number contrast was used in a repetitive pattern: 2–1–2–1–2.

2 The three zones of action were in a half circle around the camera, but at different distances, so that as the camera panned, the players were seen in a tighter composition progressing from medium shot to close shot and to close up.

3 The players in each zone altered their body positions. First they interchanged 'upstage' and 'downstage', then moved into the same plane.

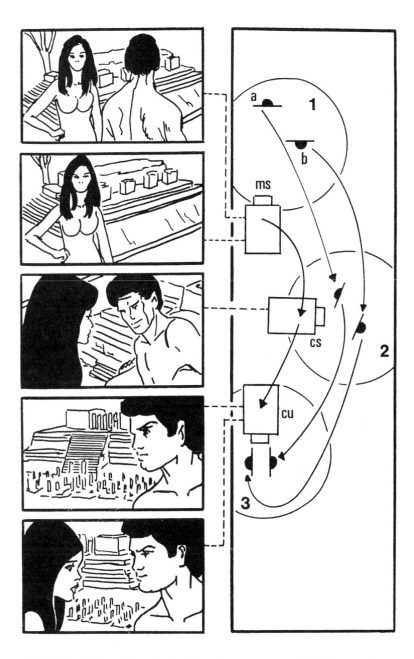

FIGURE 25.37 Several formulas for editing in camera are used in this example. Player A is always on the left of the screen, while B remains on the right.

4 There were only two camera pans. The first followed A, the second B.

This example shows the importance of using the seven techniques in combination, to obtain a smooth construction of master shots. By combining player and camera movements this technique dispenses with the need for physical cuts. But editorial emphasis or changes in the scene are achieved with complete naturalness.

Editing within the film frame

French film makers call it 'le plan sequence', in Spanish it is identified as 'montaje en el cuadro', the Americans call it 'a fluid camera style'. All these identify the same form of film language— the long master shot that flows smoothly, covering a scene completely or a large portion of it. Most film makers use it and yet there is a marked preference among European directors to avail themselves of this recourse in a more intensive way. Some of their films are constructed with numerous master shots. They seem to prefer the slower rhythm and more fluent execution afforded by this technique.

In America the technique appears to be used more sparingly. Conventional editing by cuts is much in evidence. But there are notable exceptions. Sidney Lumet and Otto Preminger, for example, often edit in the camera.

Perhaps the difference lies in the working methods employed on different sides of the Atlantic. In general, in America the film director covers a suitable scene with multiple master shots from, say, the three points of a triangle with interior reverse shots, cut-aways and some other protective shots in case some extra material will be needed later.

An experienced film editor sees the material and, using an annotated script as a guide, edits the film in sequence. He is the one responsible for the selection of the final shots, he decides when to stress a scene by cutting into a close shot or moving back to a long shot. The job of the director is to provide him with a wide pictorial coverage that allows the editor an ample scope for selection. On occasions, a film editor will assemble two or three versions of a sequence. Later the director and the producer see the sequences as edited by him and suggest changes, or decide that some supplementary shots are needed.

The editing of the film is a separate operation taking place while

538

the director is on the set shooting further scenes. The amount of film consumed in this way is quite high—an average of one foot of film might be used out of ten feet shot.

Very few risks are taken with that type of production organization. Individuality, greatly prized by European film makers, has very little chance to flower within a system that demands only competent artisans. This is not a criticism of that production method. In an industry that must show a high output of filmed material, a quick, competent worker is to be preferred to an individual artist who requires a longer period of time to obtain his results. Pressure is enormous in the film industry due to time/cost factors among others.

Independent film makers, particularly those in Europe, can afford the longer shooting schedules in which they can feel at ease, because their organization is different. They generally work with lighter equipment, often do not shoot lip-sync (only a guide magnetic tape may be recorded to help in the dubbing operations carried out later), and they take more chances. But they are not wild risks.

Moreover this type of film maker is more likely to take an active part in the editing of the film. So he shoots a lower proportion of retakes.

He may plan the different approaches to a scene in advance and then make a choice of the one he is going to shoot. This is not a rigid choice. He keeps his mind open to any improvements that the actual work on location or stage might suggest. Alfred Hitchcock's dictum: 'Good films are made on a desk—not on a sound stage' is very good advice.

Editing in the camera is exercising a choice. The scene is shot only in that version and there are no alternative cover shots to change the approach though there may be some cutaways to stress story points that could not be integrated within the master shot. Paradoxically, this system allows a faster shooting rate than multiple coverage for conventional editing purposes. The main risk is that there is less room for error. Simple dialogue, where the actors move in a limited stage space, can be covered in medium or close shot set-ups.

A television series may make an extensive use of this technique as the episodic nature of the series is well suited to it. Several film units may be working at the same time and finished film can be turned out at a high rate.

Movements with definite geometrical patterns are used extensively particularly circular and triangular patterns. Circular patterns might be around a static player, a piece of furniture, vehicle or prop on the set.

In Fig. 25.38 a player moves in a full circle around piece of furniture and another performer who remains stationary during the shot.

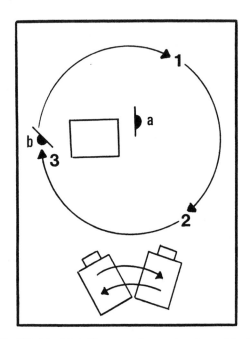

FIGURE 25.38 Circular pattern of movement around a piece of furniture and a stationary player.

The player in motion stops successively in the three positions around stationary actor A. The camera pans with B and he moves from position to position.

The static player can stand in the centre of a circle or close to the rim, or perhaps on the outside. Fig. 25.39 shows some examples of circular paths for this type of shot.

Triangular patterns are also widely employed. Fig. 25.40 shows a simple instance.

540

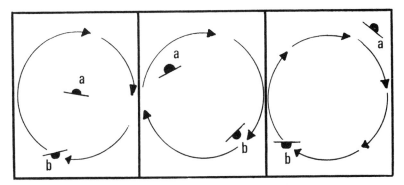

FIGURE 25.39 Different circular patterns of movement. The stationary player is either outside the circle, in the centre or close to inner rim of it.

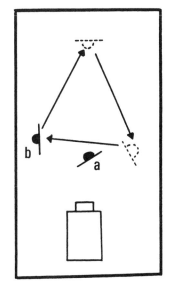

FIGURE 25.40 A triangular pattern of movement for a player.

Triangular paths may become more elaborate, with the players moving alternately in the triangle and in front of a panning or tracking camera.

26

MOVING FROM ZONE TO ZONE

In discussing approaches to groups of people in dialogue scenes it has been assumed that the group remained more or less in the same area of the set and variation and visual emphasis was achieved by physical editing patterns based on properties of the triangle principle. But moving the players from area to area also helps lend a feeling of reality to a scene though the performers are stationary in each area but their relationship is qualified by variation in body posture, distance between actors, placement in the frame, etc.

Changes of zone not only give variety to the backgrounds glimpsed behind the players but also allow the film maker to change his physical editing pattern. The audience should be unaware of the formulas used to present the scene on the screen. These may be used over and over again but the fact that they are applied to different performers in different situations helps to mask their similarity. Thus, one of the most dreadful filmic problems, handling static dialogue scenes, is covered in a natural and pleasant way. Action scenes, parallel events, lend themselves more easily to film presentation. But static dialogue, although necessary for some expositive scenes tends to bog down the cinematic properties of film. Physical editing plus changes of zone solve the problem.

General principles

With changes of zone the group can move from zone to zone, expand to several zones or contract from several to only one zone. There is no limit to the number of areas that can be employed but three to five is generally enough since each area can be used several times if the development of the story so requires.

Movement must be (or seem) motivated by something. The most natural reasons for movement are found in the dialogue of the screen play itself. The most effective movement is that which results from emotion. If there is no emotional reason for moving, a practical one must be found. The examples here involve only two people. Larger groups obey the same rules, with the difference only that the increased number allows further combinations on the screen.

A group moving from zone to zone

Zone change is primarily a technique used to obtain pictorial variation. Its second property is that it allows the scene to progress to different levels of emotion and mood. As the zone is changed so also the mood of the play alters, becomingmore intimate, tense, etc.

A change of zone should take place during the re-establishing shot used to bridge two different editing patterns. (Fig. 26.1).

Only two areas are used in this example. The editing order of the sequence is as follows:

1 2 3 2 3 1 4 5 4 5

The whole locale, with both players in it, is established at the beginning of the sequence. The first part of the scene, with both players standing, is then covered by intercutting master shots 2 and 3 in parallel, which are external reverse sites around the players.

When the first part of the sequence is finished, we return to shot 1. Now we use this camera site as a re-establishing position for the audience. Here we see the players move together into the background towards the second zone. Two additional variations are accomplished: the players exchange screen areas and their body level is lowered as they sit down. Master shots 4 and 5 resort again to external reverse coverage of the couple. The pictorial composition on the screen varies although the editing pattern used previously is repeated, because the actors have exchanged their screen positions.

The mood of the scene also changes. The performers now occupy more comfortable positions, lending the scene an air of increased intimacy in their relationships.

The formula is simple: an editing pattern is used in the first zone and repeated in the second. These editing patterns can be different in each zone, and they can make use of several combinations of master shots according to the five variants of the triangle principle

543

FIGURE 26.1 A simple case in which a group of people move from one zone to another during a conversation. Body level and position change add variety.

for camera placement. The concept that must be retained is that the group of players can be moved from one area of the set to another whatever the distance. In this way different backgrounds for the static master shots are obtained.

If a large group is involved, the central characters alone can be moved to the next area.

Two, three, four or five areas on the set can be chosen as zones where sections of the sequence will be staged. Many types of visual variation are available in each. Not only different editing patterns, but attitudes, body positions, distances, etc., are consciously planned to achieve the illusion of spontaneity.

The group expands

Moving the whole group (as just discussed) is a limited approach that can be improved by introducing group expansion, or to use a theatrical term, by using broad inter-area motions.

Expansion is achieved either by selective editing or by moving some of the figures from the central group to another area.

Selective editing can emphasize a silent player on the rim of the group or achieve pictorial variation simply by changing the editing pattern. (Fig. 26.2).

The editing order of the sequence would be as follows:

Shot 1 Full shot of the group in the room forming a circle around the two central players engaged in a discussion. The passive group is seated or reclining against diverse pieces of furniture. Only the central players stand erect, commanding our attention.

FIGURE 26.2 Group expansion by the use of selective editing, using two different zones on the set (the girl and the central group) during the second half of the sequence.

545

Shot 2; Each covers close external reverse views of the central
Shot 3 performers engaged in the discussion of a topic of
interest for the whole group. Each is a master shot and
both are edited in parallel, covering the first part of the
scene.

Shot 4 The whole group is re-established from a different position in the room. In the foreground at the left, with her back to the camera, is the seated figure of a woman looking towards the central players in the background.

She is placed on the rim of the circle surrounding the dominant performers.

Shot 5 A reverse shot of the girl seen close to the camera. She is looking off screen, right. This is a silent master shot in which the girl offers a neutral expression—no reactions are seen in her face as she listens.

Shot 6 Full shot of the two central players and part of the group around them. The dominant performers continue their discussion. This camera position has the same visual axis as shot 4, and is an advance on the axis.

In fact, what is framed in this shot represents the girl's point of view. This is also a master shot, periodically interrupted by inter-cutting shot 5 where the girl watches silently as the discussion continues on the sound track. The silent shots of the girl are very brief—two seconds each perhaps, while the segments of shot 6 are longer.

Shot 7 The scene is re-established from a new point of view and then ends. A good pretext is to have one of the central players (engaged in the discussion) start to move away from his companion as seen at the conclusion of shot 6, and cut on the action to shot 7.

In this shot the whole group is set in motion and all exit from the room to another part of the house.

As can be seen in the example quoted, the whole group, including the central characters, occupied stationary positions on the set during the sequence, and only moved at the conclusion. Master shots 2 and 3 heightened a concentrated centre of interest in one zone of the stage. The relationship between master shots 5 and 6 introduced a visual expansion of the group by relating persons occupying different areas of the set. Pictorial variation was obtained without moving any of the players.

Two further variants

If a player moves from one zone to a second while his companion remains in the first, there is, in effect, an expansion of the group. (Fig. 26.3).

In editing the first part of the sequence two external reverse master shots are intercut in parallel. When the whole scene is re-established the players movement is from one zone to another.

FIGURE 26.3 Only one player moves to another zone, while his companion remains in the first.

The editing pattern in the second part of the sequence makes use of two internal reverse camera sites, one for each zone, to relate the players visually before closing the sequence with a re-establishing shot. The editing order for this example runs as follows:

1–2–3–2–3–2–3–4–5–6–5–6–5–6–7

The expansion of a group can be combined with zone changes for the whole group to add variety to a long sequence. In such an event the sequence begins with both players in the first zone and an editing pattern of external reverse shots is applied to that area. Then both players move to the second zone and exchange screen areas in the process.

A right angle external camera coverage could, perhaps, be chosen to cover the players in this zone. Afterwards, one of the performers moves to a third zone and both areas (2 and 3) are related by the use of internal reverse camera positions. Re-establishing camera sites are employed to record each zone change. Fig. 26.4 details the movements and camera placements just discussed.

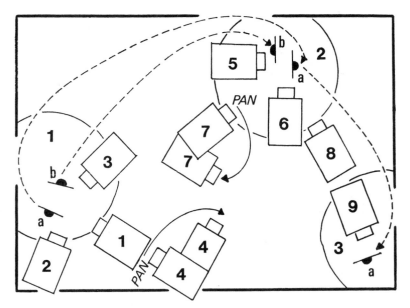

FIGURE 26.4 Two previous techniques are blended here. The group moves from zone to zone, and then expands, while one of the players moves to a third zone Meanwhile his companion remains in the second.

A player moves, the other remains still

In this variation a performer moves away from the zone common to the couple to a zone (or zones) in the background. The key variant is that he keeps moving until he returns to his partner who has replied to his spoken lines, without moving from his original position. The formula is simple:

Shot 1   Medium shot of both performers. The camera then pans to one side with the moving player as he walks away.

Shot 2   Internal reverse shot of the player who remains in one place through the entire sequence.

Shot 3   Master panning shot in which the moving actor wanders on to the set. He moves by segments, making successive stops. This master shot is intercut with two smaller master shot of the stationary player. These two small master shots have a common visual axis and are from internal reverse positions.

Shot 4   The sequence concludes showing how the wandering actor returns to his former place besides the stationary player.

Fig. 26.5 illustrates the sequence that follows, using the technique just described, with dialogue.

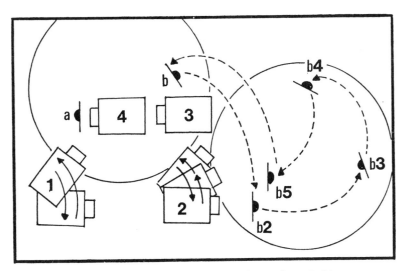

FIGURE 26.5 Floor plan of the sequence shown in the next figure. In this case one player moves from zone to zone, while the other remains in a fixed position.

Shot 1   Medium shot. A and B talk. B turns, walks to the right. The camera pans with him. B stops and turns to face A off-screen.

Shot 3   Medium shot of A facing the camera. He replies.

Shot 2   Close shot of B facing the camera. He turns and walks to the background to position B³ where he stops in medium shot facing the camera. The camera pans with him to the left. He talks.

Shot 3   Medium shot of A. He listens.

Shot 2   Medium shot of B. He moves again, walking to the left to position B⁴ in close shot. The camera pans with him to that side. He talks.

Shot 4   Close shot of A facing the camera. He listens.

Shot 2   Close shot of B. He moves to the right to position B⁵ in close shot. The camera pans with him to the right. He talks.

Shot 4   Close shot of A. He replies.

Shot 1   Medium shot of B. He walks to the left and joins A. The camera pans with him to show both actors in medium shot. They talk. The sequence ends.

It is not necessary that both performers stand up through the whole sequence. The static actor, for instance, could be sitting down. The moving player does bits of business on his movements, like lighting a cigarette, or moving a vase of flowers from one table to another—little things that justify his movements from zone to zone.

Fig. 26.6 illustrates the screen compositions reached and held for each fragment of the four master shots that were combined for the sequence.

In a long sequence the moving actor might sit down halfway through and stand up again moments later to start moving. The camera cannot only pan with the moving actor but track forward or backwards with that player as he moves alone from zone to zone.

If the sequence is extra long, we can reunite the players midway through by having the moving player re-join the other one, stay for a moment and then cross to the other side where the moving player repeats the whole pattern in full once more (Fig. 26.7).

The essential thing is that one player stays put while the other moves from area to area.

FIGURE 26.6 A simple case in which one player moves from zone to zone while the other stays put during the whole sequence.

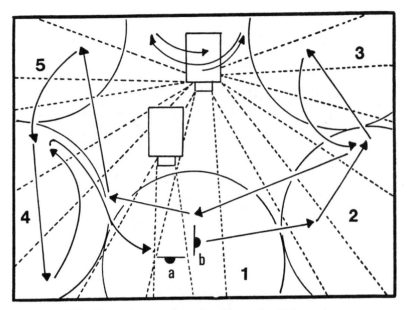

FIGURE 26.7 Diagram for a more complex sequence in which one player moves while the other remains in a fixed position during the whole sequence.

The group contracts

The group contracts in the example just discussed—players who are scattered in different zones are reunited in a single area. This recourse is very useful for concluding a sequence. Two players have been shown together moving from zone to zone. The group, having been expanded, is now contracted, bringing the performers together once more to conclude the scene. A pattern of movement that expands and contracts periodically during the sequence should be at the service of the story and not arbitrarily imposed on a scene. Rather, the most adequate editing solution should be selected.

Devices for zone change

We have stated elsewhere that changes of zone should be effected during the introduction of a re-establishing shot to show clearly the two zones involved and underline the geography of the situation. There are several formulas for making changes of zone employing various editing arrangements.

554

FIGURE 26.8 The players are first covered individually. One then walks to the other so that they now occupy a single area. A pair of external reverse shots provide coverage.

Case 1

Players A and B are seen on internal reverse shots. The master shots are edited in parallel. Then A exits his master shot. She then enters master shot 2 (which now frames both players, Fig. 26.8).

The contraction of the group was achieved simply by moving a player from his zone to his partners. Master shot 2 can now continue with both players, or a pair of external reverse shots can be introduced to cover the couple by parallel editing. By reversing the formula expansion of the group can be obtained.

Case 2

A pan movement can be used to reunite the players in a single zone. Master shots 1 and 2, covering each player separately in internal reverse shots are edited in parallel. When A moves in master shot 1, the camera pans with her showing how she approaches B and stays with him. (Fig. 26.9).

555

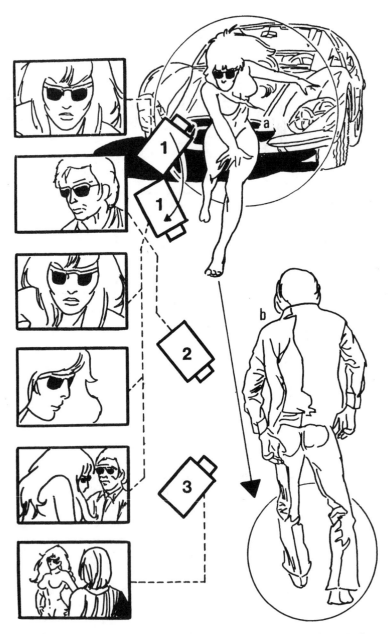

FIGURE 26.9 This is similar to the preceding case, the only difference being in the panning shot used for the change of zone. This pan accompanies the moving player to the other zone, where her companion waits.

The result is similar to the case examined previously (Case 1) and the sequel of shots equal those employed in that example.

Case 3

Two players, occupying different zones are often brought together by a short track, both players having been shown individually in internal reverse shots. The sequence is as follows:

Shot 1   Close shot of A.
Shot 2   Close shot of B.
Shot 1   Close shot of A.
Shot 2   Close shot of B.
Shot 1   A advances to the camera. The camera tracks back passing beside B and stops when it frames him from behind on one side of the screen. A stops in front of B.
Shot 3   Reverse external shot of B–A.
Shot 1   External reverse shot of B–A.
Shot 3   B and A seen together.
Shot 1   B and A in a two shot.

The solution is similar to that in the previous two cases, where the editing pattern was changed from internal to external coverage as the two actors were brought to a common zone stage (Fig. 26.10).

The illustration offers a second alternative for the last part of the sequence. In the scene just described she stops in front of him, the girl on the left and the man on the right of the screen, as seen from the last position of the camera in shot 1. The alternative is to have her move to the other side of him, so that from the last camera position of shot 1, he is seen placed on the left of the screen, with his back to us, and she faces us in the right sector of the film frame. The site for shot 3 would now be on the other side of the line of motion, providing us with a perfectly licit external reverse angle. The line of interest flowing between the players at the beginning of the scene is shifted to a new direction at the conclusion of the tracking camera motion that reunites both players on a common area.

Case 4

When two players move from one zone to another one actor might move first rather than the two together (Fig. 26.11).

Shot 1   A and B talking. A exits left, leaving B.
Shot 2   A enters from the right and turns to face B off screen.

557

FIGURE 26.10 A tracking shot accompanies the moving player when he moves from one zone to another where the other person is waiting.

Shot 1 B, alone, delivers one or two lines, then exits left.

Shot 2 B enters from right joining A.

In the example given, both players are seen in profile in both zones. But two cameras placed at right angles will introduce a pictorial variation on the same formula (Fig. 26.12).

Shot 1 B and A are talking. Actor B exits left leaving A alone in the centre of the picture. A then exits left.

Shot 2 B is facing the camera and on the left side of the screen. A enters, right, into shot and stops on that side, with his back to us.

This is a simplication of the approach detailed in the previous case.

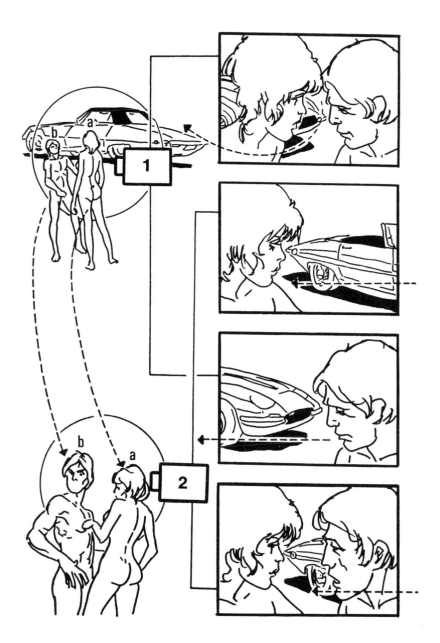

FIGURE 26.11 Both players move alternately from the first to the second. Two master shots are edited in parallel to record the effect.

559

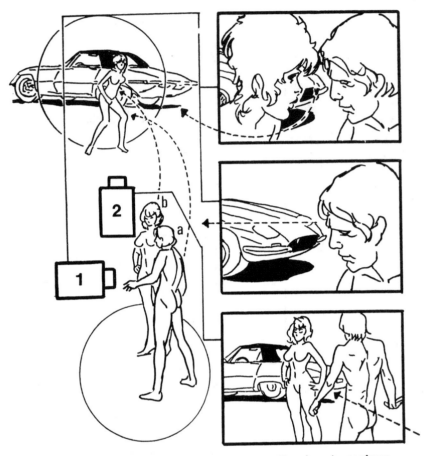

FIGURE 26.12 A right angle camera arrangement is used here for a change of zone in which the players move alternately.

Case 5

Two successive pans from the same camera site, can be used to show two players moving from zone to zone one after the other (Fig. 26.13).

Shot 1 B and A in medium shot. As B moves to the left, the camera pans with her to that side till she joins C.

Shot 2 A, still in the first position and seen in medium shot, walks to the left. The camera pans with him to that side where he joins C and B.

The three players are now in the second zone and can be covered by the triangular principle to emphasize the group as a whole or

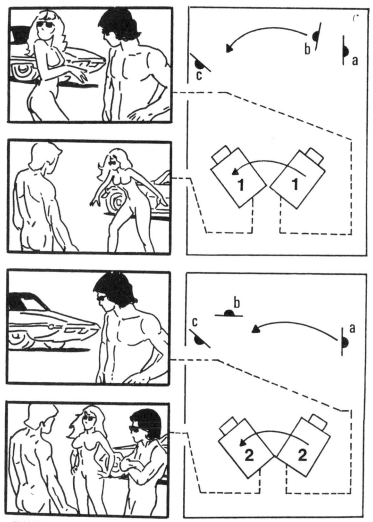

FIGURE 26.13 Two players move from one area to another covered by a panning camera. Both pans are made from the same camera position, first with one player and then with the other as they move to the new zone where a third player awaits them.

its members individually. The second pan (shot 2) can move beyond B and C, accompanying A to the third zone (Fig. 26.14).

If the pan shots of the performers are long shots, static objects or props in the foreground would add depth to the panning movement. The second may also be from a position closer to the subjects and on the same visual axis as the previous camera site.

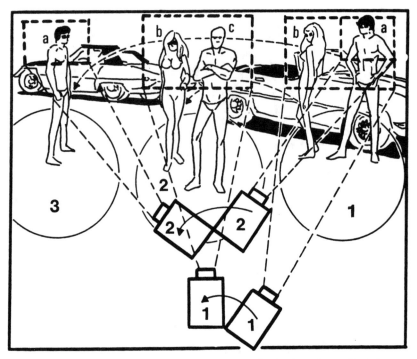

FIGURE 26.14 Two panning shots have a common visual axis, and cover the two moving players individually as they change from zone to zone.

Case 6

The second player's change of zone can be delayed by introducing an interplay of master shots in parallel (Fig. 26.15).

The sequence would be edited in the following way:

Shot 1   Close shot of players A and B.
Shot 2   Reverse close shot of both.
Shot 1
Shot 2   (As above)
Shot 1   After a moment B moves to the right. The camera pans with her to frame the girl alone in close shot.
Shot 3   Close shot of A.
Shot 1   Close shot of B.
Shot 3   Close shot of A. He walks towards us. Camera tracks back with him until it frames B from behind on one side of the screen. A stops, facing her.

This delayed approach to zone change looks less artificial and can

FIGURE 26.15 A pan and track combined in this example achieve the change of zone for both players as they move one after the other, with a pause between.

be introduced whenever the situation warrants it to move the players smoothly from zone to zone.

There are, of course, more solutions to the problems of zone changes where two, three or four persons are involved. Several of the rules and examples are outlined earlier (page 503).

27

COMBINED TECHNIQUES

Those who make fiction films will soon find that the larger part of his work concerns dialogue sequences. Dialogues serve to give information to the audience, define the conduct of the characters, give amusing relief, contribute to the development of the drama or communicate feelings, etc.

Documentary film makers also often encounter scenes that require dialogued presentation (either in a visual performance alone or with lip sync speech) to put a story point in their theme across more effectively.

In surveying the cinematic means of handling dialogue scenes we must include the combination of physical editing techniques with those edited in the camera. These combinations widen the scope of resources available by providing solutions which are very adaptable to very different circumstances. But it is the concept behind them that really matters since, of course, the range of possible solutions is almost numberless.

Shot by shot editing

With this type of approach the scene is taken in as many shots, long or short, as is felt necessary. The long shots may be static or 'edited in the camera' shots.

Dialogue scenes present some difficulty in planning because there is only one way to edit the sequence—there is just one shot for each phrase or group of lines spoken by the players.

Scenes of pure action where the performers move without depending on dialogue are easier to handle with the shot by shot editing technique. The arsenal of film rules involving cutting on action, the triangle principle for camera deployment around the player, action and reaction, etc. apply in full with this approach to film cutting. The French film director, Serge Bourginon, is a master in the use of this technique and one of the very few who has consistently applied shot by shot editing to whole films. His films *Sundays and Cybele*, *The Reward* and *15 Days in September* offer striking examples of the results that can be obtained. He has used each shot only once (with the exception of one or two occasions per film, in which he was forced to cut a shot in half and intercut an insert or cut-away). This approach to film making requires a solid knowledge of film technique, since an accumulation of errors while shooting the film will offer less opportunity for correction on the moviola when the sequences are assembled.

Partial use of this technique for different sections of a fiction full length film is employed by almost all film makers, particularly in sequences that depict pure action. But documentary film makers consistently resort to this technique.

Case 1

There is a short fragment of a sequence which gives an idea of what the technique looks like when applied to a scene with dialogue.

Shot 308   Medium shot of a couple sitting in tall grass near a tree trunk. The camera tracks in slowly towards them and gradually stops.

He: 'It is so nice, here far from the village. It makes me feel alive, full of joy.'

The young man lies back to rest on the ground. Cut on the action.

Shot 309   Side shot of the couple. The young man in the foreground completes his reclining movement and puts his hands under his head. The girl, beyond, turns to him and laughs.

She: 'You are acting like a boy, Billy.'

He smiles back and then rises. The camera pans slightly to the right with him, framing both, sitting side by side in the grass, profiled right.

He: 'Sometimes we ought to. It is good for the system.'

He begins to turn his head towards the girl. Cut on the action.

Shot 310 Both are seen from behind. He further turning towards her. He raises his right hand and gently takes her chin.

He: 'Those beautiful, innocent wide eyes . . .'

He pulls her face closer to his to kiss her lips. Cut on the action.

Shot 311 Reverse close up of both. The young man has his head in the shadow of the tree. His features are outlined against the well lit surface of the girl's face. She bends her head forward to meet him. They kiss. The camera tracks to the right behind their heads panning to the left to frame the other side of their faces, as the windswept branches of the tree cast a moving shadow over their faces. They end kissing and she pulls back her head to look at him, a smile on her face. They stare at each other. Suddenly a horse neighs nearby, breaking the spell. Both turn to look off screen.

Shot 312 Reverse. The couple in foreground, their backs to us, framed in medium shot. Beyond, in the background, a man on horseback is watching silently.

Shot 313 Close shot of the rider. Same visual axis as the preceding shot. He smiles broadly.

Rider: 'Am I interrupting something?'

Each shot in the example given covers a fragment of the scene. No camera site is used twice. None of the shots is spliced in parallel with any of the others. The example in itself is small and rather simple.

Case 2

Shots edited within the film frame can be used in accordance with the same principles. A series of medium length takes (one or two minutes each) can be cut in, one behind the other, covering a whole or part of a sequence. The example that follows adheres to such an approach. Fig. 27.1 is a floor plan of the sequence.

Shot 426 The camera tracks from right to left with player A (a woman) who joins performer B (a man), joining B and A in close shot in the second zone. After a moment of conversation player A walks to the right and the camera tracks with her. When she reaches th

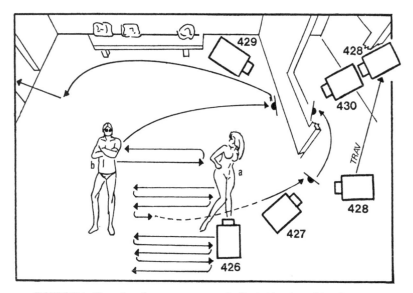

FIGURE 27.1 Floor plan of a sequence covered with shot by shot editing. Each shot is used only once, but some use the principle of editing in camera which gives the sequence pictorial variety.

first zone again she stops and turns to the left, continuing to speak. Then she moves again to the left towards the second zone. The camera tracks with her and stops profiling B–A in close shot. Bitter words are exchanged between the players. B crosses to the right, followed by the camera and reaches the first zone where he stops. Moments later, B returns to the second zone and the composition combines A–B in close shot. He hurls his last bitter insult. A crosses to the right exiting shot. Only B remains, with his head downcast.

Shot 427 A enters the shot from the left. She walks away from camera and stops with her back to it, framed in a medium shot. She turns to the left to mouth a bitter line of reproach and then turns her head away from us again. Cut on the action.

Shot 428 Reverse medium shot. B on the left of the screen in the background with his back to us. A in foreground walks right, to another room. The camera tracks with her. She stops inside close to the entrance on the left

567

side of the screen. B profiled in the background turns toward the camera and approaches player A.

Shot 429 Reverse. A on the left in the second room. B enters right and stops with his back to the camera. He speaks.

Shot 430 Reverse. Close shot of A and B. This is an advance on the visual axis of shot 428. B concludes his speech. A, left, reacts by turning her back on him and faces the camera. She replies with bitter words. B turns and walks to the background exiting by a door there. A remains alone on the screen.
Fade out.

The dialogue of the scene was omitted from the description of the shots to make the example more graphic and to concentrate on the physical action itself. Thus we can clearly observe how each shot which is edited in camera is linked with the preceding one for continuity of action. The technique employed adopts the shot-by-shot editing principle described earlier.

Case 3

It is easier to edit single shots of parallel action, than the one related by a continuous motion, such as in the preceding examples. With parallel editing the timing of the sequence can be adjusted at will by trimming down the shots or using longer versions of them. With continuous shot-by-shot editing the film maker, once his material is shot and printed, has less control in introducing any modifications. By using inserts or cut-aways, filmed as protection, he can delete parts of the master shots. But it is a repair job full of difficulties.

On the other hand, shot-by-shot editing that alternates two or more lines of narration in parallel is easier to assemble, change or delete. Here is an example of an action that adheres to the latter possibility. The fragment offered is the conclusion of a fight scene.

Shot 456 Long shot. A girl standing in the road close to a cliff. She watches the villain (foreground) flip the hero to the ground. Both fall. The villain gets up and runs to the left out of shot. The hero rises and runs to the left after the villain. The camera pans to the left with the hero excluding the girl from the shot. Again we see the villain running to the edge of the cliff. The hero catches up with him, and tackles him.

Shot 457 Close shot of the girl looking off-screen, left.

Shot 458 Long shot. The hero and the villain fighting. The hero falls under a blow from the villain. The villain reaches for a rock.

Shot 459 Medium shot. The girl comes forward and picks up the gun from the road. The camera pans down and up with her movement.

Shot 460 Long shot. A car, driven by the hero's friend speeds towards us along the road.

Shot 461 Long shot. The villain, holding the rock high over his head, moves towards the hero.

Shot 462 Close up. The girl fires the gun towards the camera, pointing it off screen left.

Shot 463 Full shot. The hero on the ground recovering slowly. The villain with the rock high over his head is hit by the shot and falls back out of shot.

Shot 464 Long shot from above the cliff. The body of the villain plunges into the sea with an audible splash.

Shot 465 The hero rises into the screen framed from below in a medium shot. He looks down.

Shot 466 Full shot. The hero's friend steps out of the car and runs along the road to the right. The camera pans with him to that side.

Shot 467 Close shot of the hero exiting shot, right.

Shot 468 Close shot of the girl. She lowers the gun out of the screen, and then comes forward towards the camera, passing out of shot, left.

Shot 469 Full shot. The hero walks to the right towards the road The camera pans with him.

Shot 470 Medium shot. The friend comes forward on the road and stops. The girl enters right, the hero, left. Both have their backs to us. Suddenly all turn towards the camera and look up to the upper right corner as they hear an explosion off screen.

Shot 471 Long shot. The lone bus on top of the hill blows up in a fierce explosion.

Each shot in this sequence portrays a different part of the event. There are three main lines of action alternating on the screen. Since each action is visually independent of the others, it is possible to adjust the duration of shots to the length desired. This is an important factor that allows the film maker to increase or slacken the tempo of his film.

Case 4

On many occasions, single shots are used to present one fact at a time to the audience. Each shot has the value of a phrase or of a short statement. These shots are sometimes linked with dissolves that serve to indicate the passage of time. We offer an example taken from Delmer Daves' film *Cowboy*.

Dissolve

Long Shot of the country. The sun rises slowly over the horizon.

Dissolve

Close Shot of a coffee pot over a camp fire. A hand enters the screen and takes off the lid. The water is seen boiling inside.

Dissolve

Full shot. The cowboys wake up to the sound of a frying pan being beaten off screen. One of the men rises close to the wagon and walks to the left. The camera pans with him, showing the others in the group and stops in the foreground on the sleepy face of Jack Lemmon.

Dissolve

Close shot of an iron grid over the coals of the camp fire. It is full of juicy steaks slowly cooking. A hand with a fork enters and picks up one of the steaks. The camera pans up and we see a cowboy distributing the steaks to his mates.

Dissolve

Close shot of the camp fire. Somebody pours the contents of the coffee pot over the hot embers, dousing the fire.

Dissolve

The wagon train passes in front of the camera from left to right in full shot.

Long shot. On the left in the background we see the cowboy's caravan coming to us. A group of pacific Indians on horseback enter shot from the right.

They ride into the background.

Cowboys and Indians cross each other in front of the camera. The camera pans to the right with Jack Lemmon (the tenderfoot of the story) who looks at the Indians.

Dissolve

The caravan follows a lazy Z path from left to right in front of the camera. Glenn Ford and his Mexican foreman ride at the head of the column. Jack Lemmon comes along behind, half asleep on the saddle.

Dissolve

At sunset. Glenn Ford at the head of the caravan stops his horse and raises his arm to signal the others to stop.

Dissolve

Around the campfire at night a new sequence begins, covering the events of a day in the march of the caravan. Each shot is the equivalent of a written phrase.

No spoken words are necessary for the sequence, which relies on its images to put its ideas across.

Merging the techniques

To the parallel editing of master shots and the editing of a scene in the camera without visual cuts, one should add a further resource based on the combined use of these two. The key combinations that can be obtained are:

1   A series of consecutive shots edited in the camera followed by two (or more) master shots edited in parallel.

2   Two (or more) shots edited in the camera intercut in parallel.

Case 5

These techniques may be applied in a repetitive way. Because there are only two possible variations the presentation may be repetitive in nature, conforming to an alternating pattern. Nevertheless it affords a very wide margin for variation since each individual technique has, in itself, a whole arsenal of combinations that will disguise the nature of the general pattern. A practical example gives an idea of what this combination of technique looks like (Fig. 27.2).

Shot 1 A enters by the door at the left and walks to his A^2 position. The camera pans with him. We see player B on the far right, sitting. A blows out a candle and then walks to his A^3 position, now seen in the composition $B-A^3$. Then B rises and comes towards the camera. She stops in the foreground, composing B^2-A^3. After a few moments, and when several lines of dialogue have been exchanged, A comes forward to his A^4 position, forming a B^2-A^4 composition on the screen. Both performers are now profiled to each other, framed in medium shot.

Shot 2 External close shot of B and A, favouring A. More dialogue is exchanged.

Shot 3 Reverse external close shot of B and A, favouring B. The conversation continues.

Shot 2 The players in close shot, A featured over his partner.

Shot 3 Both players in close shot, B visually emphasized over his partner.

Shot 1 B and A framed in medium shot again, profiled to each other. The pictorial composition is similar to that used at the conclusion of the first fragment of this take. A moves to the background and sits down. The composition becomes B^2-A^5. B then joins A in the background. She sits down beside him. Composition is now B^3-A^5.

Shot 4 Insert. Close shot of B and A seated. The shot emphasizes a phrase being exchanged between them. This shot has the same visual axis as shot 1.

Shot 1 Again, the composition on the screen becomes $B-^3A^5$. Player A rises and comes to the foreground again. The camera pans with him to the left. He stops and turns to the background composing A^5-B^3.

Shot 5 Insert. Close shot of A, seen from an internal reverse camera position. He listens.

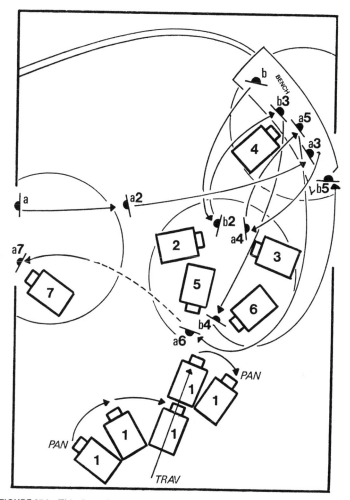

FIGURE 27.2 This floor plan view shows the several camera arrangements used to cover a dialogued sequence. Shot 1 is a long master shot covering the whole sequence. Other shots are intercut either as inserts or edited in parallel with the main master shot. Thus, several editing techniques are merged to cover the sequence.

Shot 1 We return again to the composition A^6–B^3. This is a medium shot. B rises in the background and walks to A, (foreground). As she walks to A the camera tracks in towards the players to frame a close shot of them, composing A^6–B^4. They talk.

Shot 6 Reverse external close shot of A^6–B^4. This composition favours player A.

573

Shot 1 Close shot of A^6–B^4. The composition favours B.

Shot 6 Reverse external shot of A–B, favouring A.

Shot 1 Close shot of A–B. A then exits shot left. B turns her head to the left following his movement off screen.

Shot 7 Full shot of a door in the background. A at the beginning of the shot enters from the right and walks to the door, stops there and looks back. He speaks.

Shot 1 Close shot of B profiled left. She listens in silence.

Shot 7 Player A in full shot close to the door, opens it and exits.

Shot 1 Close shot of B. She lowers her head, then turns her back to the camera and walks to the background. The camera pans to the right with her. She sits on the bench, worried.

The sequence just described, although somewhat complex at first, is structured in a simple manner, as the analysis that follows will disclose. The sequence is built using the following elements.

Shot 1 A long master take covering the scene from beginning to end. It uses the technique of editing within the film frame by panning and tracking during the shot as the players move in three zones on the set. Into this shot are intercut the shots that follow, which were designed to cover points of view different from the master shot, and replace sections of the master take itself.

Shots 2 and 3 A pair of external reverse shot. Shot 1 acts as the top of the triangle in the delta camera formation. Shots 2 and 3 are placed on the base of this arrangement.

Shot 4 This is an insert that stresses a piece of dialogue. It momentarily gives a closer view of the players, and is placed on the same visual axis as shot 1 at that moment in the sequence.

Shot 5 Silent reaction shot, covering an internal reverse position, that gives the audience a chance to observe the reaction of the player with his back to the camera in master shot 1.

Shot 6 This shot is edited in parallel with master shot 1 and covers a reverse external position on the other side of the couple involved in the scene.

Shot 7 This shot, also edited in parallel with master shot 1, differs from shot 6, which covered the players on the same zone of the set, by the fact that shot 7 juxtaposes the first zone on the set with the second seen in the last part of the master shot 1.

The sequence can be divided in four parts that use different combinations of the basic approaches already explained.

1   As can be observed, master shot 1 is first used alone within the technique of editing in the frame. The players are seen using three zones on the set: one close to the camera and the others placed at right angles.

2   Shot 1 is interrupted to give place to a couple of shots edited in parallel that stress a part of the dialogue.

3   The scene moves back to shot 1 which is again employed with the technique of editing within the frame. Two inserts, one with live sound and the other a silent reaction, cover the next section of the scene.

4   Then, in the fourth part of the sequence, shots 6 and 7 are intercut in parallel with the master shot itself. Shot 6 provides a reverse view of the couple standing in the second zone. When both players are in different zones, shot 7 presents the point of view of the performer who remains in the second zone, thus affording parallel editing of both zones.

Three techniques are used in this sequence. First, a combination of 'camera editing' master shot and fixed camera sites are intercut in parallel. Then two inserts are edited into the main master shot. Thirdly, two fixed camera lesser master shots are edited in parallel with the principal master shot.

The second technique outlined is an important one. Silent or live sound reaction shots should be intercut whenever necessary into a frame edited master. They serve to comment on events or performers not at that moment included on the master shot. These reaction shots are of two natures: cut-aways or inserts. The latter stress an action or a line of dialogue or an element or person present in the central master shot into which they are intercut.

Case 6

Two master shots edited within the frame can be intercut in parallel. The approach is quite simple. The *last part* of the first master is intercut with the *first part* of the second master. The example that follows features such an occurrence. Fig. 27.3 gives a floor plan view of motions of the players in the scene.

Shot 1   Close shot of a couple. She is standing in foreground with her back to us. He is seen beyond on the right,

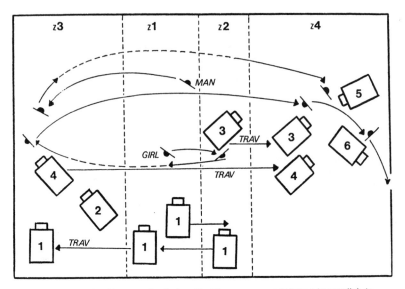

FIGURE 27.3 In this example shots edited in camera are intercut in parallel, involving a more complex technique for the coverage of a dialogued sequence.

facing the woman. She then walks to the right. The camera tracks with her. She stops in the second zone and turns to face her companion who is now off screen. The camera stops, framing her in close shot. Afterwards she returns to the first zone on the left. The camera tracks with her again and then stops, facing the man, as the girl crosses in front of him and exits shot, left. The camera holds on a close shot of the man looking off screen left.

Shot 2   Medium close shot of the girl. She turns in the centre of the screen and faces us looking off-screen right. The camera holds on her as she speaks.

Shot 1   Close shot of the man. He walks to the left to the third zone. The camera tracks with him and stops as he joins her, framing a close shot of girl and man. They talk, then he exits right, leaving the girl alone on the screen. We stay with her for a moment.

Shot 3   Close medium shot of the man walking to a railing in the background. The camera tracks behind him and stops when he reaches the railing and sits down.

Shot 4   Close shot of the girl. She talks.

Shot 3 Medium shot of the man sitting at the foot of the railing. He replies.

Shot 4 Close shot of the girl. She speaks.

Shot 3 Medium shot of the man, seated. He speaks.

Shot 4 Close shot of the girl. She speaks and then walks to the right to the fourth zone where the man is. The camera pans and tracks with her to that side, framing both together at the end of the tracking movement. She is in the foreground, left, with her back to the camera. He is seated on the right, facing her. They speak.

Shot 5 Close shot of her. This is an internal reverse shot featuring the girl.

Shot 4 Medium shot of both. The camera angle favours him.

Shot 5 Close shot of her.

Shot 4 Medium shot of both. He replies. The girl then walks to the right, going out of shot. We stay with him for an instant.

Shot 6 Full long shot. From up high through an arch in foreground, we see the girl in the centre of the screen moving away into the background. At the beginning of the shot she moved from behind one of the columns into the picture.

In the example given the master shot that illustrates the point is shot 4. Shot 3 is intercut in parallel with the beginning of shot 4 in the static camera sections of the shots. Then the camera moves in shot 4 from the third to the fourth zone, where it again becomes stationary. This last part of shot 4 is edited in parallel with an internal reverse shot of the girl (shot 5). In this example the maximum possibilities are obtained from a simple shot like shot 4 by relating the first and third zones initially and by providing reverse angle coverage on the fourth later.

Summing up

The examples given to show how the different editing techniques can be merged are in themselves simple ones. More complex editing patterns can be achieved depending on the context of the scene to which these techniques are applied. No matter how intricate the solution arrived at, two motivations must be constantly observed:

That the technique applied serves the scene and not vice versa.

That the visual results obtained seem natural and lifelike as they are projected on the screen.

Technique would defeat its purpose if it fails to convey the intentions of the film maker and the subtleties of the acting performed in front of the camera.

28

FILM PUNCTUATION

Film punctuation—separations between sequences, pauses in narration, stress of a passage—is achieved by editing, camera movement or subject movement, either alone or used in combination. The best known devices are now described.

Transitions from scene to scene: fade out—fade in
This 'time transition' device (where the screen image gradually darkens and is replaced with another image which either fades in or begins abruptly) is normally carried out in the laboratory. If insufficient film footage is available, the scene can be 'frozen' and then faded either in or out.

White-outs and colour fades
An alternative to ordinary fades is a fade out to a white screen. Fades can also employ dominant colours. The image to be faded out is suddenly tinted by a colour that grows denser till it obliterates the image completely and a flatly coloured screen remains. This colour then grows lighter and the new scene is revealed. Two different colours can be used, one to fade out and the other to fade in to the the new scene. Agnes Varda, in her film *Le Bonheur*, used this method repeatedly, employing single colours (red, blue) or combinations (blue-red; green-violet) so helping to suggest the mood relationship of the sequences connected by the colour fades.

Dissolve
A dissolve is a combination of a fade out and a fade in, superimposed on the same strip of film. It is believed that dissolves were first used by Georges Meliès in 1902 for his film *A Trip To The*

Mood. A rapid dissolve gives a fairly sharp transition from one scene to another. Slow dissolves can relate the mood of two scenes to one another. If the overlapping portion is extended the dissolve is prolonged, perhaps to stress an intense nostalgic or poetic mood.

The combination of a fade out and fade in is used to obtain apparitions on the screen. The empty set is first photographed, the camera stopped, the player moved into the shot and the camera restarted. Later, in the laboratory, when the two shots are dissolved, the player appears to materialize from nowhere and become solid.

The stationary parts of the scene retain even intensity throughout. The camera cannot be moved.

Wipe

A wipe is a laboratory effect in which a new scene is introduced on the screen as the first one is pushed or wiped to a side. There are two types of wipe. In the first the new scene enters from one side or above and pushes the other out of the screen. In the second, a thin line travels across erasing the old scene and revealing the new.

The second type of wipe, the travelling line, is the most often used for time transitions on the screen. The travelling line can move horizontally, vertically or diagonally, either from right to left or vice versa.

More complicated patterns, such as the spiralling wipe, or multiple squares, have been designed and used to achieve time transitions but their startling effects have been reserved for film trailers.

Iris

The iris effect has undergone some transformations over the years. At first it appeared as a diminishing circle that centred attention on an isolated subject or detail. Abandoned as a time transition method through being overworked, it was relegated to a closing effect for animated cartoons. It has been revived and updated from time to time. For example, in an American television series, *Batman*, a stylized figure of a bat grows from the centre of the screen towards the camera till it covers the image completely and then recedes again to a dot, revealing a new image.

Use of dark areas

For another form of time transition, the camera can pan or track behind a dark area or shape that fills the screen and then cut to a similar opening device in the next scene. If the camera moves in the same direction in both shots, the transition will be smoother than with opposed directions. Alternatively, the actor himself can move towards and away from the camera. With only one person the effect is somewhat artificial, but becomes more subtle with two performers, who approach the camera drawing closer together as they reach the foreground, and separate as they move away in the next shot in a new place and a different time.

Titles

The use of titles to separate sequences is a remnant of the silent film epoch. But today titles can identify places, the exact time of the day, or the year in which the action is supposed to take place and might appear over a typical picture of the place or over a plain background.

Some documentary films use sub-titles to designate new sequences.

Props

Time props are still used to denote the passage of time. The idea is to depict the ravage of time on an article that requires small spanses of time to show marked changes in its appearance. The complete prop is first shown and then dissolves to the final stage in which the prop has been destroyed, consumed or worn out. Such props, though now most are cliches, include lighted candles, cigarettes, fireplaces, campfires, clocks, calendars and dated newspaper headlines.

Light change

Changes from morning to evening light can suggest a time transition. The camera frames a motionless set, and the studio lights are altered to denote the change. The audience sees the light change, shifting shadows as a gradual effect, then the camera or players move into the scene to begin the new sequence.

Question and answer

This method relies on an idea to effect the time transition. For example, a character in the story asks, 'Do you think that Pamela is really beautiful?' 'Yes, she is,' replies another player in a different place at a different time and to another person standing beside him. The questioner and the person answering are not related by the direction of their looks. Only the rapport between the words spoken effects the transition.

A movement in the same direction

The player sits in the cockpit of a racing car. He is in front of his country house, surrounded by friends. He starts the car and moves out of shot, right. In the following shot the car enters a race track from the left and speeds away. The same vehicle is used, the movement is in the same direction from left to right, but the place, the time and the mood are different.

Substitution of an object

Somebody holds a glass of champagne. He is irritated by the event that has taken place and reacts by throwing the glass away out of shot. The next shot, introduced by a sudden cut, shows a pane of glass being broken by a stone. Behind this broken pane a face appears, looking down. The students of a university are stoning the windows of the faculty's quarters. The link between such sequences is provided by a similar sound or effect.

Word repetition

A character closes a sequence by speaking a word in close shot. The next opens with a new player repeating that word in a different place, at a different time. He might repeat the word with the same emphasis, or perhaps change it into a question. The new scene develops from there.

A deceptive visual match

In scene transitions that rely on an element at the end of one shot and the beginning of the next, that element may play a different

582

role in each. The viewer is led to believe that the new scene is part of the sequence he has been seeing but suddenly becomes aware that this is a new sequence bridged by a period of time.

The two basic devices employed to achieve this effect are: 1, the reaction shot and 2, movement continuity. The first recourse conditions us to expect a reaction shot after a given action but this reaction is linked to what follows in a different way. For example, in David Lean's film *The Bridge on the River Kwai*, we see a scene in which Clipton (the medic) looks up at the sky complaining of the fierce heat. The following shot shows the sun beating down. It is the subjective view of the medic. Instead of cutting back to Clipton the shot continues on the sun when suddenly from below rises the figure of Shears (the escaped American) who blocks out the sun and stands backlit and framed from below. Shears is unkempt, clothes in rags, hair dishevelled, a step away from madness. When he moves on and the sequence continues, we are in a different place at a different time.

A subject that at first cannot be properly identified until a human reference is introduced, can also be employed for such a transition.

Michelangelo Antonioni in his film *La Notte*, uses such a recourse. The main character in the story, a writer, is in his flat waiting for his wife. He lies down on a sofa in his library and looks off screen. The next shot shows an abstract pattern. It seems to be a section of the wall of his room until the small figure of a woman enters the lower left corner of the picture and the image acquires meaning. The abstract pattern is revealed as the side wall of a large building. A new sequence has begun.

Visual shock can be increased for a 'flashy' scene transition. In Frank Tashlin's film *Caprice*, Doris Day and Ray Walston meet for a secret rendezvous on a lonely mountain in the Alps. Richard Harris watches from afar and trains a hidden film camera on the talking couple. A two shot of Doris Day and Ray Walston is suddenly presented. It looks as a natural part of the scene, a continuation of it, but without warning the figure of Jack Kruschen rises from below the screen and blocks the image, which is now projected on him. The image disappears and a white screen remains and the new scene develops inside the office where the film has been projected on a screen.

A movement that continues from one shot to the next shot can be used as a scene transition even though the subject has been substituted by another. A camera movement by itself can serve for transitions from scene to scene relying on a momentary distraction supplied by a close shot or close up framing at the beginning of the second shot before the camera motion reveals the true relationship of things in the new shot. Here is an example from *The Sleeping Car Murders* directed by Costa Gavras (Fig. 28.1).

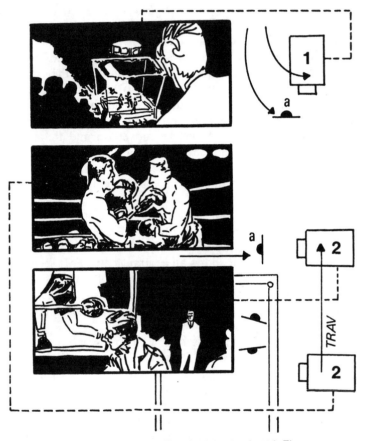

FIGURE 28.1   Time transition obtained by a deceptive visual match. The scene seems to continue from shot to shot, but a time gap is revealed.

A descends a flight of steps in a stadium. He and the camera stop in the foreground. He is framed with his back to us. Beyond, two fighters slug it out in a boxing ring. We cut to a medium shot of the boxers seen in the centre of the screen, exchanging blows. A moment later the camera tracks to the right to show A advancing through the crowd and then sitting in foreground.

The second shot seems to be an advance on a common visual axis with respect to the first shot. This would be the normal case but the surprise comes when the camera moves and discloses our main character already in the front row of the crowd. The time lapse in which he descended towards the ring was omitted by the device described. A close shot, where the surroundings cannot be identified, is used to obtain a time transition within a scene. In his film *Blow Up*, Michelangelo Antonioni uses camera movement to get the same effect. Fig. 28.2 shows both camera positions.

The shots are as follows:

Shot 1   The young photographer is kneeling in the park beside the place occupied the night before by the dead body of a man. The camera picks him up from behind as he looks towards the branches of the tree.

Shot 2   Close shot from below of the branches. It is apparently his point of view showing what he sees. Moments later the camera pans down to reveal the young man standing up near the bushes.

The disclosure comes as a surprise because the young man occupies a position that is not compatible with the subjective point of view implied by its rapport with the preceding shot. Cutting around a central character is another variant. A close up of a person serves as a bridge between two sequences in which he is seen. The camera pulls back to reveal the new location. The change is masked by using neutral backgrounds in both shots. The close up seems to be part of the first sequence but in reality belongs to both scenes.

For example:

Shot 1   A boy in the bed seen over his father's left shoulder. The boy speaks.

Shot 2   Internal reverse, the father seen in close shot. He replies, trying to calm his son.

Shot 1   Boy and father as before. The boy continues to speak.

Shot 3   Internal reverse. The father in close shot reacts painfully to his son's words and turns his head to the right. The camera tracks back to show him seated at a table in a public dining room. The sound of the noisy crowd erupts on the soundtrack.

FIGURE 28.2 Another time transition employing a deceptive visual match used by Michelangelo Antonioni in his film *Blow Up*.

This sequence, shown in Fig. 28.3, was used by director Guy Green in *The Angry Silence*.

A similar deception is played by employing dialogue to trigger an emotion that results in an idea opposite to the one expressed. A man, in close up, menacingly says to a girl, 'If you don't co-operate I will kill your sister'. The next scene is a close up of that sister opening her mouth to cry as she falls back. The camera pans with her and we see that she is in a bathing suit and is jumping back into a swimming pool, where she gaily plays with her companions.

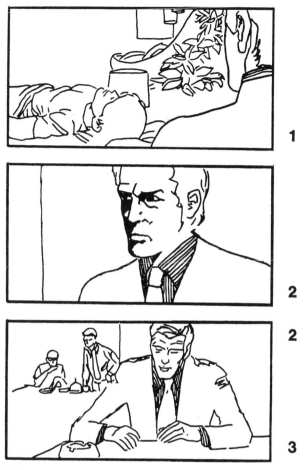

FIGURE 28.3 The second shot in this sequence is the ambiguous one. It belongs to the scene that concludes and to the one that begins after it. The background is neutral in this second shot, to integrate it smoothly within both sequences.

Cutting around a prop

An extension of the previous example, using a 'prop, is demonstrated as follows:

A man, talking to another, asks to be introduced to a third. He presents his card, which is taken by the first man. The card is seen in close up. Close shot of the third and the second man. The third man is holding the card. But the place, time and one of the characters have changed. (Fig. 28.4).

The composition of shots around the close up are similar, but the situation is not. A time gap was quickly bridged by a purely cinematic recourse.

A sudden close up

The close up used as a visual bridge need not relate to the shot that follows. It could be a simple cut to an object or person in close up and then seen in the following shot in its proper context. For instance:
A sequence concludes with a scene inside a room. The shot that follows is a close up of a lamp post with four light bulbs. The third shot is a full shot in which the lamp post is shown as part of the general scenery in a park, The new characters are located in the foreground.

The close up in the first shot was related to the whole ensemble in that which follows.

Transition by parallel editing

Brian Hutton in his film *Where Eagles Dare*, used parallel editing to introduce a flashback near the beginning of the film. Richard Burton as head of a commando group is in the plane that is taking them to their destination:

Shot 1   Richard Burton, seen in close shot, becomes aware of the green light that begins to blink on the plane (we do not see the light, only its reflection on Burton's body).

Shot 2   Close up of a green light bulb in the ceiling, blinking on and off.

Shot 1   Close shot of Burton, as before, bathed by the green light, looking.

Shot 2   Close up of the green light in the ceiling. The camera pans down revealing that the light was not located in the plane but in the underground conference room of a military outpost.

The parallel editing of these shots introduced a return to the past in a visually fluent manner. Roger Corman in his film *The Trip* used the same recourse to introduce a transition into the future. On these two occasions the cutting tempo was unhurried. But when Dennis Hopper used this effect in *East Rider* (Dennis Hopper and Peter Fonda had both worked with Roger Corman on *The Trip*) the transition between one scene and the next was achieved by quickly cutting back and forth a couple of times between the two scenes.

FIGURE 28.4 A close shot of an object is employed here to obtain a time transition from scene to scene.

Used in that way the effect looks rather selfconscious. Only time will tell if it could become a substitute for the dissolve.

Scene openers

If all scenes began abruptly, undue emphasis would usually be thrown on them and unwittingly conspire against the nature of the scene itself. It is better to begin neutrally and then move on to the main event or character. There are two ways—by moving the actor or the camera.

589

The actor

His body blocks the camera lens. He starts to move away, disclosing the scene.

Something in foreground (in sharp focus) is removed by a player. The camera shifts focus to frame the player moving away and then stopping to use the object he picked up in the foreground.

Somebody opens a window (camera outside) or slides away a closed door (camera inside) revealing himself and the scene beyond. Some of the most common props used on opening scenes are: doors, venetian blinds, window shades, curtains and room lights (turned on one by one to illuminate the scene gradually).

The camera

The scene begins with something being picked up and carried away. The camera pans or tracks to frame a new place where the central action begins. This disclosure motion can be executed by the main player himself or by a secondary person who exits view as soon as he discloses the central characters.

The camera frames an object in silhouette that blackens the screen completely, or almost, and tracks to one side to reveal the new scene behind.

The camera tracks back from an extreme close up of an object revealing the place where that object is located. That prop can be either something worn by a person such as a piece of jewellery or a wrist-watch or may be located on a piece of furniture, or even on the floor. The prop used must in some way be related to the content of the scene. The scene begins with the camera framing an empty section of the set, and the camera tracks or pans or cranes down to the sector where the players are.

The scene begins with a close shot of a person. The camera dollies back and we become aware that it was shooting through an opening in a screen that is now revealed in the foreground between the camera and our main subject. The subject then moves from behind the screen and moves into another section of the set.

A painted picture, an embroidered scene, a still picture in a newspaper, are used to begin the scene. They fade into a photograph (in the first two cases) that suddenly acquires movement. The frozen image is given life. The procedure is reversed to close a scene: the image freezes on the screen, the camera pulls back so that it is now part of a newspaper story, with caption and headlines.

Absolute stillness is another way of introducing a new scene. After a sequence concludes by a simple cut the new shot begins, but nothing moves in it for a few seconds. Then the players enter from any one of the sides, or through a door in the background, and the action begins. Stanley Kubrick in his film *Clockwork Orange* employed this device several times.

The scene openers described do not denote the passage of time between scenes. They are conventional ways of introducing an event with varying degrees of emphasis.

Introducing points of view

The subjective point of view of a character on the screen is conveyed by first showing him in close shot and following with a shot taken from his position and excluding him. This point of view can be stressed by subject movement and letting people featured in it look straight into the camera lens. Here is an example (Fig. 28.5).

A young man walks into an office. The camera pans along with him left to right. Now, for a shot taken from the man's position, the camera tracks from right to left beside a desk, and the girl behind it looks up at the camera and follows it with her gaze. We cut to a static-camera shot of the man and girl. The man (left) walks into the background, the girl looking at him.

The subjective shot, where the camera represents the view of the main player, stresses the situation. The camera movement (pan and track combined) represents the body movement.

Another possibility is to introduce a static shot within a tracking shot to show the character whose subjective viewpoint we have just seen (Fig. 28.6).

Shot 1   The camera tracks forward. Player A (right) pulls B out of the way. Cut to

Shot 2   A and B standing in the foreground, right. A car enters from the left, crosses the screen and exits right. Cut to

Shot 1   The camera continues tracking towards the wall in the background. Then we cut to

Shot 3   From one side—the car enters, left, crashes into the wall.

591

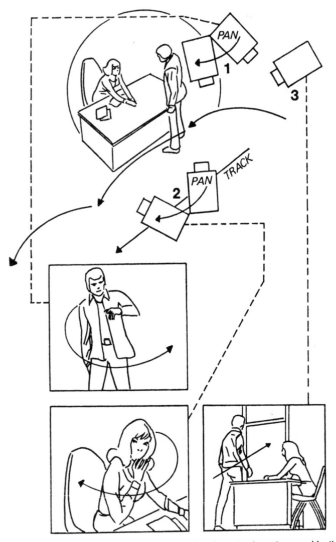

FIGURE 28.5 Emphasizing the point of view of a character by using a subjective camera shot.

Shot 3 is only a coda to the whole event. The main shot is the first, the subjective viewpoint of the occupants of the vehicle while hurtling towards the wall. Shot 2 introduced at a critical moment, re-establishes the vehicle in motion and, with its sudden lack of camera action, stresses by contrast the view from inside.

592

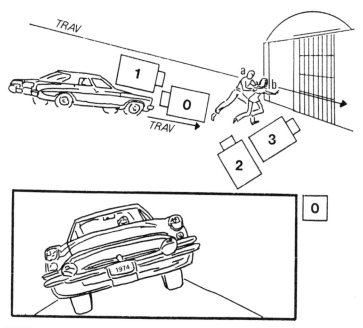

FIGURE 28.6 A subjective point of view is broken to stress its impact in the narration.

Sometimes a subjective viewpoint is introduced without first identifying the observer. Certain marks are immediately recognised as representing this such as binocular shapes or gunsights, the spectator or gunman appearing in the subsequent shot.

A dominant colour in the image can represent a subjective point of view. Robert Aldrich in his film *The Dirty Dozen*, during the final raid on the German castle, suddenly introduces a scene photographed through a red filter, and follows it by the image of a sniper pulling the trigger of his weapon. In the next shot a man from the attacking party falls dead. The second time the director uses a red coloured image we immediately identify it as the subjective viewpoint of another sniper but this time we only hear the weapon being fired and the following scene (with normal colours) shows a bullet ricocheting close to an attacking soldier.

There is yet another way of introducing a subjective viewpoint without identifying the person—a movement in the foreground with the accompaniment of hushed voices. For example, a tree branch in the foreground may be pulled aside by a hand, off screen,

revealing a distant column of soldiers moving across the forest. We hear *sotto-voce* comments from different people off screen planning how to take the enemy by surprise. As the foreground branch is released obscuring the view, the impression is given that the hidden attackers are moving away.

Abrupt jump cuts used as punctuation

Jump cuts, as the term implies, are very visible as cuts on the screen because the change from shot to shot is abrupt. They are usually done with a more or less static subject on the screen with each shot of the series placed on a common visual axis.

In *The Birds*, Alfred Hitchcock has a scene in which he uses jump cuts to stress a gruesome discovery. When Mitch's mother discovers the farmer's body lying beside his bed with his eyes pecked out by the birds, three short shots advance towards the face of the man. The farmer is a static subject and these three shots placed on a common visual axis serve to stress the impact of the discovery (Fig. 28.8).

The effect can also introduce a new element visually. Michelangelo Antonioni in his film *Il Deserto Rosso* begins a sequence showing a metallic island that rises from the sea at some distance from the coast. Three successive jump cut shots, drawing closer, show us the superstructure of the man-made island.

Documentary films sometimes use jump cuts to introduce new subjects with emphasis. Bert Haanstra in his film *The Sea Was No More* employs the device several times, but limits the effect to two shots. One is an extreme long shot and the other a full shot on the same visual axis—accompanied on the sound track by percussion music that stresses the jump cut.

On other occasions the effect can be employed as a pause before an unexpected revelation. In the final sequence of Lewis Gilbert's James Bond film *You Only Live Twice*, a plane has jettisoned rubber rafts that fall on the surface of the ocean. The survivors from the catastrophe on the island swim towards the rafts. James Bond and a young girl climb aboard one of the rafts and prepare to enjoy themselves during the long wait. Three shots follow of the raft bobbing on the sea, each closer than the other, but using relatively lengthy shots. Then comes a close shot in which Bond's

FIGURE 28.8 Rapid succession of static shots used to punctuate a situation. This example belongs to Alfred Hitchcock's film *The Birds*.

raft rises into the screen. A submarine has surfaced under the raft and lifted it out of the water. Dialogue scenes can be treated this way. In *Farenheit 451*, Francois Truffaut uses it when someone speaking on the phone receives a warning.

This effect can be obtained directly in the laboratory by enlarging a single frame. *The Spy in the Green Hat*, a film of the Napoleon Solo spy series, uses this variant in some of the shots employed for the credits.

John Frankenheimer in his film *Seconds*, reverses the technique. Mr. Hamilton is waiting for a vital phone call in his studio. The scene begins with an extreme close up of the eyes of the player and by a series of jump cuts recedes to a full shot of the room with the player looking small seated behind his desk. The phone rings and the director cuts to a tight close up of Mr. Hamilton picking it up off-screen and raising it into view to speak.

Director Gerard J. Raucamp used a series of shots on an axis line deflected to the left to cover a progression of static advancing shots towards an oil refinery in his documentary film *Holland Today*.

Jump cuts as time transitions

Another property of jump cuts is that on some occasions they can be used as time transitions from scene to scene or within the same scene. Sound judgement must be employed when selecting this mode for such a specific purpose. Not every situation lends itself to it.

Robert Enrico in *Les Aventuriers* has a car chase through the streets of Paris. The camera is shooting from the front seat of the chasing car. The other car is always framed in the centre of the screen but with each cut, the surroundings change. Several tracking shots have been spliced together and the idea of a long chase is conveyed.

Jump cuts can eliminate uninteresting segments of time as in the film *Blow Up*, where David Hemmings is photographing a model and from the same camera position we see a succession of jump cut shots of the model in various body postures representing his pictures of her.

Selected peaks of action

As mentioned earlier, the story can continue smoothly with large pieces of uninteresting action deleted even within a sequence. In *Blow Up* the photographer leaves the antique shop and gets into his car. He opens a glove compartment and takes out his camera. He closes the compartment. We cut to a reverse shot. He is standing in the street beyond his car with his camera, looking for a good angle to photograph from.

The transition is smooth because a movement is concluded in the first shot and another begins in the second. Also the fact that the camera angle is changed, a reverse in this case, helps to make a smooth cut. The same principle is used in *Les Aventuriers*. Alain Delon is testing a biplane passing through some obstacles erected by Lino Ventura on an airfield. The tests completed, Ventura rides home in a truck, and is playfully followed by the plane. Here is a section of that sequence:

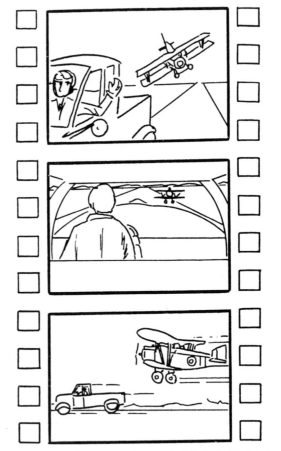

FIGURE 28.9 Fragment of a sequence from Robert Enrice's film *Les Aventuriers.*

The camera moves with the truck on the airfield. Lino Ventura is seen on the left looking into a rear view mirror and beckoning the biplane which approaches from the background, right, and then flies out of shot, right. Cut to:

View from inside the truck, Ventura in the foreground, left, his back to us. The plane, right, flies towards us at low altitude as we advance along the runway and then rises and flies out of view top left. Cut to: Panning shot, right to left. The truck runs to the left, closely followed by the plane. The plane then veers away to the background.

Observe how, without sacrificing smoothness of transition from shot to shot (the cut comes after the plane exits from each shot) the turn round movements of the plane are omitted. This concept is also applied to a transition where in the first sequence two persons, talking, are viewed separately. Near the conclusion one makes a statement but instead of splicing to a reaction shot of the other (before concluding the sequence) this last shot is deleted, and a direct cut is made to the next sequence.

Inaction as punctuation

If the screen image is rendered devoid of motion at the beginning or conclusion of a shot, it affords an easy transition between the preceding or following shot, and the shot in question i.e. the easy transition is between the two shots separated by the static view. There are two ways of using it:
1 At the conclusion of a shot.
2 At the beginning of a shot.

The static scene may take the form of a shot held on the general scene after a character moves out of it. The scene might be a landscape, a blank wall, an empty building or just a long shot of a beautiful seascape.

Single shots as pauses in narration

There are occasions where the conclusion of a sequence would be ruined by an abrupt change, especially if the one that follows has a mood totally opposed to it. A visual pause is needed as a bridge, either by a black leader inserted between the sequences, by prolonging the last shot of the sequence beyond its dramatic peak or by using a different related or unrelated shot between. With the first recourse—a black screen—the audience will be brought to a complete emotional standstill. The effect must not be overdone, which would be irritating. The next scene follows, faded in or abruptly. Michelangelo Antonioni in his film *Le Amiche* used this effect. A girl quarrels with her lover in the street and the scene fades to darkness which is held for a moment. The new scene begins abruptly and the body of the girl is being recovered from the river by the police. She has committed suicide.

Sometimes the period of darkness is accompanied by a 'curtain' of background music which increases in volume and then diminishes as the new sequence fades in.

The device of prolonging the last shot beyond its dramatic climax, often used by John Ford, corresponds to a slackening of our emotional pitch, and conveys a mood of melancholy. The next sequence normally starts with a full or a long shot. That camera framing dilutes our concentration and relaxes our attention.

The third recourse mentioned above is the most frequently employed—a single shot is used as a pause between the sequences and this shot is either related to the sequence that concludes or it has no story relation, only an emotional effect.

Let us take an example for the first case. Peter Yates in his film *Bullitt* has a sequence in which the hero and his girl park on the side of the highway and discuss their personal relationship after a particularly violent sequence in which a woman is strangled. This sequence begins with a long shot of the heavy traffic on the road. After a moment the girl's white sports car emerges from it and comes towards the camera. She parks and gets out of the car, walking to the edge of the river. Moments later Bullitt joins her. The dialogue begins. She reproaches him with his way of life— his total indifference to violent death. The scene is revealing and painful to the characters. As they reach a tentative agreement and remain silent, there is a cut to the traffic. Then a new sequence begins. The last shot of the cars is, in effect, the pause. The director uses the same effect again. A murderer has met a grim end in an airport terminal and the shot that follows is a view of an empty street in San Francisco. In the shot following, Bullitt arrives at his house on the morning of the next day. Once more a single shot, this time related to the new sequence, was employed as a pause between sequences.

On other occasions the shot intercut as a visual pause between two different scenes bears no relation at all to either of the sequences it bridges and is used solely for the emotional content of the shot itself.

In *The Girl On The Motorcycle* such a recourse bridges two

scenes that take place on the same set between the same performers, but with different moods. The central couple in the film, Alain Delon and Marianne Faithfull, are in bed in an hotel. He is telling her of his experiences as a motor cycle rider. The mood is ebullient, full of joy. As this sequence comes to an end, we see a transatlantic ship in a harbour, at dusk, with all its lights ablaze, silhouetted against the setting sun, as a smaller vessel passes in the foreground. The mood of this scene is bucolic, suggesting quietness and fulfilment. The sequence then continues with the lovers in the hotel, still in bed. But the mood has changed and they are taking stock of themselves and of their feelings and attitudes towards each other. The bridging shot provides no identification of a new place, is not reminiscent of a previous point in the story. It only has value in its visual content—an amotional catalyst that prepares us for a different mood.

An entire sequence used as a narrative pause

Often, a single shot is not enough pause between two sequences of differing moods. When two story points must not compete with each other they should be placed well apart.

In Peter Yates' film *Bullitt*, a gangster is given protection by the hero who is a policeman. He assigns a guard to the man and leaves to meet his girl, whom he takes to dinner in a bistro laden with beat atmosphere and later both go to bed. Now the killers arrive to eliminate the gangster under custody.

As can be seen, the actions of Bullitt are irrelevant to the advancement of the main plot. What counts is that an informer is given protection and that his former colleagues succeed in killing him. Both are strong scenes in the structure of the story. But if they were put together we would watch them at an emotional saturation point where we would not care what happened. It is all too pat. So, to make each sequence stand out on its own, an irrelevant sequence is inserted between. This particular sequence acts as a pause in the narration and resorts to a subject to justify its inclusion and to disguise its true role—the hero's personal life is revealed. But attention is not focused on his particular relationship with the girl. The whole thing is stated casually with more attention given to the beat orchestra in the bistro than to the central couple.

This diversionary tactic is quite useful to build up suspense as Alfred Hitchcock has amply demonstrated. In *Rear Window*,

Grace Kelly has entered the apartment of the suspected killer. She is seen from James Stewart's point of view across the inner patio, moving through the flat, examining things. Suddenly his attention is distracted by the actions of a spinster woman, previously established in the story, who seems on the verge of committing suicide. We are sidetracked into this new plot. We momentarily lose sight of Grace Kelly and her errand, so it comes as a shock when then we see the suspected killer coming to his flat. There is no way to warn the girl inside of the danger. If we had not been diverted into the secondary subplot, we would have been waiting for the killer to appear at any moment and when he did our expectations would be fulfilled and we would lose interest. In this other way, the arrival of the killer gains an emotional impact due to its suddenness. The strong scenes in the plot were isolated by an inbetween sequence used as a pause.

Out of focus images as punctuation

This effect is more often seen on live television than in films. The technique is simple. The concluding scene in a sequence is defocussed until it becomes an unrecognizable blur. We then cut to the new sequence which begins with the image completely out of focus, and then gradually grows sharp. This new image is in another place and at another time.

Michelangelo Antinioni has used another variant. A smouldering fire is seen out of focus at the beginning of a sequence. It is an intriguing pattern of colour and undefined shapes. A few seconds later a pair of bare female feet enter the foreground in sharp focus. The scene acquires meaning. Sequences can be concluded using the same recourse. A person in the foreground, in focus, leaves the screen and the out of focus background remains for a moment. (Incidentally, there is now a tendency to use out of focus images as background for the credit titles of a film.) Out of focus actions are often used on purpose to stress a point. For example, in Sidney Furie's film *The Ipcress File* the hero gets out of bed in one image (in focus) and enters in the next as a vague blurred image in the background, to open the window shutters. In the foreground and in sharp focus, is an alarm watch marking the time.

Another technique is to have one player sharp in the foreground who remains still during the take, while another moves in the background completely out of focus and comes forward into focus to join the other. John Huston in his film *Moulin Rouge* uses such an effect. Toulouse Lautrec has quarrelled with his girl friend and she departs, slamming the door on her way out. The next shot shows a dejected Lautrec in the foreground, facing the camera. After a moment the door in the background (completely out of focus) opens and the girl comes in again and slowly walks to the foreground until she is in focus beside the painter.

The sharp focus can be in the background. Two lovers seen in focus begin to kiss and move slowly forward out of focus and turn into undefined moving shapes.

When they want to suggest that a man is losing consciousness and is about to faint, some film makers use point of view shots that gradually defocus. The reverse effect is employed when the contrary situation is desired: a person coming to his senses.

To suggest that a person has trouble with his eyesight, the point of view shot of what the man sees goes from sharp to blurred and to sharp again. As mentioned elsewhere when discussing the use of split focus in a scene, there is a tendency today to have a subject sharp in the foreground and, as he turns his head to the background to shift focus there so that the foreground player becomes blurred. Mike Nichols used this in *The Graduate*. In that scene Ben implies to Elaine that it was with her mother that he had an affair. The revelation comes when she is close to the half open door of her bedroom. We see her in the foreground. Beyond, her mother appears. Elaine turns to look back and the camera shifts focus to her mother. She is wet from the rain, as Ben is. The mother goes away after a moment and Elaine turns her head to us. But she remains out of focus for a moment, then slowly the image becomes clear and sharp as she realizes what has happened and reacts angrily. Her mental process of understanding the situation fully is made clear to the audience by the delayed focus which portrays it visually.

Dark screen used as punctuation

A dark screen can be effectively employed to separate shots or scenes. The effect of isolation is total and each scene hits the viewer unexpectedly and with the fullest emotional impact. The audience waits for an image to appear on the screen but is never certain for how long it will be. This confers a certain type of suspense on the sequence, and each shot or group of shots will sink home with

603

great force. Look at an example from an Argentinian film entitled *La Hora De Los Hornos* (The Time of the Ovens) made by Fernando Solanas and Octavio Getino in 1968:

Dark screen. A drum is heard on the sound track.

Suddenly a hand carrying a torch appears on the screen. Short pan right following the motion of the arm of the running man.

Dark screen again. The drum beats continue.

A group of policemen with machine guns appear running on the centre of a street at night. Short pan to the right with the men.

Dark screen again.

A civilian throws a Molotov cocktail against the display window of a store and it bursts into furious flames.

Dark screen again.

A civilian runs along the street, right to left; the camera pans to follow. A policeman clubs him in the back and the man falls to his knees, a second policeman enters from the left and kicks the man in the kidneys. As the civilian doubles in pain, still on his knees, a third policeman enters, left, and savagely kicks the man in the face with his boot, sending him rolling backwards.

Dark screen again.

The shots employed for this sequence were all taken from newsreel coverage of disturbances in Buenos Aires and the film is an indictment, bitter and gripping, on the political situation of that time in that country as seen by the two film makers. What makes that opening sequence of the film so stunning is precisely the use of dark strips of film edited in parallel with the individual shots selected for the sequence.

The continuous sound—a percussion motif in this instance—brings unity to the sequence and helps to heighten the visual impact. Sometimes a dark screen is used to begin and a sound is heard and suddenly an image is revealed that places the sound in its proper context. Bert Haanstra in his documentary film *The Rival World* begins with a dark screen and only the buzzing of a fly. Suddenly an image appears on the screen—a close-up of a man who opens his eyes and realizes that a fly is standing on the tip of his nose. It is a striking way to open a film.

Punctuation by camera motion

An advancing or receding camera can stress or isolate a character or a situation on the screen.

Case 1

As we pointed out elsewhere, a camera movement that precedes a line spoken by a player stresses that line, but if the movement comes *after* the phrase has been uttered it stresses the reaction of the player. If the camera advances during a long speech by the main character a feeling of intimacy is gained. If it recedes the player is de-emphasized and his surroundings or lack of them become important.

Case 2

A player's movement can be combined with the punctuating motion of the camera to give the scene added visual impact. For example, somebody is challenged and in the shot that follows the camera advances towards a group of persons. As we approach one turns aside disclosing behind the challenged person. The camera stops, framing this character in close shot.

A delayed camera motion can be used too. For instance, a character framed in close shot stays in the foreground for several seconds and then walks to the background into a full shot. He stops, begins to turn and the camera tracks swiftly in, framing him again in close shot.

Case 3

Usually, when these camera punctuations are employed, the shot begins with the camera in a fixed spot and as the scene develops the camera moves but the shot concludes with the camera static once more.

A variant of this is obtained by starting the shot with movement in it and, as that ends, cutting again to a static composition similar to that at the beginning of the preceding moving shot. For example, a scene begins with a close shot of a man sitting at the head of a long table. The camera is tracking back over the table revealing the two rows of guests. It stops at the end and then we cut to a close shot of the man as seen at the beginning of the preceding shot. Musical films avail themselves of this solution where, for instance, a full shot of the couple of dancers begins the shot with the camera tracking back and booming upwards. The camera then descends vertically (framing the whole scene in long shot) to the dancer's height and stops. A cut follows to a full shot on the same visual axis and the whole movement is repeated once more.

Case 4

An approaching or receding movement can be repeated two, three or more times consecutively. With a single subject the effect is disturbing and draws attention to itself.

In the Italian film *Agostino*, directed by Mauro Bolognini, the central character, a boy whose name is the title of the film, witnesses a sexual act performed off camera by two other boys. This revelation comes as a shock to him. Visually, the scene is presented by a series of forward camera tracks that repeat six or seven times. The camera moves from medium shot to close up and suddenly cuts back to a medium shot on the same visual axis, tracking in slowly once more.

A similar use of repetitive forward camera movement was employed by Alain Resnais in *L'Année Dernière à Marienbad* but the effect of image overexposure was added in the laboratory. The girl in the film runs from a room out onto a wide terrace and stops, opening her arms in joy. The camera tracks towards her several times consecutively from the same direction adding a static pause before each camera movement.

In another example from Laurence Olivier's film version of *Hamlet*, the King and Ophelia's brother are plotting against Hamlet. The scene opens with a medium shot of both players. The camera tracks back and upwards until they are seen in small scale down below. There is a cut to another point in the triangular camera deployment around the two players and they are seen in medium shot. The camera again moves back and upwards. A cut follows to a reverse medium shot of both players. The camera holds it for a moment and again begins to track back and up. The mood of conspiracy is thus emphasized.

Case 5

Repetitive camera movement towards or away from a single player can be intercut in parallel with scenes remembered by that character and representing a subconscious return to the past. Here is a fragment of such a sequence:
Camera tracks forward to a young man sitting with his back to

the railing on a deck of a transatlantic liner. The camera advances from a full to a medium shot. There is a cut to:

A woman opening a door and facing the camera. She says something.

It is a scene previously seen in the film, during an earlier sequence. The camera tracks from medium to close shot of the seated man. There is a cut on the track to:

The young man in full shot walking in a park beside the girl. They are both talking.

The young man, in a room, with his back to the camera in the foreground, left.

On the right another man advances towards him and stops to utter some harsh words.

The young man. The camera tracks from medium to close shot on the ship.

The young girl turns away from us and walks to the background. We are in a room now. She turns to us again and speaks a few lines.

The young man on the ship's deck. The camera tracks from close shot to a big close up and stops, holding a frontal image of the young man to register a tear running down the young man's cheek.

All the shots spliced in parallel with the repetitive forward tracking correspond to images already used in previous sequences and represent a return to the past.

The cuts come while the camera is still moving except at the very end. The camera is allowed to slow down and stop tracking. The method described is also useful to stress one of two simultaneous actions. For example:

A man seated in the foreground, with his back to us. He is reading a book. A girl in the background, facing him, turns away and moves into the background.

Reverse shot. The man is reading the book. The camera tracks towards him from a full to a close shot. The scene is cut while the camera is still moving.

The girl enters shot, stops, turns and looks off screen, then she turns to the background and exits through a door.

The camera tracks forward from a medium to a close shot of the man still engrossed in his book.

The repeated tracking shots towards the man emphasizes that he is unaware of the girl's wish to speak to him.

Case 6

Forward tracking movements from two opposite reverse camera positions can be edited in parallel (Fig. 28.10).

FIGURE 28.10 Opposed camera movements edited in parallel used to stress a situation.

A man walks towards a car where a girl is waiting. The first camera position is behind the walking man and the camera tracks behind him as he walks to the car. The second camera position is located behind the car and we advance to it as the man in the background walks towards us. These two shots conclude with close shot compositions of both players and can be edited in parallel either when moving towards the static goal (the girl in the car) or when both camera sites become static themselves. Parallel editing of these opposed camera movements aids the scene with dynamic presentation.

Case 7

Forward tracking movements intercut in parallel can be applied to two separate individuals who are looking at each other or talking to each other. Speeds in the tracking motion can be varied and they will change the emotional effect of the sequence. The idea is not to make a single track towards each player and then intercut those two shots in parallel, but to make several tracks towards each character, each one closer at its end to the waiting actor. The paths of the tracking movements overlap slightly so that the area that concludes a shot is again used at the beginning of the next (Fig. 28.11).

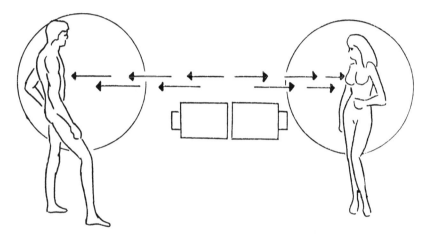

FIGURE 28.11 Overlapped camera movements for each player, later edited in parallel to pinpoint attention on the players.

The two last shots of the series (one for each player) conclude the track by coming to a stop in front of the player and holding on him.

Case 8

A further variant to two camera movements edited in parallel (where each camera covers a single player) can be achieved by introducing a reversal of direction at the end of the sequence. Here is an example:

Shot 1 Camera tracks in swiftly to player A, slowing down as it approaches, cut to

Shot 2   Camera tracks in at the same speed as before towards subject B, slowing down.

Shot 3   Close shot of A. The camera pulls back swiftly and slows down to a complete stop in full shot.

This sudden change in direction of the camera movement provides a further example of punctuation with moving camera shots.

Case 9

Two shots, in which the camera moves in opposed directions, towards one player and away from another, can be edited in parallel. By this device one of the players is de-emphasized while the other is visually stressed. In this and all the previous cases, the subjects remain static while the camera does all the moving.

Case 10

Camera movements combined with movement within the picture can be used to stress a sudden unexpected accident or disaster. Here is an example where the visual punctuation precedes the catastrophe.

Camera tracks in, fast, towards a subject who looks surprised.

A second person walks into shot, right.

Camera tracks in, fast, towards a third person.

Camera tracks back quickly from a group.

Camera tracks quickly into a person. As the camera nears him, he ducks under.

Several successive explosions shatter the place.

Observe the contrasting direction of movement from shot to shot. These motions are short and fast, while the pay off, the explosions themselves, are longer.

The second example concerns the reactions of several players to a sudden catastrophe.

An explosion seen in long shot.

Close up of a woman; she turns her head to the left.

Close up of a man; he turns his head to the right.

Close up of a man; he is rising into the screen, looking right.

Close up of a man; he approaches diagonally from right to left.

The aftermath of the explosion seen in long shot.

Here the punctuating movements are performed by the players, not by the camera. Sudden turns are among the most frequently used human movements for visual punctuation of a situation. Several successive close-up head turns can stress the arrival of a character. These movements precede the arrival of the main character. They can be overlapped or repetitive. Fig. 28.12 shows the two possibilities.

All the movements are slow ones. With overlapped turns, the three subjects turn a third of a circle—matched from shot to shot for smooth transition as the characters change.

The second possibility confines itself to a repetition of movement in the same screen area and direction. Slow, contrasting tracks or pans that cover static subjects can be used to obtain an intimate, tense mood, or to enhance the preliminaries of a task being prepared by the protagonists. Several film makers have refined this approach, notably among them the British film maker J. Lee Thompson, who in *Kings of the Sun*, *Return from the Ashes* and *The Eye of the Devil* offers excellent examples of the use of this technique.

Vertical punctuation

There are situations in which the main action moves in horizontal paths and therefore a sudden development will not have a clear visual stress, unless a helping vertical motion is introduced to accentuate that sudden event. An example taken from David Lean's film *The Bridge on the River Kwai* clarifies this point. In the battle previous to the blowing up of the bridge, two central characters in the story are killed: Joyce and Shears. Here are the fragments.

Shot 105 FS of Nicholson and Joyce struggling beside the cable that leads to the detonator.
Joyce: 'You don't understand!'
They crawl towards the background. (2 seconds 20 frames).

Shot 106 MS of Yay and Shears behind the fallen tree trunk. Shears rises and shouts to the right off screen.
Shears: 'Kill him! Kill him!'
He holds a knife in his right hand. (3 seconds 22 frames).

Shot 107 The same as shot 105. Joyce struggles towards the detonator in the background and is prevented from

FIGURE 28.12 Puntuation by players movement that precedes the introduction of an important action on the screen.

reaching it by Nicholson, who clings to Joyce's legs. (47 frames).

Shot 108 FS of Shears standing on the right. Yay crouched on the left. Shears makes a decision and jumps forward over the tree trunk and falls down to the left. (2 seconds 3 frames).

Shot 109 FS. The bridge in the background. In the left foreground Shears falls and starts to run to the right. The camera pans with him and he wades into the river. He exits right. In the background, four Japanese soldiers descend on the opposite bank of the river, close to the bridge. (4 seconds 7 frames).

Shot 110 MS of Shears swimming across the screen to the right. The camera pans with him. He is shouting.
Shears: 'Kill him!'
(3 seconds 23 frames).

Shot 111 MS of Nicholson and Joyce in foreground. They crawl, struggling towards the right. In the background two groups of Japanese soldiers are advancing. They fire. Joyce is hit and falls on his back rolling towards the camera. (3 seconds 1 frame).

Shot 112 Close shot. A beautiful, young Thai girl descends, looking to the right. (39 frames).

Shot 113 As in shot 111. Nicholson turns Joyce face up on the ground and sees blood on the lad's chest. Nicholson turns his head to the background to look at the Japanese soldier. (8 seconds 12 frames).

Observe how the crawling of Nicholson and Joyce and the running and swimming of Shears are horizontal movements. The death of Joyce would go unstressed except for that sudden shot (112) in which a girl supposedly on the ridge that overlooks the river, descends. This adds nothing to the story, except a strong vertical movement after the sudden, unexpected event. Her action pinpoints attention on Joyce's death. This recourse is used again when Shears is hit. Here is the fragment of the scene.

Shot 116 FS. Nicholson standing beside the fallen body of Joyce. The Japanese soldiers in the background are looking towards the centre of the river. They open fire. Nicholson turns to the left to look at the river. The camera pans to show Shears in LS swimming towards us. (3 seconds 12 frames).

Shot 117   As in shot 110. MS of Shears swimming to the right. (3 seconds 10 frames).

Shot 118   MS of Nicholson taken from a low angle. He looks incredulous towards the left. He advances towards the camera and stops in a close shot. (3 seconds 9 frames).

Shot 119   FS of Shears in the river. He stands and wades towards us. Suddenly he is hit and falls. (4 seconds 4 frames).

Shot 120   Close shot. Another beautiful Thai girl rises into the screen and looks off screen right. (33 frames).

The vertical motion (upwards in this case) is brought into play to direct attention on the action that preceded it. The recourse described is simple, unobtrusive and effective when punctuation is desired on a predominant horizontal action.

These examples use movement inside the screen but a strong vertical camera motion can serve the same purpose. In the film just quoted there are several such examples. When jungle birds are startled into sudden flight by gun shots, they are shown crossing the screen in flocks that move horizontally. But midway there is a vertical camera pan showing the shadows of the birds crossing the jungle foliage.

Frozen frame

With the frozen frame technique, time ceases to move physically on the screen. Many films conclude with a sudden freeze of the image on the screen, thus interrupting the flow of motion. Other film makers use the effect to terminate a sequence: the image is stopped and after a moment it fades out. In the middle of a sequence, sometimes the end of a shot is frozen to centre attention on a fact or a character. Zoom shots that move forwards have been frozen at the end with remarkable effect.

A single shot can be momentarily frozen on any frame—one or more times. Bob Fosse in *Sweet Charity* momentarily stops the flow of motion to emphasize the reaction of a character, or uses it several times during a musical number to break the exuberant rhythm.

He also uses colour changes on the frozen film frame. The normal or natural colour is changed by using coloured filters during printing.

An antecedent to this technique can be traced in Stanley Donen's film *Funny Face*, where during a musical number the image of Audrey Hepburn modelling different dresses was frozen on the screen and its colour altered several times before passing on to the next shot.

Careful judgement must be exercised in determining just how much time a frame is kept frozen on the screen.

Sound can be interrupted, slowed down or increased during these motion stops to work in contrast or in harmony with the mood of the scene.

In conclusion

The many aspects of film language discussed in the preceding chapters do not, of course, in any sense exhaust the expressive possibilities of film. But, beside the purely aesthetic aspects they include an attempt to provide some sort of basic physical structure to the interpretation of ideas and emotions in the cinema.

As with most art forms, so with the film, the best way to develop and expand your technique is to study the masters of the medium. The most obvious way would be to see as many of their films as possible. But a most profitable way to examine a film is to run through a copy on a viewer, analyzing the scenes that excite you, and noting how they were put together. It is surely then that the films or scenes that excite you will reveal their secrets and inspire your future film making.

INDEX